Peacebuilding in Traumatized Societies

AF739106

Edited by

Barry Hart

University Press of America,® Inc.
Lanham · Boulder · New York · Toronto · Plymouth, UK

4501 Forbes Boulevard
Suite 200
Lanham, Maryland 20706
UPA Acquisitions Department (301) 459-3366

Estover Road
Plymouth PL6 7PY
United Kingdom

Printed in the United States of America
British Library Cataloging in Publication Information Available

Library of Congress Control Number: 2008921688
ISBN-13: 978-0-7618-4035-0 (paperback : alk. paper)
ISBN-10: 0-7618-4035-4 (paperback : alk. paper)

™ The paper used in this publication meets the minimum requirements of American National Standard for Information Sciences—Permanence of Paper for Printed Library Materials, ANSI Z39.48—1984

Contents

Acknowledgements

The ideas and concepts in this book come from scholars and practitioners who care about the thousands and millions of people who have suffered the pain and destruction of large-scale violence, war and structural injustice. In partnership with their peers and most importantly with the citizens of places like Rwanda, Colombia and Bosnia-Herzegovina, they developed or enhanced their insights about peacebuilding theory and practice. My own experience in Northern Ireland, West Africa and the Balkans exposed me to people's great pain and sense of loss, while at the same time gave me a deep appreciation for their courage and resilience. I came to understand their commitment to peace with justice and their desire for true partnerships with international organizations to rebuild their communities and nations. In the end, though, they know it is their responsibility to build peaceful relationships and structures. It has been a privilege to work with and learn from many of these committed peacebuilders.

I want to thank my colleagues in the Center for Justice and Peacebuilding (CJP) at Eastern Mennonite University for supporting me in the development of this book. Their research and theories in the areas of justice, peacebuilding and trauma inspire me as does their practice, which applies these theories to real world and complex conflicts. I hope they will take insights from the book to further their theory building and practice. I want to thank past and current students of CJP. Their insights about violence, trauma, justice and peacebuilding shared in class and through personal conversations have helped me think more broadly as well as deeply about what I want to contribute to these fields. Special thanks goes to Ruba Musleh and Vesna Hart, the technical editors of the book. They made it seem easy when I know it was not.

Introduction

During the last three decades, theorists and practitioners in the field of peacebuilding have developed a great number of tools needed to help transform complex and violent conflicts. They have seen the need to learn directly from victims of these conflicts and work closely with them to create the means to not only stop the violence, but to "provent"' it from happening again (Burton 1990). The emergence of this practice is rooted in a nonviolent response to the global impact of large-scale violence and wars in the 20th Century. Leaders such as Mohandas Gandhi, Abdul Ghaffar Khan and Martin Luther King encouraged people to take responsibility for what was happening around them and not be 'bystanders' who contribute to direct or structural violence through their inaction. These leaders also challenged people to be intentional and compassionate witnesses (Weingarten 2004); and act against (and in the long term *for)* the perpetrators and sustainers of violence (McNair 2002). They also demonstrated a way forward by showing how essential it is to take risks in times of great need.

Through risk taking, courage and actions, these leaders and those they encouraged and empowered, set a standard that spoke against violence and for peaceful coexistence. In the last thirty years, there has been prolific advancement of nonviolent practice and corresponding conflict transformation and justice theories and practices (Lederach 1997 and Abu-Nimer 2001, van Tongeren et al 2005) that build upon these standards and continue to rely on the vision, values and practice skills of these and many other earlier leaders.

Today's peacebuilders are made up of a broad range of actors who participate in helping transform violent conflicts and building secure and just societies. They include community members, human rights activists, restorative and transitional justice practitioners, researchers, environmentalists, religious leaders, peacekeepers, relief and development workers, trauma healers, members of police forces, political and economic actors, and educators to name a few (see

Schirch 2004; Keating & Knight 2004). Their peacebuilding work is most effective when there is a solid coalitions of peacebuilders working together to help transform conflicts and peacefully sustain this transformation.

Doing the work of building a sustainable peace after the multitude of past and current conflicts in places Liberia, Aceh, Sri Lanka, Chechnya in Russia, Sierra Leone, Northern Ireland, the Democratic Republic of Congo, Bosnia and Herzegovina, Israel/Palestine and Rwanda is a complicated and long-term process. Although many of these conflicts have been transformed and peace within certain limited parameters exits, ongoing work is needed. Several of these conflicts appear to be intractable due to historical trauma, internal economic, political and ethnic or religious factors as well as regional and international pressures.

In these cases, and generally within every peacebuilding process, theorists and practitioners need to delve deeper into the reasons behind the fear, anger and violence in order to develop more comprehensive conflict transformation theories and practices; and to better understand the power of the *intangible* factors of complex and violent conflict such as identity, worldviews and trauma, as well as culture and religious belief systems (Volkan 2004; Redekop 2002; Augsburger 1992).

Peacebuilding in Traumatized Societies addresses these *intangible* issues in order to emphasize their importance in the development of comprehensive peacebuilding theories and practices (Katunga 2003). Along with the *tangible* or more measurable issues such as numbers of displaced people in war, level of infrastructure destruction, sources available to feed and house people (all critical issues), psychological issues such as stress and trauma, identity formation and threat, as well as the powerful symbolic elements of culture and religion need to be seen as part of every peacebuilding equation.

Since trauma, identity and other factors are usually hidden below the surface and difficult to deal with, building peace in traumatized societies becomes a special research and practice challenge. Trauma, for example, requires an examination of its symptoms as well as its causes; and its psychological and social interventions need to be adapted or developed to aid not only individuals but entire communities or societies (Kleber, Figley & Gerson 1995; Ajdukovic 1997; Green et al 2003). The power of identity in terms of how it is formed and manipulated is also essential to understanding the causes of violence and therefore critical to the development of peacebuilding theories and processes (Clark 2002; Druckman 2006; Volkan 2007).

When intangible factors are left out of peacebuilding practices, or not applied adequately to them, less effective peace accords and post-war reconstruction processes are the result. Similarly, if the more tangible issues are not seen to have psychological or symbolic importance in the reconstruction phase after war, this, too, may contribute to ineffective approaches to rebuilding communities and societies after large-scale violence and war.

The Peacebuilding Wheel (Hart 2007) is a model that shows the interface of the tangible and intangible elements of peacebuilding (see figure 1). As a Wheel, each section has it strength and role to play in complimenting and completing the Wheel, making it possible for it to move forward. Culture and context (social, political, economic and environmental) is always assumed in this model as is the need for gender mainstreaming—although it has its own set of challenges regarding culture beliefs and practices.

The Peacebuilding Wheel can also be used as a template for complex conflicts and post-conflict reconstruction. It helps users see what elements are required to build peace and how they must work together to do so. As a template, the Wheel shows peacebuilders with a particular focus such as trauma healing or transitional justice, who their partners are and who they must build coalitions with to be most effective. Moreover, each section of the Wheel is also a potential "entry point" to begin to deal with violence or its aftermath, but again, peacebuilding toward a more stable society requires the creative and constructive action of each section of the Wheel and the *interaction* of them all.

Finally, the values that *inflate* the tire on the rim of the Wheel come from all sectors of it and relate to human needs, rights and dignity as well as beliefs. These values, along with trustbuilding and reconciliation (also a value, process and potential outcome) inform, support and promote both human security and growth and, at the same time, challenge leadership to govern in ways that help build and constructively maintain social, political and economic systems that are just and secure.

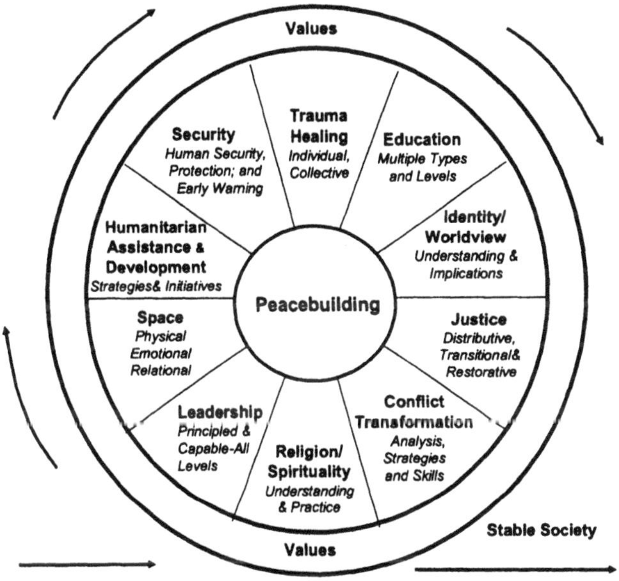

Peacebuilding Wheel

Figure 1. Peacebuilding Wheel

The Peacebuilding Wheel has also been used as a template for *Peacebuilding in Traumatized Societies*, where contributors to this volume were asked to develop their areas of expertise in relationship to the other sections of the Wheel. First, they were asked to outline their field, comprehensively explore a topic within it, and attempt to place it within the larger peacebuilding framework. For example, when examining transitional justice, authors were asked to describe how peace commissions and special or traditional courts are linked to and inform the peacebuilding process and/or contribute to healing individual and collective trauma after war. A further question for their consideration was "How do transitional justice practices use trauma healing expertise represented in the Wheel (or any other expertise from the Wheel) to enhance or expand justice processes?"

Furthermore, experts in trauma healing, for example, were asked to consider the theoretical and practical ways their field enhances the peacebuilding process and how linkages to other sections of the Wheel, such as development, leadership or the creation of a safe "space" for dialogue, aids in the psychological healing process of individuals or large groups of people. In other words, all contributors were asked to focus on a subject within their field of expertise while at the same time explore it in relation to and influence on other sections of the Wheel.

The first part of the book emphasizes the theoretical frameworks of peacebulding, trauma healing and justice. The first contribution is on peacebuilding and trauma healing within a development framework, by Riva Kantowitz and Abikök Riak. It is followed by the relationship between memory and transitional justice examined by Judy Barsalou. Humiliation, trauma and trauma recovery is explored by Evelin G. Linder. Education and post-conflict recovery is examined by Margaret E. Smith. The link between security, identity, and the arts for peacebuilding is developed by Lisa Schirch. In the final chapter in this section, I contribute an article on peacebuilding leadership in traumatized societies.

Merging theory and practice comes in the second part of this volume, where psychological recovery, reconciliation, justice and prevention in Rwanda are addressed by Ervin Staub, Laurie Anne Pearlman and Rezarta Bilali. The contribution of trauma healing to peacebuilding in South Central Europe is developed by Amela Puljek-Shank and Randy Puljek-Shank. This section also includes an arts approach to trauma healing and peacebuilding by Babu Ayindo. In the final chapter of this section, Mohammed Abu-Nimer examines the role of religious peacebuilders in societies traumatized by violent conflict.

The third section of the book includes case studies that describe trauma healing processes in three settings. Arlene Audergon looks at community trauma in Croatia: Bonnie Klassen explores the possibility of trauma healing in Columbia; and an examination of trauma and healing among Australian's 'Stolen Generation' is offered by John Bond.

In the concluding chapter "The Way Forward: Policy Development and Implementation," I suggest ideas and means to enhance the partnership between governments, civil society and international NGOs and institutions regarding policymaking for peacebuilding. A set of recommendations is presented to add to the discussion about how best to develop and implement policies that reflect both the tangible and intangible needs of people during post-conflict reconstruction.

References

Abu-Nimer, M., ed. 2001. *Reconciliation, Justice and Coexistence: Theory and Practice.* Lanham, Maryland: Lexington Books.

Ajdukovic, D., ed. 1997. *Trauma Recovery Training: Lessons Learned.* Zagreb, Croatia: Society for Psychological Assistance.

Augsberger, D. 1992. *Conflict Mediation across Cultures: Pathways and Patterns.* Louisville, Kentucky: Westminster/John Knox Press.

Burton, J.W. 1990. *Conflict: Resolution and Provention.* London: St. Martin's Press.

Clark, M.E. 2002. *In Search of Human Nature.* New York: Routledge.

Druckman, D. March 2006. Explaining National Identity: From Group Attachments to Collective Action. Sabanci University Program on Conflict Analysis and Resolution Occasional Paper Series.

Green, B. et al., eds. 2003. *Trauma Interventions in War and Peace: Prevention, Practice and Policy.* New York: Plenum Publishers.

Hart, B. February 22-24, 2007. "Peacebuilding and Trauma Recovery: Integrated Strategies in Post-war Reconstruction." Conference presentation at University of Denver. Denver, CO.

Keating T. and Knight, A., eds. 2004. *Building Sustainable Peace.* The University of Alberta Press.

Kleber, R. Figley, C. and Gersons, B., 1995. *Beyond Trauma: Culture and Societal Dynamics.* New York: Plenum Press.

Leaderach, J. P. 1997. *Building Peace: Sustainable Reconciliation in Divided Societies.* Washington, D.C.: United States Institute of Peace Press.

MacNair, R. 2002. Perpetration-Induced Traumatic Stress: The Psychological Consequences of Killing. Portsmouth, New Hampshire: Greenwood Press.

Schirch, L. 2004. *Strategic Peacebuilding: A Vision and Framework for Peace and Justice.* Intercourse, Pennsylvania: Good Books.

Van Tongeren, P. et al., eds. 2005. *People Building Peace II: Successful Stores of Civil Society.* London: Lynne Rienner Publishers.

Volkan, V. 2004. *Blind Trust: Large Groups and Their Leaders in Times of Crisis and Terror.* Charlottesville, Virginia: Pitchstone Publishing.

________. 2007. *Killing in the Name of Identity. A Study of Bloody Conflicts.* Charlottesville, Virginia: Pitchstone Publishing.

Part I

Theoretical Frameworks

1

Critical Links between Peacebuilding and Trauma Healing: A Holistic Framework for Fostering Community Development[1]

Riva Kantowitz and Abikök Riak

This chapter examines the complex relationships and critical intersections between peacebuilding, trauma healing, and development. [2] Can the task of promoting participatory development in post-conflict countries be linked to facilitating healing in these societies? What activities must take place to ensure that communities and individuals affected by war have the capacity to effectively engage in development processes? This discussion attempts to address such questions, highlighting the current challenge to academics and practitioners in these arenas: raising issues and emphasizing linkages at the intersection between peacebuilding, trauma healing, and international development, and creating programs that promote the sustainability of these themes by engaging their interrelatedness. While there are a myriad of ways to conceptualize "peacebuilding," "trauma healing," and "development," we define these concepts broadly, underscoring a basic set of values that underlie all three: promoting human dignity; creating societies of justice; and, nurturing personal and collective transformation. We suggest that conceptually, these issues are inherently intertwined and therefore, programmatically, in order to ensure effective development in post conflict areas, these three tasks must be undertaken simultaneously.

The first part of this chapter is conceptual in nature. We begin by exploring development, peacebuilding, and trauma healing separately. Next, we look at the connections between these topics, examining the way in which collective trauma can impede processes of participatory development or vice-versa, when participatory strategies might interrupt patterns of trauma.

The second part of the chapter focuses on applied work, examining how one organization, World Vision International (WV), has approached the intersection of these topics both theoretically and practically. WV's experience over the past 6 years related to integrating peacebuilding into development practices provides a unique backdrop to explore the topics addressed in this chapter, and potentially serves as a valuable example for other humanitarian assistance agencies attempting to address such issues in their programs and policies. We begin with an exploration of World Vision's development model and how belief in transformational development led to an investigation of the impact of WV programs on conflict. By intentionally incorporating peacebuilding themes into development processes, the staff of this organization felt its long-term development projects could provide a unique opportunity to support genuine transformation. How WV's approach interprets the intersection of development, peacebuilding and trauma healing in the context of post-conflict development is explored, as well as ways in which the model could be expanded and enhanced, offering specific illustrations from various field programs.

Considering the topics in this chapter has raised many questions about the ways in which development, peacebuilding, and trauma healing are linked, both as concepts and in practice, we conclude with what we feel to be the most pressing of these questions, suggesting critical areas for intervention and further inquiry.

Development

The concept of development assistance arose from the necessity of reconstructing countries after World War II and the end of colonialism around the world, which created an awareness of the need to eradicate poverty. The process of development was initially seen as a linear one, the goal of which was to bring "underdeveloped" or "third world" countries up to the same "level" as the "first" or "developed" world. This approach has been widely critiqued due to its paternalistic and colonialist underpinnings and the implication that wealthier countries fundamentally impose their systems of governance and economy on poorer countries (Rahnema 1997). Some see development as a form of Western imperialism, and contend that the development enterprise is flawed because it does not respond to inequitable distribution of wealth and power, which critics argue cannot be addressed through the giving of aid or "charity" (Korten 1995).

In the early 1990s, a shift in development paradigms occurred, prompted by an acknowledgment that despite tremendous progress in health care, education, and other standards, poverty and access to resources were still major issues in much of the world. The concept of *human development* emerged, articulated in the United Nations (U.N.) Agenda for Development. As opposed to previous linear and narrowly defined paradigms that focused on providing direct aid, human development strives to promote freedom from fear and want, emphasizing participatory processes and improving the quality of life for all peoples (UNDP 1994). This paradigm placed human needs at the center of development goals and focused on issues such as poverty reduction, employment, social integration, and environmental protection. In general, the field of international development has embraced this shift and moved towards less linear, more holistic approaches. In his seminal work, Sen (2000) redefines development not merely as access to clean water or employment, but suggests that development equates "freedom" itself:

> Development requires the removal of major sources of unfreedom: poverty as well as tyranny, poor economic opportunities as well as systematic social deprivation, neglect of public facilities as well as intolerance or over activity of repressive states. Despite unprecedented increases in overall opulence, the contemporary world denies elementary freedoms to vast numbers—perhaps even the majority—of people.

While the frameworks used to conceptualize development work have been broadened, there continues to be a sectoral approach to development aid, focusing on areas such as: infrastructure construction; health; education; economic stability; human rights; gender issues; democratization and governance; and environmental protection. International development is supported through such mechanisms as the work of International Non-Governmental Organizations (INGOs), Local Non-Governmental Organizations (LNGOs), and a process through which multi-lateral and bi-lateral agencies give money or aid to local governments to help promote those countries' ability to meet standards in each of the above sectors that are internationally recognized (e.g., the Sphere Standards and Millennium Development Goals).

Two important concepts have emerged from the field of international development over the last decade: participation and sustainability. *Participatory development* is an approach that recognizes that for a project to be successful over the long-term, it must be based on the needs, wishes, and participation of local or recipient actors. This relates to the idea of *capacity building*, the goal of which is to promote skills and develop resources that will eventually enable a country to be able to meet the needs of its citizens independently without development assistance. The concept of capacity building is also linked to the idea of *sustainability*, meaning that a development project does not consume more economic, environmental or human resources than are available in any given setting, thus limiting its long-term viability. Further, there has also been an important move towards incorporating "conflict sensitive" approaches into development processes. Such frameworks acknowledge that development assistance can have unintended negative consequences, particularly in terms of fueling extant tensions across ethnic and social lines (Anderson 1999; International Alert 2003). As will be illustrated, this shift in approaches to development also has implications for peacebuilding and trauma healing in post-conflict societies.

Peacebuilding

Peacebuilding embodies the goals of building societies based on the concept of human security, safety from direct and structural violence, and tenets of justice (Schirch 2004; Tschirgi 2005). Peacebuilding activities engage the question, how can people achieve a greater sense of justice, respect, and equality in their lives while violence is reduced? An important aspect of *strategic peacebuilding* involves the principle that building peace is by nature participatory, allowing people to "shape their environment so they can meet their own needs" (Schirch 2004). Within such a holistic framework, peacebuilding is not limited to tasks that relate directly to containing violence, mediating conflict, negotiation, or dialogue activities; rather peacebuilding work encompasses a much broader range of activities and processes that are based on the fundamental core values of promoting human security, from policy making and governance to truthtelling to training and education. These core values also underscore processes of development and trauma healing, as will be discussed further in the chapter.

Collective Trauma and Trauma Healing

Trauma can be defined as a "real or perceived threat to the survival of an individual, a support system, or a larger community or culture. Trauma leads to changes in the brain, nervous system, and related areas of the body that are essential to survival but potentially detrimental to ongoing self and spiritual development, engagement in relationships, and productive involvement in learning and work."[3] At the collective level, trauma has been further specified as a condition that results from the experience of both overt and structural violence and is characterized by three primary dimensions: an environment of ongoing dysfunction and chaos; collective social and communal narratives that are deeply ingrained and relate to perceived lack of choice/control; and, individuals' survival orientation.

Collective trauma results from the experience of living in an environment rife with fear and institutional failure, which can result in collective narratives that individuals and communities' create based on their real and perceived access to resources and opportunities. In such settings, people often continue to operate in a survival mode, making decisions based on meeting basic needs which prevents focus on long-term sustainable development mechanisms. These dynamics have important impacts because ultimately, they potentially serve to maintain the marginalization of indigenous or minority ethnic communities by reinforcing their real and perceived lack of access to choices and power (Kantowitz 2006).

Briere and Scott (2006) argue that the definition of psychological trauma "has been applied to so many contexts by so many people that it has lost some of its original meaning." In addition to the issue of "language-ing," the discussion of trauma is made even more complex by the fact that the majority of theory and research available refers only to individuals and does not include the way in which communities and society can be affected by war or other traumatic events. There is a dearth of knowledge about the nature of trauma, resiliency, and the recovery process at multiple levels of analysis. The impact of this concern on practitioners is addressed later in this chapter, reflected in the way in which organizations working in post-conflict settings often lack a systematic approach to psychosocial issues.

Both individual and collective trauma impacts individuals' and group's ability to engage in post-conflict reconstruction and development. The international community has, by and large, adopted the idea of "participation" as being critical to effective policy and programming at the local and national levels; however, there is little discussion of war-affected communities' and individuals' capacity to participate, or the way in which dynamics of trauma impact how they engage in participatory processes. One of the key components of collective trauma propagated by war involves groups' relationship to authority. This dynamic can be characterized by deeply ingrained social patterns such as dependency and paternalism, which shape group and individual behavior (Kantowitz 2006)[4].

This relationship to authority is a product of multiple factors. First, dependency is a historical and learned dynamic in many post-conflict countries, resulting from the oppressive, authoritarian and/or colonialist systems that have often existed in settings in which local communities were forced to rely on landholders and oligarchs to provide for them. Second, paternalism and dependency have been created both by the international community long before concepts such as participatory development existed, as well as by local culture that may be based on gendered conceptions of male "providers" and leaders (i.e., the existence of a cultural norm in which it is considered the role of men and male leaders to arrange for families' and communities' basic needs to be met). Finally, dependency is a result of a legacy of violence in settings where those who took up leadership roles or spoke out against authority were severely persecuted. Thus, the collective behavioral lesson learned was silence, which can mean imposed complicity with reliance on such authority.

These factors coalesce to form a "culture"—a set of group beliefs, attitudes, and behaviors—that results in a collective narrative characterized by powerlessness and a sense of lack of control. This narrative is fed by the fact that these environments often continue to be rife with ongoing fear and dysfunctional institutions (e.g., systems of governance riddled with corruption, ineffective police and judicial forces, and health care and educational systems crippled by lack of economic and human resources). Further, simply because a period of overt war has ended does not mean that historical systems of marginalization and discrimination—often the structural factors that give rise to violence—have ceased.

Issues such as ongoing fear, mistrust, insecurity, institutional failure, and continued victimization converge to maintain the aforementioned deeply ingrained dynamics of collective trauma, including dependency, paternalism, and the perception that communities and individuals do not have access to power, choices about their lives or group life, or the ability to plan for the future and have their collective needs met in ways unrelated to day-to-day survival. Such instability, fear, and institutional failure continue to shape relationships in post-conflict settings, affecting individuals' and collectives' capacity to function—and engage effectively in community development processes. Examples of this can be seen in high rates of substance and alcohol abuse, domestic violence, and a lack of communication, reconciliation, and transparency in communal processes and relationships. These elements impact community members' abilities to work together and effectively to achieve collective goals. Further, individuals and communities in post-conflict countries may also make certain choices, for example, related to leadership, which perpetuate the dynamic of trauma. Such choices may involve picking leaders who play on ingrained patterns of paternalism and dependency as well as the ongoing environment of uncertainty to maintain their power, when deep, systemic change and the transformational leadership that can affect it are needed (Kantowitz 2006).

Trauma healing involves meeting peoples' basic needs through providing safety, acknowledging the past, and restoring relationships between individuals, families, communities and society (Yoder 2004). Like peacebuilding, the work of trauma healing focuses on processes and not solely outcomes, and importantly, on changing patterns and dynamics, such as the above cultural narratives. Trauma healing or psychosocial interventions try and create space for people to find ways to meet their own needs, such as providing food and security for themselves and their families and living in communities in which there are effective communication, leadership, and institutional processes. The route to healing may vary from person to person and community to community. Interventions can encompass a range of activities, but most commonly involve, for example, inhumation and exhumation processes, truthtelling and reconciliation, memorialization, reintegration of child soldiers, and individual work with those who have suffered war atrocities (Agger & Strong 2001; Galappatti 2003). We suggest that engaging individuals in participatory community development processes to meet basic needs is also one important aspect of healing from trauma because it gives communities and groups agency. Discussed further below, this agency may counter some of the dynamics of collective trauma, such as dependency and paternalism.

How Are Development, Peacebuilding and Trauma Healing Linked?

Historical, Contextual, and Value Linkages

Despite increased focus on conflict sensitivity in recent years, the confluence of "peacebuilding" and "development" is at times contained in the task of promoting poverty reduction in the context of conflict or post-conflict settings. However, in keeping with conflict sensitive approaches, this chapter suggests a more holistic view. Logically, peacebuilding and international development are inherently interconnected due to the relationship between economic and social resources and violence. Gurr (2005) shows a dramatic association between weak states, poverty, and armed conflict.[5] Thus, eradicating poverty and creating just access to resources for all peoples is necessarily a task of peacebuilding in that such inequality is linked to so much violence in the world. Additionally, peacebuilding, trauma healing, and development and the practices associated with them inherently overlap because they share a set of fundamental core values: meeting basic human needs, promoting human rights, and eliminating structural and overt violence.

Peacebuilding, trauma healing, and development have become inter-twined over the last fifteen years due to their emergence within and response to the broader global environment. Tschirgi (2005) points to these interrelationships, stating, "As a concept, peacebuilding reflected the optimism of the 1990s when it seemed possible that the end of the Cold War would yield significant peace dividends by ending the global arms race and armed conflicts while promoting socio-economic development." This optimism was tempered by the horrific violence of the 1990s, including the massacres of Bosnia-Herzegovina and the international community's failure to intervene in the Rwandan genocide. Such events prompted the humanitarian assistance community to re-think its role in exacerbating conflict, fomented new approaches to peacebuilding and humanitarian assistance based on more inclusive concepts of participation and sustainability, and brought attention to the need for individual and collective trauma healing in the wake of mass atrocities such as massacres and the use of rape and child soldiers as tools of war.

Another paradigmatic shift in peacebuilding and development assistance occurred post 9/11, when the international communities' focus moved back to externally driven concerns predicated on security, as opposed to context driven approaches to building peace and meeting basic human needs. This security focus has created a challenge that underlies peacebuilding, development, and trauma healing work due to ideological agendas to promote certain tasks (e.g., democracy-building) in certain priority regions that compete for international attention. This has created a tension between the dire needs of particular contexts (such as the Darfur genocide) and the lack of political will to intervene in these settings.

Participatory Development and Trauma Healing Agency

Shifting from a policy to programmatic focus, there are also linkages between development assistance and trauma healing. At a general level, key development concepts like participation and sustainability have the potential to counteract collective trauma. It has been widely acknowledged that development processes are more sustainable when approached through participatory mechanisms. While "participation" alone is not a psychosocial intervention, it is a potentially important aspect of societal healing. Participatory approaches empower communities with decision-making capacity regarding their future, in this way giving individuals and communities agency and changing the dynamic of powerlessness and an orientation towards survival that may characterize traumatized communities. A piece of the individual and collective trauma incurred through war is the sense that, although perhaps overt violence has "formally" ended, people will still not be able to meet their basic needs, and further, continue to live in an inequitable society where those who have discriminated against, oppressed, and harmed them in the past still wield power. Again, involving citizens and communities in meeting their own needs in meaningful ways—such as participation in government, national and local activities; creating sustainable economic development opportunities; or reducing the level of fear in the environment through creating effective police and justice mechanisms—counteracts this sense of powerlessness and thus, helps rebuild societal bonds and heal communities.

Focus on Material Infrastructure

Development assistance and trauma are further linked by the way in which the international community focuses on providing material, "technical," or infrastructure-related resources and the possibility that traumatized communities tend to seek only material forms of development (Dichter 2004; Jackson 2001; Kantowitz 2006). At the international level, organizations such as UNDP have acknowledged this bias through stressing the aforementioned idea of *human development*, which embodies a more holistic concept of human security because it includes variables related to intangible constructs (e.g., climate, gender participation, and respect for human rights). Research has confirmed the importance of such variables in understanding communities' abilities to successfully engage in participatory development processes, while at the same time suggests that a characteristic of traumatized communities may be their focus solely on the material, tangible aspects of development (Kantowitz 2006).

First, it is possible that the members of such communities are merely behaving as "good consumers." There is a devastating reality to the fact that the geopolitical landscape in many post-conflict settings has not changed significantly enough to create access to social and economic opportunities for the majority of the population. In a climate likely still pervaded by fear and lack of choice, it does not seem surprising that communities and individuals would be hesitant to ask for, engage in or implement programs that increase intangible aspects of human development, such as justice, equality, and participation. In such settings, focusing on the tangible may appear to be the wisest survival strategy.

Second, the tendency towards building roads and water systems merely reflects a bias in the field of development itself. Dichter (2003) points out that development organizations continue to "measure" and "do" things, however:

> Increasingly, we know that the real keys to development are neither tangible nor involve much "doing." They are about institutions, attitudes, laws, and hu-

man resources. . . . If development was successful in fostering institutions, attitudes, and laws and in enhancing human resources, we—as professional developers—would not have to do things like build schools and roads. The institutions of a functioning society would see to it that they got built.

He further suggests that the task of sustainable development requires changing the "conduct of people and their governments."

Understanding the effects of trauma at the individual and collective levels is critical because these effects impact conduct—or behavior—and thus, the way in which people and groups engage in the process of development. Such an understanding sheds light on how to change behavior and attitudes, thereby building local capacity by fostering functioning institutions. As Dichter (2003) suggests, the tangible, material, "doing" paradigm must be challenged, for only attending to these aspects of development or post-conflict reconstruction is insufficient. Further, it is possible that continuing to focus on material resources maintains current dynamics of trauma and dependency by perpetuating the message that it is not acceptable to demand more—to insist on justice, equality, and participation.

Summary

In the above sections, we have seen how peacebuilding, development, and trauma healing are linked by a core set of values that have evolved in response to social, political, and historical/current realities. Further, concepts that cross peacebuilding and development, such as participation and sustainability, empower and also promote societal healing. A shift in the focus of development work from tangible outcomes to processes which promote human security can also nurture these collective goals. Recommendations for intervention are discussed at the end of this chapter. Below, we shift to exploring how one organization, World Vision, has addressed the intersection of development, peacebuilding, and trauma healing.

Programming at the Intersection of Peacebuilding, Development, and Trauma Healing: World Vision's Journey

The second half of this chapter explores World Vision's development model, focusing on the areas of intersection between development, peacebuilding and trauma healing. From a theoretical perspective, the intersection between the three sectors is laid out effectively in the framework for transformational development which emphasizes 1) well-being of children, their families and communities; 2) empowered children as agents of transformation 3) transformed relationships 4) interdependent and empowered communities and 5) transformed systems and structures. Significant emphasis is placed on individual growth and transformation in a community context. As noted in the first section of the chapter, there is clear evidence that individual and communal trauma have the potential to severely limit one's ability to participate effectively in the development process. In addition, over half of the countries where World Vision is operational have been affected by conflict and inter-ethnic/religious disputes. If we use the transformational development framework as a theoretical launching pad and combine it with the operational environment of where World Vision works, one is left asking the question: *How are individual and communal trauma addressed in the transformational development process?*

Prior to concluding with recommendations, the rest of our discussion will explore this question, looking first into more detail about how World Vision is structured and their development model as it relates to deepening an understanding of the intersection between development, peacebuilding and trauma healing. Within this model, the challenge to addressing trauma healing specifically arises when attempting to operationalize that theoretical intersection. Examples of specific project interventions will be provided with a detailed look at an integrated project in Rwanda as a possible model of how to think about the intersection.

World Vision's Organizational Dynamic

Numbers, Structure and Staffing

World Vision is the largest Christian relief and development organization in the world. In fact, it is the largest non-governmental organization (NGO) in the world, reaching some 100 million people. With an annual budget of over 2 billion US dollars and programs in over 100 countries, WV has considerable reach. WV's ultimate goal is to tackle the causes of poverty though the chosen approach of empowerment. The emphasis is on relief, development and advocacy.

There are over 21,000 staff and more than 95% of them work in their country of origin. Forty percent of national directors are nationals of the country programs that they oversee. Worldwide, there are less than 600 expatriates. This organizational demography means that WV's approach to development, peacebuilding and trauma healing take place in an environment where almost all long-term development projects are designed, managed and implemented by nationals in their countries of origin. As such staff care is a critical way in which WV addresses trauma healing at an individual and communal level.

World Vision has a federated structure. For example, staff in Kenya or Lebanon or Colombia do not report to staff in the US and visa versa. Each country office is managed independently and although they are joined together by a common mission, vision statement and other core partnership documents, each country office can approach programming in peacebuilding, trauma healing and development differently. As such, the ways in which a regional or national office interprets the intersection and therefore programs for each of these sectors can vary quite significantly. In both theory and practice, therefore, it is not possible for one office to impose programs on another, including trauma healing ones. Decisions about country level programming rest at the national and regional office levels.

In some country programs, there are staff positions specifically focused on staff care, trauma healing and peacebuilding and reconciliation. In others, there are neither. Some examples of the way in which WV has addressed these issues through specific staff roles include Cambodia where there is a Peace and Justice Program Manager. In Rwanda, there is a National Healing, Peacebuilding and Reconciliation Specialist who oversees an integrated development, peacebuilding and trauma healing project. In Bosnia and Herzegovina after the war in the 1990s, staff received specialized training on how to work with children traumatized by war. Several Asian and East African countries have dedicated peacebuilding staff. The Asia regional office has a regional peacebuilding coordinator.

At the highest levels in the organization, it is not clear where trauma healing and psychosocial interventions are housed, a function of the fact that, WV is structured along regional and sectoral lines. Peacebuilding (gender, disability and protection) are viewed as integrated global themes that are cross-cutting to the "pillars" of transformational development, humanitarian emergency affairs and policy and advocacy. There is Director for Peacebuilding and Reconciliation responsible for the development of strategy and policy for the integration of peacebuilding into transformational development and advocacy throughout World Vision. He leads networks of regional peacebuilding networks. There is also a Vice President for Transformational Development, responsible for leading a team that seeks continuous improvement of the theory and practice of transformational development in World Vision. The Director for Children in Development has staff responsible for leading World Vision in the development of sector strategies and standards for all children in crisis, including children affected by war. A new position of Director for Staff Care was recently announced. This person will report to the Vice President for Human Resources and Organizational Development. Functionally, the directors for Peacebuilding and Children in Development sit on the same team. What this means is that the three main "sectors" where trauma healing has primary relevance (peacebuilding, development and staff care) are not functionally dependent on each other and can exist somewhat independently.

The Development Model

Transformational development (TD) is core to World Vision's identity and is a common thread throughout all of its programs. TD seeks to restore and enable wholeness of life with dignity, justice, peace, and hope for all girls, boys, women, men, households and their communities. Transformation also takes place at an organizational level, stimulating change within individual staff, on teams and throughout the organization. World Vision seeks also the transformation of donors and partners. The transformational development approach is "Christ-centered, child-focused, community-based, value-based, sustainable and holistic." The model is holistic in nature reflecting an "integrated physical-spiritual understanding of human beings; the world they live in and the way people develop."[6] Resiliency is a strong theme in transformational development and all transformational development programs "aim for peace and reconciliation and employ processes and actions that reduce risks and enhance capacities of families and communities to cope, mitigate and respond to disasters, conflicts and HIV/AIDS."

Within the transformational development framework, fourteen indicators have been developed to measure development. Of the fourteen, two are key to thinking about the intersection between trauma healing, peacebuilding, and development: caring for others and emergence of hope.[7]

The *caring for each other indicator* seeks to:

Measure attitudes, actions, and values of community members which are fundamental to their relationship. Care for each other means that men, women, boys and girls perceive that they care for others and other care for them in their community. Care for each other is defined around dimensions of usc (sharing) of community resources, gender relations, protection and valuing of children, well-being of vulnerable persons and conflict prevention/resolution.[8]

The *emergence of hope indicator* seeks to:

Find out if hope for a brighter future is emerging and growing among the people. Only hope for a better future will provide necessary motivation for people to overcome critical limiting factors in their living situations. Hope for the future relates to people's perceptions: that of self, as well as perceptions of the past and present and whether past and present are seen only in negative terms, or as learning experiences or celebrations on the road to the future. Hope is essential for transformed relationships—the third domain of change in World Vision's TD framework and policy."[9]

World Vision's development model relies on a few key assumptions. One is that World Vision's role is that of a catalyst. Second, staff members are able to model transformation in their lifestyles and interaction with communities. Third, WV staff represents a unique "all embracing and impartial approach" (Calthorp). Although this is only a brief look at the framework, it clearly illustrates how critical concepts of individual and communal participation together with conflict transformation are critical to achieving transformational development.

Peacebuilding as Transformation: Six Years down the Line

World Vision has been exploring the link between peacebuilding and development since the mid 1990s. Many staff had been working on peacebuilding and developing conflict sensitive programs long before it became *de rigueur* in the field of development. That said it was not until senior leadership made the direct theoretical connection between transformational development and conflict that the organizational impetus was set to explore the linkages. With the hiring of a Director for Peacebuilding and Reconciliation in 2001, a vision for integrating peacebuilding into transformational development was laid out. Case studies were written, a framework developed, staff trained, indicators designed, projects implemented, lessons documented and shared.

iPAD: Integrating Peacebuilding into Development[10]

One of the significant successes over the past few years has been the development of a framework and a training manual to help community development workers integrate peacebuilding themes and processes into long-term development programs. After a four-year process of articulating the transformational development framework, three areas were identified as having the potential to limit the impact of transformational development: disasters, HIV AIDS and similar pandemics and conflict. In response to this, five strategic processes were developed to help practitioners understand the various elements needed to support a durable peace at the community level.

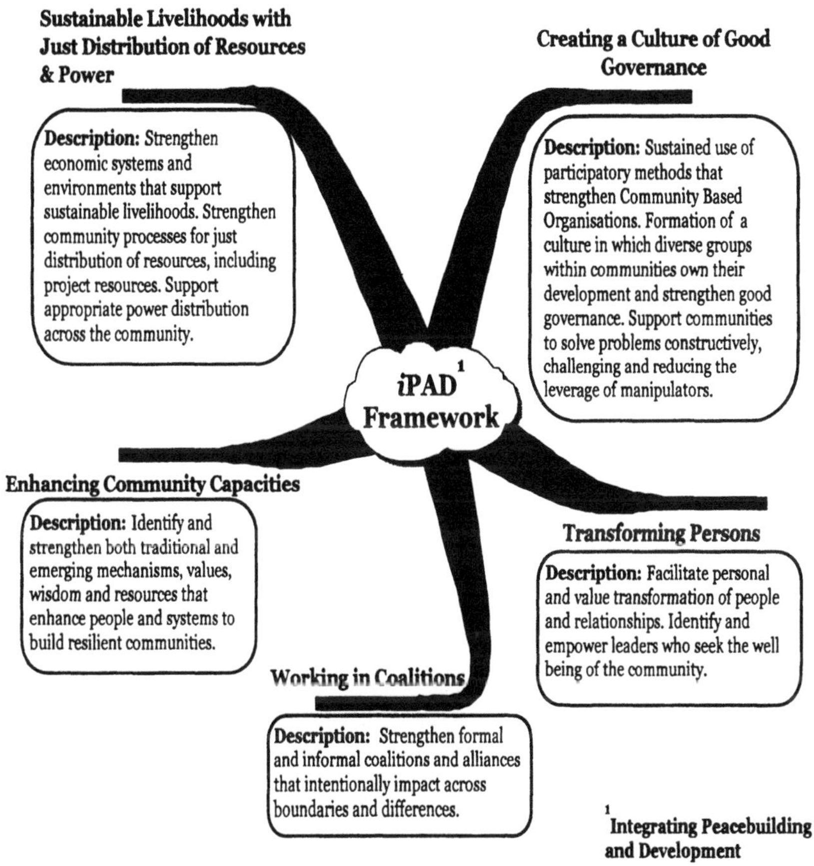

Figure 1.1. iPAD: Integrating Peacebuilding into Development

These strategic processes are:

- Creating a Culture of Good Governance
- Transforming Persons
- Working in Coalitions: Impacting beyond commonly recognized boundaries
- Enhancing Community Capacities that Generate Hope
- Developing Sustainable Livelihoods with Just Distribution of Resources

As the strategic processes were developed in part out of exploring the relationship between peacebuilding and development, that intersection is clear. The challenge again is that trauma healing is critical when thinking about the intersection between development, peacebuilding and trauma healing. However, how trauma healing links both theoretically and programmatically to the strategic processes has not been articulated.

That said, the strategic way that the intersection between peacebuilding and development were teased out and elaborated has led to a unique situation where, six years later, it is quite common for WV staff to comment that everyone can be a "peacebuilder" and everyone can support development processes that "contribute to peace." The question is still pending as to whose role is it to support trauma healing and development processes that support "wholeness of life with dignity?" The work that WV has done towards making strong theoretical and operational links and working towards mainstreaming peacebuilding in a development context is perhaps a model that can be explored when thinking about the links between peacebuilding, trauma healing and development.

Trauma Healing or Psychosocial Intervention: Does It Really Matter What We Call It?

The range of programs that have a trauma healing or psychosocial component is quite large. This is interesting given that there is no strong consensus on what to call these programs. Within World Vision, the term "trauma healing" is a controversial one. Some staff believe that World Vision should not be involved with trauma healing because the organization does not have the technical capacity to implement mental health programs. Many see it as requir-

> The World Vision International HIV AIDS team has a Regional Psychosocial Advisor who is based in Nairobi, Kenya. A counseling psychologist, he has worked with researchers from Johns Hopkins, Boston and Columbia Universities since 1999 to develop appropriate cross-cultural mental health assessment methods and tools and to measure the effect of an adapted form of group interpersonal psychotherapy (IPT-G) with depressed persons in Uganda and Rwanda (Bass 2006, Bolton 2003). The Uganda research revealed that IPT-G is relevant in Uganda. The anthropological research that was carried out to support the study revealed that there are terms in the local language to define depression.

ing very technical skills and formal training. Trauma healing makes some staff nervous because they feel it implies counseling and psychotherapy, high costs and medicines that are not easily accessible in many parts of the world. Others believe that the work of inner healing is God's work and that healing lies most importantly in our relationship with God and does not need external interventions such as counseling. For others, the fact that WV works in cultures and communities that do not have words or concepts for mental health, psychiatry or psychosocial interventions limits the cross-cultural relevance of Western-oriented psychosocial approaches and interventions. They note that clinical psychology does not cross cultures very well.

The term "psychosocial intervention" is less controversial but not entirely embraced. A psychosocial approach implies that there is something in the environment that is causing distress rather than something solely in the individual themselves. Although the terms are also debated in the field of international mental health, there is evidence to support the theory that traumatic events affect an individual's mental and behavioral outcomes (Herman 1992). In the context of a development model that rests almost entirely on relationships, the mental health of individuals, groups, and communities where World Vision operates cannot be ignored—and in many offices, it is not.

The initial research for this chapter, though not exhaustive, identified a variety of programs, each with different methodologies and each being implemented by staff with varied levels of experience and training in the mental health profession.[11] Some interventions have a strong counseling component (peer, group, individual). Others focus on creative art therapy, mentoring/coaching and life skills training. Many use a combination of approaches. In some national offices, World Vision provides these interventions directly. In others, WV partners with mental health professionals and institutions that provide mental health support such as schools and other government service providers.

> WV's Director for Child Protection is one of the few WV staff with a doctorate in Psychology. He has focused on staff care issues for many years and notes that the success to good psychosocial interventions with staff and communities rests with a three pronged approach of understanding "culture, language and context." He advocates a model that focuses on seeing people that survive disasters and wars as just that—survivors. This survivor model identifies them as survivors and identities what the community was like before the trauma event. What is beneficial about the model is that you do not need mental health professionals to implement these programs.

As a child-focused organization, World Vision is especially concerned with the impact of traumatic events on children and youth. Pynoos (1993) argues that "childhood exposure to traumatic stress impinges on the course of development by shaping children's expectations about the world, the safety and security of their interpersonal life and their sense of personal integrity (p. 205)." WV responds to the psychological needs of children in a variety of settings from post disaster, post conflict, exploitative child labor, or sexual abuse. For example, World Vision has developed a model of Child-Friendly Spaces (CFS) for children in post-disaster settings such as after the Pakistan earthquake and the Asian tsunami. Significant work has been done to address the psychosocial needs of orphans and vulnerable children affected by the HIV/AIDS pandemic. In the Philippines, WV has developed a training program for community counselors to promote wellness for children and families experiencing disasters or other forms of crises. The guiding theme of the program is the indigenous spirit of *urabayan* or unity in the common work of helping.

In Cambodia, WV runs a trauma-counseling center for girls that have been sexually exploited and abused. This center provides Non Directive Support Therapy, which involves individual and group counseling together with art or play therapy once a week. Trained caregivers, not mental health professionals, counsel the children. Focused on individual trauma, the goal of the project is to reduce a child's post traumatic stress symptoms, reduce a child's symptoms of depression, reduce children's externalizing and internalizing behaviors and reduce a child's anxiety and their distorted sexual behavior (Wallace 2007). In Aceh after the 2005 tsunami, World Vision partnered with Acehnese mental health professionals and local religious leaders to support the psychosocial needs identified at the community level.

In many post conflict settings, the effects of trauma are also being addressed. For the past six years, in northern Uganda, WV has managed center-based projects doing psychosocial work with children in preparation for their being united with their families. Programs in the North Caucasus (Chechnya and Ingushetia) provide direct psychosocial support to children and their families recovering from the effects of an especially brutal war.

World Vision's trauma healing work in post-conflict areas does not focus only on children. In Indonesia, WV implemented a small project to produce a training manual for healing and reconciliation for religious leaders in North Maluku. In the Philippines, projects have been designed to promote healing and reconciliation. The integrated trauma healing, peacebuilding and development program in Rwanda is probably the best example within World Vision of what the intersection could look like practically.

Rwanda Case Study: Where Everyone Has Pain How Can We Develop?

The 1994 genocide was not Rwanda's first experience with violence. Over a period of more than 40 years, Rwanda has experienced traumatic internal upheaval, which has included a series of massacres. This has continually fuelled cycles of ethnic hatred, fear and a resulting desire for revenge and reprisal. The genocide of 1994 resulted in the deaths of over 1 million people. Three million fled to neighboring countries and lived in refugee camps. Since 1996, most have returned to Rwanda.

Following the genocide, the World Vision response was primarily relief in nature. WV provided material goods to meet immediate needs such as food and shelter. In the implementation of these relief projects, it became evident that the move to development assistance would have to address the level of trauma that had been experienced during the genocide and leading up to it. A World Vision ethnographic study in 1999 demonstrated the effects of trauma on individual Rwandans. The report noted that "...people who carry deep pain and trauma demonstrate dysfunctional behavior in terms of social interactions and work performance. They feel lethargic, lose interest in business are weak and therefore unproductive." The report also noted that for most Rwandans, trauma, fear and guilt are more collective in nature and therefore need to be addressed communally. Much of the trauma noted by survey respondents was generational in nature highlighting the risk of renewed cycles of violence.

> Something has been released from my heart. In the program we were told to write letters to our dead loved ones and every night before, I usually had nightmares about them – especially my father. I have kept that letter and that took a lot of weight off my mind. Now I am able to sleep. (HRP workshop participant)

> I could not eat anything that came from the ground. This was where my relatives were buried and everything tasted and smelt of flesh. Now I can eat and can even work in my garden to feed my family. (HRP workshop participant)

In response to the disintegration and destruction of social capital, World Vision began a Healing, Peacebuilding and Reconciliation (HPR) program. The rationale behind the HRP was that transformational development could not occur effectively unless the community addressed the issues that had plagued the country for 40 plus years as these internal forces worked actively against any forms of community cohesion and development. Such a program was needed to enable a cohesive society where genocide survivors, perpetrators, returned exiles and refugees chose to live and work together in a reconciled and functional community.

Rwandan psychologists in Rwanda were the primary developers of the trainings and workshops. Several strategies were utilized to work towards these objectives especially the use of community workshops—usually mixing perpetrators, survivors, male and female in groups. One of the developers of these workshops used the rationale for the workshop development as "the community that destroyed itself must heal itself—not as individuals or groups but as a community." In addition, the training of community members to identify individuals in the community suffering from trauma was another strategic initiative towards the broad goals of the program. All of these approaches are based on the assumptions that the trauma experienced by Rwandese over a sustained period of time has had a detrimental effect on the community. Most commentators agree the all Rwandese experience the effects of trauma. Josephine Munyeli currently manages the trauma healing and reconciliation program. When asked about who attends the trainings, she said "everyone." "Everyone has pain. Everyone has a story."

In 2002 World Vision began a process of integrating the work of trauma healing and peacebuilding into its long-term development programs. This was an intentional move to ensure integration of trauma healing activities into World Vision's strategic plans at the community level. The results of a January 2007 evaluation noted the following about this process, much of which focused on the impact of trauma on WV staff: [12]

- The impact of their history - genocide, persecution and discrimination has had a detrimental effect on World Vision Rwandese staff as well as the community. Their ability to effectively work together as a team and to model to the wider society reconciliation and forgiveness has been affected and was evident.
- The trauma work conducted by the staff takes a toll—with examples of "vicarious traumatization" being reported. Self-care can be difficult in a work culture that encourages 'sacrificial' work practices and where most staff members are suffering from their own responses to the trauma of their experiences of the past.
- The staff have been able to use their expertise and training in providing their communities with opportunities for conflict resolution, mediation, healing and reconciliation.
- There are no societies that are free of trauma or the ensuing impact of ongoing and past trauma on individuals. No psychosocial programs achieve ongoing permanent healing for all participants. The expectations of success or degrees of success in regard to effectiveness and impact will depend on many factors that are outside what happens during the intervention of these or any psychosocial programs.

The evaluation also noted that "the pervasive Christian presence in [Rwanda] found a resonance with the language and themes of a Christian understanding of healing, peacebuilding and reconciliation." The application of WV's Christian identity and transformational development model can promote healing through an intentional focus on reconciliation and grace. Many national offices have established inter-faith programs. Lowrey (2007) describes the variety of there programs:

> In the Asia-Pacific Region, WV Development Foundation of the Philippines supports a Mindanao inter-faith religious leaders network that advises on transformational development programs at both local and island-wide levels. WV Indonesia developed an innovative training program to equip inter-faith religious leaders in North Maluku with basic skills in trauma healing. WV Cambodia has facilitated the launch of an interfaith peacebuilding initiative for youth, which is co-led by representatives of Buddhism, Islam and Christianity.

WV Kosovo has facilitated the development of a strong multi-faith and multi-ethnic Community Council of Peace and Tolerance in the divided city of Mitrovica. Additionally, WV is facilitating an interfaith religious leaders consultation process in other parts of Kosovo, and has helped create the Kids for Peace program that brings together children and youth from Muslim and Christian communities. World Vision Jerusalem-West Bank-Gaza is a mixture at both staffing and community programming levels of Muslim and Christian Palestinians. And in numerous countries in Africa, World Vision works closely in linking Christian, Muslim, and African Traditional Religious leaders and communities to build more peaceful and just societies.

Managers as Transformational Leaders

The influence and impact of leadership cannot be underestimated. To what extent do managers and senior leaders in World Vision understand the ways in which the effects of trauma impacts and pervades psychological functioning and relationships? To what extent to World Vision leaders understand that their own trauma has a potential impediment to transformational development? To what extent are managers aware of the intrinsic link between trauma and transformational development? As noted earlier, the majority of World Vision managers and leaders work in the countries of their national origin. Our argument, therefore, is that in the context of the World Vision development model, and how the organization is structured and governed, it is critical to develop a keen understanding of this intersection if World Vision is truly going to contribute to transformational development.

In March 2007 World Vision International posted a job opening for a Director of Staff Care (in the area of Stress & Trauma Management for WV staff & their families). As this position reports to the World Vision International Vice President for Human Resources and Organizational Development, the opportunity exists to find answers to those questions and create a structure where management competencies address the issue of staff care and managers are responsible for creating a team environment that allows staff to not only manage stress and trauma but also find the place where they are able to contribute to transformational development.

Although the justification for the intersection between trauma healing, peacebuilding and development can be found in the transformational development policy and frame, there are no organizational guidelines or operational mechanisms for staff to make the connection between the three sectors. For the first time in the history of the World Vision partnership, there are key staff at a global level representing the sectors of peacebuilding, staff care, children in crisis and transformational development. Although they are not on the same functional team, as they move forward and develop their strategies, the opportunity exists to 1) further explore the theoretical intersection between transformational development, peacebuilding and trauma healing and 2) the practical implications of what that intersection looks like at the field level given that the majority of World Vision staff work in their countries of origin and are not immune to trauma and its potentially debilitating effects.

As a Field, How Do We Move Forward?

Just as poverty is debilitating, so is trauma, if not addressed. As theorists and practitioners, there needs to be a more in depth and intentional analysis of the ways in which individual and communal trauma influence the development process. Discussed below are specific questions and points of intervention aimed at promoting peacebuilding, collective healing, and participatory development.

Paradigm Shift Away From Material Development. Constructing roads in underdeveloped settings are undeniably imperative; yet, it is equally vital to invest in capacity building that focuses on affecting change in the culture of communities, thus interrupting the dynamics of trauma and fostering more effective functioning of systems and procedures within communities and society.

Leadership. Leadership is an essential change point in breaking the pattern of dependency, paternalism and authoritarianism in communities. Shifting current paradigms of leadership require targeting change at the policy level through implementing democratic practices (transparency, fair elections, term-limits, etc.), and also the grassroots local level involving both leaders and followers. Regarding the former, interventions that teach leaders how to build consensus, engage in dialogue, create compromise, foster equal participation, and empower communities to break the above cycles—but through other mechanisms than strict authoritarian management—are important. Regarding the latter, the role of civil society in encouraging the exercise of civil liberties becomes critical in post-conflict settings, where these liberties may not be understood let alone exercised.

Safety. Fear is also a critical way in which communal trauma is perpetuated in post-conflict countries. When citizens feel safer, they are better able to participate in their community in more effective ways (Kantowitz 2006). Changing the external environment to create economic opportunities that would stymie the activity of gangs, and reforming police and judicial processes such that they are functional is obviously important in the macro-sense. However, focusing on interventions that create mechanisms of safety and control at the grassroots level are also potential means of moderating fear. Addressing issues of security from a grassroots perspective should be a priority for local communities and leaders.[13]

Meaningful Reconciliation. Reconciliation, a traditional focus of peacebuilding and trauma healing activities, needs to be meaningful at the grassroots level to enable communities to work together and achieve development goals more effectively. Macro-level mechanisms such as the presence of civil society leaders related to human rights and their monitoring, and the knowledge of processes dealing with reparations have brought a consciousness to healing and justice. Yet, "reconciliation" at the local level can focus on the debate about reparations (i.e., monetary compensation), without addressing deep underlying fractures in communities. These fractures have implications for communities' ability to work together and engage in participatory development processes that actually accomplish community goals. Thus, reconciliation efforts must include not only exhumation processes, attempts at justice through reparations, and individual healing, but a commitment to other mechanisms, such as dialogue and mediation, that would better stabilize the fragile equilibrium of communities that have been shattered by war.

Organizational Mapping of All Psychosocial Projects (in post conflict contexts and elsewhere). To effectively address trauma, agencies must review their programming and staff training to ensure basic level of skill which would address the intersection between staff competencies, staff care and trauma at multiple levels of analysis.

Staff Support. For those staff who are working in post conflict areas, there is a need to ensure an adequate level of training and sensitization to their own stress patterns and those of the people that they are called to serve. This should include ensuring that adequate support mechanisms are in place.

Additional Research. In general, there is a tremendous need for further research about the conceptual links between trauma at the individual and collective levels, and mechanisms that counteract and mitigate such trauma. Such investigation should focus on providing additional guidance to development practitioners on how to design projects that can lead to, for example, "enhanced capacity and value based commitment to resolve differences and conflicts without destructive or violent means."[14] In keeping with the above recommendation about moving away from solely focusing on "hard" development projects involving infrastructure, internal WV research in 2006 on developing models of community resilience recommended that additional understanding was needed on the immaterial components of development such as "hope, faith, sense of dignity and cohesiveness." There must be resources and attention focused on finding ways to integrate trauma healing and meeting psychosocial needs with other participatory development initiatives.

Further, there is a dearth of data and information regarding extant programs and interventions in many organizations. For World Vision, one research question could be related to the types of interventions that have worked for WV staff who were, for example, child soldiers in Uganda or Cambodia? What helped them to heal? Was it their faith, the service component of their jobs, support from families and communities, counseling? Are there any links between the ways in which WV staff have been able to heal themselves and how WV approaches trauma healing at a community level?

Conclusion

We have attempted to elucidate the links between development, peacebuilding and trauma healing, both conceptually and practically. It is clear that much work remains at the intersection of these topics; however, it also evident that addressing trauma and healing is becoming a central focus in the arenas of development and peacebuilding. We have suggested that the goal of promoting human dignity and peace, and giving individuals and communities tools to transform their lives lies at the intersection of development, peacebuilding and trauma healing. Acknowledging that psychological and psychosocial issues play a significant role in individuals' and communities' abilities to engage successfully in development and peacebuilding processes is a significant first step. A more nuanced, systematic understanding of the phenomenon of trauma and the relationship between theory, policy and practice that relate to traumatized and developing communities is necessary to nurture this goal.

Notes

1. The opinions in this chapter do not necessarily reflect the views of World Vision International or World Vision Inc.

2. The authors would like to thank the following people for assisting in the research, conceptualization and editing of this chapter: Mary Angelini, Susan Barber, Tony Culnane, John Fawcett, Michael Hegenauer, Josie Holcomb, Paul Jeffery, Azra Kacapor, Ashley Inselman, Bill Lowrey, Peter McKinnon, Bridget Moix, Josephine Munyeli, Lincoln Ndongoni, Jaisankar Sarma, Trudy Sharp and Teresa Wallace.

3. Dr. Julian Ford, http://www.traumamatters.org/

4. Paternalism refers to the idea that those in authority relate to their constituents in a "fatherly" manner without necessarily cultivating their capacity for self-reliance.

5. For full report, see www.humansecurity.info

6. World Vision International Transformational Development Policy. Approved by the World Vision International Board, 18 September 2002.

7. The other twelve are water, nutrition, primary education, diarrhea management, immunization, household resilience, poorest households, caring for others, emergence of hope, Christian commitment, community participation, social sustainability, HIV AIDS prevention and advocacy.

8. World Vision Development Resources Team. Transformational Development Indicators Field Guide. Volume 4 Transformed Relationships, p. 7.

9. Ibid, page 26.

10. Framework developed by Bill Lowrey, World Vision International Director for Peacebuilding and Reconciliation.

11. More research would be needed to articulate a more detailed report of programs that have a distinct psychosocial component.

12. Taken from January 07 WV Australia-funded external evaluation report written by Roslyn Leary.

13. In keeping with the tenets of peacebuilding, it is important to address security issues using nonviolent means, as opposed to mechanisms such as vigilante justice.

14. One of the illustrative indicators identified for integrating peacebuilding into development. Transformational Development Core Documents, February 2003, page 21.

References

Anderson, M. 1999. *Do No Harm: How Aid Can Support Peace or War.* Boulder, CO: Lynne Rienner.

Bass, J., et al. 2006. Group Interpersonal Psychology for Depression in Rural Uganda: 6-Month Outcomes. *British Journal of Psychiatry,* 188: 567-573.

Bodenhamner, M. 2006. Learning from the Community Resilience Research. World Vision International. Unpublished. Available online: http://www.transformational-development.org/Ministry/TransDev2.nsf/C413D9BC50DEBA9D8525711500700 6DA/$file/Learning%20from%20Community%20Resilience%20Research%20in%20 2006.pdf

Bolton P., Neugebauer R. and Ndongoni L. 2002. Prevalence of Depression in Rural Rwanda Based on Symptom and Function Criteria. *Journal of Nervous and Mental Disease,* 190:631-7.

Briere, J. & Scott. C. 2006. *Principles of Trauma Therapy: A Guide to Symptoms, Evaluation and Treatment.* Thousand Oaks: Sage Publications.

Dichter, T. 2003. *Despite Good Intentions: Why Development Assistance to the Third World Has Failed.* Boston: University of Massachusetts Press.

Everly, G. et al. 2003. Critical Incident Stress Management (CISM): A Statistical Review of the Literature. *Psychiatric Quarterly,* 73:3, 171-181.

Galappatti, A. 2003. What is a Psychosocial Intervention: Mapping the Field in Sri Lanka. *Intervention* 1 (2), p. 3 - 17.

Gurr, T. & Monty, M. 2005. Peace and Conflict 2005: A Global Survey of Armed Conflicts, Self-Determination Movements, and Democracy. Center for International Development and Conflict Management: http://www.cidcm.umd.edu/publications/publication.asp?pubType=paper&id=15

Kantowitz, R. 2006. *Healing Systems: A Multilevel Social Psychology Model of Trauma in Guatemala.* Columbia University, unpublished dissertation.

International Alert, FEWER, and Safeworld. 2003. Conflict-Sensitive Approaches to Development, Humanitarian Assistance and Peacebuilding: http://www.conflictsensitivity.org/resource_pack.html

Herman, J. 1997. *Trauma and Recovery: The Aftermath of Violence—From Domestic Abuse to Political Terror.* New York: Basic Books.

Inter-agency Standing Committee. 2007. IASC Guidelines on Mental Health and Psychosocial Support in Emergency Settings: http://www.humanitarianinfo.org/iasc/content/documents/weekly/20070620-1345/Guidelines%20IASC%20Mental%20Health%20Psychosocial.pdf

Korten, D. 1995. *When Corporations Rule the World.* West Hartford, CT: Kumarian Press.

Lowrey, B. 2006. "Introduction" In Michelle Garred, ed. *A Shared Future: Local Capacities for Peace in Community Development.* Monrovia: World Vision International.

O'Reilly, S. 1998. *The Contribution of Community Development to Peacebuilding: World Vision's Area Development Programmes.* Final Report. World Vision United Kingdom.

Pynoos, R. S. 1993. Traumatic Stress and Developmental Psychopathology in Children and Adolescents. *Review of Psychiatry* 12: 205-238.

Rahnema, M. 1997. "Towards Post-Development: Searching for Signposts, a New Language and New Paradigms." In Rahnema, M. & Bawtree, V., eds. *The Post Development Reader*. London: Zed Books.

Shirch, L. 2004. *The Little Book of Strategic Peacebuilding*. Intercourse, PA: Good Books.

Sen, A. 2000. *Development as Freedom*. New York: Knopf.

Staub, E., et al. 2005. Healing Reconciliation, Forgiving and the Prevention of Violence After Genocide or Mass Killing: An Intervention and Its Experimental Evaluation in Rwanda. *Journal of Social and Clinical Psychology*, 24:3; 297-333.

Tschirgi, N. 2004. Post-Conflict Peace-Building Revisited. IPA Policy Report: http://www.ipacademy.org/PDF_Reports/POST_CONFLICT_PEACEBUILDING.pdf

United Nations Development Programme 1994. An Agenda for Development. http://www.un.org/Docs/SG/agdev.html

Verdell, H., et al. 2003. Adapting group Interpersonal Psychotherapy for a developing Country: Experience In Rural Uganda. *World Psychiatry*, 2:2.

Wallace, T. 2007. "Treating Child Victims of Sexual Exploitation in Phnom Penh, Cambodia with Trauma-Focused Cognitive Behavioral Therapy. Intervention and Evaluation Study Designs." Unpublished.

Wessells, M. & Monteiro, C. 2004. "Culture, Healing, and Post-Conflict Reconstruction in Angola: A Community-Based Approach to Assisting War-Affected Children." In Gielan, U., Fish, J. and Draguns, J., eds. *Culture, Therapy and Healing*. Mahwah, NJ: Lawrence Erlbaum.

Yoder, C. 2005. *The Little Book of Trauma Healing: When Violence Strikes and Community Security is Threatened*. Intercourse, PA: Good Books

2

Managing Memory: Looking to Transitional Justice to Address Trauma

Judy Barsalou

In recent decades, the field of transitional justice has grown enormously. Between 1974 and 2004, 27 truth commissions operated in a wide array of countries around the world.[1] National, international and mixed legal tribunals designed to hold war criminals accountable—such as the International Criminal Tribunals for Rwanda and the former Yugoslavia, and the newly established International Criminal Court—have captured public interest worldwide. Other transitional justice interventions based on extra judicial strategies such as memorialization—have been applied in a wide variety of settings. Yet, despite substantial and ever-growing investments in transitional justice processes by the international community and countries emerging from violence, it remains unclear precisely what short- and long-term impact these interventions have. Do they help reduce the psychological trauma experienced by individual survivors? Are they effective in promoting reconciliation or social reconstruction? What relative contribution do they make in restoring a sense of normality and stability to societies compared to other reconstruction processes, such as constitutional

---

This chapter is based, in part, on a conference organized by the U.S. Institute of Peace and the American Association for the Advancement of Science in March 2004, and on a subsequent publication by Judy Barsalou entitled, "Trauma and Transitional Justice in Divided Societies." Washington, DC: USIP Press, Special Report 135, April, 2005.

and economic reform, physical reconstruction, and traditional cultural practices designed to reintegrate former combatants into peaceful social life?

These are difficult questions to answer, and only a few scholars have recently started to address them seriously.[2] Defining success, even in a single geographical context, and applying lessons learned from one context or time frame to another, is a complicated process. For one thing, it is difficult to evaluate the overall effectiveness of transitional justice mechanisms given the differing perspectives of victims and perpetrators. There are also significant methodological challenges. When, for example, is the optimal time to assess impact? How can researchers isolate the impact of one transitional justice intervention from other processes at work in a society? While it may be possible to determine that an individual's mental health has improved, how does a researcher "take the temperature" of a society to determine the degree of post-conflict reconciliation or social reconstruction?

A scholar who reviewed the literature on the psychological effect of trials of perpetrators on victims concluded that, "we know little."[3] The perception that trials, truth commissions and other transitional justice interventions have salutary psychological effects on individuals and their societies is based largely on anecdotal data and media accounts rather than on carefully constructed evidence.

The Role of Trauma

The international community now recognizes that among the most important needs of countries emerging from violent conflict is accounting for what happened during the conflict, seeking justice for those who were wronged, and promoting social reconstruction of afflicted societies. Less well understood is the role that psychological trauma plays in these processes. Clearly, some individuals emerging from long-term violent conflict remain deeply troubled and their societies are destabilized. Individuals, be they "victims" or "perpetrators," and the societies of which they are a part are essentially survivors of collective violence and gross human rights abuses. Arguably, these traumatized individuals and their societies display recognizable patterns of behavior.

On the individual level, some survivors suffer from a range of symptoms associated with post-traumatic stress disorder (PTSD)—such as flashbacks and nightmares, detachment or estrangement from family and social life, memory loss, depression, substance abuse and cognitive problems. Rates of traumatization vary. One study of Rwandan survivors of the 1994 genocide documented almost eight years later that nearly 25 percent of those surveyed still reported PTSD symptoms.[4] Another study of PTSD in four societies—Algeria, Cambodia, Ethiopia and Gaza—found assessed rates of PTSD ranging from a high of 37.4 percent (in Algeria) to 17.8 percent (in Gaza).[5] These and other studies have established that rates of traumatization are often associated with different risk factors, such as torture, death or separation within families, exposure to conflict before the age of twelve, continued terrorist attacks, poor housing quality and other factors that vary from one society to another.

The importance of helping traumatized individuals struggling with PTSD is a widely understood need, although the scale of the problem is generally vastly greater than the availability of services from either local or international sources. A number of Western practitioners have developed models and techniques for assisting those suffering from PTSD. Some, such as Eastern Mennonite University's STAR program, have been tested for use in a wide variety of cultural settings around the world. Other programs—such as the Center for Victims of Torture in Minneapolis—started initially by focusing on people who have left their countries and come to the United States.[6] And others, such as the interventions developed by the Documentation Center in Cambodia, are largely locally initiated. There are on-going debates about what approaches are best to use. Some employ the use of Westernized and medical approaches, while others deem these inappropriate when applied to non-Western settings and argue instead for traditional, "culturally appropriate" practices. Many programs opt to combine elements of both.

On the broader level, it is undeniable that many societies emerging from long-term, violent conflict display problematic social tendencies. Heightened rates of prostitution, rape, domestic violence and other forms of criminal and gang behavior are common in so-called "post-conflict" societies, such as South Africa.[7] Societies that have suffered primarily from "vertical" violence—that is, violence inflicted by the state against groups of citizens and vice versa during a period of civil war—often suffer from high rates of "horizontal" violence experienced by citizens as victims of crime after the war ends.[8]

But unlike PTSD, which is a widely accepted syndrome describing the behavior of affected individuals, there is no comparable agreement on the existence of a syndrome describing the behavior of societies affected by large-scale violence. Some psychiatrists believe that political violence causes psychological distortions in societies that affect group dynamics and interaction. For example, psychiatrist Vamik Volkan argues that large groups, not just individuals, go through a "psychological mourning process."[9] According to Volkan, the psychological consequences differ somewhat depending on whether the cause of the loss was a natural disaster (such as a flood) or violence caused by other human beings. In the latter case, survivors can manifest not only a sense of loss but also of being "singled out by others for victimization or punishment." The resulting trauma, according to Volkan, generates feelings of humiliation, helplessness and a loss of human dignity.[10]

Volkan's work is especially interesting because he makes a link between individual and group psychology in the wake of calamitous human violence. He argues that, following such events,

> A mental representation of it, common to all members, begins to take shape. This mental representation is the consolidated collection of the shared feelings, perceptions, fantasies and interpretations of the events, as well as the images of relevant characters, such as a fallen leader. When the mental representation becomes so burdensome that members of the group are unable to initiate or resolve the mourning of their losses or reverse their feelings of humiliation, their

> traumatized self-images are passed down to later generations in the hope that others may be able to mourn and resolve what the prior generation could not.[11]

According to Volkan, memories of these events, which he describes as "chosen traumas," become key elements of group identity around which groups and even whole societies rally. In the retelling of the events from one person to another and one generation to another, the events themselves often are recast or glorified and may be used to incite revenge and justify efforts to restore the honor or dignity of the victimized group or society. While some individuals distance themselves from these memories, others become susceptible to political leaders who may "reignite a dormant group memory that affects collective thinking, perception, and actions."[12] As a consequence, ethnic groups or societies organized around these defining "chosen traumas" can become engaged in highly (self) destructive political dynamics in which they become locked in unending conflict with their hated enemies and where reconciliation will not be achieved through the signing of a peace treaty alone but will also require adjustments at a more fundamental psychological and group-identity level.[13]

Others deny that psychological concepts and models appropriate for individuals apply to societies. They object to the use of medicalized images depicting "wounded" societies and their "recovery," which, they argue, psychopathologize the process of social reconstruction and over-simplify complex societies. In this connection, Rosalind Shaw asserts that, "Nations . . . do not have psyches that can be healed."[14] Michael Ignatieff argues that it is difficult to characterize an individual as having a single identity and impossible to impose a similar construct on a nation or society in the context of promoting healing after violence.[15] Stathis Kalyvas believes it depends on whether one views revenge as a norm or an emotion, and notes that a relatively small percentage of conflicts that are remembered by protagonists actually become violent.[16]

At the core of this debate is how the relationship between individuals' mental states and personal attitudes affect the beliefs and behavior of the social groups and larger societies of which they are a part.[17] A related issue is how intra- and inter-group relations affect the mental health of traumatized individuals. Clearly there is a complex interplay between individuals and the groups to which they belong. According to one set of researchers, however, "it has long been established that people behave differently in intergroup settings than they do in interpersonal settings because of a shift from personal to social identity and because of an emphasis on the in-group rather than on the self. . . ."[18]

Regardless of where one stands on this issue, it is clear that the concept of healing is difficult to define in practical or quantifiable ways in relation to societies, and even more problematic given the diversity of cultures in which political violence occurs. Some scholars and practitioners use the term "reconciliation" to describe processes through which individuals and societies recover from trauma and mete out justice, but defining exactly what reconciliation means, how it is achieved and even recognizing when it has been accomplished remains a challenge. Given the ambiguities of the term, some prefer to talk about "social reconstruction" rather than reconciliation to refer to a wide array of strategies to help divided societies become more stable, just and democratic. Social reconstruction as defined by Eric Stover and Harvey Weinstein describes a "process that includes a broad range of programmatic interventions, such as security, freedom of movement, access to accurate and unbiased information, the rule of law, justice, education for democracy, economic development, [and] cross-ethnic engagement. . . ."[19]

There is even less agreement on how to "fix" societies that display problems linked to a violent past. What priority should be given to different strategies—ranging from symbolic reparations such as public apologies and memorials, to legal accountability of perpetrators, constitutional reform, judicial restructuring, economic revitalization and educational system reorganization? Those who argue against "medicalizing" social reconstruction suggest that reliance on "healing" diverts attention away from the basic issue of how societies rebuild themselves after massive violence. From this perspective, the success or failure of those efforts depends primarily on establishing (or reestablishing) the rule of law and viable political institutions, security from violence, freedom of movement, access to unbiased information, economic and physical reconstruction, and development of high quality educational systems. All of these factors are likely to play a role in the restoration of individuals' sense that they have control over their lives. Yet, in addition to these needs, some individuals also require individual assistance either through psychological counseling or other culturally specific forms of support to recover their psychological balance.

The Role of Politics

Political considerations, not psychological needs of survivors, loom largest in decision-making processes regarding the design and implementation of transitional justice interventions. Truth telling, justice seeking and reconciliation mechanisms are inherently politicized processes heavily influenced by the nature of the societies emerging from conflict, conflicting interests and access to resources. Among the relevant factors are:

- *How those in power define their interests.* When well-known human rights abusers and war criminals continue to hold high office, they are unlikely to permit the development of processes that will hold them and others accountable.
- *Restoration of basic security.* When security is absent, witnesses and judges may be intimidated, either requiring that transitional justice processes (such as war crimes tribunals) be held out of the country or preventing the operation of those processes in the first place.
- *The institutional, professional, financial and cultural resources at the disposal of the affected country.* Some conflict-affected countries have well-developed legal systems as well as large, professional legal and mental health communities, but others may be almost entirely bereft of such resources. Likewise, some countries have more financial resources than others to spend on transitional justice and trauma relief, or they may have well-developed cultural practices, such as ritual purification ceremonies, that help promote reconciliation and trauma relief.

- *The extent to which the international community is interested and involved.* In such settings as East Timor, the former Yugoslavia and Rwanda, the international community has committed substantial financial and professional resources to develop transitional justice institutions and programs, while other countries, such as the Democratic Republic of Congo, have received little attention and support. Even in countries where truth commissions and other transitional justice mechanisms are relatively well financed, their work tends to be of fairly short duration, and they are chronically under-funded, understaffed and over-mandated.

One of the clearest cases of a transitional justice mechanism compromised by politics was the Chilean Truth Commission. Although its work was still of great value, its mandate was limited in three important respects: It could investigate only deaths and disappearances, not cases of torture or other human rights violations; all of its hearings were held in private; and it was forbidden to name perpetrators.

The design of the South African Truth and Reconciliation Commission (TRC) also was the product of a series of political compromises. Initially, the National Party demanded a blanket amnesty as a condition of a political transition, whereas the African National Congress wanted to prosecute those responsible for serious human rights abuses. The establishment of a truth commission with the mandate to extend amnesty for political crimes in exchange for full disclosure offered a middle ground. But the creation of the TRC by parliament was delayed by at least a year by South African president Nelson Mandela, who understood that the top leadership of the army and policy needed to be changed first so that the new government would be fully in control of those institutions.

On another continent, the creation of the International Criminal Tribunal for the former Yugoslavia in part reflected the fact that, when the Balkans wars ended, local war criminals were heroes among their ethnic groups and unlikely to be immediately tried by local courts. The international community recognized that if justice was to be done the court would have to be located outside of the region where judges and witnesses would be secure against attacks and where a tribunal would be, and would be perceived to be, impartial.

While political forces may be paramount, they can be tempered by cultural or religious influences that affect decision-making about transitional justice interventions.[20] The situation in Uganda—where the Lord's Resistance Army (LRA) has murdered, maimed and enslaved thousands across Acholiland and beyond—represents the interplay of conflicting political, cultural and psychological influences at local, national and international levels. The International Criminal Court has issued arrest warrants for the top five leaders of the LRA, even though the Ugandan government has promised amnesty for LRA rebels if they lay down their arms. Acholi culture, however, offers forgiveness to killers who compensate their victims (or their survivors), including sharing a meal with them—a cultural artifact from a time when conflict was managed by clans tightly bound together by intermarriage and trade relations and interested in preserving good relations.[21] In line with this thinking, an Acholi victim of the LRA said, "Only God can judge," while an Acholi chief, Colins Opoka said, "In our culture, we don't like to punish people. It doesn't really get you anywhere."[22] It remains to be seen what approach will prevail in Uganda.

Compromises made to achieve political ends following war abound. In the aftermath of World War II, the United States hastened the conclusion of the Nuremberg trials, facilitated the release of prominent Nazis from prison, and limited the lustration process in an effort to ensure that West Germany would be "a dependable ally in the Cold War."[23] In Algeria, in an effort to promote national reconciliation and stability, the government offered amnesty to Islamist extremists, as well as to government forces engaged in the struggle. In justifying this approach, which was implemented without the benefit of a truth commission to investigate and ascribe responsibility to perpetrators, the chair of Algeria's human rights commission, Mustapha Farouk Ksentini, said, "The country is tired. The national unity is very fragile."[24] This perspective was unconvincing to another Algerian—Fatima Yous, president of an NGO that traces the "disappeared"—who said, "All we want is the truth. We are ready to forgive, but we want our families back and we want the truth. We are not going to sue the guy who killed him. But I do want to know if they killed him, why they killed him and where his bones are."[25]

These examples suggest that the psychological value of transitional justice interventions may depend on a complex calculus of factors—including whether survivors are satisfied that perpetrators have accepted responsibility for their actions, even if they are not punished; how they relate to important cultural or religious values in the affected society; and whether transitional justice processes help create the framework for greater political, economic and social stability.

Timing, Sequencing and Financing Considerations

The tasks of promoting justice, legal accountability, psychological relief and physical and economic reconstruction are hugely challenging and costly, and collectively take decades or even generations to achieve. Yet transitional justice and related interventions designed to re-knit societies back together are almost always constrained by time deadlines and inadequate financial resources. Victims may pin their hopes on the restorative effect of promised reparations and experience bitter disappointment when either the reparations fall short of expectations or fail to materialize at all.[26] Communities hardest hit by political violence and struggling for economic survival in its aftermath may view with hostility expensive public memorials designed to honor victims erected in their midst when opportunities for economic advancement have not improved in the post-conflict period.[27] Given the complexity of rebuilding psychologically and physically shattered communities in the aftermath of political violence, "single-shot" approaches or one-time "fixes" usually fall short of expected goals and often raise unrealistic expectations. In short, the end goal of achieving broad-scale social reconstruction requires multiple interventions over an extended period of time.

Resource constraints and mandate limits are inevitable features of transitional justice mechanisms and trauma relief programs. Adding to the challenges imposed by resource limitations is the fact that the timing and sequencing of interventions is important. There is often a limited window of opportunity to establish particular mechanisms. For example, a lustration program to remove from responsible positions key individuals associated with the previous regime is often—although not necessarily—best implemented early in the transitional justice process. Collection of evidence and witness statements for war crimes trials and/or a truth commission is generally best undertaken quickly, while memories are fresh. On the other hand, early mandates, especially when imposed by outside actors, to set up a transitional justice mechanism may ignore political, societal and budgetary realities. The urge to act quickly must be balanced against the need to spend time on a broad consultation process, on securing resources and on developing sound mechanisms. Indeed, the implementation of a transitional justice mechanism may benefit from the passage of time as survivors—both victims and perpetrators—mentally process their experiences and adjust to the new order.

Time and resource limitations increase the temptation to over-mandate transitional justice interventions. Truth commissions are commonly expected to undertake a wide range of functions: to establish an authoritative record of the past; to gain public acknowledgement of past abuses and violence; to restore dignity to victims and promote psychological healing; to forge the basis for a democratic political order; to end violence and prevent future human rights abuses; and to promote reconciliation. Particularly the latter goal has come into question as observers challenge the broad applicability of a statement on a banner displayed by the South African Truth and Reconciliation Commissions that "Revealing is Healing." As temporary bodies with limited resources, truth commissions have limited capabilities. Under such circumstances, it is not surprising that these and other transitional justice mechanisms sometimes disappoint those who expect them to deliver more than they can realistically accomplish.[28]

No single intervention is likely to solve all the problems, and interventions that begin where others have left off may prove to be more effective. For example, war crimes tribunals may determine the culpability of individual perpetrators but fail to establish larger societal patterns of criminal behavior. Truth commissions may take on this task, but fail to meet the need of victims for compensation. Monetary compensation programs, in turn, may not address the need for symbolic reparations, such as monuments, memorials and public apologies. Each type of intervention may differentially affect individual victims and the groups with which they identify—hopefully advancing individuals' psychological recovery and stabilizing the societies of which they are a part. Further research is needed to determine how different transitional justice mechanisms individuals and collectively contribute to the psychological health of victims and social reconstruction.

Who Benefits?

There is often ambiguity about who the beneficiaries of truth commissions and tribunals are meant to be. In fact, these interventions may have a differential effect on individual victims involved in them personally versus those who view their proceedings at a distance through media coverage.

People affected by truth commissions and tribunals range from individual victims and perpetrators to their wider societies and even future generations. Clearly, truth commissions and war crimes tribunals are designed to help societies expose evidence of crimes committed against individuals and groups—in the process, setting the historical record straight about what happened during conflicts and, in some cases, holding perpetrators accountable. In so doing, the benefit to individual victims may be a primary consideration but to what extent do such mechanisms also benefit the larger society—for example, by helping to reestablish the rule of law or promote respect for it? Does the import and value of such transitional justice mechanisms change from one community to another within the affected country, or from one generation to the next? Does ascribing responsibility and blame for atrocities set forward or backward the process of normalizing social relations between formerly warring factions?

While some transitional justice mechanisms may help expose the truth and hold perpetrators accountable, their contribution to psychological recovery and reconciliation, either at the individual or societal level, is not well established. Some report that victims from such diverse settings as Sri Lanka, South Africa and Chile have found relief through testimony.[29] Others suggest that testifying in truth commissions and trials may re-traumatize some victims who re-live their terrible experiences.[30] Even when great care is taken to handle witnesses in a sensitive manner, the nature of giving testimony in trials can impair survivors' psychological wellbeing.[31] Those who testify may also be afraid of retribution—including the loss of jobs or violence committed against them or their families—following their testimony.

Eric Stover, who studied witnesses testifying before the International Criminal Tribunal for the former Yugoslavia, argues that the view that testifying has "therapeutic value" reflects "more wishful thinking than . . . fact."

> The few participants who experienced cathartic feelings immediately or soon after testifying . . . found that the glow quickly faded once they returned home to their shattered villages and towns. This was especially true for witnesses who faced uncertainties in their lives, including the loss of a job, death of a loved one, or eviction from their homes. Respondents also reported feelings of helplessness, abandonment, and anger when they learned of the light sentences meted out by the tribunal, or of the reversal of an earlier conviction on appeal.[32]

Victims' attitudes about transitional justice interventions may sometimes be linked to the type of intervention. In Rwanda, for example, respondents viewed foreign trials, including those conducted by the International Criminal Tribunal for Rwanda in Tanzania, as less likely to contribute to reconciliation than genocide trials conducted in Rwanda and the local justice process known as gacaca.[33]

Some victims in the former Yugoslavia who testified against high-level defendants said that they would only be satisfied "once they had testified against *local* war criminals whom they held directly responsible for the deaths of family members and neighbors."[34]

In designing truth commissions and tribunals, policymakers and practitioners essentially engage in a complex moral calculus in which the priorities and needs of individual victims may be sacrificed in the interest of promoting the society's larger goals of laying bare the truth. Clearly, truth commissions in South Africa, Guatemala and Peru, to name only a few examples, have played an essential role in laying bare patterns of institutional behavior that forced those societies to recognize long-established systems of discrimination and inequality at the root of political violence. Painful as testifying is for some victims, doing so can help societies acknowledge what was previously well hidden—such as a systematic policy to "disappear" political opponents or the existence of secret prisons where torture was routine. Revealing these secrets and establishing patterns of illegal behavior by state institutions or armed opposition groups makes their official deniability impossible. Laying bare the truth helps rising generations learn about and from the mistakes of the past. In Guatemala, for example, teachers afraid to teach about the civil war years after it had ended found that the publication of the Guatemala Historical Clarification Commission's report opened up political space for them to incorporate victims' stories from the Commission directly into their teaching.[35]

Even though reliving the past through a truth commission or war crime tribunals may be psychologically painful for some victims, the alternative, arguably, is worse. Countries that turn their backs on the past in an effort to "move on," and that fail to seek the truth or hold war criminals accountable remain divided and vulnerable to further cycles of conflict. Lebanon is a prime example. Only one major war criminal, Samir Geaga was tried and imprisoned after the civil war ended in 1990. Because former warlords held key governmental positions, no effort was made at the national level to account for the grueling fifteen-year civil war through the organization of a truth commission, a war crimes tribunal, a national museum or revision of school curricula on Lebanon's contemporary history. Instead, national authorities made physical reconstruction the top national priority. With the past still largely unexamined and war criminals never held accountable, Lebanon remains highly politically unstable and increasingly rent by sectarian tensions.

Whose Truth?

In transitional justice processes, "complex truths" are often hard to find in individual survivors' stories. Survivors find it hard to focus on anything but their own stories, which can be widely at variance with the perceptions of other survivors. With respect to any given conflict, one has to ask the question, "Who is the victim and who is the perpetrator?" knowing that the answer to that question will differ depending on who answers it. From a societal point of view, everyone is a survivor of the conflict, and victims and perpetrators alike can suffer from post-traumatic stress disorder.

Arguably, what is ultimately needed to promote reconciliation and social reconstruction is the revealing of "complex truths." Individual stories alone are insufficient in casting light on the complex personal and institutional relationships that led to violence, or, as one observer has put it, "the network of responsibility and shame that divides communities internally."[36] Establishing the identities of victims and perpetrators is complicated in contexts where everyone claims to be victimized. While legal trials are designed uncover and publicize the truth, punish perpetrators and thereby satisfy individual victims at some level, they may set back the process of reconciliation when the accused concerned view themselves as victims or when victims feel that justice has not been fully rendered.[37]

Even when blame can be fairly assigned, the truth can be inconvenient. For example, an ethnic group struggling to recover from years of targeted discrimination and violence will be reluctant to lift the lid on evidence of violence that members of the same group committed against each other. Crimes committed by oppressed groups in battles against a greater evil (such as apartheid or genocide) may be suppressed in the narratives that emerge once the conflict ends.[38] The effort to uncover the truth may also raise difficult issues of moral judgment: Is a crime committed by a targeted group the moral equivalent of a crime committed by an oppressor?

Historical narratives are a crucial part of getting to the truth, but the telling and writing of history reflects the perspective of the teller and can be the basis for continuing conflict.

Indeed, competing narratives of victimhood often vie with each other in countries emerging from violent conflict. Also problematic is the failure to include the voices of marginalized groups whose perspectives may be in conflict with those offered by social elites. The way out of this dilemma is by promoting processes that question the validity of prior, monolithic narratives that pitted one group against another; facilitating the emergence of alternative narratives through the collection of documents, oral histories and historical artifacts; including the voices of marginalized victims and groups in society; and teaching critical thinking skills to rising generations.

What one generation chooses to convey to the next generation through public school history texts reveals much about the extent to which a society has grappled with its past.

Many societies, such as Lebanon, Bosnia and Rwanda, find the past too controversial to teach and have suspended wholly or in part the teaching of the country's contemporary history in public schools.[39] Others, such as Colombia or South Africa, have focused largely on improving their teaching of civics, as opposed to their country's contemporary history. Still others, such as Japan, have failed to fully own up to the past in their history textbooks, which, in this case has been a source of continued tension between Japan, China, South Korea and Japan's other Asian neighbors.[40]

Local Traditions and Outside Interveners

There is on-going debate about whether the most psychologically effective methods of addressing the memory of past violence are those that draw upon local cultural traditions and amnesty rather than accountability.[41] At stake is the issue of what transitional justice approaches maximally address the needs of victims and the societies of which they are a part. A skeptic of the universal application of Westernized truth-telling and accountability processes, Rosalind Shaw argues that the work of the Sierra Leone Truth and Reconciliation Commission is problematically premised on an assumption of the "purportedly universal benefits of the verbal recounting of past violence."[42] While truth telling, she argues, is beneficial in societies in which state-sponsored violence has resulted in widespread disappearances and clandestine death squads, it is less effective in places like Rwanda and Darfur where the killings are done openly. Contrasting western approaches to trauma that rely primarily on "verbalized remembering," she argues that in Sierra Leone and other settings the most effective interventions are "widespread local techniques of healing and reintegration, which are based on the *social forgetting* of violence" through rituals that "cool the heart" of former combatants and reconnect them to their families, communities, ancestors and God.[43]

Clearly, third parties can play essential roles by introducing new or independent perspectives about the conflict, by providing needed expertise and/or by mediating among parties to the conflict. But outside interventions may also inhibit psychological healing. In this context, Shaw cites the example of Mozambique where, "rural communities incorporated ex-combatants and healed those affected by the war through spirit mediumship which externalizes past violence through ritual . . ." and where "psychosocial programs that encouraged people to remember and talk about the violence out were not effective, since verbally recounting memories of the violence opens one up to spiritual attack."[44] Helena Cobban concurs, arguing that "many or most Mozambicans seem strongly guided by a set of deeply held norms that act *against* the discussion of painful events in public." Instead, they use traditional medicines and rituals to extract "wrong spirits" from former combatants.[45]

Whatever the cultural context, when outsiders participate in interventions related to transitional justice and trauma alleviation processes, the very fact of their presence may affect relationships. For example, Anne Aghion's most recent documentary film focused on a village in post-genocide Rwanda includes footage of personal confrontations among survivors and perpetrators that they might otherwise have avoided if she and her team were not present.[46] Whether these encounters ultimately encouraged a catharsis that promoted reconciliation or merely confirmed continuing mutual enmity is hard to say.

The complexity of societies emerging from violent conflict will challenge outsiders and locals alike engaged in helping them deal with the past. Outside "interveners" in particular may have trouble identifying precisely who their local interlocutors are. They need to carefully examine what role those people played in the conflict, and what political interests they now serve; how those considerations should affect their advice about the design of interventions to promote justice, truth telling trauma relief, reconstruction and reconciliation; and whether the views of the marginalized are adequately represented.

The Role of Memorialization

Do interventions—ranging from monuments, street murals and historic site museums to parades to public apologies—designed to remember and honor victims of conflict play a role in recovery from trauma and the shaping of historical memory?[47] Little work has been done to evaluate the impact of memorialization as a tool in the psychological recovery of victims. Nonetheless, anecdotal evidence would suggest that memorialization can provide relief to some victims at the same time that it can either promote social reconciliation or stimulate further conflict.

Given the inherently political nature of public memorials, there is often disagreement about the appropriate goals of memorials and about which groups will serve as arbiters and beneficiaries of memorials and legacy projects—the victims, their communities, the wider society, the government in power or future generations. A museum that seeks to advance the process of social healing by giving voice to contending narratives may lose its ability to contribute to peacebuilding if it gives equal weight to all narratives, including those that promoted violent conflict. Memorials commemorating specific individuals, such as victims of a particular bombing, can emphasize divisions and are more likely to have a psychological impact limited to the immediate families and their communities because they narrowly reflect their loss. Memorials that focus on the larger tragedy of the conflict and acknowledge the pain of all who suffered from the violence can constitute a form of "reparation" that builds bridges between groups or parties involved in the conflict.

Timing and perspective appear to be crucial. The Working Group on Memorialization that convened at the U.S. Institute of Peace concluded that,

> The meaning of memorials often shifts over time and depends on the life experiences of the viewer. A memorial that helps one individual victim regain his or her psychological balance may be viewed by someone on the other side of the conflict as a provocation. Young children will respond differently to memorials than adults. Outsiders to the conflict and direct participants may also interpret the same memorial in diverse ways. Rising generations may have different reactions to a memorial site than their grandparents who lived through the conflict.[48]

The USIP Working Group ultimately concluded that,

> The *process* of determining what shape a memorial project should take and how memorial space should be use is essential—more important, ultimately, than the physical edifice itself. Moreover, process remains essential even after a memorial is built. Memorial projects that encourage survivors to explore contested memories of the past, promote learning and critical thinking, and facilitate on-going cultural exchange are more likely to advance social reconstruc-

tion. They are also more likely to retain meaning for rising generations than static memorials of long past conflicts and heroes that fail to interpret their meaning in ways that have contemporary relevance.[49]

Problems of Defining Success

If achieving justice, reconciliation and the psychological relief that may flow from them is conceived as a dynamic process rather than a static condition that unfolds from different interventions over time, it may wax or wane depending on the circumstances, and may look very different depending on one's individual perspective. The social and political stability that arises from real reconciliation encompasses both interpersonal and wider social relationships within and among communities. It requires accommodation among former antagonists, coming to terms with past injustices and violence, the development of new social and political relationships, and the readjustment of group identities. But these relationships and identities, by definition, are fluid, and their transformation may be more complete in some communities than in others.

A transitional justice process that may satisfy one victim may appear to be of little benefit to another. It may be enough for one victim to tell her story before a truth commission and get public recognition for her suffering, while another may find the exercise useless, or even harmful, unless the perpetrator is held to account and punished. In this connection, a participant at the U.S. Institute of Peace Conference on trauma and transitional justice said,

> Survivors bring completely different expectations to the process [of story telling]. Some of them want to be listened to by someone who cares and who takes note of their suffering. Some of them want to tell their story to their community. Some of them want to tell their story because, by telling it, they can emphasize the need for justice, the need for further investigation. It's a form of presenting their demands or their needs. . . . Sometimes it's a process that needs to happen in private.[50]

The same goes for other transitional justice mechanisms, such as compensation programs. One victim may find that any financial compensation offered for loss has value because it represents acknowledgement of wrongdoing, while another may be disappointed by the amount offered, humiliated that their loss is not worth more, or insulted by the notion that money can compensate for loss.

The perceived success or failure of transitional justice processes reflects the varying interests and perspectives of victims, perpetrators and beneficiaries of the previous regime within the affected society. Perceptions of the desirability of pursuing truth, justice and reconciliation, as well as the appropriate means of doing so, vary considerably among victims and perpetrators, and are shaped by time, group identity, location and other factors.

The social science literature offers little guidance on the best methods to evaluate the impact of transitional justice mechanisms. Clearly one method, although rarely executed, is to survey the public's views about the implementation and impact of a given transitional justice intervention.[51] Representative surveys provide a complete picture only if they are administered before, during and well after the intervention ends. Not surprisingly, such empirical evidence about the impact of different types of interventions is very limited, given the cost and difficulty of administering such surveys. Other survey data, however, may be useful—such as the World Values Survey, which provides data from a number of countries about individuals' views of current and past regimes and their feelings about the future.[52]

In designing evaluation methods, one needs to identify the various audiences for which transitional justice mechanisms have been designed, distinguish between short-, medium- and long-term impacts, and develop operational measures to discern changes in attitude and behavior before and after interventions are made. The comprehensive, long-term impact of transitional justice interventions ultimately may be too complex to measure precisely. But evaluative judgments can be made about the processes involved in implementing any given transitional justice mechanism, and the changing relationships between individuals and groups resulting from the intervention.

Conclusions

Given the slim empirical evidence available on the precise relationship between trauma and transitional justice, several conclusions seem clear.

First, more research is needed to establish if and how the operation of different transitional justice interventions affect the psychological states of survivors of violent conflict. Good baseline and follow-up studies are needed to track dynamic changes in attitudes and relationships that occur over time, and to achieve better understanding of whether and why different individuals and groups within societies have different reactions to the same intervention. Given existing evidence, it is too soon to conclude that judicial initiatives have therapeutic benefits for most survivors.[53] There is also too little empirical evidence to assume that there is a generally positive relationship between efforts to promote truth-telling, trauma relief and reconciliation either between individual victims and perpetrators or among contending groups in the broader society. Additionally, a relationship between interventions designed to improve the mental health of individual victims and reconciliation among formerly warring factions has not been established.

Second, it seems clear that trauma recovery and reconciliation are long-term processes that involve a series of carefully designed interventions and are influenced by complex events and relationships difficult to gauge or control. At best, a single transitional justice mechanism can just begin these processes and may only be successful if carried out in tandem with other social reconstruction efforts. In other words, policymakers and practitioners would be wise to assume that efforts to assist traumatized survivors and to promote broader reconciliation depend on a *number* of efforts, such as economic reparations for victims, the establishment of fair judicial systems, and the creation of political institutions that protect the rights of minorities. As Brandan Hamber has argued, trauma relief cannot be viewed as a "linear task requiring only particular interventions such as counseling and public testimony to ensure resolution."[54]

Third, the optimal order or sequencing of interventions may vary from one society to another. Should truth telling precede reorganizing a country's shattered education system? Is economic reconstruction more important than judicial reform? Most observers agree that restoring security is a first priority. But the relationship between the establishment of viable political and economic systems, the operation of successful transitional justice mechanisms and the emergence of democracy in countries previously wracked by political violence has not been established. There may be an important connection between transitional justice, political and economic reconstruction and psychological trauma to the extent that transitional justice mechanisms that contribute to reconstruction may help victims regain a sense of dignity, self worth and acknowledgement of their loss—feelings essential to citizenship in a democratic polity.

Notes

1. Brahm, Eric, "Getting to the Bottom of Truth: Evaluating the Contribution of Truth Commissions to Post-Conflict Societies," paper prepared for the Wisconsin Institute for Peace and Conflict Studies 20th Annual Conference, October 6-8, 2004, Marquette University, p. 2.

2. See, for example, Gibson, James L., "The Contributions of Truth to Reconciliation: Lessons from South Africa," *Journal of Conflict Resolution* (forthcoming); Gibson, James L., *Overcoming Apartheid: Can Truth Reconcile a Divided Nation?* (New York: Russell Sage Foundation, 2004); Fletcher L.E. and Harvey M. Weinstein, "Violence and Social Repair: Rethinking the Contribution of Justice to Reconciliation," *Human Rights Quarterly*, 2002:24:573-639; Stover, E. and Harvey M. Weinstein, *My Neighbor, My Enemy: Justice and Community after Mass Atrocity*. (Cambridge: Cambridge University Press, 2004); Pham, Phuong N., Harvey M. Weinstein and Timothy Longman, "Trauma and PTSD Symptoms in Rwanda: Implications of Attitudes Toward Justice and Reconciliation," *The Journal of the American Medical Association*, 2004; 292: 602-612; Backer, David, "Victims Responses to Truth Commissions: Evidence from South Africa," in Ndulo, Muna (ed.), *Security, Reconciliation and Reconstruction: When the Wars End*, (London: UCL Press, 2006).

3. O'Connell, Jamie, "Gambling with the Psyche: Does Prosecuting Human Rights Violations Console their Victims?" *Harvard International Law Journal*, Summer 2005: 295, p. 3.

4. Pham, Phuong N., Harvey M. Weinstein, Timothy Longman, *op cit*. p. 602.

5. De Jong, Joop T.V.M., Ivan H. Komproe, Mark Van Ommeren, Mustafa El Masri, Mesfin Araya, Noureddine Khaled, Willem van de Put and Daya Somasumdaram, "Lifetime Events and Postraumatic Stress Disorder in 4 Postconflict Settings," *The Journal of the America Medical Association*, August 2001, vol. 286, no. 5, p. 555.

6. This organization also operates trauma treatment programs in Africa.

7. See MacGinty, Roger, "Post-Accord Crime," in Darby, John, *Violence and Reconstruction* (Notre Dame, IN: University of Notre Dame Press, 2006).

8. Hamber, Brandon, "Does the Truth Heal? A Psychological Perspective on Political Strategies for Dealing with the Legacy of Political Violence," in Nigel Biggar (ed.),

Burying the Past: Making Peace and Doing Justice after Civil Conflict, (Washington, DC: Georgetown University Press, 2001), p. 140-141.

9. Volkan, Vamik, *Blood Lines: From Ethnic Pride to Ethnic Terrorism*. (New York: Farrar, Staus and Giroux, 1997), p. 38. Also see Brenner, Ira, "Terror and Societal Regression: Does Psychoanalysis Offer Insights for International Relations?" *Journal of the American Psychoanalytic Association* (2006:54/3) p. 977-988.

10. Volkan, *op. cit.*, p. 40.

11. Ibid., p. 45.

12. Ibid., p. 46.

13. Also see Pynoos, Robert S., Alan M. Steinberg, Grete Dyb, Armen K. Goenjian, Sui-Huei Chen and Melissa J. Brymer, "Reverberations of Danger, Trauma and PTSD on Group Dynamics," in Sklarew, Bruce, Stuart W. Twemlow and Sallye M. Wilkinson, *Analysts in the Trenches: Streets, Schools and War Zones*, (Hillsdale, New Jersey: The Analytic Press, 2004). They argue that "Cultural representations extend traumatic expectations among a cohort to the wider society and future generations" (p. 17). In this connection, they argue that, "The motto of the survivors of Pearl Harbor is 'Remember Pearl Harbor and Keep America Alert.' 'Never Again' is perhaps the 20th century's most poignant and powerful verbal expression of a traumatic expectation that carries a transgenerational imperative" (p. 18).

14. Shaw, Rosalind, "*Rethinking Truth and Reconciliation Commissions: Lessons from Sierra Leone.*" Washington, DC: U.S. Institute of Peace Press, Special Report 130, February 2005, p. 1.

15. Ignatieff, M., *The Warrior's Honor: Ethnic War and the Modern Conscience* (London: Chatto and Windus, 1998), p. 169.

16. Conversation at USIP, October 13, 2006.

17. As Jodi Halpern and Harvey Weinstein point out, "The medical and psychiatric literature . . . has focused on the effects of trauma on individuals, in particular, in post-traumatic stress disorder as a syndrome that results from overwhelming stressful events. While there is a burgeoning amount of research on issues ranging from measurement to treatment, the attempt to understand the effects of war has not been connected to analysis of social relationships and the building of societies." Halpern, Jodi and Harvey M. Weinstein, "Rehumanizing the Other: Empathy and Reconciliation," *Human Rights Quarterly* 26 (2004), p. 563.

18. McLeron, Frances, Ed Cairns, Miles Hewstone and Ron Smith, "The Development of Intergroup Forgiveness in Northern Ireland," *Journal of Social Issues*, Vol. 60, no. 3, 2004, p. 588.

19. Weinstein, M. Harvey and Eric Stover, "*Introduction: Conflict, Justice and Reclamation,*" in Eric Stover and Harvey M. Weinstein, *op. cit.*, p. 5.

20. Christianity, for example, emphasizes the importance and power of forgiveness. In this tradition, some contend that perfect justice can never be achieved—that the punishment of a murderer is never sufficient compensation for the loss of a loved one—and that reconciliation between perpetrators and surviving victims is most likely to occur through forgiveness, which only victims have the power to give. See Amstutz, Mark P., *The Healing of Nations: The Promise and Limits of Political Forgiveness,* (Lanham, MD: Rowman and Littlefield Publishers, 2005). Also see McLernon *et. al, op. cit.*, p. 589, who address the issue on the whether religiosity or religious group membership relate to forgiveness.

21. Gettleman, Jeffrey, "*Uganda Peace Hinges on Amnesty For Brutality,*" The New York Times, September 15, 2006, p. A6.

22. Gettleman, op cit., p. A6.
23. Buruma, Ian, "*War and Remembrance*," The New Yorker, September 19, 2006, p. 84.
24. Whitlock, Craig, "*Algerian Program Offers Amnesty, But Not Answers About Past*," The Washington Post, September 17, 2006, p. A17.
25. Whitlock, *op cit.*, p. A17.
26. For discussion about this problem in Guatemala, see Isaacs, Anita, "*Confronting the Past? The Challenge of Truth, Justice and Reparations in Guatemala*" found at www.realinstitutoelcano.org/analisis/879/Isaacs879.pdf
27. Barsalou, Judy and Victoria Baxter, "*The Urge to Remember: The Role of Memorials in Social Reconstruction and Transitional Justice*," U.S. Institute of Peace Special Report, Stabilization and Reconstruction Series, No. 4, 2007, p. 9.
28. Isaacs, *op. cit.*, p. 5.
29. Minow, Martha, "*The Hope for Healing: What Can Truth Commissions Do?*" in Rotberg, Robert I. and Dennis Thompson, eds., *Truth v. Justice: The Morality of Truth Commissions*, (Princeton and Oxford: Princeton University Press, 2000), p. 243-245.
30. Friedman, Merle, "*The Truth and Reconciliation Commission in South Africa as an Attempt to Heal a Traumatized Society*," in Shalev, Arieh Y., Rachel Yehuda and Alexander C McFarlane, International Handbook of Human Response to Trauma, (New York: Kluwer Academic/Plenum Publishers, 2000), p. 409. Also see de Ridder, Trudy, "*The Trauma of Testifying: Deponents' Difficult Healing Process*," http://ccrwebccr.uct.ac.za/archive/two/6-34/p30_deridder.html .
31. Judith Herman, writing about ordinary crime victims notes that, "The mental health needs of crime victims are often diametrically opposed to the requirements of the legal proceedings. Victims need social acknowledgement and support; the court requires them to endure a public challenge to their credibility. Victims need to establish a sense of power and control over their lives; the court requires them to submit to a complex set of rules and procedures that they may not understand, and over which they have no control. Victims need an opportunity to tell their stories in their own way, in a setting of their choice; the court requires them to respond to a set of yes and no questions that break down any personal attempt to construct a coherent and meaningful narrative. Victims often need to control or limit their exposure to specific reminders of the trauma; the court requires them to relive the experience directly by confronting the perpetrator." Herman, Judith Lewis, "*The Mental Health of Crime Victims: Impact of Legal Intervention*, Journal of Traumatic Stress, 16/159 (2003), p. 159-160.
32. *Ibid.*, p. 107.
33. Longman, Timothy, Phuong Pham and Harvey M. Weinstein, "*Connecting Justice to Human Experience: Attitudes toward Accountability and Reconciliation in Rwanda*," in Eric Stover and Harvey M. Weinstein, *op cit.*, p. 219.
34. Eric Stover, "*Witnesses and the Promise of Justice in the Hague*, *op cit.*, p. 107. Emphasis in the original.
35. Cole, Elizabeth A. and Judy Barsalou, "*Unite or Divide: The Challenges of Teaching History in Societies Emerging from Violent Conflict*," U.S. Institute of Peace Special Report, No. 163, June 2006, p. 5 and 12.
36. Barsalou, Judy, *Trauma and Transitional Justice in Divided Societies*, *op. cit.* p, 7.
37. Amstutz, *op. cit.* p. 104.
38. A good example of this is efforts by the Rwandan government to suppress discussion of Tutsi crimes committed against Hutus in the context of the 1994 genocide.
39. Cole, Elizabeth A. and Judy Barsalou, *op. cit.*, p. 7-8.

40. See Cole, Elizabeth A., ed. *Teaching the Difficult Past: Violence, Reconciliation and History Education,* 2007.

41. See, for example, Cobban, Helena, *Amnesty after Atrocity? Healing Nations After Genocide and War Crimes* (Boulder, Colorado: Paradigm Books, 2006), which discusses the different ways that Rwanda, Mozambique and South Africa have addressed their violent pasts.

42. Shaw, Rosalind, *op. cit.*, p. 2. Emphasis in the original.

43. Emphasis in the original. *Ibid.* p. 3.

44. *Ibid.*, p. 7.

45. Cobban, *op. cit.*, p. 13. Also see Nordstrom, Carolyn, *A Different Kind of War Story,* (Philadelphia: University of Pennsylvania Press), 1997.

46. Aghion, Anne, *In Rwanda We Say . . . The Family that Does Not Speak Dies*, 2005.

47. For a description of a range of memorialization strategies in one society emerging from violent conflict, see Hamber, Brandon, "Public Memorials and Reconciliation Processes in Northern Ireland," a conference paper delivered at the USIP/AAAS conference, "Trauma and Transitional Justice in Divided Societies," March 27-29, 2004, available at http://64.233.161.104/search?q=cache:cmrNCX2BeoIJ:www.brandonhamber.com/publications/Paper%2520Memorialisation%2520and%2520Northern%2520Ireland.doc+Memorialization+transitional+justice&hl=en&gl=us&ct=clnk&cd=3&client=firefox-a

48. Barsalou, Judy and Victoria Baxter, *op. cit.*, p. 17.

49. *Ibid*, p. 2.

50. Barsalou, Judy, "Trauma and Transitional Justice in Divided Societies, *op. cit.*, p. 10.

51. See, for example, Gibson, James, *Overcoming Apartheid: Can Truth Reconcile a Divided Nation?* Op. cit.

52. Brahm, Eric, *op. cit.*, p. 13.

53. Jamie O'Connell, *op. cit.*, p. 25.

54. Hamber, Brandon, "*Does the Truth Heal? A Psychological Perspective on Political Strategies for Dealing with the Legacy of Political Violence*," in Biggar, *op. cit.*, p. 143.

References

Aghion, A. 2005. *In Rwanda We Say . . . The Family that Does Not Speak Dies.* Gacaca Productions / Dominant 7 / in association with NDR/ARTE.

Amstutz, M. 2005. *The Healing of Nations: The Promise and Limits of Political Forgiveness.* Lanham, MD: Rowman and Littlefield Publishers.

Backer, D. 2006. "Victims Responses to Truth Commissions: Evidence from South Africa." in Ndulo, M. ed., *Security, Reconciliation and Reconstruction: When the Wars End.* London: UCL Press.

Barsalou J. January 2005. *Trauma and Transitional Justice in Divided Societies.* Washington, DC: USIP Press, Special Report 135.

———. and Victoria B. 2007. *"The Urge to Remember: The Role of Memorials in Social Reconstruction and Transitional Justice."* U.S. Institute of Peace Special Report, Stabilization and Reconstruction Series, No. 4.

Brahm, E. 2004. Paper prepared for the Wisconsin Institute for Peace and Conflict Studies 20th Annual Conference: *Getting to the Bottom of Truth: Evaluating the Contribution of Truth Commissions to Post-Conflict Societies.* Marquette University.

Brenner, I. 2006. Terror and Societal Regression: Does Psychoanalysis Offer Insights for International Relations? *Journal of the American Psychoanalytic Association,* 54/3.
Buruma, I. September 19, 2006. War and Remembrance. *The New Yorker.*
Cobban, H. 2006. *Amnesty after Atrocity? Healing Nations after Genocide and War Crimes.* Boulder, CO: Paradigm Books.
Cole, E., ed. 2007. *Teaching the Difficult Past: History Education and Reconciliation.* Boulder, CO: Rowman & Littlefield.
Cole, E. and Barsalou J. June 2006. *Unite or Divide: The Challenges of Teaching History in Societies Emerging from Violent Conflict.* U.S. Institute of Peace Special Report, No. 163.
De Jong, Joop T.V.M., Komproe, I., Van Ommeren, M., El Masri, M., Araya, M., Khaled, N., van de Put, W., and Somasumdaram, D. August 2001. Lifetime Events and Postraumatic Stress Disorder in 4 Postconflict Settings. *The Journal of the America Medical Association*, vol. 286, no. 5.
de Ridder, T. The Trauma of Testifying: Deponents' Difficult Healing Process. <http://ccrwebccr.uct.ac.za/archive/two/6-34/p30_deridder.html>.
Fletcher, L.E. and Weinstein, H.M. 2002. Violence and Social Repair: Rethinking the Contribution of Justice to Reconciliation. *Human Rights Quarterly*, 24:573-639.
Friedman, M. 2000. "The Truth and Reconciliation Commission in South Africa as an Attempt to Heal a Traumatized Society." in Shalev, Arieh Y., Rachel Yehuda and Alexander C McFarlane, *International Handbook of Human Response to Trauma.* New York: Kluwer Academic/Plenum Publishers.
Gettleman, J. September 15, 2006. Uganda Peace Hinges on Amnesty For Brutality. *The New York Times.* p. A6.
Gibson, J. L. 2006. The Contributions of Truth to Reconciliation: Lessons from South Africa. *Journal of Conflict Resolution.* Vol. 50, No. 3, 409-432.
———. 2004. *Overcoming Apartheid: Can Truth Reconcile a Divided Nation?* New York: Russell Sage Foundation.
Halpern, J. and Weinstein, H. M. 2004. Rehumanizing the Other: Empathy and Reconciliation. *Human Rights Quarterly,* 26.
Hamber, B. 2001. "Does the Truth Heal? A Psychological Perspective on Political Strategies for Dealing with the Legacy of Political Violence." in Nigel Biggar, ed., *Burying the Past: Making Peace and Doing Justice after Civil Conflict.* Washington, DC: Georgetown University Press.
———. March 27-29, 2004. Public Memorials and Reconciliation Processes in Northern Ireland. Conference paper delivered at the USIP/AAAS conference, *Trauma and Transitional Justice in Divided Societies.* available at http://www.brandonhamber.com/publications/Paper%20Memorialisation%20and%20Northern%20Ireland.doc
Herman, J. L. 2003. The Mental Health of Crime Victims: Impact of Legal Intervention. *Journal of Traumatic Stress*, 16/159.
Ignatieff, M. 1998. *The Warrior's Honor: Ethnic War and the Modern Conscience* London: Chatto and Windus.
MacGinty, R. 2006. "Post-Accord Crime." In Darby, J. *Violence and Reconstruction.* Notre Dame, IN: University of Notre Dame Press.
McLeron, F., Cairns, E. Hewstone, M. and Smith, R. 2004. The Development of Intergroup Forgiveness in Northern Ireland. *Journal of Social Issues*, Vol. 60, no. 3.

Minow, M. 2000. "The Hope for Healing: What Can Truth Commissions Do?" in Rotberg, R. I. and Thompson, D. eds., *Truth v. Justice: The Morality of Truth Commissions*. Princeton and Oxford: Princeton University Press.

Nordstrom, C. 1997. *A Different Kind of War Story*. Philadelphia: University of Pennsylvania Press.

O'Connell, J. Summer 2005. Gambling with the Psyche: Does Prosecuting Human Rights Violations Console their Victims? *Harvard International Law Journal*. 295.

Pham, P. N., Weinstein, H. M. and Longman, T. 2004. Trauma and PTSD Symptoms in Rwanda: Implications of Attitudes toward Justice and Reconciliation. *The Journal of the American Medical Association*, 292: 602-612.

Pynoos, R. S., Steinberg, A. M., Dyb, G., Goenjian, A. K., Chen, S-H. and Brymer, M. J. 2004. "Reverberations of Danger, Trauma and PTSD on Group Dynamics," in Sklarew, B., Twemlow S. W. and Wilkinson, S. M., *Analysts in the Trenches: Streets, Schools and War Zones*. Hillsdale, New Jersey: The Analytic Press.

Shaw, R. February 2005. *Rethinking Truth and Reconciliation Commissions: Lessons from Sierra Leone*. Washington, DC: U.S. Institute of Peace Press, Special Report 130.

Stover, E. and Weinstein, H. M. 2004. *My Neighbor, My Enemy: Justice and Community after Mass Atrocity*. Cambridge: Cambridge University Press.

Volkan, V. 1997. *Blood Lines: From Ethnic Pride to Ethnic Terrorism*. New York: Farrar, Staus and Giroux.

Whitlock, C. Algerian Program Offers Amnesty, But Not Answers About Past. *The Washington Post*, September 17, 2006, p. A17.

3

Humiliation, Trauma, and Trauma Recovery in a Globalizing World

Evelin G. Lindner

Yesterday, I met with a dear friend, a Japanese professor, an expert on mediation. She explained to me that she believes that humankind will not survive, at least not in the longer term. Humankind will die out, leaving behind a devastated planet Earth, relieved of its human plague. And, she added, it is absurd to write chapters about *Peacebuilding in Traumatized Societies*, while forgetting that we all, including all trauma experts and all readers of books for trauma experts, are doomed and ought to be thinking what to do with traumatized death-bound humankind, us, during our last days.

When I listened to my friend, I remembered the bitterness I witnessed in Africa. I started my field work for my doctorate on humiliation in 1998 in Africa—see Lindner (2000)—and among the most humiliated people I met were the helpers at lower echelons of humanitarian organizations. Many had drifted from idealism to cynicism. Michael Maren (1997) wrote a book entitled *The Road to Hell: The Ravaging Effects of Foreign Aid and International Charity*, and this book had resonated with many. Usually, most helpers began their mission inspired by human rights ideals, ideals of equal dignity for all, but soon had to realize, painfully, that they were caught in a larger context, which sometimes included their own superiors, where power was still defined in old top-down ways, frequently at the expense of human rights. Similarly, the readers of this book, while trying to help traumatized societies, face their own limits and the fact that the larger context traumatizes all.

I suggest that we have to face up to this larger context, if we wish to have a chance at all to be successful in helping traumatized societies or, for that matter, traumatized individuals. I posit that it is not elective to take large-scale global trauma into account, it is compulsory.

Michio Kaku (2005), renowned physicist and leading expert in string theory, concludes his book on *Parallel Worlds* with the following paragraph:

> The generation now alive is perhaps the most important generation of humans ever to walk the Earth. Unlike previous generations, we hold in our hands the future destiny of our species, whether we soar into fulfilling our promise as a type I civilization [meaning a civilization that succeeds in building a socially and ecologically sustainable world] or fall into the abyss of chaos, pollution, and war. Decisions made by us will reverberate throughout this century. How we resolve global wars, proliferating nuclear weapons, and sectarian and ethnic strife will either lay or destroy the foundations of a type I civilization. Perhaps the purpose and meaning of the current generation are to make sure that the transition to a type I civilization is a smooth one. The choice is ours. This is the legacy of the generation now alive. This is our destiny (Kaku, 2005, 361).

I believe we have to accept that mass trauma will increasingly define the psychological state of the human population of the globe, us, the readers of this book included. Humankind will face ever more global challenges. Already at the current point in time, mass trauma has entered world stage forcefully. Natural disasters such as the recent tsunami in the Indian Ocean, hurricane Katrina or terrorist acts in large cities such as Madrid or London, intractable violent conflicts in various world regions, as well as inner city violence and poverty are all creating large-scale trauma. Post Traumatic Stress Disorder (PTSD) is no longer a term for a few specialists, who attend to victims of pedophilia, domestic violence, or neglect of children and the elderly; it has become a definitorial term relevant for millions. New large-scale approaches to tackling trauma have to be developed that bypass the bottleneck of the availability of individual therapists.

In this chapter, I propose that the crises that humankind faces globally, at the highest macro level, may serve as a challenge that, if taken on, might even help to alleviate the effects of trauma that occur on meso and micro levels. A Canadian consultant working in Japan, after attending one of my lectures—see Lindner (2006a)—commented that my global vision of hope needs to be disseminated, not least in Japan, where more than one million young men have retreated into depressed isolation, like eremites secluding themselves in their homes, refusing to lead fuller lives (the so-called *hikikomori* phenomenon).

Trauma does not automatically lead to incapacitation—it can also lead to growth. In their *Handbook of Posttraumatic Growth*, Tedeschi and Calhoun (Eds.) (2006) attest that some trauma survivors find that their losses have produced valuable gains, even though this did not mean that their emotional distress was diminished (clearly, focus on growth through trauma should not come at the expense of empathy for the pain and suffering of trauma survivors). There is evidence from disasters that shows that the best way to overcome extreme stress and attain growth is to be proactive. Merely reacting is not sufficient, and people who allow themselves to be overwhelmed may even die, without any noticeable coping actions.

Barry Hart has developed the *Peacebuilding Wheel*, a template for trauma recovery and peacebuilding. I suggest that it has to be applied at the global level as much as at local levels, in a proactive way, so as to facilitate growth at a large scale. Hart indicates that the following important elements have to be considered if a stable society is to be achieved: identity/ worldview, justice, religion/ spirituality, leadership, relief and development, conflict transformation, and trauma healing, all on the background of values related to human security (human needs, rights, dignity, and beliefs), and informed by culture and context (social, political, economic, and environmental).

In this chapter it is argued that we can proactively harness global crises and facilitate growth, and that this can also help alleviate trauma at meso and micro levels. We can do that by understanding, proactively, that humankind finds itself in a historic transition away from old values and old worldviews, toward new values and new worldviews that represent adaptations to new circumstances. This transition is currently handled less than optimally. However, if managed more efficiently, this transition entails hope. This transition is intimately linked with human rights, humiliation and trauma, all of which, if not managed well, may undo the otherwise hopeful features. This chapter presents a frame that might be useful for constructively harnessing crisis and trauma at all levels, global and local.

Before delving into more depth, I believe, every reader has to make a personal decision. This decision is addressed in the following section.

Before doing anything else, in order to be efficient in their work, trauma experts have to take a proactive decision

I sympathize with my Japanese friend's feelings. I catch myself being envious of people who are able to close their eyes in blissful ignorance and stay uninformed of the crises humankind is facing. I also feel ashamed, ashamed of being part of the species Homo sapiens that behaves like locusts, short-sightedly destroying the resources they depend on for long-term survival. I feel ashamed when I hear that our global problems are not tackled properly because of so-called "lack of political will." Furthermore, I feel humiliated when some individuals choose to peddle their ignorance as so-called Realism and demean those others who try to fight for more far-sighted awareness. In short, I feel everything, from traumatized, to ashamed, and humiliated. I feel traumatized by global crisis, ashamed of global ignorance, and humiliated by people of short-sighted righteousness. I feel even more humiliated by people who indulge in double standards—I mean those who speak of human rights and human dignity and betray their words with their deeds. "To recognize humanity hypocritically and betray the promise humiliates in the most devastating way by denying the humanity professed" (Stephan Feuchtwang, November 14, 2002, in a personal note).

I am the founding manager of Human Dignity and Humiliation Studies (http://www.humiliationstudies.org/) and we have two annual meetings. Currently, we conduct an online discussion in preparation for a meeting in Costa Rica, in September 2006. I opened the discussion by comparing humankind to a locust-minded crew on the Titanic, just before sinking, busying themselves with conflicts and trauma inside or between the cabins, both on the luxury first floor and among the poor further down in the ship, while trying to block out the looming traumatic fact that the entire ship is sinking. The sinking of the ship is too big a trauma, too large to be fully allowed into our psyches—it is easier to concentrate on the "smaller" traumas that we think we can actually do something about. In other words, many people, like my Japanese friend, work for "bettering the world," however, in an honest moment they admit that they live in a lingering sense of hopelessness as to whether not all efforts may be pointless.

I suggest that we need to intervene here and make a proactive decision—even more, I propose that all other traumas, the smaller ones so to speak, will be easier to overcome if we succeed in facing the largest ones proactively.

If we think that it is hopeless for the world to avoid the abyss—it may indeed be hopeless—we better follow my Japanese friend's suggestion and make our last days as pleasant as possible. However, sometimes, even very ill patients may get better if treated with the proper medicine. The treatment might diminish the patients' quality of life in the short-term, in exchange for the promise of surviving in the long term. If we decide to go for this kind of "treatment" for humankind, let us hold together through the hardship of this path, without complaining, because long-term survival might be the reward.

The decision to fight in times of crisis has nothing to do with naïve optimism—as C. Richard Snyder (2002) explains in his *hope theory*. On the contrary. Hand-wringing is a luxury for good times and forecloses the optimal strategy of facing crisis, namely firm and focused proaction. It is *either/or*. *Either* we agree with ourselves on the first *or* the second strategy. We cannot have both and we better don't hover in the middle. If we wish to avoid painful interventions we will not save the world. If we wish to save the world we have to face difficult times. Whichever decision we take, it is proactive to make the very decision. Lingering in between, keeping our eyes half shut, letting simmering traumatization seep into our lives slowly, all this equals the worst strategies for facing crisis, namely merely reacting post-hoc or letting disaster overwhelm us. If we decide, consciously, for humankind to die out, deeming our own species' locust-nature to be too resistant to reform, this is a proactive and noble decision. Settling on trying to "save the world" is another proactive and noble decision. In contrast, keeping still and letting the crisis slowly overwhelm and eat us from inside, while indulging in half-hearted reactions such as indignated hand-wringing and deep sighs, forecloses both solutions.

This chapter is written for people who have decided to fight. Those of you, who have chosen otherwise—a decision I deeply respect—please disengage and, above all, refrain from discouraging those who have chosen to fight.

The Intricate Connections between Humiliation and Trauma

The readers of this book, I assume, consider themselves to be human rights advocates. The first sentence in Article 1 of the Universal Declaration of Human Rights reads, "All human beings are born free and equal in dignity and rights." This means that nobody ought to be humiliated—humiliation is a violation of dignity that is illegitimate.

It seems easy to be a human rights advocate—the ideals are so noble. Problems arise, however, when we face complex situations. Here is an example, Until 1991, I worked as a clinical psychologist (in the Middle East 1984-1991, among others), and was confronted with many complicated cases, including what is called honor killing (see for a recent case, for example, http://news.bbc.co.uk/2/hi/uk_news/england/london/5179162.stm). Imagine, a mother approaches you and explains that her daughter was raped and has to be killed to prevent family honor from being humiliated since the rapist will not marry her. As human rights defenders, you stipulate that marrying a raped girl off to her rapist, let alone killing the girl, is equivalent to compounding humiliation, not remedying it. The mother, in turn, regards your attitude as condescending, as humiliating for her cultural beliefs. In sum, we face several layers of honor, dignity and humiliation. What position do we take when we think of healing trauma? Whose honor or dignity do we protect? And which arguments do we use?

What we see as detestable humiliation today was once seen as legitimate humbling

Demeaning, degrading, or debasing: at the heart of the practice of humiliation we find a movement of holding down. Up to very recently (and still today, in some world regions), holding down a person was not necessarily regarded as illicit. The verbs *to humble* and *to humiliate* were used rather interchangeably until about 250 years ago, when the meanings of those two verbs separated and developed into diametrically opposed directions in the English language: *humility* remained to be seen as a virtue, while *humiliation* acquired the taste of an illicit violation. According to the Oxford English Dictionary, the earliest recorded use of *to humiliate* meaning to mortify or to lower or to depress the dignity or self-respect of someone does not occur until 1757.

If we ask what else happened around that historical period, we see that other features began to change as well: an awareness of One World began to emerge, the notion of an individual self unfolded, science as a moral project gained visibility, and it was soon time for the French Revolution and the U.S. Declaration of Independence, and, not least, the human rights entered mainstream stage.

As it seems, humankind, at least in the West, set in motion a process of deep cultural and social change around 300 to 250 years ago. I suggest that it is useful for trauma experts to understand this transition and to conceptualize it as part of a much larger historic discourse, namely a discourse around humiliation, or, more precisely, around the option that something or somebody can be held down or put down, that reaches back more than 10,000 years. William Ury (1999), anthropologist, and director of the Harvard University Project on Preventing War, pulls together elements from anthropology, game theory and conflict studies to describe three major types of society: a) simple hunter-gatherers, b) complex agriculturists, and c) the currently emerging knowledge society.

In Ury's system, simple hunter-gatherers lived in a world of coexistence and open networks, within which conflicts were negotiated, rather than addressed by coercion. Small groups of around 200 people enjoyed rather egalitarian social institutions. The abundance of wild food represented an expandable pie of resources that did not force opponents into win-lose paradigms.

When we study the historic facts, we find that the hunter-gatherer way of life dominated the globe until about 10,000 years ago, when it "hit the wall." Around 10,000 years ago, rather suddenly in terms of long-term history, hunter-gatherers no longer could merely wander off and find untouched abundance of wild food in the next valley; other people were already there (*circumscription* is the anthropological term). All the easily accessible parts of planet Earth were inhabited by Homo sapiens. We could call this the first round of globalization for humankind.

Humankind came up with a response to this crisis, namely agriculture (*intensification* is the anthropological term). However, as Ury spells out, there was a problem with this response. Complex agriculturalists lived in a world of coercion. They lived within closed hierarchical pyramids of power—submission/domination—on land that represents a fixed pie and pushes antagonists into win-lose situations governed by strict rules.

If we look at Ury's theory, we can add that dependence on land, with its inherent win-lose framing, also triggered what international relations theory calls the *security dilemma*. The term was coined by John Herz (1950), to explain why states that have no intention to harm one another may still end up in competition and war. Its very essence is one of tragedy. The threat of preemption with preemption is the ultimate and inevitable outcome of the traditional strong security dilemma. Fear reigns, Hobbesian fear of surprise attacks from outside one's nation's borders. Constant preparations for war drain societal resources. Stereotyped fear of outgroups (for example, of other nations) permeates ingroups and informs cultural institutions from "Ministries of War" or "Defense" to identity constructs such as patriotism, or gender division—see Goldstein (2001), and how he links war and gender division.

In other words, the world of domination/submission could be regarded as an adaptation to the security dilemma, which is an outflow of the fact that land became the resource of most of humankind, a resource that by definition is not expandable.

In a world of domination/submission, all share the view that it is God's will or nature's order that some people are born higher and ought to hold down those who are lesser beings. Myriads of social systems are invented to keep this top-down order in place, from kow-towing to regular beatings and killings so as to "remind" underlings of their due lowly place. When masters hold down underlings to keep them humble, even the most atrocious methods are seen as "honorable medicine," and the victims has no right to invoke the notion of humiliation as a form of violation. Only the masters themselves, when their privileged position is questioned, can appeal to what I call *honor humiliation* as an infringement of their honor and redeem it, for example, by going to duel.

Honor killings provide an example for practices that have their place in a larger framework of honorable domination/submission. Only an obedient daughter is a "good" daughter; a disobedient daughter is seen as a shame for the family, and the humiliated family honor "must" be reconstituted by cutting out the diseased limb, which is the daughter (this was the explanation I usually was presented with, when I was exposed to such cases during my work).

Human rights, in contrast to honorable domination/submission, represent an adaptation to new circumstances, namely to the current round of globalization leading up to a global knowledge society that removes the security dilemma as defining principle.

Humiliation gains significance as obscene violation of human rights elements

Ury posits that a knowledge society resembles the hunter-gatherer model because the pie of resources—knowledge—appears to be infinitely expandable, lending itself to win-win solutions. This type of society rejects tightly knit hierarchical structures in favor of the open network espoused by our earliest ancestors. Negotiation and contract replace command lines, and coexistence is the primary strategy.

Indeed, research shows—see, for example, Gaertner and Dovidio (1999)—that a win-win situation lends itself to cooperation, while zero sum circumstances increase the likelihood of divisions among people. If we take Ury's historic picture, we find that a rather benign period of hunting-gathering spanning the first 90% of human history was followed by a relatively short but malign period of complex agriculture, leading up to the present benign promise of a win-win framing through knowledge in a global knowledge society.

So, it seems that globalization entails positive elements. And there are more—for example, the waning of ingroup/outgroups divisions. As long as we engage in polarizing "us," or our ingroup," from "them," a host of destructive *biases* arises, such as *attributions errors* and *false polarization effect,* to name just a few, all of which are not conducive to fruitful cooperation. Humankind is being freed from those destructive biases in tact with the emergence of the idea and reality of *one single family of humankind* who is jointly responsible for their tiny home planet Earth.

However, we ask, if globalization is such a good thing, how come that we live in a world of environmental destruction and violent conflicts, with a few indulging in conspicuous over-consumption and the majority living in squalor?

Three elements are important. First, human rights redefine the notion of humiliation: humiliation transmutes from prosocial humbling to a violation of the very core of human dignity, or to *dignity humiliation.* Treating people as lesser beings is no longer admissible. On the contrary, it turns into the worst form of violation. Humiliation acquires the potential to cause deep wounds, deeper than ever before, wounds at the core of ones humanity. Wherever people are treated as lesser beings, no longer are calm and stability the result, but revulsion and upheaval.

Second, human rights move the entitlement to invoke humiliation from masters to underlings. No longer are elites entitled to cry "humiliation" when their privileges are infringed upon, and no longer are they permitted to take up the sword to defend their supremacy. In times of human rights, elites are required to descend humbly and discontinue arrogating superiority. Nelson Mandela went to the white elite in South Africa and asked them to humble themselves without crying "humiliation." He took humiliation away from the elites, and gave it to the oppressed. He went to the downtrodden and bestowed on them the entitlement to invoke humiliation. The underlings, those who traditionally were expected to quietly accept mistreatment, received the right to feel humiliated, hurt, angry, and empowered to rise up. The downtrodden masses thus were given a powerful instrument that only a few elites had before.

To formulate it differently, the Mandelas of this world, the human rights advocates, use feelings of humiliation as the very fuel for the human rights movement (I treat Nelson Mandela in an *ideal type* fashion; his achievements are not minimized by various criticisms that people may be directing at him as a person). Mandelas teach those at the bottom of the pyramid of power, the poor, the disenfranchised, and the marginalized, that their plight no longer is ordained by God or nature, but a violation of human rights. Under the security dilemma the negative emotion that ruled the world was fear, fear of attack. One community feared the other, the enemy. Human rights, in contrast, invite all human beings into one single human family where everybody enjoys equal dignity. All are neighbors, no longer friends versus enemies. Everybody learns to expect to be treated with respect. And everybody feels humiliated if this respect is failing. Thus, while the historical period of honorable domination/submission was characterized by fear as dominant negative emotion, collective fear of attack from outgroups, human rights introduce humiliation as dominant negative emotion, humiliation on the part of each individual qua being an individual, as a reaction of being treated disrespectfully.

And humiliation has awesome potency. If human rights promoters are not cautious, this "fuel" of the human rights revolution is so powerful that it can eat its children. Trauma experts need to understand the potency of humiliation. In my book *Making Enemies: Humiliation and International Conflict*—see Lindner (2006c)—chapter seven is entitled "The Humiliation Addiction." There I explain that feelings of humiliation can turn out to be as strong and compelling as an addiction. For drug addicts, self-interest is replaced by their craving for the next fix. Likewise, people who feel humiliated may hunger for revenge and might act in ways that lead to suicide and homicide. In Rwanda, not the masters, but the former underlings, the Hutus, when they had the power, attempted to eradicate their former master in a genocide. The wisdom of Mandela saved the white elite in South Africa from this fate.

As to the definition of humiliation, we understand now that humiliation has two deeply contradictory definitions—honor humiliation is not at all the same as dignity humiliation. Both share the downward movement of holding down somebody. However, in the world of honor, holding down underlings is no violation; only the elites have the right to interpret an attempt to put them down as violation, not their underlings. This situation changes with the advent of human rights that prescribe equal dignity for all and permit everybody to feel deeply humiliated if treated as lesser beings. Academia itself is part of this transition. Only a few researchers have studied humiliation explicitly so far, since it has become visible only so recently. Mostly, the phenomenon of humiliation figures implicitly, for example, in literature on violence and war. The view that humiliation may be a particularly forceful phenomenon is supported, however, by the research of some authors—Gilligan (1996), Hartling and Luchetta (1999), Klein (1991), Miller (1993), Retzinger (1991), Scheff (1990), and Vogel and Lazare (1990). There is, furthermore, a significant literature in philosophy on the *politics of recognition* and ressentiment. Avishai Margalit (1996) calls for a *decent* society, in which institutions no longer humiliate citizens. Also the notions of *domination* and *oppression* are relevant for humiliation—see Deutsch (2006). The relationship between guilt, shame and aggression is related to humiliation as well, and *hazing* and *bullying* entail humiliation at their core. *Face-saving* is a related notion, and *malignant narcissism* has been linked to humiliation. I myself have worked on humiliation in a *transdisciplinary* fashion, and include all fields from political science, sociology, anthropology, history, theology, social psychology to clinical psychology—see http://www.humiliationstudies.org/whoweare/evelin02.php.

Now we come to the third point that undercuts the otherwise hopeful promises of globalization at the current point in time. The transition from the old honor order to the new human rights order is carried out in such a haphazard way that feelings of humiliation are compounded. As we saw, the old honor order condones the ranking of people into higher and lesser beings. The human rights order of equal dignity for all squarely rejects this. Both arrangements cannot coexist, they are mutually exclusive. One cannot rank people and not rank them at the same time. Like in the case of driving, a country can have either left-hand driving or right-hand driving, but not both. If a country's leadership is too weak to carry out a clean transition from one system to the other, and some people continue to drive on the left side while others begin to drive on the right side, the mere incompatibility leads to accidents. Currently, humankind allows for precisely such accidents. And these accidents are bound to multiply feelings of humiliation on all sides.

How should a human rights worker, a helper, a trauma expert, the reader of this book, act efficiently in such a mess? The world is full of traumatized people, victimized by large-scale power play that is detrimental to a fair global economy, detrimental to a healthy global climate, and unhelpful in solving violent conflicts around the world. Should a trauma expert focus on some smaller traumas of the rich who can pay for treatment and forget about the needs of all others? Or should the trauma expert despair at the antagonisms emanating from the larger context? Here we are back to our Japanese friend.

I suggest that hopelessness and despair stem from a lack of understanding of how historic social change works and thus represent an unnecessary expenditure of energy. And, as mentioned earlier, hand-wringing and rage—rather than endured as a state of being—are best harnessed into proactive constructive action. The human rights movement needs to be more aware of the fact that we live in the middle of a large-scale social transition, which does not realize itself instantaneously and automatically, and surely not through indignation-entrepreneurship or rage, but requires wise guidance.

Mass Healing through Egalization

At the current point in time, so far, globalization has led to deep global humiliation and trauma. In order to disentangle malign and benign influences at the current point in human history, I have coined the term *egalization*. Humiliation and trauma can only be prevented and healed through "marrying" globalization with egalization, or, in other words, through putting into practice, beyond mere rhetoric, the ideals of human rights.

The term egalization is meant to match the word globalization and at the same time differentiate it from words such as equality, equity, or egalitarianism. The main point is *equal dignity* as stipulated in the Human Rights Convention. As discussed above, human rights ideals oppose hierarchical rankings of human worthiness that were once regarded as "normal" (and are still "normal" in many parts of the world).

The term egalization is also meant to avoid claiming that everybody should become equal or the same and that there should be no differences between people. *Egality* can coexist with functional hierarchy that regards all participants as possessing equal dignity; egality can not coexist, though, with hierarchy that defines some people as lesser beings and others as more valuable.

Egalization, at international, national, intergroup, intragroup, interpersonal and intrapersonal levels, is called for, if trauma prevention and recovery shall be successful. Let me begin with interpersonal and intrapersonal levels and then work my way up to international, national, intergroup, intragroup levels.

Formerly, when underlings staged revolutions, they merely replaced their former master and kept the hierarchical system in place—upcoming inferiors soon acted as new tyrants. The human rights revolution is different, and recognizing this fact is essential for efficient trauma recovery to work. The human rights revolution entails two parts, first the dismantling of tyrants and second the dismantling of the very tyrannical system. And this tyrannical system is not merely a characteristic of the larger social environment; it is also to be found within ourselves.

Many in the peace movement overlook this fact—in Lindner (2006b) I address this point. Many human rights defenders are angry people, not least because they are frustrated at the uncoordinated slowness of the human rights revolution. They accumulate frustration and some fall back on old-fashioned authoritarian top-down behavior and behave aggressively, lashing out even at their own friends and colleagues. In other words, some try to achieve the first part of the human rights revolution by forgetting the second. They compound trauma by not recognizing that humiliating humiliators and demeaning co-workers is not a strategy that is commensurable with human rights. They need to learn to walk their talk and understand that human rights bestow dignity on every human being, including those who are slow to grasp that new times have come. Tyrants, supremacists, adherents of the old honor order, they all must be humbled with respect. Whenever humiliating strategies are employed, supposedly to achieve human rights aims, the effect is counterproductive because moderates are being radicalized, rather than extremists becoming more moderate.

Human rights can be implemented only through proactive non-humiliating interventions, not through hand-wringing, and not through indignation-entrepreneurship or worse. Trauma experts need to follow the example of Mandela, who emerged from 27 years of humiliation without losing hope, without lashing out at his humiliators in blind rage, and without paying back by inflicting humiliation on his humiliators. In the spirit of Jean Baker Miller (1986), we need to learn how to "wage good conflict."

Mandela waged a good conflict by stopping cycles of humiliation, with toughness and firmness, so that space is opened for new ways of dignified connectivity. The Mandelas of this world can be called the moderates. Hitlers are extremists, who, under the pretext of toughness and firmness, wage bad conflict and keep turning spirals of humiliation deeper into the abyss.

The example of Mandela shows an important feature of human rights, namely that they are not just a fancy Western idea. All the downtrodden around the world respond with joy if told that they are entitled to live a better life. Usually, only their elites hesitate, rejecting human rights as foreign ideas in order to hold on to their privileges. Elites often have a hard time recognizing the fact that a world of equal dignity for all is not only the new adaptation required by new global circumstances, but that it would also benefit them. Human rights are not just a moral call; they also entail straight forward practical advantages, advantages that went unused under the conditions of the security dilemma. A world of equal dignity for all is beneficial for everybody because the old division of masters presiding over underlings handicaps all players: underlings are prevented from contributing to larger society with their creativity and leadership, and elites are prevented from enjoying caring and nurturing. Egalization is beneficial for all.

If we look at the global level, realizing egalization means building a *decent* global community, in the spirit of Margalit's (1996) call for a decent society. In practice, this means working for the Millennium Goals and for building global institutions that are based on human rights and free the highest global level from the current might-is-right ranking that contravenes equal dignity for all at every lower level.

As part of this endeavor institutionalized humiliation has to be undone. A senior adviser in the European Union Delegation of the European Commission in Kenya explained to me how humiliation is institutionalized in the relations between the international organizations and the recipient countries (this discussion took place on December 2, 1998, in Somaliland and I quote from my notes). He explained that though the principles of empowerment are widely known and accepted, they are not followed. What is needed today is the exercise of empowerment: "We need cooperation, not assistance!" he said:

We need joint management of projects, together with local partners, with international organization slowly phasing out. . . . Of course humiliation should not now be moved from the recipient to the donor, there must be a balance. The bottom line is always: avoidance of corruption, where does the money go to, transparency, good governance, and accountability. Humiliation is now institutionalized in the way international organizations approach the recipients and what is needed is the operationalisation of ways how to change that.

Apart from undoing institutionalized humiliation, cultural resources for trauma recovery need to be used more systematically and at larger scales. All cultures of the world need to be "harvested" for constructive practices of healing—see for a discussion Lindner (2006a). Many cultures know about art, for example, and how it can express trauma and facilitate healing. From Africa we can learn to apply *ubuntu* philosophy—following the Zulu maxim of *umuntu ngumuntu ngabantu* or "a person is a person through other persons"—Michael Jesse Battle (1997) explains how Archbishop Desmond Tutu based his concept of Truth and Reconciliation Commissions on ubuntu. Or, the Great Lakes in Africa can teach us *gacaca* reconciliation meetings, also based on ubuntu.

From Japan we might learn communal apology. I am writing this paragraph on July 25, 2006, in Japan, while watching the news on television. I watch two officials of the Paloma group (producer of water heaters) apologize to the family of a 21-year-old man who died of carbon monoxide poisoning in 1996 due to a malfunctioning water heater (see http://www.yomiuri.co.jp/dy/national/2006). Both officials are shown how they first pay their respects to a shrine in the living room of the family, which displays the picture of the young victim. Then the officials kneel on the carpet in the living room, facing the victim's father and mother who kneel in front of them. The officials are shown to bow with their heads almost touching the floor, staying in this position while the victim's father and mother ask them why this accident took so long to uncover, and why so many water heaters malfunctioned over the years. In other words, here we see a public display of mourning, reproach and atonement between a company and a family hurt by one of the company's products. (So far, the old honor code prevents similar deep apologies from the Japanese side at higher international levels; however, the cultural template is there to be used and facilitating this wisely, in Mandela-like ways, is precisely the task of human rights advocates.)

Conclusion

Barry Hart's *Peacebuilding Wheel* can help us to proactively face crisis and facilitate growth, both with respect to mass trauma and individual trauma. This chapter discusses how humankind's current large-scale historic transition touches upon every single element in Hart's *Peacebuilding Wheel*, upon the cultural, social, political, economic, and environmental contexts of societies around the world, and how we define human needs, rights, dignity, and beliefs. All definitions are embedded into the present all-encompassing movement toward human rights ideals which stipulate equal dignity for all, a movement that leads away from a culture where human worthiness and value are ranked. This transition permeates all world regions and all levels, from global levels to everybody's psyche.

Global warming and global lack of peace are as much part of this transition as any lack of proactive resolve in my inner psychological world. Among the pitfalls of this transition is the fact that human rights forcefully introduce feelings of humiliation into this world, feelings of humiliation when dignity is not respected. And since the transition toward human rights is so dismally slow and incoherent, feelings of humiliation are rife everywhere. And since these feelings are potentially so strong and have the capacity to lead to ravaging traumatization and hatred, they often undo the otherwise hopeful elements.

If we translate Hart's terms into the world of ranked honor, the identity of a "good" woman, for example, is to be a respectful and subservient daughter and wife and thus protect the honor of her men; her worldview is that it is nature's order that she is born as lesser being and that justice is being done when she is being chastised in case of disobedience; she sins against her religion and her spiritual orientation when she does not know her due lowly place; for her to demonstrate leadership is to show her daughters the path of due respectful subservience; relief and development need to underpin this framing; and conflict transformation and trauma recovery are successful when unruly underlings are made to quietly and thankfully accept the authority of their patrons.

In contrast, if we translate Hart's terms into a human rights framing, the identity of a "good" woman is to be treated as equal in dignity with her brothers and her husband; her worldview is that it is nature's order that she deserves to be treated as equal in dignity with everybody else and that justice is being done when her dignity is respected; she sins against her religion and her spiritual orientation when she allows humiliation to occur, both for herself and others; for her to demonstrate leadership is to show her sons and daughters the path of respect for equal dignity for all; relief and development need to underpin this framing; and conflict transformation and trauma recovery are successful when underlings are given a voice and elevated to the same level of dignity as everybody else.

When we see those two worldviews, and what they entail, we understand that the current transition toward building an ethical and institutional framework that is based on human rights at global levels is at the core of trauma prevention and recovery work, both for global and local communities and for each individual. We understand that the transition in itself is very difficult—powerful feelings of humiliation drive the human rights movement—and that the current incoherence and slowness of the process compounds humiliation and trauma. This chapter presents a frame that might be useful for harnessing crisis and trauma at all levels, global and local, through humanizing globalization wisely, patiently, calmly, intelligently, and far-sightedly—by imbuing *globalization* with *egalization* (equal dignity for all).

In a first step, before focusing on the trauma of others, trauma experts, the readers of this book included, are advised to turn their eyes both more inwards and more outwards than usual and invest part of their time in learning how to walk the talk themselves (this is the inward, micro level), and on helping to build global institutions for a decent global society (this is the outward global macro level). Only on the background of such an engagement can helpers uphold their own motivation and remain efficient helpers. If helpers try to evade the trauma entailed in the larger global context into which we all are embedded, by focusing on "smaller" traumas at national, communal or domestic levels, the interference from the larger world will undermine their motivation. And if they fall back on old top-down behavior in their ways of dealing with themselves and others, they will compound humiliation and trauma.

Globalization is powered by technology and our use of it for shrinking the world, while egalization depends on our moral decisions. Egalization is about how we treat others and ourselves, whether we uphold a system of domination/submission or whether we believe we ought to treat everybody with respect for equal dignity. Egalization is about whether we use fear as the "glue" for coercive hierarchies or prefer to live in creative networks held together by mutual respect and the avoidance of humiliation. A friend wrote to me yesterday: "As you know, for example, academia in the U.S. seems to require many individuals to employ power-over maneuvers to gain recognition. It is a tradition that rewards individual, competitive achievement, while discouraging and devaluing creative, collective efforts" (personal message, July 26, 2006). This is an example of a culture that has to be overcome.

"Globalization critics" do not necessarily wish for less globalization, but for a different kind of globalization. They want this world not only to shrink in "width," but also to become "flatter"—see Thomas L. Friedman (2005). Human rights advocates wish to do more than bring down tyrants (and let them be replaced by new tyrants); human rights promoters aim at dismantling the very system that keeps supposedly higher beings above lower beings. Egalization means dismantling oppressive hierarchies and building institutions, both locally and globally, that respect that every citizen is equal in dignity, while healing, preventing and avoiding humiliation. This vision is in line with Margalit's (1996) vision of a *decent* society, or, in the case of the whole world, a *decent global village*—a world based on human rights, extending the opportunity for dignified lives to all.

This is not a dream. In former times, only rulers counted. My grandmother said to me once, "Wir kleinen Leute können ja sowieso nichts tun. Die da oben machen ja doch was sie wollen, "meaning that the masses, the "little people" as she called it, had no power. And she was right, then. However, today, this has changed. Globalization and its technology give virtually everybody the tools to become a global Mandela or a global Hitler. Trauma experts have a responsibility to help everybody to become Mandelas and help us all create decent and dignified living conditions for humankind.

Today I received a message from Cairo from an Israeli scholar, who had overcome his hesitation and traveled to Cairo to give his paper at a conference there (personal message, July 27, 2006). He writes, "The next day, one of the people at the conference who had heard my presentation approached me and complimented me on the paper. He introduced himself as a Professor at the American University in Beirut. He had also come to the conference in spite of the 'situation,' a word that has become a euphemism for the death and destruction, the agony and the pain that we all share." The Israeli then describes how both shared their dismay at the situation and how they expressed compassion for the other side's suffering. A little while later they met again, and my Israeli friend told his colleague from Beirut that his remarks had brought tears to his eyes. He writes, "We looked at each other and embraced." The Israeli then read the paper written by his colleague from Beirut and he shares his feelings as follows, "In the prologue he [the Professor from Beirut] noted the words of two Egyptian artists, Ahmad Fouad Negm, and the Oud player, Sheikh Imam. He brought forth only four lines which stress the power of words, the main tools of communication. These words echo and reverberate in my mind, refusing to leave me, to allow me any rest or respite:

> Should the sun drown in the sea of clouds
> And should the world be engulfed in waves of darkness
> You who search, and care, for meaning
> Shall find nothing to guide you, but eyes made of words

References

Battle, M. J. 1997. *Reconciliation. The Ubuntu Theology of Desmond Tutu.* Cleveland, OH: Pilgrim Press.

Deutsch, M. 2006. A Framework for Thinking about Oppression and Its Change. *Social Justice Research,* 19 (1), pp. 7-41.

Friedman, T. L. 2005. *The World Is Flat: A Brief History of the Twenty-First Century.* New York, NY: Farrar, Straus and Giroux.

Gaertner, S. L. and Dovidio, J. F. 1999. *Reducing Intergroup Bias: The Common Ingroup Identity Model.* Hove, UK: Psychology Press.

Gilligan, J. 1996. *Violence: Our Deadly Epidemic and How to Treat It.* New York, NY: Putnam.

Goldstein, J. S. 2001. *War and Gender: How Gender Shapes the War Systems and Vice Versa.* Cambridge, UK: Cambridge University Press.

Hartling, L. M., and Luchetta, T. 1999. Humiliation: Assessing the Impact of Derision, Degradation, and Debasement. *The Journal of Primary Prevention,* 19 (5), pp. 259-278.

Herz, J. H. 1950. Idealist Internationalism and the Security Dilemma. *World Politics,* II, pp. 157-180.

Kaku, M. 2005. *Parallel Worlds: A Journey through Creation, Higher Dimensions, and the Future of the Cosmos.* New York: Doubleday.

Klein, D. C. 1991. The Humiliation Dynamic: An Overview. *The Journal of Primary Prevention,* 12 (2)87.

Lindner, E. G. 2000. *The Psychology of Humiliation: Somalia, Rwanda / Burundi, and Hitler's Germany.* Oslo: University of Oslo, Department of Psychology, Doctoral Dissertation in Psychology.

———. 2006a. *Avoiding Humiliation—From Intercultural Communication to Global Interhuman Communication.* Tokyo, Japan: Lecture at the Society for Intercultural Education, Training and Research (SIETAR) Japan, Reitaku University Tokyo Kenkyu Center, June 9, 2006.

———. 2006b. *Is It Possible to "Change the World"? Some Guidelines to How We Can Build a More Decent and Dignified World Effectively: The Case of Dignifying Abusers.* Human Dignity and Humiliation Studies, see http://www.humiliationstudies.org/whoweare/evelin02.php.

———. 2006c. *Making Enemies: Humiliation and International Conflict.* Westport, CT, London: Greenwood Press and Praeger Publishers.

Maren, M. 1997. *The Road to Hell: The Ravaging Effects of Foreign Aid and International Charity.* New York, NY: Free Press.

Miller, J. B. 1986. *Toward a New Psychology of Women.* 2d ed. Boston, MA: Beacon Press.

Miller, W. I. 1993. *Humiliation and Other Essays on Honor, Social Discomfort, and Violence.* Ithaca: Cornell University Press.

Retzinger, S. M. 1991. *Violent Emotions: Shame and Rage in Marital Quarrels.* Newbury Park, CA: Sage.

Scheff, T. J. 1990. *Bloody Revenge: Emotions, Nationalism and War.* Chicago, IL: University of Chicago Press.

Tedeschi, J. T. and Calhoun, L. G., eds. 2006. *Handbook of Posttraumatic Growth: Research and Practice.* Mahwah, NJ: Lawrence Erlbaum.

Ury, W. 1999. *Getting to Peace. Transforming Conflict at Home, at Work, and in the World.* New York, NY: Viking.

Vogel, W. and Lazare, A. 1990. The Unforgivable Humiliation: A Dilemma in Couples' Treatment. In *Contemporary Family Therapy,* 12 (2), pp. 139-151.

4

Education and Post-Conflict Recovery

Margaret E. Smith

The range of issues that arise at the nexus of education and violent conflict provides a rich, and to a considerable degree untapped, field for research (Davies 2004; Sommers 2002). Clearly, as a core institution of communities, schools are an available and important tool for reconstruction after war.

Education can be, and usually is, complicit in perpetuating the attitudes and social divisions that encourage conflict. Uneven provision of education can preserve privilege. State-imposed curricula may undergird authoritarian systems and the denial of minority voice. School segregation contributes to broader social segregation. The language in which lessons are conducted, level of willingness to engage in controversial discussions, and schools' willingness to offer religious instruction to all religious groups are measures of the wider society's recognition of pluralism. Textbooks may perpetuate stereotypes of the "other," focus on history that legitimates those who have seized power unjustly, or simply support hostile behavior by emphasizing warlike images.

Education can be a target of conflict. Schools may be destroyed or commandeered for military purposes during war. Sabotaging a school is one way to mobilize or kidnap children to become child soldiers. Teachers, often regarded as leadership figures in small communities, may have been killed or injured, and will undoubtedly have suffered their own share of deprivation and trauma in the course of the conflict.

The author thanks her research assistant Jennryn Wetzler for her help with this chapter.

Education can become politicized by war. At the university level, in the name of critical thinking, vocal student unions or teachers' unions may speak out against the authorities and then become the targets of oppression, as was the case in El Salvador (Marques and Bannon, 5). But educational institutions can also be the core of social resistance. In eighteenth century Ireland when Catholicism was outlawed, Catholics developed a hidden school system known as "hedge schools," and succeeded in maintaining a high level of education for their people. A similar and recent example is the hidden, alternative schools run by Kosovar Albanians between 1989 and 1999, when Albanian-language schools in Kosovo were shut down. Education can supply a base for recruitment to a political cause as was the case with the Nicaragua Literacy Campaign that mobilized the sympathies of teachers, government agencies, religious groups and young people for the Sandinista regime in the 1980s (Marques and Bannon).

Education can help whole communities recover from war by reintroducing routines, helping people to process, understand and psychologically recover from what happened during the war, teaching attitudes and behaviors that support new institutions, imparting skills of nonviolent conflict resolution, training people for employment, and preparing citizens to function in a plural, democratic society.

Education's role in rebuilding is the focus of this chapter. The chapter discusses ways education plays this role and then explores seven aspects of post-conflict education. The first three address the immediate needs of traumatized people: emergency response, education for women and girls, and the special concerns of ex-combatants. The next three address the challenge of creating a multicultural society that honors difference: school integration, history teaching, and citizenship education. Finally, peace education addresses the skills needed to introduce a culture of nonviolence.

Education as a Tool for Recovery

When we think about education's role in rebuilding traumatized societies, we can consider education's structural role, its substantive role, and its symbolic role.

Structural role: Functioning schools offer all members of a community a sense of routine and a hub for common action. It has been documented that in the wake of the Southeast Asian tsunami in 2004, as well in response to Hurricane Mitch in 1998, affected communities that started by rebuilding their school had a more effective recovery overall than other communities (Moseley). The school can be a place for training community workers in how to address post-traumatic stress. For children, schools function as an extension of the family, a place where they find predictability as their minds expand and they discover the world. Keeping children in school during a war, or getting children back to school quickly at the end of a war can offer them stability in the midst of chaos.

According to a recent World Bank study, schools rarely cease operations totally during war, and primary schools in particular are generally quick to start up again after war, with or without outside support (Buckland 7-8). At the same time, the disjuncture caused by war is a chance to bring long delayed reforms. One aspect of these reforms can be the decision to give parents, teachers and local authorities more say in the running of schools, as has been the case in a number of Central American countries. Another aspect can be to introduce more "child centered" forms of teaching. A third can be making schools more gender sensitive. Thus from a structural standpoint, a key tradeoff is the relationship between restoring and revamping. Given the exhaustion that communities face after war, how much reorganization is helpful in the immediate aftermath? Families may feel even more loss when they see big changes in schools. And yet, if reforms are not made immediately, old ways return rapidly.

Substantive role: In the wake of war, children need to be given a way to understand what happened that allows them to get past their sense of disempowerment. They need help to grieve. Moreover children may have suffered neurologically, so that their ways of learning may themselves be impaired. Schools are a place where such needs can be identified and children can be given mental health care. But mental health services are rarely adequate to address the trauma that large numbers have experienced. Schools themselves could be developing curriculum that is sensitive to mental health needs of children following war, but apart from the occasional art or drama program, they rarely do so. Presumably the "do no harm" philosophy is a major restraint: emergency workers and teachers are, rightly, cautious about attempting more than they are trained to do.

In the classroom, revised curriculum and textbooks can help children rehumanize their view of the "other," or enemy, group and offer a new frame of reference on which they will base their sense of identity. Textbooks can teach young people to think critically and open-mindedly so that they need not be prisoners of ideological thinking. Children can also learn how to make use of democratic principles and human rights and to understand citizenship as a set of values common to all. Schools can give special instruction in ways to address conflict through peer mediation, learning about other cultures and religions, and understanding the principles of nonviolent protest to bring social change. Schools and adult education projects prepare the young, women and ex-combatants to find jobs and contribute the economic advance of the country as a whole, which is a significant means of avoiding recurrence of conflict.

New approaches to teaching history, citizenship education, and peace education are obvious ways to give content to the notion of a plural society. A concern about these new approaches to teaching is that children are required to be pioneers for the new society. Is it fair to place the burden on children to achieve what adults have failed to achieve? Surely this is only acceptable if children see similar efforts in other areas of life.

Symbolic role: Governments regard education as a means to express, enact and impart their over-arching plan for the society. In the wake of a newly minted peace, education is a symbolic way of declaring a new beginning. Education provisions may appear in peace treaties, because education is an obvious way to translate the vision for a post-conflict society into everyday life. The degree to which educational provisions in peace treaties become the springboard for new education policy is not entirely clear. One problem among many can be that international actors have been the ones who insisted upon the insertion of educational clauses into treaties without having adequate understanding of domestic realities (Marquis and Bannon 10).

Communities like to have control over their schools. At the same time, reforms that support pluralism or multiculturalism in a post-conflict regime may not always be popular among teachers or parents. In Northern Ireland one problem that emerged was teacher exhaustion in the face of numerous curriculum reforms. A more difficult challenge, one faced currently in Bosnia and Herzegovina, is bringing school integration to mixed areas after war. Parents will lead resistance to school integration, and teachers will be afraid of classroom discussions on political or war-related issues in integrated settings. Thus, we see a tradeoff between increasing community ownership and control of schools on the one hand, and, on the other, introducing reforms needed to enforce a plural society.

Education and Emergency Response

> *Emergency education programs alone are the largest psychosocial intervention in an emergency as they establish a familiar learning environment, provide a regular schedule and instill a feeling of hope for the future.*
>
> – *INEE Good Practice Guides*

First responses to humanitarian emergencies, whether in the context of war or natural disaster, involve efforts to reassure all involved that normal life is still possible. Schools follow close in the wake of housing and food in the order of tasks for first responders. Populations returning home to devastation and bereavement will be helped by seeing the local school starting up again as quickly as possible.

Many of those who have worked in such situations emphasize the importance of community involvement in setting up education programs, so that the needs of the community are fully identified and local resources are mobilized. The elderly, disabled, women and children should be consulted. Responders therefore need to know how to listen and facilitate dialogue.

Safety is a huge issue. A first consideration is whether the school itself has been, or now is, a place of recruitment of child combatants. If so, then protections against this practice must be in place before the school reopens. The structural safety of the school building must be verified. In addition, the distance children must travel to get to the school and hazards along the way are key concerns.

While it is a good strategy to build on programs that existed before the catastrophe, it is also important to make sure schools offer classes that are relevant to the current needs of the population. Adolescents, for example, may find sitting in a classroom tedious after all they have been through, and may be more interested in vocational training that can lead them quickly into the workforce. Minority groups and others who are displaced will be keen to have education in their own language but will also need help to learn the language of their new locality. Women who are widowed will need job training to support their families. Girls who have not had the chance to go to school will need special attention and instruction in child care, hygiene, HIV-AIDS issues, immunization, and pregnancy prevention.

Typically an emergency environment lacks trained teachers, and in particular teachers who have had training that prepares them to work in such an environment. People with no teacher training may have stepped forward in refugee camps and other settings to create ac-hoc schools. These people must be acknowledged for their work, and indeed may have useful insights about ongoing needs. At the same time, teacher training is an urgent matter. Teachers who have been traumatized will need time to talk about what they experienced and to give each other support, so that they do not burn out or abandon their work.

Children who have been traumatized will be coming to school with anxiety, aggression, depression and grieving. They will often have difficulty concentrating. Teachers must therefore have clear learning objectives, with a definite beginning and end to their classes. They can help withdrawn pupils to speak by asking open ended questions and calling on all pupils in the class. Teachers should be trained to recognize stress symptoms both in their pupils and themselves, and to have techniques they can draw on for stress relief. They need a referral system for the children who need more care, and a trustworthy body that provides this.

In 2004 the Inter-Agency Network for Education in Emergencies (INEE) produced a set of minimum education standards as goals for humanitarian assistance in emergencies. The guidelines were the result of a two year consultation process with groups in Africa, Asia and the Pacific, Latin America, the Middle East, North Africa and Europe. The document built off of international goals for education laid down by the World Education Forum meeting in Dakar, Senegal in 2000, entitled "The Dakar Framework for Action: Education For All: Meeting Our Collective Commitments." The INEE guidelines respond to the fact that the Dakar Framework says very little about the special difficulties of providing education in conflict regions. The new guidelines highlight three aspects of supplementary education which INEE refers to as "Life Skills" that can be offered in school, or can be offered in after-school sessions. These are Health Education, which includes personal hygiene, building latrines, water purification, and HIV-AIDS; landmine awareness; and peace education – tolerance, conflict management and human rights. (INEE)

Among other organizations that have developed manuals for addressing the needs of children affected by war and displacement are International Save the Children Alliance, UNICEF, Oxford University's Refugee Studies Center, Concern Worldwide and UNHCR.

Women's Education

> *Gender dynamics . . . are a critical dimension in the complex interaction between education and conflict.*
> – Bouta, Frerks, and Bannon

"Educate a boy and you educate one person; educate a girl and you educate a nation" (Badis). Women are educating all the time. As mothers, teachers, and civil organizers, women are at the core of community response to war and will be the principal teachers of future generations about alternatives to violence. The aftermath of war presents women with a unique opportunity. Largely excluded from the decisions that brought their communities to war, and usually playing little role other than victim in the conduct of the war, women assume a much larger role in post-conflict reconstruction. The education sector is a place where women can quickly gain political influence.

International bodies are giving a new level of recognition to the link between women and conflict recovery. UN Security Resolution 1325 (2000) on Women, Peace and Security, recommends that women in war zones receive special treatment as victims and be made partners in negotiating the peace. This resolution followed from the Beijing Declaration and Platform for Action (1995), and thus shows that women's activism is meeting with increased success (Corrin 2001, 94).

Women's workload grows during war. Their responsibilities to their family include not only child care but caring for the elderly who have previously received social assistance, fetching firewood and water, and generating income. In addition, mothers often educate their children at home when travel to school is unsafe, or schools close due to conflict.

In spite of the load they carry, women still have to deal with paternalism, even from international NGOs and foreign governments who presume to know what development techniques work best for women in post-conflict communities. In Kosova, for example, tractors were awarded by the UN to all of the families that owned tractors before the war. However, UNMIK officials decided that families represented by female heads of household would receive hired labor for plowing instead, assuming women could not drive farm tractors. UNMIK officials made the decision without consulting the women. This decision overlooked the fact that women were entitled to the tractors, and that in fact many of the women wanted to learn to drive farm machinery (Corrin 2001, 81).

Women have their own needs during war that largely get overlooked: needs for gynecological care and counseling (especially for rape victims), psychological and social support services, repatriation assistance, and help to find employment, particularly for women who are heading households. During war, many women have gained self-confidence because of the extra responsibilities they have taken on. Some have had, of necessity, to become breadwinners. NGOS should be helping women gain professional recognition for their skills, but sadly, much of women's extra care-giving and teaching is labeled an extension of domestic responsibilities. Adult education programs need to offer women basic administrative, management, teaching and health care skills so they can earn more and find recognition in the public arena (Corrin 2001, 95).

Women's and girls' access to education and vocational training often remains restricted by traditional attitudes. Families may take their girls out of school to help with the increased workload resulting from poverty, reconstruction efforts, or loss of family members. Attending school can pose security threats, such as rape or physical attack. Increased transportation costs in a post-conflict community can stop girls from going to school. Families reason that marriage, which may have been delayed by the war, will be delayed further by education. Decreased enrollment numbers for girls means the whole community will pay a price in the future in reduced coping and fewer possibilities to reach out and understand the world.

At very minimum, education in post-conflict societies must endeavor to increase girls' enrolment. In addition, peace studies curriculum introduced in schools after war can offer more gender sensitive teaching. This usually begins by removing gender bias from textbooks but can be pursued further by underlining how war experiences of men and women differ. (Bouta et. al 2005, 121) Such education should help pave the way for women to find greater self-confidence and voice in postwar society.

Education for Ex-Combatants

UNICEF estimates 300,000 children under age eighteen currently participate in over thirty conflicts worldwide (UNICEF 2007). Children may perform non-combative work serving as porters, guards, cooks, spies, medics, laborers, messengers, or sex slaves. However, most serve as combatants. While the rehabilitation and post-conflict education for child soldiers must cater to their needs as children, ex-combatant programs must also address the special needs of adult soldiers, including the disabled, women ex-combatants, and those prone to criminal behavior. Many ex-combatants return home with severed limbs or wounds from gunshots or landmines. Incidence of HIV/AIDS rises steeply among the active military and women in refugee camps, and this has repercussions long after the conflict is over. Depression and alienation can be acute. Education programs must promote condom use, voluntary testing, medical care, and counseling.

Many ex-combatants have had little or no formal education. Rehabilitation workers must choose whether to send ex-combatants to regular schools or to specially designed programs. The former approach offers ex-combatants a sense of normality and gives "time out" rather than engaging them in activities designed to respond to their recent experiences. The latter approach requires special organization, and its adoption is less likely with limited funding. In most cases, some combination of vocational training, literacy and numeracy classes, and counseling coupled with conflict resolution skills has been adopted. The partnership between UNICEF and the Belgian NGO Solidarité Afghanistan Belgium (SAB) is an example of a program that has worked well in providing Afghan children at risk and former child-soldiers with basic education and vocational training.

Some women who become soldiers do so voluntarily, but many are abducted or coerced. Non-combative positions are more common for women, including roles as nurses, cooks, messengers, administrative personnel, spies, or sex workers. Disarmament, Demobilization, and Reintegration (DDR) programs often have narrow definitions for ex-combatants, and assistance may only be available to ex-combatants who carry weapons, leaving out most women. Another problem is that aid organizations often categorize ex-combatant women as "dependents," which automatically disqualifies them from ex-combatant benefits. In addition women have greater problems than men to gain acceptance in their home areas after combat, and are at particular risk of prostitution upon return to their communities. Women's post-conflict needs are slowly gaining international recognition, in governmental and non-governmental sectors. UNIFEM in Liberia was relatively successful in offering women a gender-sensitive DDR process, which included services and counseling on reproductive health, HIV/AIDS awareness, as well as maternal and child health.

Success stories are gratifying, but strained post-conflict economies mean that most rehabilitation efforts lack the official recognition and funding necessary to provide comprehensive help. Assistance to ex-combatants largely depends on international humanitarian efforts. After educational or vocational training, ex-combatants often face a very limited job market for their new skills (Harshe, 1). Further challenging ex-combatants are the often hostile communities into which they must integrate and the fact that former soldiers get blamed for the war. Aid programs mediate the tentative balance between both groups' needs, but aid workers' focus on ex-combatants can breed discontent in the rest of the community. "The provision of targeted assistance to ex-combatants has often been perceived as rewarding the perpetrators of violence, and not as an investment in peace and security" (Ginifer 42).

Creating a Multicultural Society: The Unity-Diversity Paradox

In deeply divided societies, a core issue in post conflict reconstruction is deciding how the society will handle its diversity. After a civil war defined by ethno-national identity, politics is war by other means. Politicians recognize that they can make political capital out of the fact that, at the grassroots, a residual fear of the other group has been exacerbated by the war. Populations that, before the conflict, lived in mixed neighborhoods, now want to live in areas with their own ethnic group. This polarization impacts schools: schools will tend to be more homogeneous purely because they represent the demographics of the locality. In areas where the population remains diverse, people will look for ways to shore up separation.

From the mid-nineteenth century when public schools were first introduced, up to the late twentieth century, education in plural societies traditionally promoted cohesion. In the late twentieth century, democratic values have challenged the myth of national cohesion in plural societies. Now countries have to promote recognition of their plural nature in order to satisfy the democratic, participatory aspirations of their citizens. At the same time they still require common norms and values for the functioning of society. While honoring diversity, governments must strive to find ways to pull the citizenry together around a national vision. This unity-diversity paradox has become a core preoccupation for Australia, Belgium, Bosnia and Herzegovina, Canada, Fiji, France, Israel, Malaysia, Northern Ireland, South Africa, Sri Lanka, the UK and the US. In all cases, education ends up being at the heart of the debate. Education systems, which in the past promoted cohesion by promulgating a language, a set of assumptions, a literary canon, or by inculcating loyalty, have had to rethink their mission. Now education in plural societies has a two-fold goal, where the goals can seem antithetical. On the one hand education must introduce common norms and ideas that knit the society together, on the other it must give due recognition to difference.

In deeply divided societies emerging from violent conflict, this paradox is weightier because the centrifugal force pulling the sub-state groups apart is greater in the aftermath of war. If the country has not split as a result of the war, the peace treaty will, of necessity, enshrine a vision of a plural society held together by values of openness while recognizing diversity. The education system will be called upon to teach the citizenry how to live in such a society. But it is bound to meet resistance.

One of the first questions to be addressed in the unity-diversity paradox is whether government funded schools will be "common" schools, where all groups attend together, or whether groups will be educated separately. The second question is how the plural nature of the society will be presented and discussed in the classroom, whether or not all groups are represented there.

School Integration

During the civil rights struggle in the US, African Americans saw that their best interests lay with school integration: true equality would never be attained with separate schools. The same argument held in South Africa and is borne out by recent statistics: even in 1999, seven years after official school segregation was ended, 52% of blacks had no education beyond primary school, compared with 2% of whites (Gallagher, 2004).

In Northern Ireland, by contrast, segregation is not viewed negatively by the less powerful group, because they do not see school integration as a means of achieving equality. The chief incentive, therefore, for school integration is social mixing. An integrated school movement began in the 1970s and now about five per cent of children in Northern Ireland attend integrated schools, but significant numbers of Catholics and Protestants have reservations.

The case of Bosnia and Herzegovina is different again, in that up to 1991 in Yugoslavia, all children attended government schools, and education was not perceived as a focus of discrimination. Now, because of population movement during the war, people are living in more homogeneous regions than before. Most Serbs are bunched together in the Serbian entity known as Republika Srpska. Bosniaks and Croats are somewhat more intermingled in their entity – the Federation of Bosnia and Herzegovina – though cantonal divisions conform to group concentrations. Municipalities that are large enough to have several schools are providing separate schools for the respective ethnicities. Busing is also used to take students to schools of their own group. Other municipalities are allowing what has come to be known as "two schools under one roof." In such cases, children of different ethnicities are educated on different floors of the school building by teachers of their own ethnic group. Recess and lunch breaks are arranged to be at different times to avoid interaction. Hence, school segregation is seen, as in Northern Ireland, as a means to reinforce social boundaries. The Bosnia and Herzegovina education authorities have declared such schools illegal, but have made scant effort to enforce the ruling. Latest figures indicate that the Federation has fifty-four such schools (OSCE Mission).

School integration as a means to create co-existence in a plural, multicultural society has proven to be problematic. All countries that have attempted it have found it more difficult than was initially expected. In the US, we now see a tendency towards resegregation (Orfield and Yun, 1999; cited in Gallagher 2004). In Northern Ireland, the likelihood of a growth of integrated schools is questioned, partly for lack of funding, but also because most schools are too homogeneous to have the potential to make this change, which requires raising the ratio to 3:7 within a given number of years. The alternative to common schools is to create separate schools as a means of giving greater cultural recognition to separate groups. Such a step seems retrograde to all who put store by the value of diversity, and experience in the US and South Africa provides strong arguments against it. But research indicates that "no specific structural arrangement provides a guaranteed outcome" (Gallagher 2004). Creating plural institutions out of segregated institutions has not proven to be a straightforward undertaking.

Segregation probably has a less harmful effect in societies where the separation is a matter of choice, such as in Northern Ireland. (Gallagher 2004). This would also be the case for Bosnia and Herzegovina. But, accepting school separation increases the likelihood of ongoing social bifurcation unless curricula and teaching can be designed to address and overcome this.

History Teaching's Contribution to the New Narrative

All deeply divided societies have their examples of the way ideas about history represent the differing mentalities of the society. Eamonn McCann (1974), a Catholic from Northern Ireland, describes his history classes in the 1950s,

> History lessons did not always rigidly follow the curriculum laid down by the Northern Ireland Ministry of Education. One teacher, admittedly regarded as something of an eccentric, was at pains to discredit English propaganda. . . . At the beginning of a new school year he would lead the class through the set text books instructing them to tear out pages of fiction. . . . That done, lessons could begin.

Wherever we find political contestation, we find differing histories, because groups co-opt elements of history in order to develop a narrative of the group. Often this narrative's power depends on villainizing another group. All groups in a deeply divided society believe the other group is imparting a biased, uncomplimentary, and dehumanizing account of their group, and that this is fuel for the conflict.

The idea that a common history can be written, based on proper historical methods and verifiable facts, is held up as a salve to this problem. Surely the truth is not impossible to establish, we argue, and we imagine that this *truth* will become the overarching standard, the transcendent expression of the history of a postwar region. Such common history, it is hoped, will provide the basis for a common identity. This hope, or vision, has some value, though in certain respects it is completely unrealistic. It has value to the degree that egregiously incorrect elements in textbooks can be removed, and children can be taught how to pursue historical research in ways that observe the best scientific rigor. It can be unrealistic because in a deeply divided society, people have great unwillingness to alter their ideas about their own group or about the other group.

Several strategies to address the challenges of teaching history after war have emerged. The first strategy is to teach as little history as possible. This policy was pursued in Bosnia and Herzegovina and also in South Africa, more by default, in the immediate aftermath of conflict. In Northern Ireland the story was slightly more complicated, but teachers found a range of reasons to complain about a proposed curriculum that asked them to teach the history of the state of Northern Ireland from its inception in 1922 through to the 1980s, to the point that this curriculum policy was abandoned in favor of something that was less demanding.

A second strategy, pursued currently in Bosnia, is to recognize that some subjects are "national" subjects, in other words they will be taught differently according to what group is doing the teaching and learning. "National" subjects in Bosnia include history, geography, literature and religion. A third strategy, one appearing recently in Israel-Palestine, is to produce a textbook where the separate narratives of the different groups are recorded side by side on the same page. A fourth is to focus history teaching more on social history, where political discussion is less likely to arise. A fifth is to discuss how the past affects the present by demonstrating how historical events are treated in politics and popular culture.

Some key considerations when addressing history teaching after war include the following:

First, nothing stated above speaks to the personal trauma that the pupils and their parents and teachers have experienced in the recent war. Group solidarity hardens during war, and supporting the narrative of one's own group represents psychological safety. Pupils, or for that matter their parents and teachers, who are asked to acknowledge elements of the narrative of the other group can feel very threatened. Such discussions may also interfere with personal grieving and with the natural need to repress frightening experiences until a person feels fully secure. For this reason, it could be completely justified to have some kind of pause before talking about recent history in the wake of war. But how long should this pause last?

Second, teachers need training to prepare them to teach new material, or to give a different spin to old material. Most particularly they need training in how to speak about the historical memory of groups that are not their own, and how to facilitate a discussion on controversial issues among young people of different groups.

Third, the search for a common history is not necessarily the correct goal. Writing textbooks that satisfy all sides at the end of a conflict may be achieved by leaving out the most controversial material. Thus those working on history teaching in post-conflict societies are recognizing that some way must be found to acknowledge that different groups experienced events differently, and their accounts will inevitably differ in emphasis. The best way to write a true account of a civil war may be to write two or more parallel accounts.

Fourth, societies that remain deeply divided must find a way to discuss how historical events and experiences get co-opted in contemporary literature, theatre, movies, and politics and contribute to ongoing societal divisions. This is tricky territory for teachers because these issues arouse intense emotions that may be hard to handle in a classroom.

In segregated schools, the key point is to hold schools accountable to teach more than their own group narrative. Schools must adhere to basic requirements of objectivity and a willingness to show some criticism of the behavior of their own group. Strategies to address this include talking first about other conflicts, in order to help children be comfortable speaking about differing views of the conflict; talking about local history or social history, which tend to be less politicized; or studying the history of a larger collective, such as European or African history, to reduce the salience of the chosen group identification. Proper historical methods, investigative attitudes and evidence-based accounts are key skills to emphasize.

In the end, history teaching must engage with contentious issues of the past, demonstrate the interaction between past and present, and acknowledge the emotional resonance of the past in personal and family memory.

Citizenship Education

International norms have moved to the place where the appropriateness of teaching citizenship should no longer have to be debated. The 1989 UN Convention on the Rights of the Child lays out, among the agreed aims of education,

> The development of respect for human rights and fundamental freedoms and for principles enshrined in the Charter of the United Nations . . . [respect for] his or her own cultural identity, language and values, for the national values of the country in which the child is living, the country from which he or she may originate, and for civilizations different from his or her own; . . .[and] the preparation of the child for responsible life in a free society, in the spirit of understanding, peace, tolerance, equality of sexes, and friendship among all peoples, ethnic, national and religious groups and persons of indigenous origin. . . .

An array of bodies including UNESCO, UNICEF, the Council of Europe, governments, and NGOs has produced curricula on citizenship education. The Council of Europe has epitomized the content of citizenship as human rights, democratic values and, tolerance (Council of Europe). UNESCO's list is less focused on democracy and more on conflict resolution skills, and includes instruction geared towards skills and attitudes for personal autonomy; employment; living together; respecting social and cultural diversity; peace building; and conflict resolution. (UNESCO 2004; Quoted by Osler and Starkey 2005. See Osler and Starkey 2005 for a review of many proposals of core skills and ideas to be taught in citizenship education.)

Citizenship education that has emerged in recent years is an ideal way to hold in tension the unity-diversity paradox. In the past, citizenship education would have contained a message of patriotism that is now considered passé. In its current manifestation, citizenship is decoupled from ethno-national affiliation.

Concerns raised about the new enthusiasm for citizenship education include the question: are schools, which are generally authoritarian in structure, capable of teaching about democracy? Davies's research indicates that many teachers perceive that good citizenship is linked with obedience to authority (Davies 2004). Hence, the content of citizenship education quickly brings up discussions of school culture and teacher training. If Davies' critique is one likely to come from the left of the political/cultural spectrum, the likely critique that will come from the right is that teaching about citizenship is a distraction from teaching the basics and will get in the way of teaching children about their own culture: children will simply learn that other cultures are beyond criticism (Osler and Starkey 2005).

Those who teach these courses wrestle with the question how to use citizenship education as a means to make more of a connection between schools and communities. Using community sites for learning about citizenship, getting parents involved in discussing the meaning of citizenship with teachers, mobilizing pupils for volunteer work within the community are ideas that have been put forward. Research is scarce on the results of such endeavors. Another question is whether citizenship education courses developed for multicultural societies like the UK and the US, are usable in post-war and post-totalitarian environments. In a society recovering from war, people relate to the other group with a level of fear that is much greater than in a plural society with relatively little violence. When ethnic identity has been mobilized as a factor of the war, people will have been exposed to propaganda that totally negates the other group. The process of beginning to think of the other group as having the right to exist is a huge stretch immediately after war. Thinking about the other group as having moral equivalence with one's own is an even further stretch. The dilemma invites a stage theory on how to open people's minds to the other group sufficiently to engage or respect them. Here peace education has some special contributions.

Peace Education

Peace education is designed to mobilize the citizenry for war prevention by teaching nonviolence. It takes on a different cast according to the context in which it is being taught.

The anti-war movement in the United States developed peace education to address the militaristic nature of US policy during the Cold War. It advocated banning nuclear weapons and the arms race; values of co-operation, inclusion and creativity in contradiction to authoritarianism and conformity; and empowerment through such ideas as Friere's "pedagogy of the oppressed" (Friere 1970). Subsequently peace education has acquired other foci. Salomon creates a three level typology: peace education in regions of tranquility, peace education in regions of interethnic tensions, and peace education in intractable conflict regions (Salomon 2002). In places where little or no outright violence is involved, the goal, he argues, is to pursue a culture of harmony in all human relations. Peace education might focus on peer mediation and other conflict resolution skills that address interpersonal relationships. Here Galtung's vision of "positive peace" (Galtung 1975) seems a viable vision. In Salomon's second group, countries experiencing interethnic tensions, Third World countries and countries that are newly democratizing, the focus for change is unequal power relations or prejudice among groups. Here peace education will concentrate on human rights education.

In places of open or intractable conflict, reaching total harmony seems unrealistic, and the definition of peace becomes one of peace as the absence of war. In such places changing mindsets sufficiently to create dialogue among adversaries is the main aim of peace education. In such conflicts Salomon (2002, 9) offers a set of four interrelated and desirable outcomes for peace education: "accepting as legitimate the other's narrative and its specific implications; being willing to critically examine one's own group's actions toward the other group; being ready to experience and show empathy and trust toward the other; and being disposed to engage in nonviolent activities."

Sometimes peace education is confused with peace studies. The latter examines peace processes, and began as a college discipline after World War II. "Peace studies tend to focus on the causes of war, and alternatives to war, whereas peace education is more generic, attempting to draw out of people their natural inclinations to live in peace" (Harris 2002).

Developments in the field of conflict resolution in the past twenty-five years have fertilized the field of peace education. Conflict resolution training is generally understood as teaching skills of good communication, negotiation and mediation, as well as consciousness raising about the dynamics of conflict itself.

With the developments of global citizenship education as described above, some of the ideas of peace education have been included in citizenship education. It is probably safe to say that many of the same people, or at least constituencies, promote both. Peace education gathered momentum in the 1960s, '70s and '80s. A critical mass of citizenship education promoters emerged in the 1990s in the context of the collapse of communism and numerous identity-based civil wars where the common goal of democracy seemed like the best way to reunite the country.

The distinction may be more semantic than substantive. In countries where a longstanding, intractable conflict has been, and indeed still is, in play, using the term *peace education* may have been avoided in order to prevent people from feeling the curriculum proposed had political motivations behind it. This was certainly true in Northern Ireland, where many labels were considered for the new curriculum of the 1980s focusing on lowering barriers between groups. Rather than a label like *education for peace,* the label adopted was Education for Mutual Understanding (EMU), which seemed more positive and forward-looking. In Northern Ireland, EMU has now morphed into citizenship education. Once again, the term *citizenship education* seems to look beyond the conflict and offers a common vision for the future.

Peace education keeps some potential aspects of the curriculum on the table that might be lost with citizenship education. In order to overcome psychological barriers vis à vis another group, people need to absorb certain concepts: the human tendency to differentiate and devalue the other; destructive ways of addressing conflict by projecting hostility on the other; origins of and influences that lead to violence; and the role of bystanders. Children need to experience affection, nurturing, and guidance presented in a positive manner, learning by doing, engaging in activities on behalf of people not in their group, the meaning of moral courage (Staub 2002). Peace education may be a more natural place to address these concerns than citizenship education. Storytelling, art, and drama can be a means of helping people talk about their own experience and develop empathy towards the other.

Conclusion

The subject of post-war education is rife with possibilities for debate, even though the nature of the situations it addresses calls for action, and the speedier the better. Those embarking on projects to reform education need considerable cultural awareness, a willingness to devote time and effort to honor an inclusive community process, and a judicious recognition of the appropriate role for the central government in setting norms, assisting in teacher training and developing teaching materials.

Post war education is not simply a matter of helping children get back to some former state of concord that existed before a war. In many societies, the outbreak of war was simply the ongoing expression of hostility that has existed over decades, even centuries. Children have to be offered ways to conceptualize themselves differently, and to develop entirely new group narratives that do not negate the other (Bar-On 2002). Schools will be hard pressed to offer a new narrative if the society itself is not exploring this in other ways. Truth commissions, memorialization, documentation and history writing will contribute to the process.

References

Allport, G. 1954. *The Nature of Prejudice.* Reading, Mass: Addison-Wesley.
Audergon, A. 2004. Collective Trauma: The Nightmare of History. *Psychotherapy and Politics International* 2(1): 16 – 31.
Alic, A. 2003. Doing Away with Segregation. Transitions Online website:

http://www.tol.cz/look/TOL/article.tpl?IdLanguage=1&IdPublication=9&NrIssue=1&NrSection=1&NrArticle=10548

Apfel, R. J. and B. Simon. 1996. *Minefields in Their Hearts: The Mental Health of Children in War and Communal Violence.* New Haven and London: Yale University Press.

Arnhold, N., Bekker, J., Kersh, N., McLeish, E., and Phillips, D. 1998. *Education for Reconstruction: The Regeneration of Educational Capacity Following National Upheaval.* Wallingford, Oxfordshire: Symposium Books.

Azar, E. E. 1990. *The Management of Protracted Social Conflicts.* Hampshire, UK: Dartmouth.

Badis, Sheikh Abdelhamid Ibn. Founder, in 1932, of the Association of Algerian Muslim Scholars to spearhead resistance to the French in Algeria. Quoted on the website of The Citizens Foundation.
http://www.thecitizensfoundation.org/impact/index.php?id=6&query_dir=impact.

Bar-On, D. 2002. "Conciliation Through Storytelling: Beyond Victimhood," in Gavriel Salomon and Baruch Nevo, eds. *Peace Education: The Concept, Principles, and Practices around the World.* London and Mahwah, N. J.: Lawrence Erlbaum Associates.

Bouta, T., G. Frerks, and I. Bannon. 2005. *Gender, Conflict, and Development.* The World Bank Group, Washington, DC.

Buckland, P. July 2006. Education and Conflict: Research, Policy and Practice. *Forced Migration Review*, Supplement.

Burgess, G. and H. Burgess, eds. Posted January 2007. "Education and Conflict." *Beyond Intractability.* Conflict Research Consortium, University of Colorado, Boulder. http://www.beyondintractability.org/essay/educ_and_conflict/

Bush, K. D. and D. Saltarelli. August 2000. *The Two Faces of Education in Ethnic Conflict.* Florence Italy: UNICEF, Innocenti Research Centre.

Cairns, E. and A. Dawes. February 1996. Children: Ethnic and Political Violence—A Commentary. *Child Development*, Vol. 67(1): 129-39.

Corrin, Chris. April 2001. Post-Conflict Reconstruction and Gender Analysis in Kosova. *International Feminist Journal of Politics*, Vol.3 (1): 78-98.

Council of Europe. 1998. *Education for Citizenship: The Basic Concepts and Core Competencies.* Council of Europe, DECS/CIT (98), 7 def.

Crisp, J., Ca. Talbot, and D. Cippolene, Eds. 2001. *Learning for a Future: Refugee Education in Developing Countries.* Geneva: UNHCR.

Davies, L. 2004. *Education and Conflict: Complexity and Chaos.* London: Routledge Falmer.

———. December 2005. Teaching about Conflict through Citizenship Education *International Journal of Citizenship and Teacher Education.* Vol.1(2): 17-34.

Errante, A. 1999. Peace Work as Grief Work in Mozambique and South Africa: Postconflict Communities as Context for Child and Youth Socialization. *Peace and Conflict: Journal of Peace Psychology.* Vol. 5(3): 261-279.

Feinberg, W. 1998. *Common Schools/Uncommon Identities: National Unity and Cultural Difference.* New Haven, Conn: Yale University Press.

Friere, P. 1970. *The Pedagogy of the Oppressed.* New York: The Continuum Publishing Company.

Galtung, J. 1975. *Essays in Peace Research*, Vol. 1. Copenhagen: Christian Ejlers.

Gallagher, T. 2004. *Education in Divided Societies.* Basingstoke, UK: Palgrave Macmillan.

Gonzalo, R. and R. Aedo-Richmond, eds. 1998. *Education as a Humanitarian Response.* Herndon, Va.: Cassell.

Graybill, L. S. 2004. Pardon, Punishment, and Amnesia: Three African Post-Conflict Methods. *Third World Quarterly*. Vol. 25(6): 1117-1130.

Harris, I. 2002. "Conceptual Underpinnings of Peace Education," in Gavriel Salomon and Baruch Nevo, eds. *Peace Education: The Concept, Principles, and Practices around the World.* London and Mahwah, N. J.: Lawrence Erlbaum Associates.

Howe, K.R. 1997. *Understanding Equal Educational Opportunity: Social Justice, Democracy and Schooling.* New York: Teacher's College Press.

Inter-Agency Network for Education in Emergencies (INEE). *INEE Good Practice Guides.* http://www.ineesite.org/page.asp?pid=1238

Marques, J. and I. Bannon. April 2003. "Central American: Education Reform in a Post-Conflict Setting, Opportunities and Challenges," CPR Network, Social Development Department, Environmentally and Socially Sustainable Development Network, Paper No. 4. Washington, D.C.: The World Bank.

Mazarana, D. and C. Khristopher. 2004. "From Combat to Community: Women and Girls of Sierra Leone." Hunt Alternatives Fund. http://www.smallarmssurvey.org/files/portal/spotlight/disarmament/disarm_pdf/2004_Mazurana_Carlson.pdf

McCann, E. 1974. *War and an Irish Town.* Middlesex: Penguin.

Moseley, S. F. Retrieved March 2, 2007. "Rebuilding Schools Will Help Tsunami Victims Recover," Academy for Educational Development. http://www.aed.org/Events/tsunamioped.cfm

Ndaruhutse, S. 2004. *The Financing of Education in Post-Conflict Reconstruction: The Need for Partnership between Economists and Educationalists.* The British Association for International and Comparative Education (BAICE).

Osler, A. and H. Starkey. 2005. "Education for Democratic Citizenship: A Review of Research, Policy and Practice 1995-2005." In Research Papers in Education, 2005. British Educational Research Association.

Orfield, G. and J. T.Yun, 1999. *Resegregation in American Schools.* Harvard Civil Rights Project. Cambridge, Mass.: Harvard University.

OSCE Mission to Bosnia and Herzegovina website. Retrieved March 5, 2007. http://www.oscebih.org/education/2schoolsunder1roof.asp?d=2

Quinones, A. 2004. "Gender and Post-Conflict Reconstruction: The World Bank Track Record." Heinrich Boll Foundation panel discussion report. http://www.genderaction.org/images/Boell%20Brookings%20Gender-Conflict%20Report.pdf

Salomon, G. and B. Nevo, eds. 2002. *Peace Education: The Concept, Principles, and Practices around the World.* London and Mahwah, N. J.: Lawrence Erlbaum Associates.

Salomon, G. 2002. "The Nature of Peace Education: Not All Programs are Created Equal," in Gavriel Salomon and Baruch Nevo, eds. *Peace Education: The Concept, Principles, and Practices around the World.* London and Mahwah, N. J.: Lawrence Erlbaum Associates.

Silove, D. 2004. The Challenges Facing Mental Health Programs for Post-Conflict and Refugee Communities. *Prehospital Disaster Medicine*. Vol. 19(1): 90-96.

Sinclair, M. 2002. *Planning Education in and After Emergencies.* Paris: UNESCO.

Smith, A. and T. Vaux. 2003. *Education, Conflict and International Development.* Report prepared by the Department for International Development, UK.

Smith, M. E. 2005. *Reckoning with the Past: Teaching History in Northern Ireland.* Lanham, Md: Lexington Books.

Sommers, M. 2002. *Children, Education and War: Reaching Education for All (EFA) Objectives in Countries Affected by Conflict* .The World Bank Conflict Prevention and Reconstruction Unit Working Paper No.1. Washington, D.C.: The World Bank.

Sorenson, B. 1998. *Women in Post-Conflict Reconstruction: Issues and Sources*. Geneva: UNRISDI and PSIS.

Staub, E. 2002. "From Healing Past Wounds To the Development of Inclusive Caring: Contents and Processes of Peace Education," in Gavriel Salomon and Baruch Nevo, Eds. *Peace Education: The Concept, Principles, and Practices around the World.* London and Mahwah, New Jersey: Lawrence Erlbaum Associates.

Tomlinson, K. and P. Benefield. 2005. *Education and Conflict: Research and Research Possibilities*. Slough, UK: National Foundation for Educational Research.

United Nations, 1989. *United Nations Convention on the Rights of the Child.* New York: United Nations.

United Nations Education, Scientific and Cultural Organization. 2004. Message for the 47th session of the UNESCO International Conference on Education and proposed priorities for action to include the quality of education for all young people. Geneva: International Bureau of Education.

United Nations Development Program. 2004. *Practical Guide to Multilateral Needs Assessment in Post Conflict Countries*, A joint Project of the United Nation Development Program, the World Bank, and the United Nations Development Group.http://www.undp.org/bcpr/documents/prevention/integrate/Post_Conflict_Needs_Assessment_methodology.pdf

United Nations Development Program. 2006. *UNDP Liberia Programmes*. UNDP report. http://www.lr.undp.org/ddrr.htm

Wessels, M. Child Soldiers, Peace Education, and Postconflict Reconstruction for Peace. *Theory into Practice*. Vol. 44(4): 363-369.

World Bank. 2001. *A Chance to Learn: Knowledge and Finance for Education in Sub-Saharan Africa.* Africa Region Human Development Series. Washington, D.C.: The World Bank.

———. June 14, 2005. Bosnia and Herzegovina: World Bank Supports Restructuring the Education System. Staff Connections – World Bank Intranet.http://web.worldbank.org/WBSITE/EXTERNAL/TOPICS/EXTENERGY/0,,print:Y~isCURL:Y~contentMDK:20541263~menuPK:64615830~pagePK:166745~piPK:459740~theSitePK:336806,00.html

———. 2005. *Reshaping the Future: Education and Postconflict Reconstruction*. Human Development Network Education Hub (HDNED), led by Peter Buckland. Washington, D.C.: The World Bank.

———. 2005. Youth Development: Youth in Post-Conflict Settings. *Children and Youth* Vol. 1(1):1-4. Washington, D.C.: The World Bank.

5

Trauma, Identity and Security: How the U.S. Can Recover from 9/11 Using Media Arts and a 3D Approach to Human Security

Lisa Schirch

"Security doesn't land in a helicopter. It grows from the ground up." In the summer of 2005, I traveled to Iraq to work with an NGO integrating peacebuilding into their community development efforts. In a conversation with these frontline peacebuilding experts, they shared important insights on the links between trauma, identity, and security. They told me:

> The young men in Iraqi villages have little to look forward to – unemployment, humiliation, and war. The insurgents find them easy to recruit. Community development projects in partnership with communities offer them job opportunities and a chance for earning respect and dignity in ways other than through the gun. But our development work in Iraq not only builds wells and job opportunities. With our development projects, Sunni, Shia, and Kurdish community leaders work together—each village forms a council to operate the water wells. We help lay the political foundations for communities that can solve their own problems through dialogue rather than guns. Do the Americans know that they have made the situation worse with their focus on the military while neglecting employment, education, the real stuff that builds security? There was no Al Qaeda here before the war, but now our cities are full of terrorists. Why do they focus on hunting down the terrorists rather than civilian security and real programs that build security from the ground up? It's a backwards strategy, and it only helps the insurgents in their recruitment."

While in other places in Iraq Sunni and Shia leaders foment hatred toward each other's identities, peacebuilding programs are fostering respectful interaction between ethnic and religious groups. These community development workers in Iraq see the links between security and trauma. The more a community in Iraq suffers trauma, the more likely they are to respond to their trauma with revenge-based support for the insurgency and local militias. Peacebuilding in this traumatized society requires development and diplomacy programs to build sustainable security. With 50-70% unemployment in many cities in Iraq, even the top U.S. commander in the region, General David Petraeus, pleads that there is "no military solution" in Iraq. General Petraeus and other military leaders instead point to reopening factories and intensified national and regional diplomatic work.[1]

Yet for years U.S. leaders have insisted that there is a military solution in Iraq and have conflated security with an identity battle between "good" and "evil" people rather than seeing the economic and political roots of the violence. On a muggy evening in June of 2005, U.S. President George W. Bush addressed the U.S. public with these words:

> The terrorists who attacked us—and the terrorists we face—murder in the name of a totalitarian ideology that hates freedom, rejects tolerance, and despises all dissent. Their aim is to remake the Middle East in their own grim image of tyranny and oppression—by toppling governments, by driving us out of the region, and by exporting terror. . . . Our mission in Iraq is clear. We're hunting down the terrorists.[2]

With his words he sculpted a threat narrative of an enemy with a logic of terror and tyranny. The entirety of President Bush's speech communicates the simple message: Americans are essentially good and as such, we must fight and destroy those who are evil. For many Americans who have had little interface with Islam or Muslim people, this narrative fosters a conflation between Islam, terrorism, and "evil."

This chapter contributes to the book's themes by exploring the U.S. as a traumatized society, and the role of peacebuilding within U.S. security policies following the tragedies of 9/11. The chapter explores how a sense of trauma confirms these dual identities of self and other, and how those identities then impact security policy-making. It begins by examining the important role of regressive leadership in perpetuating trauma and insecurity by shaping an "Aggressor Cycle" response to trauma. The U.S. trauma of 9/11 resulted in several years of revenge-based security policies heavily reliant on military solutions.
The second half of the chapter explores a "Survivor Cycle." It proposes that artistic processes may be particularly effective in transforming and adding complexity to the fixed, dualistic understanding of good and evil identities, in particular perceptions of U.S. and Muslim identities post 9/11.[3] The chapter ends by describing a "3D" approach to human security based on development, diplomacy, and defense, giving readers a conceptual framework for a new vision of security. Gradually, Americans are shifting to a more long-term approach to security that reflects a more transcendent approach to the trauma of 9/11.

Trauma and Identity Formation

Trauma is an event or series of events that causes severe physical, emotional, or spiritual injury. Traumatic experiences will often initiate a cycle of trauma in the traumatized person's life or in whole societies. While the cycle of trauma and victimization is usually unique to each person or group, it is often characterized by periods of shock, denial, shame and humiliation, loss of meaning, feelings of helplessness, anger and the suppression of grief and fears. Since these feelings are often quite painful, the traumatized person will sometimes try to numb themselves to the reality of their suffering through a desire for revenge or acts of violence against oneself or another. A cycle of violence can result, where people act out their sense of trauma on each other. As acts of violence are perpetrated in response to trauma, the cycle of trauma is continued.[4]

Trauma comes not only from the experience of victimization. Trauma can also come from the experience of participating in the perpetration of violence on others. In his book *On Killing: The Psychological Cost of Learning to Kill in War and Society,* Lt. Col. David Grossman surveys research about the debilitating psychological effects of combat on military personnel.[5] Rachael MacNair's book *Perpetration-Induced Traumatic Stress: The Psychological Consequences of Killing* makes similar arguments. People who engage in or support the use violence in a context where it is socially sanctioned or even legal, such as policemen, soldiers, or executioners, suffer from "perpetration-induced trauma syndrome" or PITS. For the purposes of this article, this concept is adapted to "participation-induced trauma syndrome" to enable discussion of the trauma that results from sharing the responsibility for participating in violence against others.[6]

The experience of trauma requires people to make challenging choices about how they will respond. In the cycle of aggression, people respond to trauma by acting out in ways that harm themselves or others. Responding aggressively to threats with short-term revenge-based strategies is a sign of trauma.[7]

Understanding the biological impact of trauma requires a quick lesson in neurobiology. The human brain is divided into two lobes or halves and three segments: the reptilian, limbic and neo-cortex. The oldest, reptilian core of the brain controls basic functions such as instinctual functions such as digestion and perspiration and the impulse when faced with a threat to freeze, fight, or flee. The limbic system is the emotional core of the brain, enabling humans to feel angry, sad, happy, etc. The neo-cortex offers humans control over the older parts of the brain through logical thought and reflection.[8] However, experiences of conflict and trauma often overwhelm the neo-cortex or rational brain. In the midst of a crisis, people revert back to the mammalian, emotional core of the brain so that they can react quickly.[9] If people experience repeated traumatic or threatening events, the brain's patterns of thinking and feeling become physically engraved.

The diagram below shows the path some take in reaction to their experience of trauma, including dehumanizing the enemy, developing a good versus evil narrative to make sense out of their trauma, acting out feelings of shame and humiliation onto others, and developing an identity centered on the trauma itself.

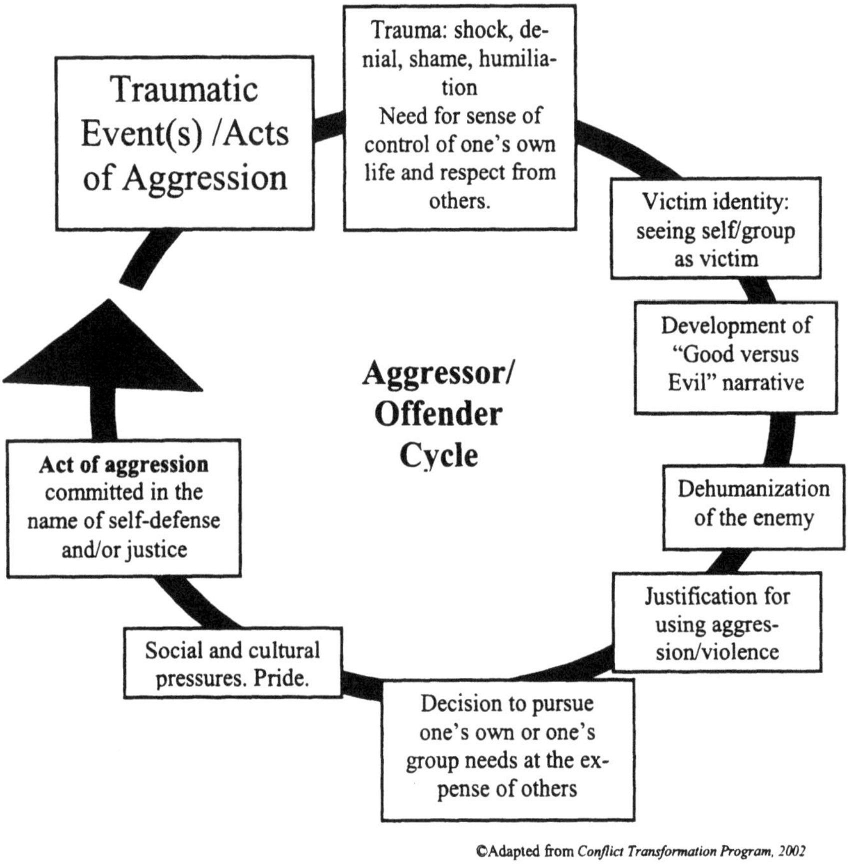

Figure 5.1. The Aggressor/Offender Cycle[10]

In the cycle of aggression, people's sense of identity becomes frozen into self/other categories. People can become obsessed with their trauma or the historical events surrounding a traumatic event. Their sense of identity can become attached to their victim status. Whenever they are threatened, they cling to their group identity and the divisions between "us" and "them." People identify themselves according to a basic mythological narrative structure revolving around "good guys," "bad guys," and "victims."[11] They see themselves in the role of victim or benevolent savior (aka "good guy") and come to define themselves in relationship to their enemy. Some scholars call this a "negative identity" where one only knows oneself by who one is not.

The Effect of Post-9/11 Trauma on U.S. Identity

After September 11, 2001, the Center for Justice and Peacebuilding (CJP) at Eastern Mennonite University began a series of weeklong workshops called STAR—Strategies for Trauma Awareness and Resilience. Through these workshops we have trained hundreds of religious and civil society leaders from the U.S. and other traumatized regions of the world in the skills of trauma healing, restorative justice, security and peacebuilding.

The workshops provide an opportunity to interact with community leaders from the United States and around the world who report how their communities are responding to 9/11 and the ongoing war on terror. The testimonies to Americans' experience at the individual and societal level are clear: We are a nation of people continuing to express a wide range of symptoms, from depression and denial, to anger and a desire for revenge, to a sense of fear and inability to recover and regain a sense of meaning and order. The literature on trauma and the path to recovery and resilience hold important insights for understanding the dynamic interaction between identity and security. This section of the chapter connects theories of trauma with the experience of September 11 and the War on Terror.

U.S. Americans experience a variety of sources of trauma stemming from September 11, 2001. There were immediate victims of the horrific events of 9/11. Then there was a growing acknowledgement of the trauma of the suffering of U.S. soldiers and their families. U.S. trauma may also relate to U.S. military, political and economic policies that have harmed civilians in Afghanistan, Iraq, and other countries. U.S. citizens support these policies through tax dollars and voting for politicians who fund and decide to go to war. Though most Americans do not pull the trigger, drop the bomb, or order the attack, there is growing evidence that American society as a whole is suffering from participation-induced trauma syndrome or PITS.[12]

Evidence of the prevalence of trauma among Americans begins with who Americans turn to for leadership. Noted conflict psychiatrist Vamik Volkan claims leaders can choose regressive or progressive ways of helping societies respond to trauma.[13] A regressive response to trauma allows for the denial, suppression and manipulation of trauma, which contributes to an ongoing cycle of trauma and victimization and provides justification for an increasingly aggressive and violent foreign policy. A progressive response to trauma promotes a collective exploration of trauma, as well as outlets for the societal expression of grief and mourning of the tragedy. A progressive response would encourage action directed toward exiting the cycle of trauma, exploration of the root causes of the violent act, realistic evaluation of the dangers of the enemy and ensuring the safety of the American people and the promotion of a collective journey toward healing.

In the 2004 November election, a majority of Americans voted for political leaders that favored what Vamik Volkan names as a regressive response to the threat of terrorist attacks. These candidates articulated a "strong and steadfast" approach to terror based on retaliation, revenge through superior military strength, and an offensive strategy to "either deal with terrorism and this extremism abroad, or deal with it when it comes to us."[14] The election of these leaders signaled an increasing turn toward "support for an aggressive military stance against potential enemies of the U.S." and turning away from diplomacy and multilateral strategies according to the Pew Research Center for the People & the Press.[15] This turn toward a retaliatory security response to terror is a symptom of societal trauma.

In the first few years of the war on Iraq, U.S. leaders responded to criticism of the war in a regressive fashion by limiting dissenting voices and denying the trauma facing soldiers and Iraqi civilians. Denial of wrongdoing can also be a sign of trauma. While the facts about U.S. human rights violations are increasingly known around the world, many in the U.S. instead sought to deny or suppress the reality of events at Abu Ghraib. Political and public space for democratic dialogue on national security issues also decreased in the years after 9/11. President Bush's assertion that everyone is either "with us, or against us" in the War on Terror sought to draw lines between "patriotic" blind acceptance of the war in Iraq and what was identified as an "unpatriotic" critique of the war.[16] This simplistic spin on identity formation creates a global division of Us versus Them. Many Americans seemed to find the clear cut division between those in the U.S. and those who support Al Qaeda appearing in the initial years after 9/11, as evidenced by increasing support for the President's political party.[17] During the 2004 election process, John Kerry's charge that the war in Iraq was the "wrong war at the wrong time" was met with a concern that this questioning would hamper the war effort and the soldier's morale.[18]

There was also denial of the deaths in Iraq. There was little media coverage of the report issued in the Lancet medical journal that the war on Iraq had resulted in approximately 650,000 Iraqi civilian deaths as of July 2006.[19] The Sinclair news network refused to air a *Nightline* program that discussed the number of U.S. soldiers killed in Iraq.[20] Even more shocking was the censorship of photos of flag-draped coffins returning the American soldiers who died in Iraq to their American families.[21]

While it is normal and natural to respond quickly when faced with an imminent threat, a long term strategy for U.S. security should be based on a more complete analysis of the roots of terrorism and a deeper appreciation for why groups such as Al Qaeda fight.[22] The experience of trauma seemed to be keeping many Americans and their leadership in a constant "low brain" state where they respond to the threat of future trauma with an emotional "fight or flight" reaction rather than a well-thought out long term strategy for addressing the roots of terror.

When Americans hear a terror alert rose to "Code Orange" it may serve as a trigger to remind them of their feelings on September 11, 2001. In response, their heartbeat may race, they may begin to perspire, or they may reinforce their sense of "us/them" identity and lash out angrily at Arab Americans. Research shows that when the President raises the threat level, his popularity among the U.S. public increases.[23] The experience of trauma, fear, or threat then becomes a trigger for the ongoing formulation of dualistic identities of "the good" versus "the evil."

This examination of trauma and identity in post-9/11 U.S. discourse illustrates the impact of trauma and regressive leadership in the formulation of threat narratives that construct a purely good self-image and an evil image of the other. The simplistic formulation of "us against them" gets reinforced through leaders who advocate revenge-based responses. These regressive leaders attempt to consolidate and strengthen national identity by limiting dissenting voices and hiding information and images that would challenge their response. Trauma remains unrecognized and unprocessed. Identities become frozen and the ability to reflect critically on one's own behavior and motives and those of others declines. The next section of this chapter further explores the mobilization of self/other identity divisions between Americans and Muslims.

The Impact of Trauma and "Good vs. Evil" Identities on Security

This simple good versus evil formulation creates a road map for the war on terror's strategy to "hunt down and kill the terrorist." There is widespread evidence now that the methods of waging the war on terror to exterminate the insurgents and terrorists are having the opposite effect. They are in fact serving to recruit further moderate and non-violent people around the world into a more extreme and violent anti-American worldview.

Many security experts now agree that the war in Iraq is increasing the number of Al Qaeda recruits and increasing the risk of future terrorist attacks rather than decreasing them.[24] The 2007 National Intelligence Estimate warns that the Iraq war provides a theater for Al Qaeda to train insurgents, mobilize the broader Sunni extremist community, and raise funds for further attacks on the U.S. It states "We assess that the spread of radical—especially Salafi—Internet sites, increasingly aggressive anti-US rhetoric and actions, and the growing number of radical, self-generating cells in Western countries indicate that the radical and violent segment of the West's Muslim population is expanding, including in the United States."[25] Some leaders conclude the Afghan population has turned against the U.S. presence in that country as well following the growing number of civilian casualties in Afghanistan.[26]

In September 2004, the Pentagon's Strategic Defence Board issued a strategic communications report written for then Secretary of Defense Donald Rumsfeld in which they state that the war in Iraq has led to the vast majority of people in Arab and Muslim countries holding an unfavorable view of the US.[27] "Negative attitudes and the conditions that create them are the underlying sources of threats to America's national security and reduced ability to leverage diplomatic opportunities." In other words, the war in Iraq has decreased American security. In "the war of ideas or the struggle for hearts and minds," the report says, "American efforts have not only failed, they may also have achieved the opposite of what they intended."[28] The report concludes that Muslims do not 'hate our freedoms,' but rather they hate U.S. policies.

> Muslims see American policies as inimical to their values, American rhetoric about freedom and democracy as hypocritical, and American actions as deeply threatening [to their interests]... it seems that in two years [since the beginning of the war on Iraq] the Jihadi message—that strongly attacks American values—is being accepted by more moderate and non-violent Muslims... Muslims are moving from "soft opposition toward "hard opposition" [toward the United States]. In Saudi Arabia, a large majority believes that the U.S. seeks to "weaken" and "dominate" Islam itself...[29]

This Pentagon report makes important observations about U.S. and Muslim identity, warning against any simplified understanding of some groups of people being good and some being bad. The Pentagon's strategic communications report notes that "Islam is a cacophony of competing and crosscutting groups, subcultures, and whole societies. A Muslim may be balancing up to five identities: as a Muslim, as a sectarian Muslim (Sunni, Sh'ia, Ismaili, etc.), as a national citizen, as an ethnic "citizen" (Arab, Kurd, Turkmen, etc.), and as a tribal or clan member."[30] The portrayal of Muslims in U.S. political rhetoric often conflates terrorism and Islam itself, which has led to increased levels of discrimination and threat against Muslim Americans.[31] In the name of furthering U.S. security, the nation and particularly Muslim Americans, have experienced a severe rollback of civil liberties. The USA Patriot Act created new laws that authorize secret searches and the indefinite detention of both citizens and non-citizens, again, particularly for Muslims and those of Arab descent.

This report also makes an important clarification that the war on terror should be more than a "war on the tactic of terrorism." It argues U.S. actions should be consistent with a message that seeks to "reduce, not increase, perceptions of arrogance, opportunism, and double standards."[32] Others in the U.S. and abroad perceive U.S. military, political, and economic policies themselves as threats to democracy and freedom. They point to the well-documented proof that the U.S. funded and directed efforts to militarily overthrow democratically elected leaders in Latin America, Africa, the Middle East, and other parts of the world for decades when democracy and freedom threatened U.S. business interests.[33] For those people who travel widely, it is no great surprise to learn that American identity is seen by many as tied to acts of perpetration and aggression against others. While Americans tend to see ourselves as "freedom fighters," others clearly see the U.S. itself as using terrorism in pursuit of its security.

When dictatorial regimes offered their cooperation with U.S. interests, the U.S. responded by supporting these dictators and suppressing democratic efforts within these countries.[34] In the fall of 2003, President George Bush acknowledged that the policy of supporting dictatorial regimes in the Middle East, such as that of Iraqi leader Saddam Hussein, had failed. He announced a new policy to support democracy in the region and around the world.[35] In announcing this policy shift, he subtly acknowledged the negative effects U.S. foreign policy has had on people in the Middle East and, in turn, also on American security today.

While it is tempting for many people to ignore the underlying causes of insurgency and terror, and to simply see the War on Terror as a war to get rid of "evil" people, a more complex understanding of why Al Qaeda and Iraqi insurgents fight and why they have growing appeal to be able to recruit hundreds if not thousands of people to their movement is essential.

Psychological dynamics of trauma create mirror images of victimhood and good versus evil perceptions of identity. One people's freedom fighters are another people's terrorists. The image of the enemy is flat or uni-dimensional, and each perceives the other's use of violence and terror as defining their essential nature as evil. Both the U.S. and Al Qaeda, in mirror images of each other, condemn each other as evil, as terrorists, and as unable to understand anything but the language of force.[36] For both sides, unprocessed trauma seems to fuel an ongoing denigration of the other and an inability to look at how their own behaviors appear equally violent to their victims.

A growing number of Muslims make the same simplistic diagnosis that conflates American people with evil. Al Qaeda members have tried to articulate why it is they fight and what it is they want. In his *Letter to America*,[37] Osama bin Laden takes away from any complexity or diversity of thought within U.S. society by holding all U.S. citizens accountable for U.S. foreign policy.

> American people are the ones who choose their government. . . . Whoever has killed our civilians, then we have the right to kill theirs. . . . America does not understand the language of manners and principles, so we are addressing it using the language it understands.[38]

In Iraq, the insurgent movement has routinely kidnapped civilian staff of international nongovernmental agencies as a way of also indicating that they make no distinction between civilian, humanitarian workers, military, etc. It appears they have equally constructed an "us versus them" sense of identity where they see themselves as good and everyone else as evil.

The foreign policies in the War on Terror, which have been based on the foundation of the good versus evil identity equation, are leading to greater insecurity for both U.S. Americans and for people in the Muslim world and beyond.

Toward a Survivor Cycle

As illustrated in the trauma cycle diagram earlier in this chapter, acts of aggression often lead to new acts of revenge that perpetuate insecurity and violence. Preventing or interrupting the cycle of trauma is essential to building the foundations for sustainable security.

The "Survivor Cycle" diagram below illustrates how people can successfully move away from revenge-based approaches to trauma and instead form their identities around their personal ability to transcend and transform their experience of trauma. When on a cycle of survival rather than revenge, people understand themselves and others as complex human beings with multiple dimensions. The trauma is processed by acknowledgement of the trauma, appropriate expression of angry emotions, and the choice to transcend the traumatic event, work toward a restorative sense of justice between victim and perpetrators, and build relationships across the lines of conflict that may have caused the trauma. In order to address the roots of terrorism, it will be important to complexify and humanize those who commit acts of terror, for all people have a logic to their violence.[39]

The remainder of this chapter examines how arts-based programs and new approaches to security assist victims in moving along this Survivor Cycle.

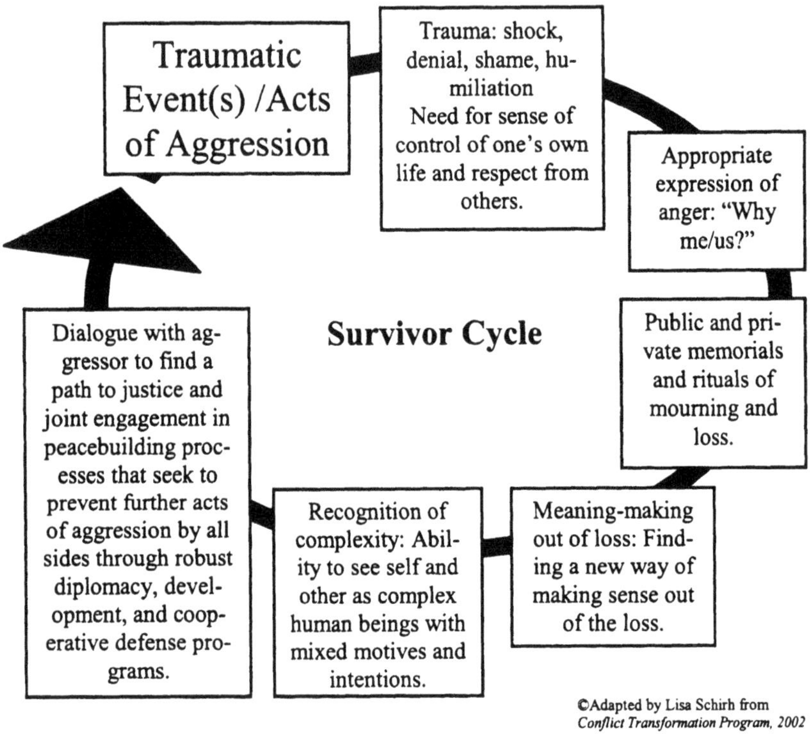

Figure 5.2. Survivor Cycle

Media Arts as Identity-Transformer in Trauma Healing

Peacebuilding in traumatized societies requires processes that communicate at the mass level. Individual approaches to trauma healing cannot reach the magnitude of traumatized societies. Mass media and the arts – here called "media arts"—are tools for trauma healing because they can be used at this mass level to impact large numbers of people.

Media arts can be tools for transforming perceptions of self and other. While trauma can foster good versus evil perceptions of identity, peacebuilding efforts using the media arts can reverse these dynamics. By appropriate mourning and processing of trauma, people can move beyond good versus evil identities and toward a more complex understanding of their own and their adversary's identity.

Arts-based approaches to trauma healing and identity transformation have a long history. Traumatized groups have used media arts to discover and recover their sense of self since the beginning of time. Case studies in this section detail an arts-based strategy for transforming trauma-influenced self/other identity categories.

One of the first steps of trauma healing is acknowledgement of trauma and the emotions that accompany it, including both pain and anger. This requires coming to terms with a highly emotional, difficult to articulate, complex, and ambiguous experience. Western communication models favor "referential" forms of communication where people use words rather than symbols to communicate directly about an object, feeling or activity. While verbal communication is limited by the nature of words and their definitions in each language, the arts 'speak' cross-culturally in a multi-vocal way that allows different people to make sense of the artistic form in different ways.[40]

The arts do this by engaging people's emotions, senses, and physical selves. These modes are significant, as communication researchers estimate that between sixty to ninety percent of communicated meaning comes from nonverbal cues.[41] The arts make use of this nonverbal knowledge. Artistic representations such as music, dance, theatre, or the material arts use symbolic references to communicate something about the real world that is missed when communicating through the direct logic of words. Art can explain emotions, ideas, or feelings that words alone cannot. Art-based tools communicate in a way that maximizes non-verbal, symbolic modes. People can communicate their identity to others in a way that uses their bodies, emotions, and senses.[42]

Earlier in this chapter, the physical effects of trauma on the brain were discussed. Trauma can result in an inability to process complex thoughts or hold together complex ideas. Cognitive theorist Jean Piaget claims learning is an integrative process where people combine new ideas and experiences with previous ones.[43] Trauma healing and identity transformation are a learning process; they require integration of new ideas and experiences. Artistic mediums like TV shows, movies, music, and novels can pave a new pathway for people's perceptions of their own and other's identity and to symbolically mourn and process their trauma. This may require creating new biological pathways in the brain to enable people to break free from trauma-habituated thought processes that have conditioned a good versus evil understanding of identity. It is particularly important in the trauma healing process for people to complexify their own and other's identities. The arts help to integrate the brain and allow people to communicate this complexity.[44]

Art can substitute for violent forms of communication and thus interrupt the cycle of trauma and violence. People in conflict often take on a victim identity that comes to serve as a justification for aggressive actions against those perceived to be their oppressors. Art is a vehicle to restore a more complex understanding of identity for groups that have been victimized.

The arts play a special role in communicating a positive sense of identity that is not dependent or defined by trauma or an evil other. In examining the role of art in the conflicts in Northern Ireland and Palestine, Irish author Eóin Murray argues that public art can play a positive role in shifting identities. In his article "The Art of War" he claims that public murals in his home town of Derry in conflict-rife Northern Ireland served an important function for people living there. Murray believes public murals "expressed the fears and memories of the people and, in so doing, assisted them in their struggle for human and civil rights, for peace and for justice."[45]

Murray also describes how Palestinian artists express, escape, or at least cope with the misery of warfare through these public art displays of the images of martyrs and victims of occupation. They use public murals with images like doves or flowers and portrayals of "huddled crowds" to represent both the collective suffering and survival of the people. In a time when Palestinians are eager to demonstrate their collective identity and self-determination in the face of occupation, art communicates a positive Palestinian identity. Murray suggests art is "a tool for nation building through the public affirmation of an imagined community. . . ."[46] The "Art of War" that Murray discusses is a strategy of resistance, revolution, memory, and identity-affirmation. The arts provide a mode of expressing a positive sense of identity that does not require a denigration of the other. Positive portrayals of identity are important in dissociating one's sense of self from the definition of an evil other.[47]

African Americans have harnessed the power of the arts, particularly music, in their journey of recovery out of the trauma of slavery and racism. Cornel West claims humans create culture in order to convince themselves not to commit suicide.[48] Art expresses culture; the systems of meaning that help people make sense of the world. Indeed, the arts have played an essential role in the cultural and physical survival of African Americans. According to Black theologian James Cone, "the slaves' problem was not sin—that was a luxury only white folk could afford—but the suffering that was being inflicted upon them through what they knew was a monstrous injustice and absurdity. Their problem was to keep from submitting to existential despair. . . ."[49]

Since the time of slavery, African Americans have expressed their humanity through artistic forms that, for the most part, did not denigrate the humanity of white people and served to strengthen their culture and identity. African American authors document the remarkable way the arts, particularly music, are used to embrace a 'survivor' identity in the midst of a racist society.

In his book on African American spirituals, Arthur Jones' notes that singing for slaves was "cathartic and therapeutic . . . many of them were able to transcend an experience of extreme degradation, emerging from it as spiritually, morally and emotionally evolved human beings."[50] Jones claims "I know of no method of meditation or therapy that could have a more potent impact on the human spirit. We have to marvel at the ability of the ancestors to provide themselves and us . . . such effective channels for emotional and spiritual healing."[51]

The history of African-American music, both sacred and secular, is the history of efforts by African Americans to name and define their identity and place in the world by telling their histories. "Our music is a creative activity that affirms our very right to be creative. A black version of Descartes' definition of human being might very well be *I sing, therefore I am.*"[52] Lawrence Levine claims black secular song is therapeutic because it allows African Americans to communicate their own worth and identity to themselves and to their oppressors. While creating music was most often not lucrative for African American musicians, Levine claims it gave them a sense of power and control and impacted their "psychic state and emotional health."[53]

These examples demonstrate the role of the arts in aiding the recovery from trauma along the Survivor Cycle.

Transforming U.S. Trauma with Media Arts after 9/11

In the days after September 11, 2001, Americans responded to their trauma in a variety of ways that also used the arts to move along the Survivor Cycle. Many people used artistic memorials to mourn the dead and connect with others in their community. In Manhattan, massive memorials of flowers, photos, candles, and other symbols of those missing or dead grew larger by the hour as people searched for some way to make meaning out of the chaos and connect with others. For many people, there were no words to communicate their feelings of loss, confusion, fear, and pain. The arts provided a way for people to share their common humanity with each other. The public memorials also gave people an avenue for expressing the identity of the victims. Photos of the dead and missing at these public memorials gave a human face and not just a number in the statistics of people who died that day.

The arts continue to be a vital component of people's recovery from the events of 9/11 and in addressing the ongoing challenges posed to people's identity. In *Hollywood as Mirror: Changing Views of "Outsiders" and "Enemies" in American Movies*, a variety of authors show how movies spawn changing views of the identities of groups of people who have been culturally treated as outsiders or enemies such as immigrants, ethnic groups, African-Americans, women, Russians, and communists.[54] Television programming since 9/11 has served a similar function. Morgan Spurlock's reality television series "30 Days" took on the issue of Muslim American identity. Using documentary-style filming, they followed David Stacy, a young Christian man from West Virginia as he lived with a Muslim community, practiced and learned about Islam for 30 days in Dearborn, Michigan. The show uses the popular artistic medium of reality television to portray anti-Muslim discrimination in America and how one person learns to appreciate the struggles and joys of being Muslim in America.

This type of media arts programming contributes to trauma healing in a variety of ways. First it gives an honest assessment of the ways in which one American has conflated Islam with terrorism. David Stacy is frank in his lack of understanding and stereotypes about Muslims at the beginning of his 30 days. By creating a safe space for examining stereotypes, it helps Americans name their own prejudices. Naming of the prejudices is the first step in transforming these flat notions of identity.

Secondly, the show gave a space on prime time television for American Muslims to talk about their lives, their beliefs, and their frustration with being accused of supporting terrorism. It gave Muslims the space to speak about and define their own identity. The show combats simplistic formulations of good versus evil identities by mainstream Americans by showing the diversity among Muslims in the U.S. The show challenges Americans to complexify their understanding of identity and creates an emotionally riveting experience that may alter the engraved misperceptions that all Muslims support terrorism. The show is also, in effect, a testimony to the power of relationship in identity transformation. When people of different cultural backgrounds are able to meet and understand each other, they begin to view each other's identity in different ways. It becomes impossible to conflate all Muslims with terrorism and evil.

The more Americans can understand Islam and their Muslim neighbors, the better able they may be at understanding the frustration many Muslims feel at current U.S. domestic and foreign policies. Spurlock worked to get the episode out to every member of Congress in an effort to make "folks on the Hill laugh and think."[55] "30 Days" is an example of the kind of artistic programming that could be a powerful aid to recovering from the trauma of 9/11 and for designing better security strategies to prevent further terrorism.

Public memorials are another way the arts are being used to address the trauma of 9/11 and the war on terror. While the effect of participation-induced trauma has led to wide-spread denial of the deaths in Iraq, groups throughout the country have developed arts-based approaches to illustrate the effects of the U.S. war on terror. Perhaps the most well-known of these efforts is the American Friends Service Committee's Waging Peace campaign. It includes the widely-acclaimed arts exhibition *Eyes Wide Open* on the human cost of the Iraq War. It features a pair of boots honoring each U.S. military casualty, and a field of shoes and a Wall of Remembrance to memorialize the Iraqis killed in the conflict. These multimedia displays explore the history, cost and consequences of the war. People are invited to leaves notes of commemoration, photographs of lost soldiers, identification tags, flowers, and American flags to accompany the boots on their journey.[56] *Eyes Wide Open* helps Americans memorialize the dead, and in doing so also helps to remind them of the identity of all those who have died in Iraq- both American and Iraqi. By remembering the Iraqi dead simultaneously with remembering U.S. soldiers who have lost their lives, *Eyes Wide Open* challenges Americans to see the inherent human identity of both groups and break free from "good versus evil" perceptions.

With similar intentions, members of an activist peacebuilding group called JustVoices found a theatrical way to bring the death toll of the war on Iraq onto U.S. soil. They began a weekly political theatre of ritual mourning in the small town square of Harrisonburg, Virginia. The group members symbolically laid dead under white sheets as an artistic portrayal of funerals in Iraq. Others in the group wore black and dramatically mourned those that had died. This silent, dramatic act of public mourning took place in front of a sign reading "Mourning all Deaths in Iraq." Others in the group distributed flyers with the numbers of people, U.S. soldiers and Iraqi civilians, who had died in the U.S.-led war on

Iraq at that date. Through the vehicle of theatre, the group again brought the human identity of Iraqi's to the attention of local residents in a small, conservative town, urging sympathy for the losses and trauma experienced by both Iraqis and U.S. soldiers.

These examples illustrate how artistic mediums can be vehicles for transforming identities, healing from trauma, and laying the foundations for a different approach to security. These efforts to use media arts to address U.S. societal trauma give evidence of the desire of many in the U.S. to move forward on the Survivor Cycle response to trauma. The last stage of the Survivor Cycle includes a range of efforts to establish positive engagement between adversaries. The last section of the chapter offers a human security approach to illustrate that positive engagement.

Human Security: Development, Diplomacy, Defense

Traditional discussions of national security focus on the protection of territory and national economic interests. In public discourse, this approach to security is communicated as a struggle between good versus evil; those who threaten state territory or economic interests are labeled "evil." This traditional focus on state security is wearing away in the face of new threats and a growing focus on the well-being of people.

The concept of "human security" focuses on threats facing individuals and communities, rather than the state or national business interests. Human security develops from the protection of human rights, sustainable development, and peacebuilding. People and communities are secure when "they live in freedom, peace, and safety; participate fully in the process of governance, enjoy the protection of fundamental rights; have access to resources and the basic necessities of life; and inhabit an environment which is not detrimental to their health and well-being."[57] The chart[58] below illustrates the shifts in security paradigms over the last ten years. Traditional national security paradigms hold a limited understanding of what makes for security. Human security approaches broaden the focus, approach, number of actors and the time span for judging success.

	Traditional National Security Paradigm	**Human Security Paradigm**
Focus	Territory and economic interests of the nation state	Well being of individuals and communities
Approach	Top-down military imposition	Multi-track efforts at top, mid, and community levels using creative efforts in development, diplomacy, and defense
Actors	Primarily military	Military, government, civil society, business, individuals
Time span	Short-term	Long-term

Human security means freedom from fear and freedom from want. Around the world, most people feel secure when they have adequate education, employment, healthcare and other basic needs for their families and when they don't have to fear the impact of environmental disasters, infectious diseases or attacks on their communities or their dignity. At the state level, there is growing recognition that today's environmental, health, nuclear and terrorism threats require a larger set of tools than currently held by most militaries. In Australia, Belgium, Canada, France, the Netherlands, Sweden, and the United Kingdom, a "whole of government" or "joined-up" institutional approach is being used that devotes greater resources and coordinated government infrastructures to address the problems of failed states.[59 and 60] In many more countries, development has been "upgraded" to a security strategy.

In the last few years, there is a move in the U.S. toward security strategies that lean more toward the "survivor cycle." There is growing public, military, and Congressional support in the U.S. for progressive leadership and non-military approaches to security. The failure to achieve a quick military victory in Iraq is contributing toward a wide-spread loss of faith in firepower and a re-examination of U.S. security strategy.[61] In the 2006 U.S. National Security Strategy, President Bush argues that today's security threats are just as likely to come from "weak" states as they use to come from strong states like the former Soviet Union thus requiring a broader array of security tools.
The U.S.'s 2006 National Security Strategy states:

> A world where some live in comfort and plenty, while half of the human race lives on less than $2 a day, is neither just nor stable. Including all of the world's poor in an expanding circle of development- and opportunity – is a moral imperative and one of the top priorities of U.S. international policy.[62]

Increasingly, the security policy-making community is talking about the problems of economic inequality and poverty, climate change, deadly diseases, and energy dependence alongside the more traditional concerns of nuclear proliferation and terrorism as root causes of insecurity.[63] The expansion of security policy to include Development, Diplomacy and Defense is sometimes referred to as the "3D" approach to security and foreign policy.

Development refers to efforts that build economic, social, and political foundations and stabilize communities and societies. Weak states (also known as failed or fragile states) are statistically linked to a vulnerability to trans-national crime; weapons trafficking in weapons, drugs, and people; the spread of deadly diseases; genocide; civil war; regional conflicts; and terrorism.[64] Development programs address the root causes of terrorism by strengthening fragile and failed states. Development programs create jobs, strengthen local democratic political institutions, and address competition over natural resources. Many conflicts can be prevented by international partnerships that work to relieve the conditions of poverty, corruption, and indignity that extremists exploit. Government and non-governmental organizations (NGOs) work to improve the quality of life through development programs like building schools and healthcare centers, digging wells for clean water, providing funds for people to start small businesses, and training community leaders in democratic processes for decision-making. A 3D security approach includes not only *more* development aid, but also *better, more effective* development policies and programs. Effective forms of sustainable development support local people in their efforts to better their lives.

Diplomacy refers to negotiation, political, and legal channels to address conflicts. Official government negotiations are widely referred to as "Track I" diplomacy. Unofficial diplomacy, known as "Track II" diplomacy, refers to negotiations, dialogue or relationship building by religious, business, or other civil society leaders. Track I and Track II diplomatic efforts have successfully prevented violence between groups in many parts of the world by creating a space for leaders to work out their problems through democratic dialogue. A 3D security approach uses diplomacy as a tool of foreign policy, not as a reward for good behavior. A 3D security approach requires increasing investments in "multi-track diplomacy" to involve more people at all levels and in all sectors of society in constructive negotiations to address challenging issues and prevent violence.

Defense currently refers to a wide range of military tasks including the logistical coordination of humanitarian aid, peacekeeping operations, policing, deploying special units to security zones and conflict areas, as well as waging a full scale war. However, many military and political experts believe military personnel around the world require new tools and training. They say militaries are overly reliant on force and do not have the capacity to use other forms of persuasion to achieve their goals. Many recognize the ineffectiveness of using overwhelming military force for addressing many – and perhaps most – of the security threats facing the world today.[65] To be effective in a 3D security framework, defense strategies need to change to adapt to the new global security challenges.

During the last twenty years, there has been an expansion of explicit "peacebuilding" through more robust efforts at development and diplomacy. These interventions into conflict regions have the explicit intention of reducing or preventing violence, building relationships across the lines of conflict, and increasing community's capacity for a culture of peace. As the upsurge of international peacebuilding through the UN, World Bank and civil society efforts grew through the 1990s, the number of deaths from violent conflict, crises, wars and genocides declined. The 2005 Human Security Report claimed that "With additional resources, and a greater commitment to conflict prevention and peacebuilding, far more could be achieved."[66]

Development and security personnel have often ignored or opposed each other's work in conflict areas and each has seen the other as getting in the way of the "real" efforts to build security. Military actors still tend to see 'hard' security as coming first and allowing development to come in later. While development workers see the necessity of having local humanitarian and development projects at all stages of a conflict. Mid and community level leaders often critique a military approach to security, noting that it often seems to cause further trauma and perpetuates a cycle of violence.

As an appreciation of the central role of economic, political, and social inequality in fueling violent conflict has grown, civil and military actors are increasingly coordinating their work and development programs, peacebuilding, reconstruction and stability programs are increasingly linked in post-war contexts. There are numerous efforts to train military personnel in peacebuilding skills and to teach peacebuilding actors the language and frameworks of security personnel.[67]

Security Policy-Making Should Be "Wide" and "Deep"

Security policy-making in traumatized societies requires a "wide and deep" approach to creating and implementing security policies. The peacebuilding pyramid below illustrates three tiers of decision-making in most countries. At the top level, government leaders make national and international policies that impact global economies, war, and relative decision-making power of other countries. At the mid-level, business, media, religious, and academic leaders help shape the discourse or story that sets the stage for policy decisions. Community level leaders make decisions with their communities.

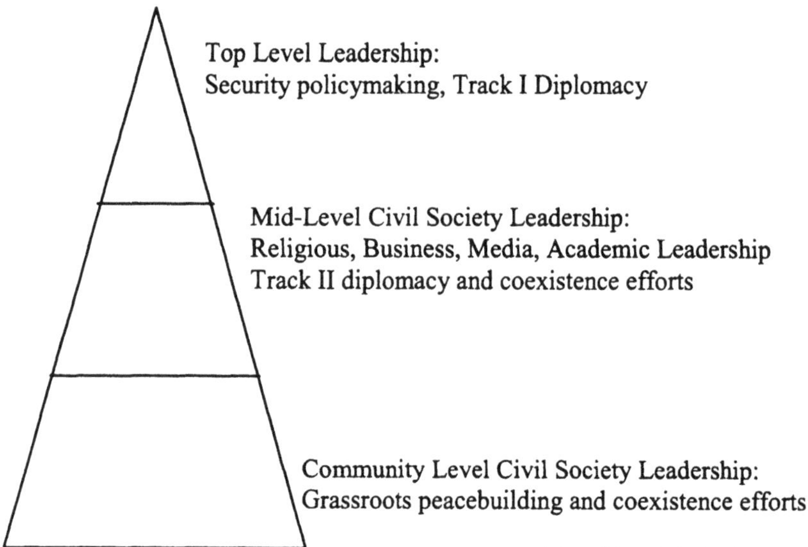

Adapted from John Paul Lederach

Figure 5.3. Peacebuilding Pyramid

People at all levels of the pyramid talk about security, but traditional state approaches to security put the responsibility on those at the top, who initiate the use of armed force on behalf of the protection of the state. Security requires partnerships between legitimate state institutions and a healthy civil society. Whole of government approaches and international efforts at coordinating security policies and developing "cooperative security" arrangements help ensure a "widened" top-level, inter-agency coordination between government units responsible for development, diplomacy, and defense.

Security policy-making should be "deepened" by including stakeholders from all levels of the pyramid. Mid and community-level leadership should be actively engaged in peacebuilding processes. These leaders often have a front-line understanding of the links between trauma, traditional security forces, and what is required to move forward out of the cycle of violence.

Toward Co-Existence

The cycle of trauma is like a spiral circling outward, with more and more people caught up in its swirling confusion. The Global War on Terror, which is an example of a security policy that relies heavily on military might, is leading to greater numbers of civilians experiencing trauma from military strikes and, in turn, to growing numbers of insurgents and terrorists who further threaten U.S. security. The shared experience of trauma in the post-9/11 world will require humanity to improvise their way toward a future of coexistence.

This chapter argues that many people around the world are suffering from unprocessed trauma that keeps them in the grips of fear, unable to plan strategically about how to improve their security. Regressive leadership uses the widespread sense of trauma to continue revenge-based security policies that rely almost exclusively on military approaches. These short-sighted policies are based more on simplistic understandings of good versus evil identities rather than a deep and complex understanding of the roots of terrorism.

This chapter suggests that the arts can be useful to the process of trauma healing to re-shape our identities to pave a path out of trauma and its simplistic formulation of identity. It proposes the use of sustainable development, multi-track diplomacy, and a more conservative use of military force as methods for building global security. Like artists, we have the capacity to improvise a path toward a new future. We can create the world in an image of either coexistence or perpetual war.

Notes

1. No military solution to Iraq, U.S. general says. CNN. March 9, 2007. http://www.cnn.com/2007/WORLD/meast/03/08/iraq.petraeus/index.html
2. President George Bush's "Remarks on the War on Terror." Fort Bragg, North Carolina. June 28, 2005.
3. In this paper, the term "Americans" refers to U.S. Americans and the term "Muslims" refers to people who follow the Islamic faith in different countries. The author urges readers to recognize that there are many Muslim-Americans and therefore the terms "American" and "Muslim" are not exclusive categories.

4. *Mass Trauma and Violence: Helping Families and Children Cope*. Edited by Nancy Boyd Webb. New York: Guildford Press, 2004.

5. Grossman, Lt. Col. David. *On Killing: The Psychological Cost of Learning to Kill in War and Society*. New York: Back Bay Books, 1996.

6. McNair, Rachel M. *Perpetration-Induced Traumatic Stress: The Psychological Consequences of Killing* Psychological Dimensions to War and Peace. Praeger Publishers, 2002.

7. Volkan, Vamik. *Blind Trust: Large Groups and their Leaders in Time of Crisis and Terror*. Charlottesville: Pitchstone Publishing, 2004.

8. Paul D. MacLean, *A Triune Concept of the Brain and Behaviour*. Toronto, Canada: University of Toronto, 1972.

9. Peter A. Levine. *Waking the Tiger: Healing Trauma*. Berkeley, California: North Atlantic Books, 1997.

10. Adapted from Olga Botcharova by the Center for Justice and Peacebuilding, Eastern Mennonite University 2002.

11. Adapted from Walter Wink, *The Powers That Be*. New York: Doubleday, 1998.

12. While more research is needed to explore societal level PITS, our experience working with traumatized groups has led us to believe that the model of individual PITS described by Rachel Macnair and Lt. Col. David Grossman can be applied to societal trauma.

13. For a deeper exploration of societal regression and the role of leadership in responding to societal trauma and regression, please see Volkan, Vamik. *Blind Trust: Large Groups and their Leaders in Time of Crisis and Terror*. Charlottesville: Pitchstone Publishing, 2004 (p 13).

14. Quote from General John Vines included in President George Bush's "Remarks on the War on Terror." Fort Bragg, North Carolina. June 28, 2005.

15. Balz, Dan. "Poll Cites GOP Gains Since 9/11." *Washington Post*. May 11, 2005. Page A02.

16. Jordan, Michael J. "With or against us' war irks many UN nations." *The Christian Science Monitor*. Global Issues, November 14, 2001.

17. Balz, Dan. "Poll Cites GOP Gains Since 9/11." *Washington Post*. May 11, 2005. Page A02.

18. The Second Bush-Kerry Presidential Debate Transcript. St. Louis, Missouri, October 8, 2004.

19. "Mortality after the 2003 invasion of Iraq: a cross-sectional cluster sample survey," Gilbert Burnham, Riyadh Lafta, Shannon Doocy, and Les Roberts, *The Lancet*, October 11, 2006. http://www.thelancet.com/webfiles/images/journals/lancet/s0140673606694919.pdf

20. "Hiding the Toll of War Again: Iraq War Casualty Families Call for Immediate Reversal of Sinclair Decision to Block Airing of Nightline Program. April 27, 2005. http://www.mfso.org/PreSinc.pdf

21. Milbank, Dana. "Curtains Ordered for Media Coverage of Returning Coffins." *Washington Post*. Tuesday, October 21, 2003, Page A23.

22. "Effective and Faithful Security Strategies." Lisa Schirch and J. Daryl Byler. *Tracing the Grain of the Universe: Public Order, Security, and the Gospel of Peace*. Pennsylvania: Herald Press, In press.

23. Willer, Rob. "The Effects of Government-Issued Terror Warnings on Presidential Approval Ratings." Current Research in Social Psychology. Volume 10, Number 1. September 30, 2004. http://www.uiowa.edu/~grpproc/crisp/crisp.html.

24. "War Helps Recruit Terrorists, Hill Told." By Dana Priest and Josh White. Washington Post. February 17, 2005. and "Occupation Made World Less Safe, Pro-War Institute Says." By Kim Sengupta. Independent. May 26, 2004

25. National Intelligence Estimate. "The Terrorist Threat to the US Homeland." Washington DC: National Intelligence Council. July 2007. pg. 7.

26. Losing the 'other war' in Afghanistan? By Karl F. Inderfurth. International Herald Tribune. May 29, 2007. http://www.iht.com/articles/2007/05/29/opinion/edinderfurth.php

27. "Report of the Defense Science Board Task Force on Strategic Communication." U.S. Department of Defense Office of the Under Secretary of Defense for Acquisition, Technology, and Logistics. Washington, D.C. September 2004. pg. 40. pg. 15. Based on research from a variety of respected sources, including the following: *Impressions of America 2004: How Arabs View America; How Arabs Learn About America*, Zogby International, 2004; *Views of a Changing World 2003: War With Iraq Further Divides Global Publics*, Pew Research Center for the People & the Press, June 3, 2004; *A Year After Iraq War Mistrust of America in Europe Ever Higher, Muslim Anger Persists*, Pew Research Center for the People & the Press, March 16, 2004; *Iraq One Year Later: Global Media Assessment Largely Negative,* U.S. Department of State, Office of Research, April 29, 2004; *Views from the Muslim World: Opposition to U.S. Foreign Policy Contrasts with Admiration for American Innovation and Education*, U.S. Department of State Office of Research, March 31, 2003.

28. Ibid, pg. 40.

29. Ibid. pg 45.

30. Ibid, pg. 42.

31. See the Muslim American Society website for examples: www.masnet.org. July 2005.

32. Ibid, pg. 30.

33. Noam Chomsky. *Hegemony or survival: America's quest for global dominance.* New York: Henry Holt, 2004.

34. Armstrong, Karen. "Our Role in the Terror." The *Guardian* September 18, 2003.

35 "President Bush Discusses Freedom in Iraq and Middle East." Remarks by the President at the 20th Anniversary of the National Endowment for Democracy. United States Chamber of Commerce, Washington, D.C. November 6, 2003. http://www.whitehouse.gov/news/releases/2003/11/20031106-2.html. July 2005.

36. For more discussion of enemy images, see Sam Keen, *Faces of the Enemy: Reflections of the Hostile Imagination: The Psychology of Enmity*. San Francisco: Harper & Row, 1986.

37. While Bin Laden's letters have been published in European newspapers, they have not been published in the U.S.

38. "Full Text: Bin Laden's Letter to America." United Kingdom: Observer Worldview. November 24, 2002.

39. For more discussion of the logic of violence, see James Gilligan, *Preventing Violence*. New York: Thames & Hudson, 2001.

40. David I. Kertzer, *Ritual, Politics, and Power*. New Haven: Yale University Press, 1988.

41. Julia Wood, *Spinning the Symbolic Web: Human Communication as Symbolic Interaction*. New Jersey: Ablex Publishing Corporation, 1992.

42. Lisa Schirch. *Ritual and Symbol in Peacebuilding*. Bloomfield, Connecticut: Kumarian Press, December 2004.

43. Jean Piaget, "Intellectual Evolution from Adolescence to Adulthood," Human Development 15, 1972.
44. Charles D. Laughlin, Jr. and John McManus. *Brain, Symbol, and Experience: Toward a Neurophenomenology of Human Consciousness.* New York: Columbia University Press, 1992.
45. Murray, Eóin. "The Art of War" Palo Alto, California: Peninsula Peace and Justice Center. Electronic Intifada. January 13, 2005. http://peaceandjustice.org/article.php?story=20050118210912308
46. ibid.
47. Volkan, Vamik. *The Need for Enemies and Allies: From Clinical Practice to International Relationships.* Northvale, N.J.: J. Aronson, 1994.
48. West, Cornel. *Race Matters.* New York: Vintage Books, 1994. p. 24.
49. Small, p. 86.
50. Jones, p. 23.
51. Jones, p. 34.
52. Trulear, p. 79.
53. Levine, Lawrence. *Black Culture and Black Consciousness: Afro-American Folk Thought from Slavery to Freedom.* New York: Oxford University Press, 1977, p. 297 in DeSilva, p. 66.
54. Robert Brent Toplin, editor. *Hollywood as Mirror: Changing Views of "Outsiders" and "Enemies" in American Movies.* Westport, Conn.: Greenwood Press, 1993.
55. Morgan Spurlock archives website http://blogs.indiewire.com/morganspurlock/archives/004224.html. July 2005.
56. American Friends Service Committee website http://www.afsc.org/eyes/about-the-exhibit.htm. July 2005.
57. Helping Prevent Violent Conflict: The DAC Guidelines. Organization for Economic Co-operation and Development (OECD) Development Assistance Committee (DAC). Paris, France. 2001. p. 38.
58. Lisa Schirch. *Guide to Security and Coexistence.* Massachusetts: Brandeis University's Coexistence International. July 2007.
59. "Whole of Government Approaches to Fragile States." Organization for Economic Co-operation and Development (OECD) Development Assistance Committee (DAC). Paris, France. 2006.
60. Patrick, Stewart and Kaysie Brown. Greater than the Sum of Its Parts? Assessing "Whole of Government" Approaches to Fragile States. New York: International Peace Academy, 2007.
61. "What Kind of Foreign Policy Does the American Public Want? Washington DC: Program on International Policy Attitudes October 20, 2006. http://www.worldpublicopinion.org/pipa/pdf/oct06/SecurityFP_Oct06_rpt.pdf
62. The National Security Strategy of the United States of America, Washington, DC: The White House, 2006. http://www.whitehouse.gov/nsc/nss.html
63. "A Development Co-operation Lens on Terrorism Prevention." Organization for Economic Co-operation and Development (OECD) Development Assistance Committee (DAC). Paris, France. 2003. www.oecd.org.
64. J. Brian Atwood. The Link between Poverty and Violence. New England Journal of Public Policy. Fall/Winter 2003, vol. 19, no. 1
65. General Tony Zinni. *The Battle for Peace: A Frontline Vision of America's Power and Purpose.* New York: Palgrave Macmillan, 2006.

66. Human Security Centre, *Human Security Report.* New York: Oxford University Press, 2005.

67. The Development Assistance Committee of the Organization for Economic Co-operation and Development, *OECD DAC Handbook on Security System Reform: Supporting Security and Justice*. Paris: 2007.

6

Peacebuilding Leadership in Traumatized Societies

Barry Hart

The focus of this chapter is on the role of leaders involved in trauma recovery processes after large-scale violence and war. It concentrates on the type of leadership that is framed by the concepts and practices of peacebuilding, the central theme of the book. Peacebuilding leadership, therefore, is explained in theoretical and practical terms that include the meaning and nature of this kind of leadership and how it is most effective in trauma recovery after complex and violent conflicts. Gender and power roles are examined, as well as the role of *followers* in the leader-follower relational dynamic. An overview of peacebuilding leadership is included in order to examine attributes of peacebuilding leaders—and to see how these attributes and a myriad of other personal and contextual factors help leaders be more effective in helping communities and societies deal with collective stress and trauma. Finally, suggestions are presented for educating peacebuilding leaders in regard to their roles as catalysts for healing societal trauma.

Leadership: Meaning, Nature and Context

Leadership has many meanings and is found at every level of society. Current interpretations of leadership understand its function in relationship to context, culture and timing; and more and more see it as a partnership with other leaders as well as followers or citizens of a community or state. According to one of the key figures in modern leadership studies, James MacGregor Burns, it is also "one of the most observed and least understood phenomenon on earth" (1995).

The English word "leadership" has its origins in the ancient root *Leith* which means "to go forth and die," as in doing battle with an enemy (Gerzon 2003). The nature of the leader in this context was one of warrior-leader, a person who had certain attributes to lead a group to dominate or eliminate other groups. In more recent times this leadership 'model' exists in highly contextual forms as demonstrated by Hitler, Mussolini and in the last twenty years by Liberia's Charles Taylor and Bosnian Serb leader General Ratko Mladic.[1] These are just a few examples of types of leadership that reflects context and historical events, as well as psychological issues that have familial and/or greater societal causes.[2]

"[A] leader is someone with the power to project shadow and light" onto the world around him or her with the results being "as light-filled as heaven or as shadowy as hell" (Palmer 2000). Unlike the leaders mentioned above, who contributed greatly to the suffering of millions of people, more light-filled leadership is found in people like Tanzanian president Julius Nyerere, Civil Rights leader Martin Luther King Jr. and Burmese opposition leader Aung San Suu Kyi—among many others.[3] Their "light" reflects another kind of *nature* and psychological profile—one that compels them to engage people and their environment in constructive and reparative ways.[4] It is leadership that understands the power of engaging others empathetically and helps repair or restore relationships that have been fractured by violence. Reparative leadership or light-filled leadership also directs followers by example and often uses a teaching process that encourages and expects constructive change in members of the community or larger society.

These leaders are defined by the psychological and even spiritual impact they have on others and they recognize their dependence on other trusted leaders and those whom they lead. This interaction and interdependence raises both leaders and followers to a level of recognition of and accountability to each other that opens the way for the development of new ways of thinking and acting collaboratively. Of course, institutional structures and pressures, as well as choices made by a particular leader based on a particular worldview or identity need, becomes the reason he or she often makes less than constructive policy and/or relational decisions. No leader "gets it right" all of the time, but those who attempt to lead from the light rather than the shadows are usually aware of both personal and institutional factors that cause them to compromise their role as leader. They are also usually self-reflective enough to know that their struggle against these factors requires openness to critique by colleagues and followers and enough patience to struggle for change over the long-term.

Leading from the Shadows

Leaders of both *light* and *shadow* understand their leadership is dependent on what is happening around them in terms of social, political and economic issues, events and structures as well as meeting followers' interests and needs. Leaders understand that historical timing is a factor that has placed them in positions of power and authority. Moreover, they know that they must adapt to these situations by making decisions that challenge the status quo and expose them to ridicule and danger. An example of this type of leadership is found on its *shadow* side in Yugoslav communist leader Slobodan Milosevic. He adapted to the economic, social and political changes that were taking place in his country in the late 1980s. Milosevic took personal and political risks while at the same time making calculated decisions to increase his power in the communist party of Yugoslavia.

Milosevic's two speeches to large groups of his fellow Serbs in April 1987 at Kosovo Polje's *Dom Kulture* reflect this tension between risk-taking and desire for power (see LeBor 2004). The people he initially spoke to demanded that their rights and lives be protected from the Albanian Muslim majority; and in his second and most important speech that April, Milosevic faced 15,000 angry and "revolutionary" Serbs who were ready to go to war with their Albanian neighbors.[5] He was afraid and knew that he was playing for the highest stakes. Milosevic also sensed that he was at and somehow in control of a *turning point* in Yugoslavia's history.

Milosevic told the crowd "No one should dare beat you again." He was referring to both the current physical abuse they experienced from members of the Albanian community and the historical defeat of Serbs by the Ottoman Muslims in 1389. Time collapsed in that moment—1987 became 1389—and Milosevic, through a short speech and several months of political manipulation created the foundation for a new political, social and institutional reality in Yugoslavia—Nationalism. It was to be used by Milosevic as a rationale for protecting Serbian large-group identity in Kosovo and throughout the region and as a vehicle for realizing the age-old dream of a 'Greater Serbia.'[6]

Nationalism replaced Yugoslavia's historical communist structure of governance with Milosevic leading the way. But, his power interests (and those of many who surrounded him) as well as his complex personality and psychological factors that may have stemmed from childhood and early adult life experiences, caused him to make decisions that led him and the people of Yugoslavia down a very dark and destructive path.[7]

Effective Leaders

Milosevic *was* an effective leader—one whose intelligence, convictions and understanding of his people's culture and problematic history of oppression by the Ottomans and other foreign powers gave him power to bring change to Yugoslavia. His leadership, framed by these circumstances, made him the top decision-maker in his country. However, his decisions were made under highly stressful circumstances and his pragmatic leadership philosophy was constantly being challenged—and refined—by the national and international politics and social environment of the times.

As we have seen, large-group identity needs were at stake in regard to the Serbs in Kosovo and for other segments of the Serbian population in the region—at least those who identified with the historical and religious meaning of Kosovo in Serb history.[8] Milosevic, like other leaders in complex moments of history, made decisions that were based on the protection (and promotion) of Serbian identity and in his case these decisions inflamed large-group regression and destructive patterns (Volkan 2004).[9] The result was a series of wars and a continuation of the historical cycle of violence and victimization among the Serbs, Croats and Bosniaks in the region.[10]

Effective leadership—the *shadow* kind that Milosevic demonstrated—happens at every level of society. This type of leadership, as well as a more reparative and therefore constructive leadership, requires the ability to adapt to a set of circumstances which include determining what constituents desire, how they perceive their needs and addressing these issues in ways one believes to be effective and historically meaningful. Factors that differentiate destructive leadership from the reparative or *light* informed kind are multi-faceted. When decision-makers are deeply reflective and perceive themselves to be serving others—and truly wanting to hear the voices of those they serve—more reparative and progressive leadership models emerge.[11] Their effectiveness stems from a natural as well as cultivated respect for one's *followers* and a deep desire for the accomplishment of a group's vision and purpose (Gardner 1995).

In more pragmatic or technocratic terms, progressive leaders can be seen as managers who work in leadership "teams" and who bring into balance the internal and external socio-political and economic factors of the community or society, while at the same time meeting the needs of the people.[12] These are both structural needs related to economic and political development and social and identity needs related to human development and security. According to Mintzberg (2007), "change is happening and needs to be carefully managed—this is why we need leaders to manage the change that is happening [around them]." Liberian president, Ellen Johnson-Sirleaf (2007) echoes this understanding when she says that leaders need to accept responsibility, listen to people and "be effective managers with [good] managerial skills."

Transactional and *Transformative Leadership:* These are two categories of leadership that point in a similar direction in terms of effectively helping small or large groups of people meet their needs, gain a sense of purpose and attain certain goals. Yet, they differ in important ways. Transactional models speak to a bargaining process, but where the bargainers "have no enduring purpose that holds them together; hence they may go their separate ways" (Burns 1995). This indicates that leadership happened, but there is no relationship or higher purpose that binds leaders to his or her fellow citizens. This contrasts with the type of leadership that helps transform the situation in ways that impact both the leader and followers and implies a "higher level of human awareness and relationship" (Couto 1995), and often a moral and value-based framework and reality that indicates trust and interdependence.

In order to effectively lead in a transformative and by implication a just and sustainable manner, leaders must attempt to understand the human element of their role in regard to the importance of interdependence across groups and levels of society. They need to find ways to *integrate* this fact of interdependence in ways that lead to building relational and structural stability within a community or a society. As Mary Clark (2002) writes concerning egalitarian societies:

> [T]he leader or elder is . . . simply the interpreter of tradition. When there is a grave problem affecting the whole group, everyone meets together to discuss the situation, nonstop, until a decision is agreed upon. Men, women, children—all participate, speaking as they wish, one at a time.

This statement tracks well with the *palaver hut* tradition in Liberia found throughout the country prior to its 14 year civil war. There was a chieftaincy and/or eldership system of governance and problem solving—where leaders and community members met to settle conflicts and make important decisions. The entire community would gather inside and around a special hut within their village designated for "talking." The members of the community would have their say about the conflict or issue at hand as the leadership listened—and listened. Decisions were then made by the chief and/or elders based on this listening and information gathering process. In Benin, among the Fon ethnic group, a similar problem solving process has been used, where the most difficult problems are dealt with in the very early morning when the earth was still and the malevolent spirits were resting. These are examples of how *spaces* have been created by leaders for constructive problem solving and change to take place.[13]

Leadership effectiveness in this traditional context was demonstrated in ways that reflected leaders' awareness of their social and physical environment and an ability to interpret their culture and tradition. This was done in a manner that acknowledged the importance of everyone's opinion and involvement in the life of the community. Through the process these chiefs and elders offered a system of leadership that says that every person has a role to play in decision making and caring for as well as sustaining community life and practices.[14]

This example may not reach the level of complexity or match the political, economic and social issues that Milosevic dealt with (see above), but it points to the values and actions taken by persons in leadership that might be adapted for these more complex situations. More progressive leadership—that respects and involves followers in the decision-making process—knows that an important part of meaning-making for members of a community or society is found in the "active involvement of its citizenry" (Saunders 1999). Therefore, to be an effective leader under this rubric of "active involvement" means that one's actions and interactions with citizens or followers assumes that their ideas and participation are acknowledged and fully considered in the overall decision-making process. Through this relationship, which can best be described as an *effective partnership*, motivation is created to maintain important traditions as well as change relational and structural systems to enhance the safety and well-being of all.

Spoiler leaders: These are leaders who fall into the destructive or non-reparative categories and fail their people when they don't foster and participate in partnership models of leadership. They literally *spoil* this critical relationship by placing their personal needs above the needs of members of their community or larger society. Also, to meet these needs and to increase their power or at minimum maintain the status quo, they often create or escalate conflict within or across ethnic, religious or other groups in their context or with outsiders (Reychler and Stellamans 2005). Spoiler leaders further fail in their roles as leaders when they don't grasp the importance of the synergy needed between followers or fellow citizens and themselves that helps create the unity, hope and sense of purpose needed to build and sustain a stable society.

Effective Citizens and Followers

The responsibility of citizens of a nation or followers in less-democratic or traditional contexts needs to be examined for a more complete understanding of this leader-follower synergy. The importance of the interaction between citizens or followers in regard to leadership is expressed in Gardner's statement: "We must know how we can strengthen and support good leaders; and we must be able to see through the leaders who are exploiting us…." (1995). If this awareness is cultivated and monitored, citizens or followers and their leaders will participate more constructively in a partnership model of mutual trust with a similar vision for the future.

Leaders and followers "don't act in a vacuum," but are "propelled, constrained, and buffeted by their environment" (Wren 1995). Culture, political and economics issues—local as well as regional and international ones—place both leaders and followers in situations that if not fully analyzed and evaluated (with strategic plans created and active engagement expected) will prevent the objectives of both groups being met. Therefore, citizens or followers should be clear about what kind of leadership they *currently* need, intentional about whom they select to lead them, and know what short and long-term social, cultural, economic and political issues they want their leadership to address. They need to keep their leaders accountable when promises are made and not kept. Citizens or followers must also be in a position to choose to restrict their leader's power when necessary.

Leaders, therefore, should not be chosen to "fix" situations, or be seen as a "savior-leader" who will replace the current "devil-leader" in their midst.[15] Instead, citizens and followers need to be engaged in the selection of their leaders as well as the leadership process itself and not abdicate responsibility to a new or the most charismatic leader. If not engaged in this manner, the *power* given the leader by his or her followers will be misused with the end result being no accountability in either direction.

Accountability: In many democratic societies, accountability is best experienced through a strong civil society whose leaders understand the power of citizen involvement and the responsibility they have to engage citizens in the governing process. According to Global Partnership for the Prevention of Armed Conflict (2005), civil society can be understood in the following way:

> [It] is essentially the *political* side of society, creating the social organization to engage citizens with public life that is necessary for democracy…[This idea re-

> fers] to non-state and non-profit making sections of society, which include, but is not limited to, those groups explicitly concerned about public matters.

Civil society leadership is meant for the public good and acts to build mechanisms of understanding and exchange across mid-level actors and between top-level and grass-root actors (Lederach 1997). Civil society leadership, in its most constructive sense, helps societies function in just and equitable ways and is geared toward helping people take control of their own lives by challenging and aiding them to assume responsibility as members of society (Reychler and Stellemans 2004). Civil society leaders, therefore, give people a voice in governance by empowering them to act in their own best and *collective* interest.[16]

Civil society models (and leader-follower models) are found across the globe but many cultural, economic and political systems still do much to prevent their engagement in social development. Greed, fear of change and corruption across all sectors of society, along with the normal difficulties in modifying attitudes and behaviors, militate against a revolutionary shift in this direction. Grass-roots and mid-level leaders and citizens who desire something transformational in terms of social change and development will find that their path is not an easy one. However, if this path is taken and encouraged by UN agencies, International Non-governmental Organizations (NGOs) and financial institutions such as the World Bank and the International Monetary Fund (IMF) acting in the best interest of community members and/or members of the larger society, the potential for grass-roots and mid-level leaders helping their communities build strong relationships and more just structures will emerge. Eventually, more top-level leaders will to see the wisdom of participating in a partnership leadership model, one based on people-in-relationship across a community or society determining their own future.

Leadership and Power

Power can generally be defined as *the capacity to produce effects on others.* Redekop (2002) states that "there are two kinds of power: a positive power to make things happen and a negative power to disrupt." French and Raven (see Hughes et al. 1995) identify five sources or bases of power that can be constructive or disruptive. They are adapted below and are organized from the leader's perspective but have application for understanding the power of followers as well.

1. Expert Power: The power of knowledge—the ability to influence through the relative expertise in a particular area. This power is a function of the amount of knowledge the leader possesses relative to the rest of the members of the group. In certain situations, such as when a new leader comes on the scene, followers may hold this power because they have more knowledge and expertise than their new leader.
2. Referent Power: The type of power that refers to the potential influence one or one's group has due to the strength of the relationship between

leaders and followers. The stronger the relationship is the more mutual influence leaders and followers exert over each other.

3. Legitimate Power: Power that depends on a person's organizational role. In this context it is thought of as one's formal or official (leadership) authority. Followers use this power when they actively resist a leader's influence through the use of legal procedures or polices.
4. Reward Power: Using power that will potentially influence others due to one's control over desired resources. Leaders and followers may wield this kind of power—the former being more obvious, but the latter when followers control resources, requiring leaders to act in a manner they want.
5. Coercive Power: Power that has the potential to influence others through the administration of negative sanctions or the removal of positive reinforcement or benefits. It controls others through fear or punishment or the loss of valued outcomes. It may be used appropriately or inappropriately by both leaders and followers, with the latter using it to physically or psychologically threaten leaders in ways that disrupt social, political or economic systems.

Another important source of power is found in the moral authority of leaders, citizens or followers. This kind of power focuses on meeting the emotional and relational needs and goals of all concerned. Its source is a set of beliefs and values that compel people to act in a manner that perceives others as critical to one's own physical well being and social development. The Liberian group *Women in White*[17] exemplified this moral, even spiritual, authority in its effort to change relationships and structures during Liberia's 14 year civil crisis. These grass-roots and middle-level leaders mobilized their fellow-citizens (mainly women) to stop the war in Liberia. This was done through extended peace vigils and effectively pressurizing political authorities and the international community to end the violence. Their moral authority in real and symbolic terms as "mothers" of all Liberians gave them the *power* to challenge the repressive and destructive leadership of the country, call for an end to killing and the initiation of peace talks.

Liberia's *Women in White* combined many of the above mentioned types of power, especially coercive power (used nonviolently) with a moral strength and set of practices that brought social and political change to their country. Their power also changed (or expanded) how women related to each other as they saw that their unity was an important force for challenging the status quo in Liberia, including its male-dominated leadership structures.

These women, as leaders *and* citizens effectively led their people into a new post-war era of peace and social responsibility in Liberia. They continue their work today with Ellen Johnson-Sirleaf, the first elected woman president of an African country, as the head of state. According to one of their founders, though, *Women in White,* as an organization is currently struggling to keep its focus as advocates of peace and social justice. The new and politically charged atmosphere of Liberia is challenging the momentum of its earlier actions (Gbowee 2007). The members of this organization will need to find new ways to continue their moral leadership and effectively exert their power for the benefit of all Liberians.

Gender Issues in Leadership

Traditionally, men have been given or taken the key leadership roles in most organizations, communities and societies. As we have seen, Liberia's *Women in White* perceived a need to change this equation in order to survive physically and emotionally during the war as well as politically in post-war Liberia. Women in this and other contexts have demonstrated their ability to act in ways that parallel men's styles of leadership while at the same time show themselves to be more communal and supportive than male leaders. Of course, context, culture and personality factors of these women (and men) need to be seriously considered in any analysis of gender leadership styles and roles.

Recent empirical research to attempt to understand the roles of women and men in leadership has mainly been done within the realm of organizational management (Business and Education). A seminal study in this area was conducted by Eagly, Johannesen-Schmidt, & van Engen (see Eagly 2007). The study integrated the findings of 45 other studies done mainly in the United States (53%) with the rest (47%) done in other nations or with mixed global samples. This meta-analysis revealed:

1. Female leaders were more transformational than male leaders. Women most exceeded men on individual consideration, which encompasses supportive, encouraging treatment of subordinates.
2. Female leaders were also more transactional than males in their contingent reward behaviors, whereas male leaders were more likely than female leaders to manifest the two other aspects of transactional leadership (active and passive management by exception) as well as laissez-faire leadership.

These differences between male and female leaders were small, but according to the study, "women, somewhat more than men, manifest leadership styles that relate positively to effectiveness, and men, more than women, manifest styles that relate only weakly to effectiveness or hinder that effectiveness." This same study concludes that women more than men "appear to lead in styles that recommend them for leadership." Men, compared to women, "appear to lead in less advantageous styles by (a) attending to subordinates' failures to meet standards, (b) displaying behaviors that entail avoiding solving problems until they become acute, and (c) being absent or uninvolved at critical times."

Although women more than men fall into the transformational category of leadership, women also engage in destructive leadership patterns. Their personalities, the context and culture they find themselves in and the systems used to select leaders can cause them to lead from the *shadows* and not the *light*. In most cases, though, women face obstacles that men do not based on context and bias within an organization or society and because of this are prevented from assuming most leadership roles where their transformational style of leadership can be used. On the other hand, men, historically, have not always led by building relationships based on empathetic responses towards others. This being the case, there may be wisdom in promoting a more comprehensive and global study of the different leadership styles of women and men—not so much to show that one group leads better than the other—but a study whose outcomes could help focus on ways their similarities and differences might compliment each other. Such a study, therefore, may point to ways to integrate and activate the unique characteristics of both women and men as well as improve both in order that more balanced leadership models might emerge.

Gender mainstreaming: It is being promoted by the United Nations[18] and major national and international non-governmental organizations. These organizations have rightly pointed to the need for an acknowledgement of women's' rights and demanding that they be honored. These organizations have also promoted women for leadership roles at all levels of society. In war and post-war situations it is women who have lost male members to the violence and find themselves as head of house-holds. They have also been raped and tortured and experienced extreme discrimination. An example of this discrimination is found in the statement by a Bosnian woman after the war in her country: 'Women came last—after everything else came women' (Abdela 2003).

This abuse and exclusion must be changed into an awareness of the social and professional skills (including leadership) that women bring to their communities and societies. Educating men and women in these issues and the potential complimentary roles they can play in leading their societies may be the next critical step in gender mainstreaming and leadership development. (See below suggestions for educating leaders in *Peacebuildilng Leadership for Trauma Healing*.)

Peacebuilding Leadership

Within the peacebuilding field a deeper understanding of effective leadership is beginning to emerge (see Lederach 1997; Gerzon 2003; Reychler and Stellamans 2005). The leadership depends on and helps create the "five peace building blocks," which are "mutually reinforcing and therefore need to be present or installed simultaneously" in any peacebuilding process (Reychler and Stellamans 2005). These five blocks are summarized as follows:

1. An effective communication, consultation and negotiation systems between the conflicting parties. It is a system that gives ample time to creatively generate mutually beneficial agreements between the parties.
2. A set of peacebuilding structures that meet political, economic, judicial as well as security needs of all people.
3. An integrative climate that stresses the importance of a favorable political-psychological and social-psychological environment. This climate would include the expectation of an attractive future as a consequence of cooperative attitudes and actions.
4. A supportive regional and international environment. The stability of a peace process is often highly dependent on the behavior and interests of neighboring countries or regional powers.

5. A critical mass of peacebuilding leadership in different domains such as politics, diplomacy, defense, economics, education, media, religion, etc., at all levels of society.

Peacebuilding further requires conflict analysis, early warning and environmental protection systems, monitory and advocacy systems and ongoing research and evaluation practices (Schirch 2004). Peacebuilding leadership is most effective in regard to these "blocks" and other requirements when:

- Leaders understand and believe in the importance of partnership models that fully engage citizens or followers—and practice this belief.
- Leaders work with other leaders who hold similar values to develop a "team" approach to leadership and challenge upcoming leaders to integrate these values and practice them.
- Citizens and followers identify their need to participate in the peacebuilding process, choose to be fully involved and are aided by their leaders to maximize this involvement.
- Leaders and citizens or followers have a deep desire for the accomplishment of their vision and purpose to build peaceful and just societies.

The Peacebuilding Wheel model (see book Introduction) is another way to understand peacebuilding leadership. The Wheel is an integrative model of some of the most important factors needed for building peace after large-scale violence. Leadership is one section of the Wheel, yet is understood as essential to all its sections. Seen in this way, peacebuilding leadership is reflected in humanitarian assistance and development work, where leaders in these fields bring a set of values to their work that speak to and help meet the needs and interests of the people they serve. This is also the case for religious leaders whose beliefs and skills inform inter-religious dialogue to help transform conflict or prevent it from escalating. There are similar values and criteria for those leaders who understand that they are doing peacebuilding in the disciplines of security and justice through truth and reconciliation commission or special courts.

Leadership is also part of the field of conflict analysis and transformation where historical, cultural, political and economic research critical to peace and capacity building is examined and interpreted, with this information shared across the disciplines represented in the Wheel. There are also good educator-leaders who educate for peace and justice and participate in the development of educational material—for example, those persons taking the lead in trauma awareness and recovery work. These trauma healing leaders (and other leaders) effectively lead as they create the *space* for people to heal after violent conflict. Leadership in all sections of the Wheel also recognizes the importance of peoples' worldviews related to culture and belief systems; and leaders study the impact of threat to individual and large-group identity in conflict situations and how this insight helps in post-war reconciliation and reconstruction processes.

Returning to our starting point, the section of the Wheel called "Leadership," is where we find the high quality diplomatic and political leaders who know that their service to their constituents is more than promoting or attempting to uphold a particular ideology. Instead, they know as leaders they are meant to engage others in ways that honor their interests, needs and rights, recognizing that this may be the best way to meet their constituents' needs and help them gain a sense of safety or overall security. In other words, *our safety depends on how safe you feel.* Finally, leaders within *each* section of the Wheel recognize their dependence on actors (leaders and citizens) in all other sections of the wheel. They grasp the complexity of how interdependence and related action helps move citizens toward a more stable and just society—and their work as leaders is to build capacity to maintain this stability for people across all levels of society.

Leading from the Light

The style of leadership described above is not the *norm* since a more hierarchal or power-oriented style has dominated leadership models throughout history and is still practiced in most parts of the world. But, the partnership approach to leadership has occurred regularly and emerged in times of crisis and need. Examples of extraordinary leaders who have embodied this partnership approach to leadership are Martin Luther King, Jr. and Nelson Mandela. These men's leadership style and set of circumstances caused them to "do the right thing" within their particular historical, social and political context. Dr. King, for example, spoke to the powers (local and national leaders) directly and empowered his followers to do the same through nonviolent demonstrations and actions. He analyzed the history of the black/white divide and current reasons for racism in the United States and educated others about these issues. Dr. King took risks to act nonviolently under violent and racially motivated circumstances and showed moral courage in his leadership of both black and white Americans. As a peacebuilding leader, he created *space* for dialogue and action as well as for the healing of a people and nation.[19]

Nelson Mandela has demonstrated peacebuilding leadership as a teacher-leader (Volkan 2004). Although an effective resistance leader before his incarceration, much of this leadership ability was shaped over the twenty seven years he spent in prison. During this time Mandela developed his ability to not hate whites, but rather their oppressive system of apartheid. Through much self-reflection and seeing small but important acts of human kindness in the whites who guarded him, Mandela gained deeper insight to the needs of South Africans—which helped him understand and solidify how he should lead all the people of his country. Volkan (2004) tells the following story about an African National Congress (ANC) executive committee meeting regarding South Africa's National Anthem as a salient example of his teaching and leadership style:

> The country's first full democratic election would be held in April 1994, and it was clear the ANC would win. The existing anthem, *Die Stem*, seemed obviously unacceptable to the committee members, as it celebrated the triumphs of nineteen century Afrikaner trekkers as they fought and conquered the indigenous people. Mandela was slated to preside over the meeting in which the issue was to be discussed, but he was called away soon after the meeting began. During his absence, an overwhelming majority of the committee members ex-

pressed their wish to replace *Die Stem* with *Nkosi Sikelele*, which expressed the suffering of indigenous people. Tokyo Sexwale, a leading ANC figure who had spent time with Mandela in prison, vividly remembers the mood at the meeting during Mandela's absence. 'We were enjoying ourselves. It is the end for the *Die Stem* song,' we said. 'The end. No more.' When Mandela returned to the meeting, however, he responded much like a correcting schoolmaster: *Well, I am sorry, I don't want to be rude...but this song that you treat so easily holds the emotions of many people whom you don't represent. Yet, with the stroke of a pen you would make a decision to destroy the very—the only—basis that we are building upon: reconciliation.*

After the ANC was elected to lead the country that April, South Africa did adopt *Nikosi Sikelele* as their national anthem—at least as one of them, since it was played in succession with *Die Stem* at every official event. This action by Mandela and his support for the nearly all white Springbok rugby team (which he understood to be another potential unifying force for South Africans), helped the citizens of the country experience a sense of pride in themselves and hope for their country. He shared his vision and deep desire for reconciliation between the people of South Africa and large numbers of them accepted as their own this vision and need for healing and reconciliation. Together, Mandela and his followers began their work to unify a people and a nation.

Nelson Mandela's leadership, along with another South African peacebuilder leader, Desmond Tutu, inspired the development of new political and justice systems needed to start a post-apartheid reconciliation and reconstruction process.[20] The fact that this process experienced difficulties and set-backs does not take away from its positive and transformative results. Its success is in large part due to the leadership of these men who embodied the meaning of the South African Xhosa word *ubuntu* or "a human being is a human being through [other] human beings" (Malan 2006).[21] The peacebuilding leadership of Mandela and Tutu (and many other men and women) depended to a great extent on helping people see not only the need for the *other* but that humanity itself is only fully found and experienced in and through other people. Their roles as leaders were to help people understand and live out *ubuntu* for the sake of all South Africans and the future of the country.

Peacebuilding Leadership for Healing Trauma

Trauma due to war or other forms of large-scale violence is one of the *intangibles* that peacebuilding leaders need to understand to help move their community or the larger society toward a more just and sustainable peace. Like the rebuilding of political, economic, judicial or infrastructure systems (some of the important *tangible* factors of post-war reconstruction),[22] trauma and related identity issues need to be understood by leaders and their citizens or followers. Moreover, peacebuilding mechanisms and intervention strategies need to be put in place that will constructively aid the trauma healing process.

It is often difficult to get a handle on these emotional and psychological issues, but it is essential for leaders as well as followers to have an understanding of trauma and its impact on their physical, emotional, cognitive and spiritual states, along with insights to its historical and/or most recent causes. This insight tied to a set of trauma recovery actions plays an important role in healing people who individually *and* collectively have suffered great loss. This may be the loss of loved ones, their homes, villages and cities and trust in themselves as well as others. In most cases, they have also lost hope in any meaningful future.

Trauma comes in many forms, but is generally known to be something an individual or group experiences or witnesses through an event—or a series of events—that involve actual or threatened death or serious physical, emotional, cognitive, behavioral and spiritual injury. For an individual, the traumatic event's complexity and level of injury depend on the person's unique characteristics, such as personality and individual resilience, their familial experience, social context or social support systems, as well as their previous exposure to traumatic events. Collective trauma with its myriad issues and greater complexity related to culture, political, economic, environmental as well as worldview and large-group identity issues complicates both an understanding of the trauma and how healing can begin for thousands, often millions, of people. Nevertheless, its complexities are being analyzed and more fully understood (see Kleber et al. 1995; Ajdukovic 1997; Green et al. 2003; Volkan 2006).

Leaders, those with the vision and courage to practice effective reparative and partnership peacebuilding models, need to know about individual and collective trauma, its effects and methods of recovery and the important role they play in providing the physical and emotional space for healing to take place. They also need to know that healing requires the empowering or creation of social systems and institutions for deep healing to begin and be sustained. To effectively respond to traumatic events and experiences, related theories and practical information should be integrated into existing educational programs on leadership (Heifetz et al. 1989) and incorporated in trainings that target peacebuilding leaders.[23] This awareness will help them understand the importance of healing collective trauma in rebuilding communities and whole societies after complex and violent conflicts. Essential points to include in these educational programs for both men and women are:

- Leaders at all levels of society need to become aware of their own high-level of stress or trauma and be willing to speak about it to their followers. Culture and other social and environment factors should be considered in regard to this "openness," but in most cases it should be seen as a strength rather than a *weakness*.
- Political will is essential for individual and societal healing to take place. When political leaders acknowledge the existence of individual and collective trauma, they begin to create the emotional and social space for people to deal with it.
- When the pain, fear and anger of a traumatic event is denied and/or suppressed, it will usually emerge in various forms at a later time and may be used as a political tool by spoiler leaders to mobilize their followers against those who inflicted the pain.

- Historical trauma is real and has its roots in violence or oppressive acts against individuals and groups that have never been healed. Past victims become perpetrators at subsequent point in history—continuing the cycle of violence.
- Justice processes need to be created that allow victims to tell their stories in safe environments—and possibly meet those who victimized them in similar contexts. This *rehumanization* process may be helpful in healing both individual and large group trauma.
- Establishing justice processes that call for both accountability on the part of perpetrators as well as their healing.
- Religion, spiritual practices, rituals and ceremonies help individuals, communities and potentially entire societies heal from the effects of traumatic events.

There are other issues peacebuilding leaders need to be aware of such as the power of memorialization in healing trauma—and how it should not be used to glorify victories, but to speak to the needs of all people impacted by violence and loss. Leaders wanting to help their followers or citizens should also educate themselves about resilience factors that exist within communities or society. Examples of resilience are: Positive large-group identity and collective self-esteem; spirituality, humor, music and dance; and the ability to collectively solve problems.

During and after the most complex and violent situation, resilience is present in people and should be *tapped* by the leadership as a tool for healing and transformation. It can also be developed through educational processes and/or trainings.[24] Furthermore, knowledge of the power of symbols and rituals in the world of individuals and large groups helps peacebuilding leaders aid others in the healing process.[25]

Historical trauma, noted above, should be given special attention in the education process of peacebuilding leaders. It concerns individual and collective trauma that if not acknowledged and healed may lead to more violence. Recall the story about Milosevic and how "time collapsed," when in 1987 he reminded Orthodox Serbs (of Serbia and its autonomous region of Kosovo) about the most traumatic event in their history—the lost to Ottoman Muslims at the Battle of Kosovo in 1389. Milosevic turned the key of the Serbian people's pain as well as fear and anger and changed the history of Yugoslavia in the process. "Pain not transformed will transmitted" (or transferred)[26] and in this case it was transferred across generations of Serbs through their oral and written history, songs and poetry to a point in time where a leader used it to manipulate the identity of millions of people. In a very real sense Milosevic was also manipulated by his followers who demanded that he deliver them from their current pain, experienced at the hands of Kosovar Albanians, but also their deeply felt historical trauma experienced at the hands of the Ottomans.

Nelson Mandela, as we have seen, took a more progressive and restorative path regarding the past and current history of his people. South Africans were given an understanding of their pain explained in symbolic terms—anthems and the national rugby team for example—and through Mandela's moral teachings and actions.[27] He, unlike Milosevic, faced historical issues and current social and political events by exposing them and their meaning and challenging South Africans to be part of healing their past and working toward a more just and stable future.

Conclusion

Peacebuilding leadership is more than the values and actions of leaders; it is influenced by context, circumstances and history. But, leadership of this kind can not happen without flesh and blood persons taking on leadership roles. It is up to these leaders to be self-reflective and practice well the art of leading. It is also up to them to inform and call those they serve to an understanding and practice of peace with justice for all members of their community or state. These leaders, who want to build peace in their communities and societies, need to surround themselves with other leaders whose integrity and vision for the future closely matches their own. This *collective of leaders*, in partnership with their followers and fellow citizens, are then able to carry out their joint vision and goals. This is the leadership 'web,' 'fabric,' 'community' that builds peace most effectively and strengthens the social fabric after violent conflicts.[28]

After war or other large-scale violence, peacebuilding leaders and their followers, whether members of victim or perpetrator groups, begin effective partnerships when they take intentional steps to heal wounds and acknowledge wrongs done.[29] Leaders within the perpetrator groups have a special part to play in this and need to be in the forefront of a process that acknowledges the humiliation and destruction of lives they, previous leaders and members of their communities and societies have caused the other group. They and members of their community need to take responsibility for their violent actions or bystander roles. To do this requires education about what violence does to a people socially, psychologically and spiritually. It further requires deep personal and collective reflection leading to acknowledgement of what happened and repentance for the violence and destruction caused.[30]Leaders and followers in the victim group have their responsibility as well: They need to not "forgive and forget" but be willing to "remember and change" (along with the perpetrator group) in order to begin the process of addressing pain and loss and developing relationships of trust with their former enemies.[31]

Through these actions and other restorative processes such as payment of restitution to victims, setting up scholarship funds for young people, creating memorials for the dead from both sides as well as addressing in restorative manners the acts and needs of perpetrators, the *reconciliation process* is put into motion. This happens within a larger peacebuilding framework that includes dialogue processes held throughout society about what has occurred, why violence was used to attempt to 'resolve' the conflict and what is needed to prevent similar or even worse conflicts in the future.

Finally, peacebuilding leading to more stability and just relationships and structures in society after large-scale violence will not occur without leaders becoming more fully aware of the impact trauma has on the overall health and well-being of their followers. It is a healthy people within a safe environment who are best able to heal relationships and construct stable societies. This health in large part comes through leadership that is aware of the current as well as past trauma's impact on their followers. When these factors are understood, leaders can then encourage the use of existing healing systems or recommend the development of new ones to provide for the healing of their people's physical, psychological and spiritual needs. It is also the case that a more healthy society comes into being as citizens work with their leaders in the creation of these healing systems. Peacebuilding leadership, in this *collective* sense of citizens working in partnership with their leaders, helps lift a community or an entire society of people to new levels of relationship, well-being and overall social, political, economic and human security.

Notes

1. In late 1989, Charles Taylor led the first attack on the military forces of Samuel Doe—the first indigenous, but highly ineffective and corrupt president of Liberia. What followed was a 14 year civil crisis that led to the death of approximately 250,000 people and displaced over 1 million people. Taylor, through threat and intimidation, eventually became president of the country, but was exiled and after several years turned over to the Special Court in Sierra Leone for war crimes committed by his fighter in that country. He is currently on trial in The Hague. Ratko Mladic, a Bosnian Serb general was charged by the Hague Tribunals for the former Yugoslavia for his leadership role in the massacre of 8,000 men and boys in Srebrenica, Bosnia in 1995. He is still at large.

2. Hitler and other regressive leaders such as Mladic were impacted by their family and/or nation's histories, desire for power and people who were looking for "savior type" leaders or those who would lead them out of their humiliation and loss of identity—WW I for the Germans and to a somewhat lesser degree, but with a similar power, the loss of the Battle of Kosovo for a significant number of ethnic Serbs in the region that was to become Yugoslavia.

3. Julius Kambarage Nyerere of Tanzania was officially called "*mwalimu,*" or "teacher" "who used teaching to elevate [his] followers' emotional and physical conditions and provide self-esteem for their identity" (Volkan 2004). Aung San Suu Kyi, a Noble Peace Prize laureate whose long-term struggle for democracy in Burma has kept her in prison or under permanent house arrest for several decades. This has not stopped her struggle for freedom from a corrupt and oppressive government. Leadership of this kind is found at all levels of society since there are individuals who understand the need to teach and serve others in order to help them achieve their needs, rights and dignity—whether as members communities or as a people at the level of a state or nation.

4. Reparative in these cases means that relationships are restored or renewed, where amends are made and reparations may be paid to symbolically heal the divisions between people.

5. LeBor (2004) writes, "The angry mobs of Serbs and Montenegrins outside Kosovo Polje's *Dom Kulture* roughly conformed to Canetti's concept of the 'Reversal Crowd.' A Reversal Crowd is a revolutionary phenomenon, dedicated to overturning the established order." In other words, the angry mob was more than a 'mob' and had leaders, a central one being Miroslav Solevic who harangued the audience about stopping the Serb exodus from Kosovo and led his 'boys' to take the stones "we had parked there . . . [and] pelt the police."

6. Greater Serbia: A summary of what this (controversial) Serbian nationalist idea has meant can be found at http://www.pbs.org/wgbh/pages/frontline/shows/karadzic/bosnia/serbia.html

7. Milosevic's personality was probably shaped by his childhood and early adult experiences. They included the loss of family members and the breakup of his biological family. His favorite uncle committed suicide; his father left the family when Milosevic was a young boy—and then later killed himself, as did his mother when he was in his early 30's. See Vamik Volkan's *Blind Trust* (2004) for a psychological 'profile' of Milosevic and how his personality development may have helped shape his leadership attitude and style.

8. Kosovo was the religious center (symbolically) of the Orthodox Christian Serbs. But Croatian Serbs, for example, where more greatly impacted by the genocide perpetrated by the Germans during WWII.

9. Milosevic did what he did "at the expense of human lives. He killed the curiosity and joy of his people." Anonymous (2007).

10. Bosniaks are Bosnians who traditionally adhere to Islam and/or have historical and cultural roots in Muslim tradition. The majority of Bosniaks live in Bosnia and Herzegovina, but are found throughout the former Yugoslavia.

11. Progressive leaders help develop policies and systems that provide for the needs and well-being of their followers/partners. They regularly take steps toward improving conditions and expanding trust between themselves and those they serve.

12. Good managers plan, organize coordinate and control outcomes. They lead in ways that directs a process and achieves results. In the best sense, they are *effective* leaders, but may not always be the most analytical, reflective or reparative leaders for the transformation of complex conflicts and post-conflict healing and reconstruction. These situations require leaders whose courage, risk-taking and vision go beyond a set of managerial skills—although the latter are also important for bringing about change and producing results.

13. Sam Gbaydee Doe, Liberian peacebuilder and scholar, first told me about the problem solving practices of the Fon people in Benin.

14. Approximately 60 percent of Liberians adhere to traditional cultural and religious practices. In post-war Liberia, the revival of traditional "scared bush" (bush schools for both men and women to learn about their culture and what is expected of them in it) and other methods of viewing and being in the world are occurring. They therefore have an important role to play in the emotional and spiritual healing of this significant segment of the Liberian people. The Palaver Hut and honoring ancestors as well as appeasing malevolent spirits will continue to exert influence on traditionalists and these practices need further study to see what parts of the traditions need to be kept, what needs to be discarded and what role the positive traditional understandings and practices offer for the development of a 'modern' Liberia.

15. Liberians, like many national groups, have often looked to the next leader to "fix" their economic and political situation; or in the case of Charles Taylor they were *forced* to vote for him to prevent further violence. During the presidential election process in 1997 they sang the following words about Taylor: "You killed my pa, you killed my ma, but I will vote for you." Taylor became president and spent the next six years *leading* Liberia deeper into violence and political and economic chaos.

16. Civil Society actors play a critical role in nation building, but not all of them have the good of the people in mind. The new United Nations Peacebuilding Commission, for example, should form strong partnerships with civil society actors in Sierra Leone and Burundi, the first countries chosen for the Commissions post-war reconstruction work,

but it must also vent civil society organizations for their commitment to the goals of nation building.

17. Formal name: *Women of Liberia Mass Action for Peace Campaign*

18. See the United Nation's Inter-Agency Network on Women and Gender Equality at http://www.un.ort/womenwatch/eanwge/gm_facts/

19. In "A Testament of Hope" (1986) Dr. King wrote, "The struggle for freedom on the part of oppressed people in general and of the American Negro in particular has developed slowly and is not going to end suddenly. Privileged groups rarely give up their privileges without strong resistance. But when oppressed people rise up against oppression there is no stopping point short of full freedom." He taught his followers that non-violence resistance was the only path for this rising up to be successful, since it "does not seek to defeat or humiliate the opponent, but to win friendship and understanding."

20. Archbishop Desmond M. Tutu was Chair of South Africa's Truth and Reconciliation Commission (TRC). He literally *shepherded* the people of South Africa through a process that exposed the evil of apartheid and his support for restorative justice processes through an amnesty provision in the Commission's mandate was both controversial and healing.

21. Tutu understood reconciliation as an ongoing process that requires remorse and repentance by perpetrators and forgiveness by victims. More than that, though, he believes, "We are made for goodness. We are made for love. We are made for friendliness. We are made for togetherness" (Helmick and Peterson 2001).

22. John Katunga (2003), referring to conflicts and conflict transformation in Africa says that "tangibles refer to all what is objectively measurable. They include the visible actors and perceived concrete issues (usually sharing of power and resources) . . . [and the] intangibles refer to what is often hard to 'objectively' measure. They include anonymous actors, the masses that are often reduced to statistics; the 'real' issues often related to identities, perceptions, self-esteem or recognition. . . ."

23. The Woodrow Wilson Center's Howard Wolpe writes, "One of the most distinctive elements in Burundi's transition—and perhaps its most instructive—is the extent to which national leaders have embraced the importance of leadership training as a key to reconciliation and good governance. Indeed, Burundi may be the first case of a country just emerging from conflict in which key leaders have integrated into their peace process a national training program explicitly designed to rebuild capacity to work effectively together in advancing their country's postwar reconstruction." *Training Leaders for Peace*, Journal of Democracy – Vol. 17, Number 1, January 2006. p. 132.

24. Argentina passed a law regarding resilience which "led to a resilience curriculum in schools of medicine, public health, nursing and social work. And as a minister of health in the Provence of San Luis, Dr. Suarez-Ojeda [also director of the International Center for Studies of Resilience] was able to demonstrate the effectiveness of resilience programs, especially for youth" (Grotberg 2003).

25. "In rituals, humans learn from and about our emotional responses to an experience… The ritual of a funeral [for example] can allow people to express emotions jointly in a symbolic, transforming space. Ritual helps people find ways of expressing what they feel together with other people" (See Schirch, 2005, for a comprehensive examination of ritual and symbolism in peacebuilding.)

26. Father Richard Rohr made this statement (See Kruk 2006). The transmission or transferal of pain to others happens when an individual and even a large group of people do not *choose* to transform or heal the pain. Education about the pain is important, as is a space or environment to talk about this pain. Also, support from others is essential, but

the person or group "holding" the pain must choose to face it and over time psychologically (and spiritually) integrate it into who they are.

27. Moral values (of leaders) come from an inner consciousness that reflects a responsibility to do for others what is right and just. "Responsibility," says Derrida, "is excessive or it is not a responsibility" (1991). According to James MacGregor Burns, "Moral values lie at the heart of transforming leadership, which seeks fundamental changes in society, such as enhancement of individual liberty and the expansion of justice and of equality of opportunity" (See Odom, L. et al. 2005).

28. Gerzon's reference in "Leaders and Leadership" http://www.beyondintractability.org/essay/leaders/

29. Often perpetrator groups do not see themselves as perpetrators at all but *victims*. Their historical victimization by the other side or outside groups causes them to see their acts toward others as a defense against further humiliation and defeat. This complicates issues of accountability which in turn impacts the healing for members on all sides of the conflict. Any healing and accountability process must take this into consideration in order to be effective in transforming complex conflicts and building stable societies that will prevent future violence.

30. Repentance is a strong and complicated term, which has specific religious, cultural and contextual meaning connected to it. In other contexts, *deep regret* may have a similar meaning for victims; and in other contexts, the real and symbolic act of giving animals or meaningful material objects may have as much meaning for members of the victim group.

31. Joseph Campbell, a peacebuilder from Northern Ireland, coined the phrase "Remember and Change."

References

Abdela, L. 2003. Kosovo: Missed Opportunities, Lessons for the Future. *Development and Practice* 13(2&3)" 208-216.

Ajdukovic, D. 1997. *Trauma Recovery Training: Lessons Learned.* Zagreb: Society for Psychological Assistance.

Burns, J. M. 1995. "Transactional and Transforming Leadership." In J. Thomas Wren, ed. *The Leaders Companion: Insights on Leadership through the Ages.* New York: Free Press.

Clark, M. 2002. *In Search of Human Nature.* New York: Routledge.

Couto, R. 1995. "The Transformation of Transforming Leadership." In J. Thomas Wren, ed. *The Leaders Companion: Insights on Leadership through the Ages.* New York: Free Press.

Derrida, J. 1991. *'Eating Well', or the Calculation of the Subject. Who Comes After the Subject. E. Cadava.* New York: Routledge.

Eagly, A. 2007. Female Leadership Advantage and Disadvantage: Resolving the Contradictions. *Psychology of Women Quarterly* 31 (1): 1-17.

Gardner, J. 1995. "Leaders and Followers." In J. Thomas Wren, ed. *The Leaders Companion: Insights on Leadership through the Ages.* New York: Free Press.

Gbowee, L. 2007. Interview with author, Eastern Mennonite University.

Gerzon, M. September 2003. "Leaders and Leadership," Beyond Intractability, http://www.beyondintractability.org/essay/leaders

Global Partnership for the Prevention of Armed Conflict Reader. 2005. *Global Conference--From Reaction to Prevention: Civil Society Forging Partnerships to Prevent Violent Conflict and Build Peace.* UN Conference Headquarters, New York, July 19-21.

Green, B., Friedman, J. et al. eds. 2003. *Trauma Interventions in War and Peace: Prevention, Practice and Policy.* New York: Plenum Publishers.

Heifetz, R., Sinder, R., Jones, A., Hodge, L., and Rowley, K. Teaching and Assessing Leadership Courses at the John F. Kennedy School of Government. *Journal of Policy Analysis and Management* 8 (3): 563-562.

Helmick, R. and Peterson, R. eds. 2001. *Forgiveness and Reconciliation.* Philadelphia: Templeton Foundation Press.

Hughes, R., Ginnett, R. and Curphy, G. 1995. "What is Leadership?" In J. Thomas Wren, ed. *Leaders Companion: Insights on Leadership Through the Ages.* New York: Free Press.

Johnson-Sirleaf, E. 2007. Presentation at "Leadership Development Conference—Capacity Day." World Bank, April 19.

Katunga, J. 2003. African Capacities of Intervention, Mediation and Conflict Resolution: Civil Society Intervention in Ituri, Bunia, DRD. Paper presented at The Challenges of European-African Relations: An Agenda of Priorities conference, October 23-24.

Kleber, R., Figley, C. and Gersons, B. eds. 1995. *Beyond Trauma: Cultural and Social Dynamics.* New York: Plenum Press.

Kruk, E. 2006. Child Custody, Access and Parental Responsibility: The Search for a Just and Equitable Standard. *Policy Paper on Father Involvement, Child Custody and Access.* The University of British Columbia.

Lebor, A. 2004. *Milosevic: A Biography.* New Haven: Yale University Press.

Lederach, J. P. 1997. *Building Peace: Sustainable Reconciliation in Divided Societies.* Washington, D.C.: United States Institute for Peace Press.

Malan, J. 2006. Interview with author, Caux, Switzerland.

Mintzberg, H. 2007. Presentation at "Leadership Development Conference—Capacity Day." World Bank, April 19.

Odom, L., Garcia, A. and Milburn, P. 2005. The Ethicality of Capping Non-Economic Damages against Physicians, Hospital and Insurance Companies: Waging a Holy War against a Perceived Unfair Process. *The Internet Journal of Healthcare Administration,* 2 (2).

Palmer, P. 2000. *Let your Life Speak.* San Francisco: Jossey-Bass.

Redekop, V. 2002. *From Violence to Blessing: How an Understanding of Deep-Rooted Conflict Can Open the Paths to Reconciliation.* Ottawa: Novalis.

Reychler, L. and Stellamans, A. 2005. Researching Peace Building Leadership. *Cahiers Internationale betrekkingen en vredesonderzoek* Jg.23, Vol.71, 2.

Saunders, H. 1999. *A Public Peace Process: Sustained Dialogue to Transform Racial and Ethnic Conflicts.* New York: Palgrave.

Schirch, L. 2004. *The Little Book of Strategic Peacebuilding.* Intercourse, Pennsylvania: Good Books.

———. 2005. *Ritual and Symbol in Peacebuilding.* Bloomfield, Connecticut: Kumarian Press.

Suarez-Ojeda, E., and Autler, L. 2003. "Community Resilience: A Social Approach." In Edith H. Grotberg, ed. *Resilience for Today: Gaining Strength from Adversity.* Westport, Connecticut: Praeger Publishers.

Volkan, V. 2004. *Blind Trust: Large Groups and Their Leaders in Times of Crisis and Terror.* Charlottesville, Virginia: Pitchstone Publishing.

———. 2006. *Killing in the Name of Identity: A Study of Bloody Conflicts.* Charlottesville, Virginia: Pitchstone Publishing.

Washington, J. ed. 1986. *A Testament of Hope: The Essential Writings of Martin Luther King, Jr.* San Francisco: Harper Collins Publishers.

Wolpe, H. 2006. Training Leaders for Peace. *Journal of Democracy, 17 (1): 132.*

Wren, J. ed. 1995. *The Leaders Companion: Insights on Leadership through the Ages.* New York: Free Press.

Part II

Merging Theory and Practice

7

Psychological Recovery, Reconciliation and the Prevention of New Violence: An Approach and Its Uses in Rwanda

Ervin Staub, Laurie Anne Pearlman, Rezarta Bilali

In this chapter, we describe an approach to promoting post-genocide psychological recovery and healing, reconciliation, the development of positive relations between groups, and a peaceful society. We describe a number of projects we conducted in Rwanda between 1999 and 2006, in which we developed, evaluated and applied this approach. We have used components of this approach with varied groups. These include the staff of local and international non-governmental organizations (NGO's) whose work ranges from community-building to reconciliation, leaders and field staff from survivor organizations, trauma counselors, journalists, high-level national leaders, commissioners of the Rwandan National Unity and Reconciliation Commission (NURC), and others. We have also used this approach in a large-scale public education campaign through radio which has been extended to Burundi and the Democratic Republic of the Congo. In the course of describing this work, we discuss some issues important in reconciliation and the prevention of new violence, such as understand-

---

This chapter uses some material from Staub, 2006; the authors are grateful to Political Psychology and Wiley-Blackwell for their permission. Projects described in the chapter have been supported by grants to Ervin Staub and Laurie Anne Pearlman from the John Templeton Foundation, the Dart Foundation, USIP, USAID and the University of Massachusetts and to the Dutch NGO LaBenevolencija from the Netherlands and Belgium.

ing the influences leading to violence and a shared understanding of history (or collective memory) and comment on some current conditions in Rwanda that appear to facilitate or create problems for reconciliation and the building of a peaceful society.

Our work has been a response to a fundamental question that arises in the aftermath of genocide or intractable, violent conflict: after such violence, how can groups that continue to live together build a better, non–violent future? While the approach we describe here was developed and used primarily in Rwanda, it seems applicable to other places where violent conflict, mass killing, or genocide has taken place.

In recent years, especially since the activity of the Truth and Reconciliation Commission in South Africa, the necessity for reconciliation in the aftermath of violence between groups and ways to promote it have received a great deal of attention (Lederach 1995, 1997). It has become apparent to many observers that violence between groups often resumes (de la Rey 2001), even when it has ended with peace treaties and agreements. Segments of one or both of the groups may find the agreements unacceptable, and/or deep feelings of insecurity, hurt, anger and hostility may remain. The resumption of violence seems an even greater danger when genocide ends with victory by the victim group over the perpetrator group, as in Rwanda.

While structures and institutions that promote and serve reconciliation are important, the essence of reconciliation is a changed psychological orientation toward the other (Staub and Pearlman 2001). Reconciliation implies that victims and perpetrators do not see the past as defining the future. They come to accept and see the humanity of one another and see the possibility of a constructive relationship. Following great violence between groups, especially genocide, reconciliation is a profoundly difficult challenge. It can only develop gradually, with likely setbacks along the way (Staub and Bar-Tal 2003). Montville (1993) has suggested that healing from past wounds is important to reconciliation; we see it as an essential aspect of reconciliation.

A Brief History of the Genocide and Its Aftermath in Rwanda

Starting on April 7, 1994, the day after snipers shot down the plane carrying the President of Rwanda, over a 100 day period Hutus killed about 700,000 Tutsis, as well as about 50,000 politically moderate Hutus (des Forges 1999; Mamdani 2002; Prunier 1995). The killings were accompanied by rape, the mutilation of women, and other forms of physical and psychological violence and torture. Among the perpetrators of this government-organized violence were parts of the military, young men in paramilitary groups, and ordinary people. This was an "intimate genocide" (Staub and Pearlman, 2001), neighbors killing neighbors, and people in mixed families killing family members and occasionally even their own children (des Forges 1999; Mamdani 2002).

The genocide in Rwanda evolved out of a past history of conflict and violence. The Hutus and Tutsis in Rwanda live next to each other and share the same language and religion, primarily Catholic. Although, originally they may have been different ethnic groups, the primary differences over time became those of occupation, class, power and social identities. Tutsis tended cattle, were wealthier and had power, while the Hutus were agriculturalists (des Forges, 1999; Mamdani 2002).

A long history of dominance by the minority Tutsis (about 14% of the population) over the majority Hutus (about 85%) greatly intensified under the colonial rule of the Belgians who, starting with a so-called white paper in 1916, developed a racist ideology of Tutsi superiority (Mamdani 2002). Hutus took power in 1959 by a rebellion in which about 50,000 Tutsis were killed. Several waves of violence and mass killings of Tutsis by Hutus took place in 1960s and 1970s. In 1990, the Rwandan Patriotic Army (RPA) composed mainly of children of Tutsi refugees entered the country from Uganda. A civil war began, with a cease fire in 1993, followed by the Arusha Accords that delineated plans for a government shared by Tutsis and Hutus.

Among the Hutus an ideology of "Hutu power" developed and was propagated by elements of the government and media, intensifying fear and devaluation of Tutsis. The genocide began in April 1994. With the world watching but remaining passive it continued until the RPA defeated the government army (des Forges 1999; Prunier 1995; Staub 1999a).

Since then, the power has been in the hands of the minority Tutsis. With many Tutsis who were refugees in neighboring countries returning, the distribution of the population is about the same as before the genocide. Members of the groups live next to each other as neighbors, as before. The government initiated a policy of unity and reconciliation, a rare, intentional societal process to help people heal and reconcile. However, as part of unity, people are expected to consider themselves Rwandans, and discussion of differences between the groups has been called "divisionism." This policy does now allow Hutus to express their concerns and identity. While in Rwanda there is a justice process (see below), this policy is a source of potential conflict.

The Impact of Victimization on Survivors, Perpetrators, and Bystanders

1. *Impact on survivors*. Victimization tends to create intense trauma symptoms such as nightmares, flashbacks, and emotional numbing, as well as disruptions in survivors' world view, relationships with self and others, and identity (McCann and Pearlman 1990a; Pearlman and Saakvitne 1995). Genocide deeply affects survivors' perceptions of themselves and shatters their assumptions about the world. They feel diminished and vulnerable as their basic needs for security, for feelings of effectiveness and control over important events in their lives, for positive identity, for positive connections to other people and communities, and for a comprehension of one's own place in the world, have all been deeply frustrated (Staub 1989b, 2003; Staub and Pearlman 2001; 2006). The world is experienced as dangerous, and people, especially those outside one's group, as untrustworthy (Staub 1998).

The psychological consequences of victimization include extreme sensitivity to new threat. When conflict with another group arises, it may be more difficult for survivors to take the perspective of the other and consider the other's needs. In response to new threat or conflict they may believe they need to defend themselves even when violent self-defense is not necessary, and may strike out, in the process becoming perpetrators (Staub 1998). Healing from psychological wounds, from the trauma that can result from victimization, is important to prevent such defensive violence and to enhance the capacity of the group for reconciliation.

2. *Impact on perpetrators.* Often perpetrators *themselves, or the perpetrators' group,* have endured victimization or other traumatic experiences as part of the cycle of violence, which in turn has contributed to their actions. Unless others acknowledge and help them address their injuries, perpetrators may be unable to shift from a defensive stance of self-justification to a position of accepting responsibility for their actions. In addition, recent studies have shown that people who engage in intense violence against others tend to be psychologically injured by their own actions (MacNair 2002; Rhodes, Allen, Nowinski, and Cillessen 2002). Perpetrators distance themselves from victims in order to protect themselves from emotional consequences of their actions such as empathic distress, guilt, and shame. This distancing begins to develop in the course of the evolution of increasing discrimination and violence that usually precedes genocide (Staub 1989) and continues even when the violence has ended. Perpetrators often continue to blame victims and hold on to the ideology that in part motivated, and to them justified, their violence.

3. *Impact on bystanders.* Although once genocide starts some people endanger themselves to save lives (Africa Rights 2002; Oliner and Oliner 1988), passivity by witnesses/ bystanders in the course of the evolution of harmdoing is the norm (Staub 1989). The psychological effects of passivity are similar to but less intense than the effects of perpetration. To reduce their own distress, passive members of the perpetrator group tend to distance themselves from victims, in part by accepting justifications offered by perpetrators, and by blaming and devaluing victims. This reduces empathy and inhibits guilt, perhaps with the help of the commonly held belief in a just world, where innocent people do not suffer (Lerner 1980). As bystanders change, at least some of them join the perpetrators (Lifton 1986; Staub 1989).

While the nature of psychological wounds of survivors, perpetrators and bystanders varies greatly, as does the moral meaning of their woundedness, healing by each group can facilitate reconciliation. Healing from wounds that result from being harmed (see also Montville 1993), having harmed others, or being a member of a group that has harmed others (Staub and Pearlman 2001, 2006) seems important for reconciliation. Healing processes are underway in Rwanda, and apparently, many people feel safe enough to engage in such processes. As reconciliation begins, it increases the feeling of security, which makes further healing easier. Progress in one realm fosters progress in the other in this cycle.

An Approach to Promoting Healing and Reconciliation in the Community

In Rwanda, our first goal was to develop a training that practitioners could readily integrate into their programs for healing, reconciliation, and community-building. Our approach engages the expertise of local staff, is concerned with cultural adaptation and appropriateness of the material, and allows users to focus on a range of goals (e.g., healing, reconciliation, forgiving, other aspects of prevention, and group coexistence).

Developing a group, rather than an individual, intervention seemed essential for a number of reasons. First, the genocide affected most of the population of about 8,000,000 in Rwanda, making an individual approach to healing impractical. Second, the genocide was a community disaster, and healing as part of a group seems more appropriate and potentially more effective in these conditions. A group approach also seems more appropriate to Rwandan culture, which, like many African cultures, is community- rather than individual-oriented (Wessells and Monteiro 2001). Further, group healing can help people reconnect with others, thus functioning as an important antidote to disconnection from other people which is one of the consequences of victimization (Saakvitne, Gamble, Pearlman, and Lev 2000). Finally, reconciliation between groups requires the engagement of the whole population, and group healing is a way of involving more people in interventions.

The development of our approach began in the U.S. and continued in Rwanda in early 1999. We first used the whole approach in the summer of 1999 in a two-week seminar/workshop in Kigali that we conducted with about 35 Rwandese staff of local and international NGOs that engage in healing and community building. This workshop included brief psycho-educational lectures based on theory, research and experience with mass violence and complex (Allen 2001; Herman 1992; McCann and Pearlman 1990a; Pearlman and Saakvitne 1995; Esterling, L'Abate, Murray and Pennebaker 1999; Saakvitne et al. 2000; Staub 1989, 1998, 1999, 2003), extensive large- and small-group discussions after each lecture and an experiential component that gave participants opportunities to apply the material to their personal experience. The objective was to provide participants with information that they could later use in their work with groups in the community, as well as with opportunities to reflect on and process some of their own genocide-related experiences.

There were four elements of the training which remained components of our subsequent work in Rwanda:

1. *Understanding the effects of trauma and victimization and avenues to healing.*

This approach blends an understanding of complex psychological trauma with a community-centered approach to recovery. Research has shown that understanding psychological trauma, including both the symptoms of post-traumatic stress disorder (American Psychiatric Association 1994) and the profound effects of traumatic experiences on the self, perceptions of people and the world, and one's spirituality, can contribute to healing (Allen 2001; Rosenbloom and Williams 1999; Saakvitne et al. 2000; Staub 1998). Understanding the psychological consequences of victimization on oneself and others can normalize these consequences and make it easier for people to engage with and support each other.

Traumatized people often carry their pain and sense of danger into the present. Engagement with their painful experiences—remembering the events and feeling the emotions related to what happened--under empathic, supportive conditions, can help people move constructively into the future. Providing people with a framework for recovery offers hope, a fundamental aspect of healing (Saakvitne et al. 2000), and can also help them gain new trust in, and reconnect with, people. Giving meaning to one's painful experience is another important aspect of healing and indeed, some research has shown that traumatic experiences stimulate a search for meaning (Tokayer 2002). Encouraging people to talk about their painful experiences, or exposure, can overcome the avoidance that maintains trauma symptoms (Foa, Keane, & Friedman 2000). While there is some disagreement about the need for survivors to talk about their traumatic experiences (Bonnano, Noll, Putnam, O'Neill, and Trickett 2003), the preponderance of clinical and empirical evidence suggests that doing so is helpful for many survivors. Survivors of sudden, traumatic loss also require a framework for understanding traumatic grief and the need for mourning (Rando 1993). Victims can create meaning by symbolizing or representing traumatic experiences through narratives, dramatizations, or art (Harvey 1996; Herman 1992; Lantz 1996; Newman, Riggs, and Roth 1997; Pennebaker and Beall 1986).

We provide a broader understanding of the psychological aftermath of traumatic experiences, "beyond PTSD," helping people understand the behavioral, cognitive, emotional, interpersonal, spiritual, and physiological sequelae of violence. We also convey to participants that trauma does not imply psychopathology or dysfunction. Furthermore, communities can use a neighbor-to-neighbor approach to address trauma: we support people in participating actively in their own recovery, and in empathically engaging with and supporting each other. This framework seems to have energized and empowered the people with whom we have worked in Rwanda.

2. *Understanding the roots of genocide.* People often see genocide as incomprehensible evil and their own suffering as unique. Examining the societal, cultural and psychological influences that lead to extreme violence shows that such violence is the outcome of a human process. This humanizes the victim, as well as the perpetrator, and point to avenues for prevention. Understanding the roots of violence and learning about similar ways that others have suffered can both help survivors see their common humanity with others, mitigate negative attitudes toward themselves, and help them see perpetrators (as well as passive bystanders) as human beings, in spite of their horrible actions. It can also reduce the defensives of perpetrators (and passive bystanders) and make it more likely that they acknowledge their responsibility.

We hypothesized that exploration of the influences that lead to genocide, based primarily on the conception developed by Staub (1989; 1996; 1999; 2003) and enriched by other conceptions (see reviews in Chorbajian and Shirinian

1999; Totten, Parsons and Charny 1997) would contribute both to healing and reconciliation. In our brief lectures about the origins of genocide, we did not discuss how the influences we noted apply to Rwanda (see, however, Staub 1999). Instead, we presented the concepts and their application to other genocides (Staub 1989), and then asked the participants to apply them to Rwanda. They did so very effectively.

3. *Understanding basic psychological needs.* The frustration of basic psychological needs by social conditions is one cause of groups turning against other groups (Burton 1990; Kelman 1990; Staub 1989). Traumatic experiences frustrate or disrupt basic needs (McCann and Pearlman 1990a; Pearlman 2003), and healing promotes the fulfillment of those needs. Based on this, we hypothesized that understanding basic psychological needs could contribute to understanding the origins of genocide and its impact on people, and further promote healing. Basic psychological needs on which our approach focuses include security or safety, trust, esteem, positive identity, feelings of effectiveness and control, positive connections to other people, a comprehension of reality and of one's own place in the world, and transcendence (or spiritual needs) (McCann and Pearlman 1990a; Pearlman and Saakvitne 1995; Saakvitne et al. 2000; Staub 1989, 2003).

4. *Engagement with experience.* We had participants engage with their experiences during the genocide and share their stories with each other, in an empathic context (Jordan, Walker and Hartling 2004). Initially, we planned to have participants engage with their experiences during the genocide by first writing about them (Pennebaker and Beall 1986). However, since about 50% of the population in Rwanda cannot write, and many have not even used writing instruments for drawing, we had them simply think about their experiences during genocide. Then we discussed the importance of empathic responding to others' experience. We provided limited training by modeling inappropriate responses such as offering advice or interrupting to tell one's own story, and by discussing genuinely empathic responding. After this, participants told their stories in small groups--and often cried with others in this process.

Informal Observations

The information we provided in our workshop about the origins of genocide and mass killing, exemplifying principles by reference to various cases, and the discussions that followed in the course of which participants applied the principles to the genocide in Rwanda, had a visibly powerful impact on participants. Learning that people elsewhere had suffered similarly and coming to understand how certain influences contribute to genocide seemed to help participants feel that they were not outside history and human experience. They seemed moved and rehumanized by the understanding that what had happened in their society is a human, albeit horrific, process. One woman said, "If this has happened to other people, then it doesn't mean that God abandoned the people of Rwanda." Echoing several others, another person said, "If we can understand how this happened, we can act to prevent it in the future." Applying the influences leading to genocide to what happened in Rwanda, participants seemed to gain a deep, *experiential understanding* of the roots of genocide in Rwanda.

Two aspects of the trauma material we presented seemed especially useful for participants. The idea that the widely varied behavioral, emotional, cognitive, interpersonal, and spiritual impact they experienced and observed in others are normal responses to abnormal events was depathologizing. And the notion that traumatized people can be effective in their lives seemed to provide hope.

We intended our participants to use the new material with groups in the community, in combination with their traditional methods or approaches, the latter presumably reflecting their understanding of the community, its history and needs (see Wessells and Monteiro 2001). Part of the seminar focused on integrating our approach with the participants' own varied approaches. We encouraged them to develop further this *integrated approach* in their work with groups in the community.

Measuring impact

The evaluation of interventions to reduce conflict between groups is mostly informal, anecdotal, rather than systematic research (Ross & Rothman, 1999). We conducted an experimental study to assess the impact of our intervention on the members of community groups that the practitioners who participated in our seminar worked with (Staub et al. 2005).

Following the seminar, some of the participants used their *integrated* approach in their work with community groups comprising the different segments of the community: Tutsis, among them women who were tortured through rape; widows; HIV-affected persons; Hutus; and Twa (about 1 percent of the population). In our evaluation these groups comprise the experimental condition. Other staff from the same organizations who had not participated in the workshop used their usual or *traditional* approach with equally diverse community groups. Both types of groups (integrated and traditional) were newly created for the purpose of the study, meeting three hours, twice a week, for three weeks. Participants were 194 people, with approximately 60 percent self-identified as Tutsi, 16 percent as Hutu or Twa, and 23 percent provided some changes in self-identification across measurements. *Control* groups were also created, which did not receive any treatment but were evaluated for changes over time.

The activities of the groups were diverse, some focusing on healing, others on community-building, with the seminar material integrated into these activities in the experimental groups, and the nature of these groups balanced in the *integrated* and *traditional* groups. All groups filled out questionnaires at three points in time: before they began to meet, just after facilitators stopped working with them, and two months after that. Members of the *control* groups filled out the same questionnaires at about the same times.

In the *integrated* groups led by the facilitators who participated in our seminar, trauma symptoms decreased both over time and in comparison to the other groups. Symptoms increased somewhat in both the *traditional* groups led by practitioners who did not participate in our seminar and the *control* group. We also found an increase in positive orientation toward the other group in the groups led by facilitators we trained, both over time and in comparison to the groups in the other conditions. The elements of this positive orientation included (1) seeing the genocide as having complex origins (rather than simply resulting from the evil nature of the perpetrators, or bad leaders), (2) expressing willingness to work with the other group for important goals (e.g., a better future), and (3) expressing willingness to forgive the other group if its members acknowledged what they did and apologized for the group's actions (see Staub et al. 2005; Staub and Pearlman 2006).

In summary, relatively limited participation in groups led by facilitators/practitioners who participated in our seminars contributed to both healing and to a more positive attitude by groups toward each other. We subsequently further developed elements of this approach, which we used in our work with varied groups.

Working with National Leaders

We conducted two seminar/workshops with high-level national leaders in August 2001 and January 2003, both organized in collaboration with the National Unity and Reconciliation Commission (NURC). The participants in the two workshops included government ministers, members of the supreme court, heads of national commissions (electoral, constitutional), the heads of the national prison system, commissioners of the NURC, heads of political parties, members of parliament, etc. The seminars were ethnically mixed, including both Tutsi and Hutu leaders.

These seminars aimed to advance leaders' understanding of the impact of genocide both on themselves and on the people of Rwanda, and to consider avenues to healing and reconciliation that leaders might promote. Three important goals were to provide an understanding of (1) how genocide and mass killing originate, (2) the impact of the genocide on the population and the leaders themselves and some avenues to healing and (3) policies and practices in the society that might reduce the likelihood of renewed violence and promote positive relations between groups. The social context and the pressing problems facing Rwanda during each of the seminars were different. In 2001, in the context of the planned gacaca, or community justice process, leaders were concerned that one undesirable byproduct would be retraumatization of the population. Another related concern was that the testimonies of horrible actions in front of the gacaca would create renewed anger and possibly renewed violence. By January 2003, a large number of prisoners were released earlier that month, and Rwanda already had its first experiences with some pilot work with gacaca.

In both seminars we discussed the important roles in generating group violence of scapegoating, destructive ideologies, devaluation of members of another group, unhealed wounds from past traumatic experiences, excessive respect for authority, the absence of pluralism, the gradual evolution of increasing violence, and the role of bystanders--both people inside a group and outside groups and nations. However, in each of the seminars the leaders worked on the specific issues important at that time. In the second seminar we provided leaders with a form (see Table 1) to help them shape and evaluate policies and practices.

Table 7.1. The origins and prevention of violence between groups (from Staub 2006)

A: Starting points:

Difficult life conditions (economic, political, social change, war)
Conflict between groups

Consequences:
The resulting frustration of basic psychological needs;
Turning to a group for identity and support;
Scapegoating; (Destructive) Ideologies

B: History, culture and current practices:

Devaluation of the other	Humanizing the Other
Destructive, Exclusive Ideology	Constructive, Inclusive Ideology
Unhealed wounds	Healing of past wounds
Uncritical Respect for Authority	Moderate Respect for Authority
Monolithic Society	Pluralism (structures; processes)
Unjust Societal Arrangements	Just Social Arrangements
Passive Bystanders	Active Bystanders

C. Continuous Processes:

The evolution of harmdoing (changes in perpetrators, bystanders, institutions, social norms and culture).
The role of leaders (The role of followers)

One endpoint of each of the dimensions in table 7.1. shows influences that would make violence between groups more likely, while the other endpoint shows influences that would help prevent violence, make it less likely. We also talked about influences that would make reconciliation more or less likely (and later formulated Table 7.2. as a representation of this, see Staub 2006).

Table 7.2. Reconciliation and the prevention of new violence (from Staub 2006)

Lack of Truth	Truth (complex: shared)
Lack of Justice	Justice
Unhealed wounds	Healing of past wounds
Conflicting views of history	Shared views of history/ Shared collective memories
Lack of Contact, Superficial Contact	Deep Contact, Shared Goals
Raising children as obedient followers	Raising inclusively caring children with moral courage
Lack of understanding the roots of violence	Understanding and actions guide it

The group members considered whether particular policies and practices they have just introduced or were planning to introduce would make violence more or less likely and what they could do to shape them so that they would reduce the likelihood of future violence. Examples of how leaders dealt with some important issues/policies in Rwanda are the following:

The meaning of group. Guided by government policy of "unity," and the strong commitment of individual leaders to this policy, the use of the terms "Hutu" and "Tutsi" has been strongly discouraged and people rarely used these terms in 2001. In response to our discussion of devaluation of the "other group," seminar participants stated that there were no groups in Rwanda and that the Belgian colonizers artificially created divisions. In our discussions, participants moved toward acknowledging that, whether or not there is a biological basis for the differentiation between Hutu and Tutsi, there has been differentiation socially (in terms of interpersonal behaviors such as discrimination) and psychologically (in terms of seeing themselves and others as belonging to one or the other group). A high-status participant said at one point, "I wonder what they say about each other in their homes." Over the years in Rwanda the possibility of using the designations Hutu and Tutsi eased, but only to a limited extent. The government considers an emphasis on these group differences as divisionism. While there is not enough research and experience to offer much guidance, our understanding of the impact of victimization, group relations, and reconciliation suggests that acknowledging feelings of hostility between groups and working to overcome them is more likely to lead to reconciliation and peace than is asserting unity and not addressing such feelings.

Creating a shared history of Rwanda. After violence, each group tends to see the other as at fault and each blames the other for its own violent acts claiming these acts as necessary reactions to the other's actions or to the danger the other represents (Staub and Bar-Tal 2003). The conflicting views about what happened can rekindle hostility and violence.

Especially when groups live together, creating a history that is acceptable to both sides may be central to reconciliation (Bar-Tal 2002; Cairns and Roe 2002; PRI 2004; Staub and Bar-Tal 2003). A French-German commission of historians did this after World War II, with a focus on showing that the two countries had not always been implacable foes (Willis 1965). In our first leaders' seminar, some participants expressed the belief that history is objective, that there is only one correct factual account of events. Predominantly, however, the group recognized that there can be different perspectives on historical events and agreed that creating a shared history acceptable to all groups in Rwanda is important. They noted that the government had just convened a commission to create a history to be taught in the schools. The hope was that this history curriculum would lay the groundwork for a more peaceful future. In our seminar in 2001, in small group discussions participants considered different ideas about how such a history could be created. These included each group taking the role of the other in describing history, as well as the recognition of earlier peaceful coexistence. However, in the end many participants expressed skepticism that it would be possible to create such a history at this time, in light of the feelings generated by the recent genocide.

In our subsequent seminars/workshops in Rwanda, we experimented with our approach to understanding the roots of genocide in creating a shared history. We attempted to make past historical events comprehensible, identifying the social and psychological forces that led to discrimination and violence. By bringing understanding and empathy to historical events and actions, we hoped to help people begin to accept the other group and acknowledge their own group's blameworthy actions.

For example, in the second leaders' seminar, one of the participants referred to the "genocide" in 1959. In response to this comment, we said that as we understood it, what happened in 1959 was mass killing but not genocide (see Staub 1989 and Staub and Bar-Tal 2003 for a discussion of this distinction). We noted that the Belgian colonizers elevated the Tutsis, who ruled in their behalf. The situation of the Hutus was extremely bad and the societal arrangements unjust. We also noted the difficulty of correcting unequal relations between groups and that, lamentably, attempts to correct such injustice often include violence (Davis 1969). We noted that under the Hutu rule that followed, there was discrimination and violence against the Tutsis. Had the Hutus created more just social arrangements, the subsequent evolution toward genocide would have been less likely. In the daily anonymous written evaluations that we collect in all of our seminars, one participant wrote that this was the first time that he or she learned that the violence in 1959 was not a genocide, that it was a response to injustice. As another example of using our "understanding approach," in various seminars we applied the general conception of the origins of genocide to the evolution of the psychology and behavior of members of the Interahamwe, groups of young men in militias who were one of the primary perpetrators of the genocide (Staub 2006; see below).

Challenges of the Gacaca as a Vehicle for Justice and Reconciliation

In the gacaca process, the populace elected 250,000 people from the general population in October 2001. These people would serve as judges, in panels of 19 (their number was later reduced), in about 9,000 locations around Rwanda. Their task was to judge the large majority of the approximately 115,000 people who were in jail since 1994, accused of perpetrating the genocide. The gacaca law requires the population to be present and participate. The process moves from identifying the crimes committed—ranging from property theft to rape, murder, and the planning of violence—to establishing what community members know about the crimes committed in that community, to judging alleged perpetrators. In the course of this process, people give and hear testimonies about killing, rape, and atrocities of many kinds. Communities gather in the fields each week to engage in this process.

Members of our group agreed that, while it could have great potential positive effects, the gacaca process was likely to reactivate trauma for everyone. It might also generate renewed hostility in both groups. They expressed concern that everyone—witnesses, alleged perpetrators, judges, families of victims, people who knew alleged perpetrators as neighbors and now see them as enemies, and so on—would need support. The participants requested our help in shaping the gacaca process to promote reconciliation. We responded by initiating a seminar with community leaders and a public education campaign, which we describe below.

Work with Local Community Leaders

In June 2002, we facilitated a four-day seminar/workshop, with approximately 35 Rwandese community leaders from around the country. They were mid-level leaders and staff primarily from Ibuka (the main survivor organization, of which several constituent associations were represented, such as Avega, a widows' organization, and Profemmes, an umbrella organization for women's associations throughout the country), the Ministry of Health, and the NURC. This was the only group we worked with whose members were all Tutsi.

Our purpose was to help participants to lessen the potential negative effects and promote the potential positive effects of the gacaca, which was in its pilot phase. We, as the facilitators, and the NURC, which organized the workshop, agreed that the purposes of the gacaca process—justice, healing, and reconciliation—might be advanced if people had ways of understanding how genocide comes about. In addition, understanding psychological trauma and healing might help to minimize the retraumatization that seemed likely to occur as a result of the gacaca hearings and enable people to support each other in the process. Before we addressed these goals in the seminar, we asked participants to describe the positive effects of the gacaca they anticipated and hoped for, and the negative effects they feared.

Some examples of the anticipated positive effects included:

- The truth will be established (how relatives were killed, who should be punished);
- The process will create justice;
- The whole population will respect the decisions made because they will have taken part in the process;
- When perpetrators are punished, reconciliation will be possible;
- Over time, the effects of trauma will diminish;
- People will find out where their relatives died and can bury them with dignity, which will enable them to mourn properly;
- Those sentenced and their relatives will know their fate and can turn to the future;
- The whole society will gain closure.

Some of the potential negative effects resulting from the gacaca that people anticipated or feared included the following:

- Retraumatization may occur as people give or hear testimonies;
- Hatred will increase between families that testify and the guilty;
- Some perpetrators may testify without any spirit of repentance, just telling of their "heroic" deeds;
- Trauma may occur among people who committed genocide who feel ashamed because of their terrible crimes.

Some potential negative effects that we added, to which the group agreed, were as follows:

- New trauma as people learn about something (e.g., rape) that happened to or that was done by someone close to them;
- Renewed anger and rage by survivors, especially if they see perpetrators not sufficiently punished;
- Hostility from members of the perpetrator group who were not perpetrators, as they feel constantly accused in the course of testimonies about horrible acts by members of their group.

One additional experience important to note from this meeting is that the group rejected the notion we presented to them that there was significant conflict between Tutsis and Hutus in the pre-colonial period, even though historical analyses indicate this (see Mamdani 2002). In contrast, a report by Penal Reform International (2004) describing comments by released prisoners who went through a reeducation ("sensitization") camp before returning to their communities, show that some of the prisoners objected to the presentation of history in the camp, according to which the Belgians created differences and difficulties between Hutus and Tutsis, as a significant distortion of the truth. This is an example of conflicting views of history which, because of their apparent importance to members of the two groups, need to be addressed as part of the process of preventing future violence.

Directly presenting particular views of history, as we did in the seminar with community leaders, is less useful than exploring them in the course of discussion. This exploration is best done in the framework of understanding how certain historical events and conditions developed, which we did in all our other work in this and other seminars.

Seminars for Journalists

The way media report events can have many significant effects, either intensifying group differences and hostility or help people understand others' actions (Staub 1989; 1999). We conducted two seminars for journalists and included journalist participants in two other week-long seminars.

The first seminar, in August 1999, included 35 journalists and aimed to inform reporting by journalists, by helping them understand trauma and the roots of violence between groups. The purpose of the second, two-day seminar, in June 2002, was to help the 40 journalist participants to develop constructive ways to report on the gacaca, and thereby to promote healing and reconciliation. Understanding the origins of the events—robbery, rape, murder, killing of neighbors, and so on—investigated in the gacaca could help journalists report on them in ways that generate comprehension among the Rwandan public. Both such understanding, and understanding trauma and retraumatization can help reporters inform people about the ways they can support each other as individuals and as members of communities as they are exposed to the gacaca proceedings. Our seminar also aimed to lessen the retraumatization and vicarious trauma of journalists themselves that is almost certainly generated as they are exposed to stories of great violence and cruelty in the course of interviewing highly traumatized people (McCann and Pearlman 1990b; Figley 1995; Pyevich 2002; Saakvitne and Pearlman 1996).

Following a lecture and extensive discussion of the origins of genocide, we asked the participants to generate news stories. As an example, we applied information about the roots of genocide to understanding how a young man might have become a participant in the Interahamwe, the militia composed of young men that did a great deal of the killing. In this example, we noted the difficult economic conditions in Rwanda and lack of prospects for young men; the political parties creating youth arms, which provided connection and community as well as identity for such young men (fulfilling basic psychological needs); the history of devaluation of Tutsis and the strong propaganda against them at the time; the power of the political group they joined, and the small group of young men they became part of over them; as well as other elements (see also Staub 2006). We suggested and they developed other story ideas about how a man came to kill his own son, about someone who tried to save lives and was killed, about children of rape, about a perpetrator confessing at gacaca with no sign of remorse, and others. They worked in small groups, each group working with one scenario or story idea.

In addition to discussing ways to create stories that promote healing and reconciliation, they expressed the belief that part of their role was to promote constructive social change. They expressed concerns about and discussed limitations by the government on their freedom to report and the government's concerns about what may be considered incitement to violence.

Public Education Campaign via Radio Broadcasting

We have been working on a public education project we initiated and developed in collaboration with George Weiss, a producer, and the organization he directs, the Dutch NGO La Benevolencija/Humanitarian Tools Foundation. We developed extensive radio programs for Rwanda on the themes we have described. Radio is the most important means by which Rwandese receive information. We initiated a radio campaign that began to broadcast in 2004, consisting of a soap opera with embedded educational content as well as direct informational/educational programs. The aims are to educate and inform the Rwandan population about the roots and evolution of violence, the trauma symptoms and complex trauma that violence creates, approaches to community healing, the prevention of violence and reconciliation including justice processes. We hoped that the radio programs, which extend our approach to a large segment of the Rwandan population, will help the population find ways to recover from the psychological impact of the past, which is essential in post-conflict societies, and lead them to engage in reconciliation processes. We hoped that thereby they will help prevent new violence and build a peaceful society (Staub 2006; Staub and Pearlman 2005; Staub et al. 2005).

The goals of the program are embedded in 12 educational messages which are inserted and portrayed in implicit and creative ways in the soap opera and are explicitly discussed within a Rwandan context in the debate programs. The following are examples of these messages or "communication objectives":

1. Devaluation increases the likelihood of violence while humanization decreases it.
2. The healing of psychological wounds helps people live more satisfying lives and makes unnecessary defensive violence less likely.
3. Passivity facilitates the evolution of harm doing whereas actions by people inhibit it.
4. Varied perspectives, open communication and moderate respect for authority in society make the evolution of violence less likely.

Radio dramas can be excellent educational tools for several reasons. First, rather than using a persuasion model of learning in which people are taught by direct arguments, dramas provide an alternative form of learning by providing knowledge and promoting understanding, and modeling constructive behavior and active bystandership. Second, they provide a safe space to bring to public attention, in subtle ways, sensitive issues, possibly opening a space for discussions. Third, the entertainment element appeals to people of diverse background, thereby making the messages accessible to a large population. More specifically, radio drama is an excellent way of introducing and portraying a new community-based approach on trauma healing by informing the public about the symptoms of trauma, understanding of the trauma, and modeling appropriate ways to support and help the traumatized person.

The soap opera being broadcasted in Rwanda is called "Musekeweya" ("New Dawn"). Musekeweya is broadcasted twice weekly by the national radio station, Radio Rwanda. The main storyline portrays the evolution and cycle of conflict and violence between two villages, representing the violent story of the two groups in Rwanda, with all the influences that can lead to or prevent violence present, and with actual violence between the villages. However, the story has been developed such that while reminding the Rwandese of the past of their country, it is not possible to identify one village in the drama as either Hutu or Tutsi. The sub-storylines include themes of love, trauma, and social justice, portraying issues that Rwandese society is currently facing. A nationally representative survey showed that Musekeweya is extremely popular, with 90.6% of the population reporting that they either knew or listened to the drama, and 92 % of radio listeners reporting that they listened to the program either regularly or occasionally.

The separate journalistic programs include a debate program called "Kuki" (Why?) and a justice program called "Akuzu". These programs complement the soap opera by explicitly talking about and elaborating on the educational messages. The aim is to inform and open debates among an educated audience in Rwanda. In Kuki, every month experts are invited to elaborate and debate on how different messages apply to the situation in Rwanda. The leading journalist first introduces the topic by elaborating our approach to understanding of mass-violence, trauma, and healing, and then opens up the discussion by raising questions to the invitees. In Akuzu, one or two experts on justice related issues are invited to discuss issues related to current justice processes in Rwanda, challenges to these processes, and different aspects of the relationship between justice, trauma, healing, and reconciliation.

To ensure the quality of the programs, all the staff, including script writers and journalists, are trained on our approach on mass violence, trauma and healing and reconciliation. In addition, before broadcasting, all programs are edited not only by journalists and communication experts, but also by the academic team who gives feedback on the scripts from the perspective of the underlying psychological theories. Some of our programs have been broadcast in Burundi as well. Starting in early 2006, new programs, both a drama series and an informational program, have begun to broadcast in the Democratic Republic of the Congo. In these programs the conceptions we have been using have been adapted to the history and conditions in the Congo.

Research Evaluation of "Musekeweya"

This public education campaign includes two research elements. The first research element is based on a series of listener groups consisting of 40 participants in 10 locations around the country. A representative sample of persons now living in Rwanda is included in these groups. Listener groups are being queried over time to provide comments to the radio team about how the programs are being received and whether the communication messages are being understood (Radio La Benevolencija 2004). Radio personnel refer to such a process as "formative research," as it shapes the programs on an on-going basis.

To understand Musekeweya's social and psychological impact, an impact evaluation of the program was conducted by an independent researcher at Yale University. The evaluation team started working one year prior to the broadcast of the drama, identifying a representative sample of population in Rwanda (Paluck 2006). Two sets of communities, matched according to regional and demographic characteristics, were randomly assigned to two conditions, listeners of Musekeweya and listeners of Urunana—another educational soap opera broadcasted in Rwanda on health issues. The listeners of Urunana agreed not to listen to Musekeweya for one year. Evaluation of Musekeweya was conducted at the end of the Year One and at the end of Year Two of broadcast through 425 interviews, community discussions, and focus groups (Paluck and Green 2004). The evaluations after the first and second year of broadcast revealed several positive impacts of the drama. Listeners of Musekeweya demonstrated higher level of trust and a greater belief in the importance of trust in community, a belief on the importance of meaningful contact, on the importance of sharing one's past experiences for trauma healing, they expressed ideas more openly, invited more open debate and cooperation in their communities, and were more likely to act as active bystanders (egg. speaking up when they disagree) (Paluck 2006).

Conclusions

Our work in Rwanda has aimed to contribute to healing from psychological wounds, to foster reconciliation, and to help to prevent violence and build a peaceful society. One major issue is the evaluation of the benefits of such work; another is, if there are benefits, how they can be maximized.

The experimental evaluation of our first project and the independent evaluation of the radio drama showed positive effects, as summarized above. Less formal and anecdotal indicators suggested that our later work also had positive effects. In anonymous evaluations that we conducted both every day and at the end of each seminar/workshop, participants overwhelmingly said that their experiences were very useful to them. Frequently, they commented that all Rwandans should receive the information they gained.

We organized our first project in collaboration with a local NGO, le Mouvement Chretien pour l'Evangelisation, le Counselling et la Reconciliation (MOUCECORE). Our later seminars, in collaboration with the NURC, were all formally opened and closed by high-level officials. In introducing a seminar with journalists, the speaker, who had participated in our first leaders' seminar a year earlier, gave a detailed and highly accurate summary of the key points from that seminar. In conversations with participants in our prior seminars, including leaders, we have heard them express ideas and discuss policy matters using concepts and orientations we have presented and developed in our seminars. The continued interest of the NURC, leaders, and journalists to work with us is another positive indicator. Not long after the January 2003 leaders' seminar, a BBC interviewer asked the head of the NURC, who participated in the seminar, what the curriculum in the reeducation camps for released prisoners would include. She replied that they intended to teach them about the origins of genocide, about the psychological damage to both survivors and perpetrators as a result of the genocide, and the need for everyone to heal (However, we don't know whether these intentions, apparently influenced by our work with NURC, have actually been fulfilled).

An important and often difficult issue for those who engage in third-party efforts is to extend the benefits of their work beyond the small numbers of people with whom they work directly (Ross and Rothman 1999). We have worked with leaders, whose willingness and interest in working with us has been astounding, and with facilitators who work with groups in the community, in order to maximize the reach of our work. The creation of the public education campaign mentioned is another very effective way to extend whatever beneficial influence our approach might have to the whole society.

The success of limited interventions like ours will depend on the political and social processes in the country. By working with leaders and journalists, by extending the reach of these efforts through radio programs and training trainers, we hope to have some positive influence on these processes. But of course the social and political processes depend on many factors. The challenges to the creation of a viable social, political, and cultural system are great in Rwanda. Some of the challenges include the psychological consequences of past history and the genocide; the destruction of basic infrastructure, social institutions and the impact on culture (like the justice system and communal relations) of the civil war and genocide; social problems like profound poverty and HIV/AIDS; and the social upheavals mentioned above.

The more the government ensures security, allows the expansion of pluralism, and succeeds in ensuring that people can expect just relations between groups (Leatherman, DeMars, Gaffney and Vayrynen 1999), the more hope people will have for a better future. Improving economic conditions in the country would also help. While there are many constructive government policies and practices along these lines, including equality in access to education, some others that we have mentioned, which may be the result of past events and their consequences, limit open discussion and political processes and are likely to make reconciliation more difficult. The international community, whose passivity in the face of the genocide (Powers 2002) was so extreme that it might be regarded as evil (Staub 1999), could help in varied realms. The indications are, however, that increasing passivity again characterizes the behavior of the international community.

A final issue is the relevance of the approach we have developed to other places and times. Information about the impact of violent victimization and other traumatic experiences and about avenues to healing; coming to understand roots of violence against one's group and oneself as part of the group, as well as one's group's violence against others and the nature of one's own role in it (as perpetrator, passive bystander, and so on); and engagement with painful experiences under supportive conditions are important for promoting healing and reconciliation between groups in many places around the world.

Presumably this approach or elements of it could be applied to the Israeli-Palestinian conflict, to reconciliation and peace-making between Sunni and Shiite Moslems and Kurds in Iraq with their history of antagonism, as well as to Serbs, Croats, and Muslims who lived in the former Yugoslavia. We invite and encourage others to adapt the approach we have developed to other situations, and to assess its effectiveness. In applying this approach we believe that it is important to offer, not to impose; to augment, not to replace; to collaborate, not to dominate. Practices based on such attitudes are more likely than their converse to open doors and to assist people.

References

African Rights 2002. *Tribute to Courage.* Kigali, Rwanda: African Rights.

Allen, J. G. 2001. *Traumatic Relationships and Serious Mental Disorders*. West Sussex: John Wiley and Sons, Ltd.

Arvay, M. J. 2001. Secondary Traumatic Stress Among Trauma Counsellors: What Does the Research Say? *International Journal for the Advancement of Counselling, 23*, 283-293.

Bar-Tal, D. 2002. "Collective Memory of Physical Violence: Its Contribution to the Culture of Violence." In E. Cairns and M. D. Roe, eds., *Memories in Conflict*. London: Macmillan.

Bonnano, G., Noll, J., Putnam, F., O'Neill, M., and Trickett, P. K. 2003. Predicting the Willingness to Disclose Childhood Sexual Abuse from Measures of Repressive Coping and Dissociative Tendencies. *Child Maltreatment 8*(4), 302-318.

Burton, J. W. 1990. *Conflict: Resolution and Prevention*. New York: St. Martin's Press.

Cairns, E., and Roe, M. D. 2002. *Memories in Conflict*. London: Macmillan.

Chorbajian, L., and Shirinian, G. 1999. *Studies in Comparative Genocide*. New York: St. Martin's Press.

Davis, J. L. 1969. "The Curve of Rising and Declining Satisfactions as a Cause of Some Great Revolutions and a Contained Rebellion." In H.D.Graham and T.R. Gurr, eds. *Violence in America*. New York: Bantam Books.

De la Rey, C. 2001. "Reconciliation in Divided Societies." In D.J. Christie, R.V. Wagner, and D.D. Winter, eds. *Peace, Conflict, and Violence: Peace Psychology for the 21st Century*. Upper Saddler River, New Jersey: Prentice Hall.

Des Forges, A. 1999. *Leave None to Tell the Story: Genocide in Rwanda*. New York: Human Rights Watch.

Esterling, B. A., L'Abate, L., Murray, E. J., and Pennebaker, J. W. 1999. Empirical Foundations for Writing in Prevention and Psychotherapy: Mental and Physical Health Outcomes. *Clinical Psychology Review, 19*(1), 79-96.

Figley, C. R. 1995. "Compassion Fatigue as Secondary Traumatic Stress Disorder: An Overview." In C.R. Figley, ed. *Compassion Fatigue: Coping with Secondary Traumatic Stress Disorder in Those Who Treat the Traumatized*. New York: Brunner/Mazel.

Foa, E. B., Keane, T. M., and Friedman, M. J., eds. 2000. *Effective Treatments for PTSD: Practice Guidelines from the International Society for Traumatic Stress Studies*. New York: Guilford Press.

Harvey, M. 1996. An Ecological View of Psychological Trauma and Trauma Recovery. *Journal of Traumatic Stress, 9,* 3-23.

Herman, J. 1992. *Trauma and Recovery: The Aftermath of Violence from Domestic Abuse to Political Terror.* New York: Basic Books.

Jordan, J. V., Walker, M., and Hartling, L. M., eds. 2004. *The Complexity of Connection: Writings from the Jean Baker Miller Training Institute.* New York: Guilford Publications.

Kelman, H. C. 1990. "Applying a Human Needs Perspective to the Practice of Conflict Resolution: The Israeli-Palestinian Case." In J. Burton, ed., *Conflict: Human Needs Theory.* New York: St. Martin's Press.

Lantz, J. 1996. Logotherapy as Trauma Therapy. *Crisis Intervention and Time-Limited Treatment, 2*(3), 243-253.

Leatherman, J., DeMars, W., Gaffney, P. D., and Vayrynen, R. 1999. *Breaking Cycles of Violence: Conflict Prevention in Intrastate Crises.* CT: Kumarian Press, Inc.

Lederach, J. P. 1995. *Building Peace: Sustainable Reconciliation.* Tokyo: United Nations University.

———. 1997. *Building Peace: Sustainable Reconciliation in Divided Societies.* Washington, D.C.: United States Institute of Peace Press.

Lerner, M. 1980. *The Belief in a Just World: A Fundamental Delusion.* New York: Plenum Press.

Lifton, R. J. 1986. *The Nazi Doctors*. New York: Basic Books

MacNair, R. M. 2002. *Perpetration-Induced Traumatic Stress: The Psychological Consequences of Killing.* Westport, CT: Praeger Publishers/Greenwood Publishing Group, Inc.

Mamdani, M. 2002. *When Victims Become Killers.* Princeton: Princeton University Press.

McCann, I. L., and Pearlman, L. A. 1990a. *Psychological Trauma and the Adult Survivor: Theory, Therapy, and Transformation.* New York: Brunner/Mazel.

———. 1990b. Vicarious Traumatization: A Framework for Understanding the Psychological Effects of Working with Victims. *Journal of Traumatic Stress, 3* (1), 131-149.

Montville, J. V. 1993. "The Healing Function in Political Conflict Resolution." In D.J.D. Sandole and H. Van der Merve, eds., *Conflict Resolution Theory and Practice: Integration and Application.* Manchester, England: Manchester University Press.

Newman, E., Riggs, D. S. and Roth, S. 1997. Thematic Resolution, PTSD, and Complex PTSD: The Relationship between Meaning and Trauma-Related Diagnoses. *Journal of Traumatic Stress, 10*(2), 197-213.

Oliner, S. B., and Oliner, P. 1988. *The Altruistic Personality: Rescuers of Jews in Nazi Europe.* New York: Free Press.

Paluck, E. L. 2006. The second year of a "new dawn": Year Two evidence for the impact of the Rwandan reconciliation radio drama Musekeweya. *La Benevolenciya Evaluation Report.* Unpublished manuscript.

———. and Green, D. P. 2004 (May/June). *Overview and Working Plan for the LaBenevolencija Impact Evaluation Study: The Impact of Musekeweya: Changes in Knowledge, Attitudes, And Behaviors. A Randomized Controlled Trial.* Unpublished manuscript.

Pearlman, L. A. 2003. *Trauma and Attachment Belief Scale Manual.* Los Angeles, CA: Western Psychological Services.

———. and Saakvitne, K. W. 1995. *Trauma and the Therapist: Countertransference and Vicarious Traumatization in the Treatment of Incest Survivors.* New York: W. W. Norton.

Pennebaker, J. W., and Beall, S. K. 1986. Confronting a Traumatic Event: Toward an Understanding of Inhibition and Disease. *Journal of Abnormal Psychology, 95*, 274-281.

Powers, S. 2002. *A Problem from Hell: America and the Age of Genocide*. New York: Basic Books

Penal Reform International 2004 (May). Research Report on the Gacaca VI. From Camp to Hill, the Reintegration of Released Prisoners. PRI Rwanda. BP 370. Kigali, Rwanda.

Proceedings of Stockholm International Forum on Truth, Justice and Reconciliation, 2002.

Prunier, G. 1995. *The Rwanda Crisis: History of a Genocide*. New York: Columbia University Press.

Pyevich, C. M. 2002. *The Relationship among Cognitive Schemata, Job-Related Traumatic Exposure, and PTSD in Journalists*. Doctoral dissertation, University of Tulsa.

Rando, T. A. 1993. *Treatment of Complicated Mourning*. Champaign, IL: Research Press.

Rhodes, G., Allen, G. J., Nowinski, J., and Cillessen, A. 2002. "The Violent Socialization Scale: Development and Initial Validation." In J. Ulmer and L. Athens eds., *Violent Acts and Violentization: Assessing, Applying, and Developing Lonnie Athens' Theories*, vol. 4. Elsevier Science Ltd.

Rosenbloom, D. J., and Williams, M. B. 1999. *Life after Trauma*. New York: Guilford.

Ross, M. H. and Rothman, J. 1999. *Theory and Practice in Ethnic Conflict Management: Theorizing Success and Failure*. New York: Macmillian.

Rutagengwa, T. 2004 (November). *La Benevolencija Radio Listening Clubs Rapport de Feedback sur les Episodes 22, 23, 24 et 25*. Unpublished manuscript.

Saakvitne, K. W., Gamble, S.G., Pearlman, L. A and Lev, B. T. 2000. *Risking Connection: A Training Curriculum for Working with Survivors of Childhood Abuse.* Lutherville, MD: Sidran Foundation & Press.

———., Pearlman, L.A. and the Staff of the Traumatic Stress Institute 1996. *Transforming the Pain: A Workbook on Vicarious Traumatization*. New York: W.W. Norton.

Staub, E. 1978. *Positive Social Behavior and Morality: Social and Personal Influences* (Vol. 1). New York: Academic Press.

———. 1989. *The roots of evil: The origins of genocide and other group violence*. New York: Cambridge University Press.

———. 1996. The Cultural-Societal Roots of Violence: The Examples of Genocidal Violence and of Contemporary Youth Violence in the United States. *American Psychologist, 51*, 17-132.

———. 1998. "Breaking the Cycle of Genocidal Violence: Healing and Reconciliation." In J. Harvey, ed., *Perspectives on Loss*. Washington, DC: Taylor and Francis.

———. 1999. The Origins and Prevention of Genocide, Mass Killing and Other Collective Violence. *Peace and Conflict: Journal of Peace Psychology, 5*, 303-337.

———. 2003. *The Psychology of Good and Evil: Why Children, Adults and Groups Help and Harm Others*. New York: Cambridge University Press.

———. 2006. Reconciliation after Genocide, Mass Killing or Intractable Conflict: Understanding the Roots of Violence, Psychological Recovery and Steps toward a General Theory. *Political Psychology (December)*.

———. and Bar-Tal, D. 2003. "Genocide, Mass Killing and intractable Conflict: Roots, Evolution, Prevention and Reconciliation." In D. Sears, L. Huddy, & R. Jarvis, eds., *Handbook of Political Psychology*. New York: Oxford University Press.

———. and Pearlman, L. A. 2001. "Healing, Reconciliation, and Forgiving after Genocide and Other Collective Violence." In S. J. Helmick and R. L. Petersen eds., *For-*

giveness and Reconciliation: Religion, Public Policy and Conflict Transformation. Radnor, PA: Templeton Foundation Press.

———. 2005. "Advancing Healing and Reconciliation." In Barbanel, L & Sternberg, R. eds., *Psychological Interventions in Times of Crisis.* New York: Springer-Verlag.

———., Gubin, A., and Hagengimana, A. 2005. Healing, reconciliation, and the prevention of violence after genocide or mass killing: An Intervention and Its Experimental Evaluation in Rwanda. *Journal of Clinical and Social Psychology. 24* (3), 297-334.

Tokayer, N. 2002. Spirituality and the Psychological and Physical Symptoms of Trauma. (Doctoral Dissertation, University of Connecticut, 2002). *Dissertation Abstracts International, 63*, 1052.

Totten, S., Parsons, W. S. and Charny, I. W. (Eds.) 1997. *Century of Genocide.* New York: Garland Publishing.

Uvin, P. 2003. *Wake up Some Policy Proposals for the International Community in Rwanda.* Unpublished manuscript, June 2003.

Wessells, M. and Monteiro, C. 2001. "Psychosocial Intervention and Post-War Reconstruction in Angola: Interweaving Western and Traditional Approaches." In D. J. Christie, R. V. Wagner, & D. D. Winter eds., *Peace, Conflict and Violence: Peace Psychology for the 21st Century.* Upper Saddler River, New Jersey: Prentice Hall.

Willis, F. R. 1965. *France, Germany, and the New Europe, 1945-1963.* Palo Alto: Stanford University Press.

8

The Contribution of Trauma Healing to Peacebuilding in Southeast Europe

Amela Puljek-Shank and Randall Puljek-Shank

In August 2002 we arrived in Sarajevo to begin coordinating the peacebuilding, relief, and development work of Mennonite Central Committee (MCC). Based on our experience and that of MCC's partners who are engaged in long-term peacebuilding work in Bosnia and Herzegovina, Croatia, Serbia, and Kosovo/Kosova, we see healing of psychological trauma as an increasingly important and often-overlooked factor in peacebuilding. The implementation of trauma education as a peacebuilding strategy in societies that have experienced widespread violent conflict is necessary in this healing process.

Certain experiences, values, and theoretical frameworks led us to a conviction of the importance of trauma healing. Narratives and shame are useful perspectives for understanding the effects of trauma on society. Also, a look at the cultural and societal context in which we are working shows how this affects the possibilities for and modes of trauma healing. A section of this chapter, on the types of trauma healing work, covers approaches and methodologies used in the trauma healing process. The conclusion integrates the ramifications of our experience for ongoing peacebuilding work in Southeast Europe (SEE) and in other post conflict situations.

Two groups that we have worked with are people in helping professions and peacebuilders, who have the potential to be multipliers. We work on developing participants' awareness of their own trauma and making elements like narratives and shame more visible. Since trauma healing at a broad societal level requires changing narratives, steadily developing a critical mass of individuals with this awareness, through partnerships with similar local organizations across the region, is an important way to extend our effectiveness.

We began our work with certain values and approaches. The importance of these values and our understanding of them have become clearer as we make decisions about which initiatives to support and what approaches to use. Values also become clearer as we contrast our work to other peacebuilding efforts. It is difficult to separate values from approaches, as each reflects the other. They are values in the sense that they are beginning points and initial assumptions which inform the approaches that we have used in peacebuilding and trauma healing. As approaches and strategies of supporting local peacebuilding efforts, these are subject to evaluation and revision, based on their effectiveness.

Key Values/Approaches

Key values that influence and guide our work are a *grassroots focus*, concentration on *long-term processes*, and an emphasis on *local ownership*, *contextualized projects*, and the importance of *relationship*. These values are guided by the Anabaptist[1] religious background of our work, the values of MCC which have developed over its more than 85 years of work, and our own life experience and training.

The importance of these values is echoed in an analysis of Mennonite peacebuilding by anthropologist Sally Engle Merry (2002). She identifies two key features of Mennonite peacebuilding efforts as leaving control in the hands of local parties and an emphasis on grassroots participation. Merry also identifies key terms and practices from Mennonite peacebuilding work worldwide, including the importance of witness and presence, following the lead of partners and not seeking control of projects, a commitment to long-term presence, an emphasis on working from the edge (in the sense of working with marginalized individuals and organizations), and entry into conflict settings through relationship-building.

We will try to explain these values in a bit more detail as we see them being relevant in our work. In its projects, Mennonite Central Committee strives to address basic human needs. These needs, or the lack of fulfillment of human needs, are most acutely felt at the margins of society. In the case of Southeast Europe this means that many of our projects are focused on refugees, elderly, and children. Because of our *grassroots focus*, we work with local partner organizations that are in direct connection with these populations. While our peace projects include a broad range of the population to strengthen key peace constituencies (i.e.: religious communities and veterans), we work mostly with grassroots organizations. This value impacts our support of trauma healing in that we attempt to strengthen and empower those who are in contact with traumatized populations.

A focus on *long-term processes,* guided by John Paul Lederach's (1997) peacebuilding framework, identifies a strategic emphasis on initiatives at the level of subsystems and 5-10 year time frames. In terms of peacebuilding and trauma healing, 20+ year generational work is required. This is longer than many Non-Governmental Organization (NGO) projects that focus on trauma through individual or group therapy, and the interest is at the level where both individual and collective trauma affects society. Some of the ways that this impact happens are in patterns of communication, identity narratives, and relationships. Change at these levels is only visible when looking over a longer period of time.

Local ownership is both a value and an orientation towards working in other cultural contexts. It is connected to MCC's work as a development organization over many years and includes understandings of the conditions needed to create substantive change in societal systems. We often encounter foreign organizations creating or attempting to create new institutions. By institutions we mean NGOs or other organizations which have a distinct identity and mission that are sustained over a period of years or decades. While creating new institutions is critical, our work supports and encourages existing institutions (mostly NGOs, although not exclusively) that are innovators in their own societies. A recent critique on the emphasis on local ownership by Hannah Reich (2006) questions whether it is possible for outside organizations that provide funding to truly develop partnerships with local peacebuilding organizations. Although this is a valid concern, a smaller monetary value of grants, over several years and careful selection of partners, allows local ownership to be maintained.

Encouraging existing local initiatives and change agents brings certain consequences and methods of working, as well as difficulties. A frequent challenge for foreign organizations is having the patience and willingness to allow local initiatives to develop. Such initiatives often need encouragement and certainly depend on financial resources, but the key question is how foreign organizations can avoid becoming "owners." By owners we mean the ones who are perceived as being responsible for the program or projects, and whose support if withdrawn means that the program or the projects will end.

This value of local ownership is reflected in the way that MCC's work in trauma healing has developed since 2002 in which an important component is first to listen and understand what is already happening in the region in the field of trauma healing. Once this process happens, it is possible to sense how to augment these existing initiatives. However, this approach takes time and careful listening to understand the needs and how best to meet them.

When we speak of the value of *contextualized projects,* we mean adapting methodologies for working in the local cultural and societal context and even developing our own methodologies through a constant process of learning and evaluation. We find a frequent importing of new concepts and theoretical frameworks to guide peacebuilding work, even at the level of incorporation of English terms. This "importing" process often does not recognize the existing professional terminology or the importance of the process of developing new concepts and terminology to describe both the current societal reality and ways to move forward.

Relationship as a framework for understanding conflict transformation has been written about and supported by many other writers, among those who have influenced us is John Paul Lederach (1997). In the work of MCC, this has been reflected by a strategic emphasis on presence among all "sides" of the conflict in SEE, even in Serbia when it was subject to international sanctions. In understanding how relationships impact our projects, we see paying attention to the long-term connection between MCC and its partner organizations, more so than one built around concrete projects. Relationship is also an important value for working in SEE, and many other parts of the world, where cultures emphasize attention to first knowing about a potential partner (background) and only then focusing on working together.

These values and approaches are interconnected and support each other. Local ownership leads naturally to contextualized projects, and contextualized projects can lead to local ownership. A focus on relationships is conducive to fostering long-term processes and local ownership. In a later section, we will explore how these values are put into practice in concrete projects.

Personal and Theoretical Framework

Before continuing it may be helpful to say a bit about our own backgrounds. Amela grew up in Bosnia and during the war experienced the trauma of being a refugee. Experiences in the war taught her many life lessons and one of the major ones was how to move from being a victim to surviving and to thriving (Herman 1997). Personal work has deepened her understanding of trauma and its affects on society and thus prompted her to continue to learn and work in this field. Randall was born in the United States and first came to Bosnia during the war. His exposure to trauma healing was first through accompanying Amela and after returning to Bosnia with a sensitization to trauma. Randall slowly became convinced of the importance of trauma in the process of peacebuilding.

Our training and perspective is not in therapy but rather in peacebuilding training and facilitation. Because of this, we do not look at trauma healing from only an individual perspective. To be sure, trauma impacts individuals deeply and trauma healing is likewise both very personal and individual. As peacebuilders and trainers, we are interested in the wider societal impact of trauma. We have found that this impact on society is large, whether it is considered from the lens of working in a traumatized society (a society that has experienced collective trauma) or a society made up of traumatized individuals. For us the term *collective trauma* is helpful for understanding the impact of certain traumatic events on groups and group identity (Thompson 2000; Volkan 1990). Collective traumas are events which impact a large number of individuals, for example the 3-year siege of Sarajevo, or the mass refugee exodus of Serbs as a result of Operation Storm in Croatia in August of 1995.

Several key concepts have been instrumental in shaping our own understanding. One of these is the trauma healing model of Olga Botcharova (2001).

This model is helpful for understanding the connection between traumatic events that happened to individuals and the role of narratives about the other (perpetrating) group. Based on the assertion that from the perspective of the perpetrator, an act of violence is often justified because of a perceived hurt which is amplified through a process of dehumanizing the other, reconciliation in this model requires the willingness to grieve the loss, rehumanize the enemy, and eventually create new narratives for understanding the joint history of both perpetrator and victim.

Another helpful concept is the distinction between reconciliation of the head and that of the heart (Kraybill 1998). Kraybill's model starts with the understanding that hurt takes place in the context of an existing relationship. The initial reaction is often one of withdrawing from contact with others. Sometimes there is an intellectual (head) desire to reconcile even though there is not yet emotional (heart) readiness. This can be seen in SEE where people do often talk about reconciliation, but it is frequently a quick and intellectual form of reconciliation. We understand the difficulty of creating real reconciliation and the many conditions that need to be created, but still hold out the possibility that reconciliation of the heart is eventually possible.

A third helpful concept is the Enemy/Aggressor and Survivor/Victim Cycle (Yoder 2005) which helps in understanding how the victim can become an aggressor and how aggressors many times are victims as well. The perspective of those locked in violent conflicts is often black and white; where one side is good and the enemy side is evil. However, the cycles broaden understanding of conflicts and encourage reexamination of where and who an individual's group is in this model.

We began this work with a conviction of the importance of narratives as a way for understanding conflict, peacebuilding, and trauma healing.[2] While this was a bias from the beginning, the functional role of narratives in trauma education has only been confirmed during these years of living in Bosnia and offering seminars about trauma. Accordingly, Vamik Volkan's work (1990) related to the connection between key events, group identity, and trauma has been helpful. "Chosen traumas" and "Chosen glories" are key concepts in this approach, which refer to the importance attached to particular historical incidents in a group's narrative. In fact Volkan uses the importance placed in Serb narratives on the loss to the Ottomans at Kosovo Polje in 1389 as a key example of a "chosen trauma" around which the meaning of subsequent Serb identity has been constructed. Another helpful concept is "Egoism of victimization" (Mack 1990). In SEE, it is expressed as the strong sense of victimization among many groups and the strong identity as victims, without the ability to critically look at the participation of their own group in the various regional wars or the possibility of becoming perpetrators in future acts of large-scale violence.

Another important connection between trauma and peacebuilding is transgenerational transmission of traumas. One way that this can happen is through narratives related to particular events which function as "chosen traumas" and "chosen glories." Another is transmission from parents who were traumatized to children where symptoms of trauma can be observed (Volkan 2000). A final method of transmission is secondary traumatization, which can affect caregivers as well as people who are close to traumatized individuals. We have encountered a high degree of secondary traumatization among people who work with traumatized individuals—even among professionals who are aware of the risks of secondary traumatization.

Why is Trauma Healing Essential for Peacebuilding?

Long lasting peace cannot be built without work on traumas that have been created through violent conflicts. The plural is used since rarely do we find only one violent conflict and only one trauma. The most common experience is that there were multiple conflicts that lasted for generations, which thus created multiple traumas within society. Trauma healing is an essential part of the peacebuilding process, and work on trauma includes the work on individual and collective trauma through therapy work as well as trauma education. Therapy can be used on both individual and collective levels through different kinds of therapeutic frameworks. Trauma education consists of seminars/trainings or classes that focus on teaching what trauma is, how it happens, what its symptoms are, and how to help traumatized individuals or groups. At this level of education, the key is to offer space for learning about trauma rather than on creating a diagnosis. In this learning environment the participants come to understand, many for the first time, what trauma is and that it is natural to have certain reactions and symptoms as a result of traumatic events during and after violent conflict. Please see the section "How we work at trauma education" for more details.

Working on these key concepts of trauma education creates space for listening and understanding from the group about where their conflict comes from, what was and is the most painful for them, how their own group contributed to the conflict, and what needs to happen for peace to be created. This process needs to take place for all the groups involved in the conflict and thus the creation of space for transformation and change is essential. These processes are difficult and complex, do not happen overnight, and cannot offer a quick fix. If society is looking for the "fast" healing of traumas, they may be disappointed, because many parts of the process will not be thoroughly worked through (that will create a mask of "things are OK") before the next violent conflict.

We often encounter the perception that trauma is a phenomenon that is experienced by a small group of people in society. People who live in the post-war societies of Southeast Europe can be often heard to say that they do not have any trauma or Posttraumatic Stress Disorder (PTSD). There is an increasing general level of awareness about the symptoms and treatments for PTSD. However, much of the focus is on small groups of people with the strongest symptoms (flashbacks, panic attacks, anxiety). These populations are also identified by their experiences, for example former soldiers, rape victims, or concentration camp survivors. In these identifications they often are seen as meriting special treatment but at the same time there is a distancing of the rest of society from them.

Most people who lived in Sarajevo during the war and many people throughout Bosnia, Croatia, Serbia, and Kosovo/Kosova experienced some kind of traumatic stress. This does not mean that they experience PTSD and in fact many of them do live productive lives. However, we find a large population that has some symptoms related to their traumatic experience. Many of these people are not aware of the connection between the symptoms and the war, and do not want to seek psychological assistance for their symptoms. Often we assure those people who share these symptoms with us that their reactions are normal reactions to the abnormal situation that they were in (STAR Manual 2002). While the symptoms of some individuals and groups are the strongest, trauma impacts much of the population. Especially given the lack of resources (counselors or therapists, societal acceptance of therapy, reliance on antidepressants and other medicines), we find that there is an important role for trauma education.

In a context like SEE, many helping professionals (therapists, psychologists, social workers, clergy, and teachers) have experienced traumatic stress themselves. This primary traumatization is augmented by secondary traumatization from hearing the stories of the individuals with whom they work. This can lead to compassion fatigue (Figley 1995) that in the long run creates an environment in which professionals themselves do not have the energy to continue with those who are hurting. This is problematic since the outlets to work on trauma healing constructively are lessened. Also, many professionals do not have sufficient training in understanding trauma and what is required for this kind of work. Individuals who seek help often times are referred to somebody else and frequently the only treatment offered is medication as a way to deal with the symptoms. Many professionals also get locked into their respective therapeutic approaches and try to fit trauma healing into one therapeutic framework that cannot deal fully with the issues. One therapist told us that work on trauma is so complex that it requires a huge amount of flexibility from the therapist to seek different approaches and understandings in how to deal with various painful issues that arise during the process. Also, the same therapist said that symptoms of trauma are tricky, and if the therapist does not have a wide range of experience, individuals can be easily misunderstood and therefore misdiagnosed.

For those who are doing peacebuilding work, it is essential to understand the meaning assigned to certain traumatic events. The predominant approach to dealing with traumatic events on a societal level in SEE is one of separating from other groups and memorialization of the loss. These two aspects combined together serve to emphasize the identity of each group as victims in the conflict. One good example is the annual commemoration of the fall of Srebrenica, which is largely attended and reported on in the media where Bosniaks[3] form the majority. More recently this has received increased attention in other areas as well, and the attendance of Serbian president Boris Tadić on the occasion of the 10th anniversary in 2005 was greeted by suspicion from groups like the Mothers of

Srebrenica[4]. Similar events also take place in Croatia each year connected to the fall of Vukovar.

Memorialization also happens on a small scale. In Sarajevo, in the last two years, each part of town erected a bronze plaque for each civilian who was killed in that area. Such memorials are often decorated with nationalist symbols, for example in Jajce a memorial with a cross was erected only for fallen Croat soldiers. Moreover, it was placed on confiscated land in the center of town. The challenge is that so much symbolism and energy is invested into memorials and the anniversaries of key events, which only serve to accentuate divisions in society. The process of how these events became "chosen traumas" and are reinforced in this role will be discussed in the next section on narratives.

Frequently these events are organized and used by nationalist politicians who benefit from continued fear and division. The misuses of the losses is clear, to the point where political parties abuse the memory of losses for their own benefit which in turn locks the groups into themselves and perpetuates the feeling of victimhood over and over again—and thus groups are trapped in their losses without ever being able to mourn. The more the groups are trapped into individual losses, the stronger the feeling of victimhood. Trauma education allows for the recognition of both individual losses as well as those of the group. In raising the awareness of losses, it becomes possible to choose to grieve the losses and to embark on the process of creating new narratives.

Narratives and Trauma in SEE

One challenge for understanding the interaction between trauma and peacebuilding is that society is composed of groups of individuals, and each individual brings his or her own understandings of violent conflicts, feelings of pain, and desire for justice. Thus, the understanding of what happened is multiple—since everybody has his or her own story and experience. However during violent conflicts certain events become the "chosen ones" that signifies the collective trauma and represent many individual traumas. Two examples are the events in Srebrenica in 1995 and in Vukovar in 1991. These chosen traumas become the major story of trauma for each group which explicitly contain all that that group and individuals from that group have experienced.

In seminars, it is often difficult for people to identify these narratives initially, because they exist at the level of metaphor and symbol. Narratives in terms of group identity address fundamental questions about who each group is, what defines them, and also who the "other" is. These narratives focus around certain key events, many of which are connected with past wars. Although the events might not be visible at first, they are very visible when one adjusts perspectives. For example, in the region, it is clear which group "owns" which color—Serb color is red, Croat blue and Bosniak green. This even went so far that in the town of Jajce in 1996 (where there was a Croat majority), it was unpopular to wear anything green. These associations with colors as symbols developed over time. However, now they are so much a part of the interpretation of social reality that *why* this is so, is rarely questioned.

Another example of narratives in terms of group identity is the way that certain names are known as belonging to one group or another. Although some people before the various wars in the region did not have this understanding of the meaning of certain names, it became very important during the war. This shows that narratives about the different groups and differences between them were present despite many years of living together in "brotherhood and unity" (a socialist-era slogan). People might not have paid much attention to these little things in the time of peace, but in a time of crises these symbols clearly communicate that they are part of the group or not, and if they are supporting the group's actions or not.

So, in looking at the region of Southeast Europe, these last wars have brought forth the major stories that each group has used as a vehicle to communicate their victimhood and thus their trauma. Also, these same stories are used as a justification for not trusting the enemy at present and for any possible future violence that might be committed. Narratives from earlier conflict were significant in creating and strengthening divisions in the lead up to the most recent wars. Table 8.1. shows significant events related to loss and trauma and the narratives that are currently connected with the events. This is a list developed by participants in our seminars. It is not exhaustive, but a beginning.

Table 8.1.
Significant events and related narratives for primary identity groups in Southeast Europe

Group	Significant events	Narratives
Bosniaks	Medieval Bosnia (1180-1527)	Source of legitimacy for modern Bosnia, source of pride in distinct Bosnian identity
	Ceding of Bosnia to Austro-Hungarian Empire (1878)	Loss of favored status and being taken over by a long-term enemy (which was Catholic)
	Independence and aggression on Bosnia, (1992-1996)	Chosen trauma—sense of violation, also anger at other countries for not doing anything
	Fall of Srebrenica (1995)	Chosen trauma—represents victimhood and loss throughout period of 1992-1995
Croats	Arrival of Ottomans (1526)	Chosen trauma—a period of repression, emphasize their role as heroic defenders of Christian Europe.
	Independent State of Croatia (NDH) (1941)	First modern independent Croatia
	Massacre at Bleiburg (1945)	Chosen trauma at the hand of Tito's Partisans, commemorated in recent years as a pilgrimage
	Vukovar/Dubrovnik (1991)	Used as examples of Serb barbarism, chosen trauma

	Operation Storm (1995)	Redemption and restoration of Croatia as a country
Serbs	Defeat at Kosovo Polje (1389)	Chosen trauma, used as justification and explanation for modern wars.
	Arrival of Ottomans (1371)	Period of repression, their role as heroic defenders of Christian Europe.
	Janissaries (young men given/taken for the Ottoman army)	Chosen trauma—feeling of violation because sons became Muslims and served the Ottomans
	Balkan Wars I and II (1912-1913)	Fighting against Ottomans and eventually freeing Serbian land of them.
Albanians	Victories by Skenderbeg (1443-1468)	Chosen glory—point of national pride, independence of Albanians against the Ottomans
	NATO bombing (1999)	Chosen glory—heavy losses but return of refugees because of NATO action

People working in the peacebuilding field have reacted to our presentation of a framework of narratives by saying that people are not *forced* to reenact events from the past and that the widespread repeating of historical narratives during the rise of nationalism was an intentional strategy using mass media by a small elite. While both of these perspectives have some truth, we see narratives primarily as a descriptive tool to explain how individuals in a divided society interpret what is happening around them. Likewise narratives are useful in that they helped to shape acceptable ways of dealing with previous losses. While narratives can be changed, they do impact how social reality is interpreted and understood. Since we are sensitized to narratives, we see them being reinforced and reinterpreted, but in familiar ways, in public discourse around us every day.

An example of this process can be seen in the public discussion around key events like Srebrenica. Groups like the Mothers of Srebrenica have a particular legitimacy in Sarajevo as they represent both a large group of victims, but also symbolically the victimhood of ethnic Bosniaks. Recently a commission of the Republika Srpska (one of two Bosnian entities) established that a horrific crime had been committed at Srebrenica and placed the number of those killed at approximately 8,000 (2004). Shortly thereafter renewed accusations of the war death of 5,000 civilian Serbs in Sarajevo were made. Although it is certain that many Sarajevo Serbs were killed during the war, such a high number is not likely and many of these Serbs suffered at the hands of the Bosnian Serb Army surrounding Sarajevo. The point, however, is the indirect but clear message of victimhood which can be understood in this way: "Yes, you [Bosniaks] may have suffered but we [Serbs] suffered too."

Shame and Locked Positions

In addition to narratives, shame is an important concept helpful for understanding peacebuilding in SEE. Some scholars that have influenced our understanding are Vamik Volkan (1996) and Rafael Moses (1990b). Each writes from a perspective that acknowledges the importance of narratives and how they communicate a system of meaning. This system of meaning is created in each culture and it explains the culture itself that in turn explains human or group behavior in a given historical moment (Blechman et. al. 2000). Within the narrative, group behavior is explained through language that is not straight forward, but rather hidden—and that is the language of metaphors. Metaphors explain something indirectly, through symbols and images which augment a story. In this case we are interested in the story of the shame that a group has survived.

In Southeast Europe, shame is not named clearly, it is rather named indirectly through various stories that have in them images and symbols of different kinds. Shame is not communicated clearly since it is shameful to talk about it publicly. So, in order to talk about shame publicly it has to be told in a space that is allowed for by the group. For example, the narrative of the Battle of Kosovo is told in the epic form in the "Mountain Wreath" by Petar Petrović Njegoš II, where the images and symbols talk of betrayal that had tremendous consequences. Through reading the story, one gets the picture of what is shameful in this narrative—losing the Kosovo battle at the hands of the infidels (Ottomans) where the ancient Serbian and Christian land has been desecrated by their presence, which is associated with them as Christ killers (Sells 1995). This brief summary saliently captures the explanation of the whole epic narrative.

In relation to shame and locked positions, it is important to say that ". . . narrative discourse is one of the most important systems of understanding that we use to make sense of reality . . ." (Vila 2000). Narratives help us to explain *to ourselves* why certain things happened and thus help us as a group to construct "the correct group response" in connection with a shameful experience. The overarching culture of Southeast Europe is one of rich narratives that explain history up through present time conflicts. These narratives were important for the survival of the groups and they helped build a strong communal connection. From this source, collective identity has been constructed, which has led to a strong collective rather than individual identity. These sources have created prescribed modes of conduct and action in how to deal with individuals within the group that shame or make a group proud.

So, if one member of the group has done something good, it reflects on the whole. Likewise, if a member of the group has done something shameful, the whole group is shamed as well. The same rule applies in the situation where somebody has shamed "my" group—eventually I or someone from my group needs to cleanse the shame from us—and this is usually done through inflicting shame on the other group. The infliction of shame in this region has been done through violent means and thus in itself presents a never ending cycle of revenge.

One example of this is *blood revenge* which was practiced in some areas into the 20th century (Malcolm 1998). Historically throughout Southeast Europe, each group had ways and processes by which shame was cleansed from the group. If someone from one group was killed, it was expected by the victim's family that the murderer's family would kill the murderer. If not, the victim's family had the right to kill the murderer. Thus, honor would be restored. This practice highlights the following elements: that shame needs to be "washed off" through revenge, that honor needed to be restored no matter what the cost, that retaliation was the natural way to do this, and the socially acceptable way to do this was through blood revenge.

We can see how this framework got adapted to collective trauma. A battle or war lost brought shame upon the whole group and thus there was an explicit need stated—the honor of the group has to be restored and thus revenge must take place. The wars in Southeast Europe had many starting points—meaning that every group had their understanding when the last wars started. The interesting thing was that all groups identified with a different place in history when the wars of 1990's started—for Serbs the year was definitely 1389 and the battle of Kosova; for Croats it was WWII and the establishment of Croatian Independent State (NDH-Nezavisna Država Hrvatska) and for the Bosniaks the 1800's when the Austro-Hungarian empire annexed Bosnia and Herzegovina. Each of these collective memories that throughout the centuries and decades have become "chosen traumas" or "chosen glories," depend on how each group has worked out different understandings of what happened. Sometimes the same historical event would become both a source of trauma and a source of glory. For more details about these narratives please see the earlier section on "Narratives and Trauma in SEE."

Southeast Europe has experienced repression at the hands of many empires (Ottoman, Austro-Hungarian, and German). In order to be able to survive these oppressive regimes, groups retold their stories and created a group memory as a survival mechanism. This survival mechanism has in it elements of the group perceiving itself as the victim that suffered tremendous loss and shame. The feelings of shame have been created by the destruction the enemy did to the group's property (personal home and most sacred of all religious objects like churches and mosques), and destruction of the group's culture by forcing a different language to be used and forbidding the use of native language (During this process an enormous literature and group memory was lost). This shame deepened when group members were put into concentration camps and tortured and when women were raped. In some cases, for the first time, certain groups gained the upper hand in society at the expense of other groups. Regardless of the source of shame, the memory of the events remained and helped shape the life and actions of the group.

This mechanism of never forgetting translated into never having constructive healing of traumatic events. The wounds continue to be re-opened without being able to be healed, and they became a source of negative energy from which the group got its sense of identity and strength to take revenge at a future point in time. The deeper the injury, the stronger the sense of shame became which strengthened the sense of group identity. Thus, it is not strange that a Serbian soldier said, "We are living history right now, it is not just something that happened in the past" (Šubar 2006). For a Serbian soldier fighting the wars in Bosnia in 1990's meant fighting not with Bosniaks but fighting with Ottomans and having the chance to right the wrong and finally win the battle of Kosovo/Kosova, after 600 years of carrying the burden of shame of losing the war.

Narratives have played a key role in constructing history in a way where within each group permission was given to the group members to cleanse the shame and restore the honor of the group through any means necessary—allowing atrocities, torture, mass killing and mass rape to take place without any questions being asked. Justification was clear as well as the fact that *all things* were allowed in war. However, the wars have now ended. The crazy times of "no rules of conduct" have passed, and now each group is called to admit, acknowledge and apologize for the crimes done. No group is able to step forward to do this since the groupthink does not allow for confession.

Battles were won in the last war but at what expense and why? Everybody in the region knows that killing, torture, rape, and ethnic cleansing are shameful and terrible acts; but since the violence was done in the name of safety and for the betterment of the group it is easily justified, excused and put aside. The problem with denial in this case is that nobody will forget what happened to their group in this last war and the traumas survived in this war will just be piled up on top of all the others. The "culture of fear," inherited from generations past, is continuing to be passed on as well as a "culture of shame" and a "culture of guilt" that have not been dealt with and resolved (Šubar 2006). Thus the cycle of violence continues.

In order to pass on the "culture of shame" to one's children and subsequent generations, one needs to be prepared. In order to be ready, one needs to experience feelings of shame so deeply that *humanity* gets stripped away. Once this process happens there is a small step to shame the other, or to dehumanize the other. Rafael Moses (1990a) has described this state in the following way:

> Dehumanization, then is a state in which one human being or group so brutalizes the others that the victim loses self-respect and human dignity. I postulate that the dehumanizer must already have lost the quality of humanness—and, therefore, of self-respect and human dignity. He could not carry dehumanizing acts otherwise. . . . I believe that in the individual must be interpsychic readiness to be dehumanized in order to dehumanize another; this cannot happen however, unless certain processes in the large group (often nation) pave the way for it.

The above analysis is helpful since it provides another entry point to focus work on trauma healing and reconciliation. The key question here is how to work on narratives—how to allow space for memories and stories to come to light that would help each group to understand their culture of fear, shame and guilt that have perpetrated violence for centuries.

How We Work at Trauma Education

By trauma education, we mean education of both people in helping professions as well as others about the physical, biological, spiritual, and psychological symptoms of trauma. An important component is equipping people to recognize burnout and secondary traumatization which can come from working with traumatized groups. A second important component is being able to reassure individuals suffering from PTSD symptoms that their reactions are normal and common. A final important component is to know when referral to mental health professionals is necessary and to have some suggestions about how to receive this assistance.

Trauma education is the main focus of the trauma healing work that we do together with our partner organizations. For example, the Center for Education and Psychotherapy in Belgrade, Serbia offers trauma therapy but also offers trauma education to the general population as well as to its clients. The organization has provided trauma seminars to teachers, psychologists, psychiatrists, pastors, lay leadership and parents. For the teachers it was a revelation to understand why students were more aggressive, less focused, depressed etc. if they were coming from families where the father is a former soldier. For psychiatrists and psychologists, the complexity of trauma and how difficult at times it is to distinguish between PTSD and other diagnoses was new information. Pastors and lay leadership in the church also learned what trauma is and how it affects individuals and how to help individuals and families begin the recovery, process.

In our seminars, once the basics of trauma have been covered, a key moment happens when we offer information and understanding on how traumas from the past have been passed from generation to generation and thus created cycles of violence that have been repeated over decades. This is the moment when it becomes clear that trauma healing is a key component in the process of any kind of future reconciliation, work on possible forgiveness, and work on bringing about justice. It often becomes clear that in order to collectively heal from the traumas, society at large needs to become aware of the inherited stories from past generations that helped to create understanding of who the enemy is, what they are like, and how to deal with them—this includes working on narratives, chosen traumas and chosen glories, and transgenerational transmission of trauma.

During seminars with people that are in helping professions, there is a common point where many participants realize that according to what they are learning, they themselves have experienced traumatic stress. One example was a teacher who had barely survived the fall of Srebrenica and fleeing as a refugee, but at first did not identify herself as a trauma survivor. Slowly throughout the seminar we could see her awareness begin to change. Even if they have been living without any serious consequences of this trauma, there is a natural phenomenon where discussing others' trauma naturally touches their own. By touching it we mean that the trauma is stirred up, and participants can start to remember what they experienced. In order for this surfacing to occur, an atmosphere of safety has to be established that the individual can effectively process their experience in order to move on to help others. The balance that we try to achieve is to have a place to share difficult experiences if people choose. This is trauma education and not therapy, and it is a challenging balance to maintain. One way to put this is that the seminars are not therapy but they can be therapeutic.

One of the challenges in doing the kind of trauma education work that we are doing is how to work at the level of understanding and possibly "rewriting" history and group narratives which do not allow for the possibility of coexistence. One approach is to focus on individual healing, with a belief that healed and whole individuals will be able to reassess their own involvement and that of their group, and create new narratives which do allow for the possibility of coexistence. One successful strategy is raising peoples' awareness. This means introducing the idea of narrative and having them work to identify group narratives. One participant (in a seminar organized together with the Franciscans) made a connection with the stories that she had learned as a young girl. She had never placed too much importance on these stories but in retrospect realized that they were an important component of passing on "chosen traumas" from earlier generations and creating the background for the current conflict. By giving examples (for example American narratives about their own country), as well as contrasting conflicting narratives belonging to the various groups in SEE, it becomes clear that narratives are not simply objective truth but include an important component of interpretation. This awareness allows the space for critical reflection on group narratives, and finally the possibility to choose which parts are helpful and to create new narratives.

Our seminars also attract people who had traumatic experiences and have been diagnosed with PTSD. Some of these were soldiers or people who had been detained in prison in difficult circumstances. They often feel that someone coming from a psychological and educational perspective does not really understand what it means to be traumatized. They have a natural desire to want to talk about what happened to them. Often they do not have other supportive environments in which to do so. The challenge is how much to let them do so without subjecting other participants to secondary traumatization and at the same time not opening up their own trauma so that it is harder for them to go back to their home environments. It is important as facilitators and trainers to check in with these participants during the seminar to make sure that they are doing OK and that they can return to their regular life afterwards.

The key moment that connects group trauma healing with the process of building peace is when we discuss narratives. Usually, it is difficult for participants to understand what is understood by narratives. However, once they are assigned to identify the stories that have been passed from generation to generation about the other side (both positive and negative), a long list of these stories emerge. The surprise on the participants' faces tells all—realization of how deeply engraved into individuals and groups these stories are and how difficult it is to get out of them. This exercise creates the understanding why someone from the other side, their enemy, hates them and does not trust them.

Now we have laid the groundwork to summarize the framework in which we do trauma education seminars as a component of peacebuilding. First of all, the focus is on people in the helping professions as potential multipliers who work with large numbers of people. Many of these people work in educational, social work, or religious institutions and will continue in these positions over many years. Secondly, there is an emphasis on building broad awareness, helping individuals to examine their own trauma and the roles of narratives related to key historical events. Our goal is to influence and develop "critical yeast" (Lederach 2005) which will lead to broader changes in these narratives. We try to help participants in the seminars to become aware of metaphors and narratives, as well as elements like shame that may not be immediately visible in society but are nonetheless potent. Lastly, we work together with local organizations that share a common vision, both to introduce these perspectives to them and to continue learning from their experience.

The Context of Southeast Europe

Before we describe some of the projects related to trauma healing that are happening in SEE, it may be helpful to elaborate on the context as we have begun to do above. Yugoslavia was a Socialist country where people's material and security needs were secured. This is important and often misunderstood by people from outside who come with the lenses of former Soviet-bloc, politically-restricted, economically-poor countries. In contrast, residents of the former Yugoslavia had higher standards of living, often oriented themselves towards the West, and were able to travel both in Eastern and Western Europe freely. Many people experienced the wars as a double loss of identity, first as Yugoslavia disintegrated and then their new "homelands" (particularly Bosnia). They experienced a loss of economic security and around 3.6 million people became refugees or internally displaced (UNHCR 1995).

The countries of SEE continue to recover slowly from the wars of 1991-1999. This recovery in economic, political, and social terms affects trauma healing as well. The 10th anniversary of the Dayton Agreement was observed in Bosnia in 2005, however, significant questions about the political structure of Bosnia (the importance of the national, entity, cantonal, and local governments) are still being defined. Politically, Bosnia has progressed from being under the significant control of nationalist parties in the immediate aftermath of the war, passed through a period of colonial rule by the internationally-appointed High

Representative, and is now in a phase of return to complete control by elected officials within what many hope is a framework of EU accession.

Socially many of the basic agreements and forms of cooperation have broken down. For example, retirees live on minimal pensions, while young people find it difficult to find jobs and many workers work in the "gray" economy without pension or medical insurance. The medical system that used to provide good care for all now requires significant payments under the table in order to get quality care. Several years ago a poll showed that 62% of young people in Bosnia said that they would immigrate if given the opportunity (UNDP 2000).

Developments in the other former Yugoslav republics are similar. We have also experienced that there is a significant difference between the few large cities and small towns. For example, in Sarajevo and Belgrade, the capitals of Bosnia and Herzegovina and Serbia, there is more economic activity and better basic services. In contrast, small towns frequently have much higher unemployment and fewer opportunities. We have found that the lack of economic perspectives often contributes to a lack of hope for residents of these towns. This seems to extend beyond the individual's personal situation and affect a general atmosphere in the town. Some of the characteristics that we have noticed in depressed small towns are lethargy and even depression in its residents, lack of initiative or belief in any change, and continued talk about the war. Sometimes it seems that residents of these towns are "stuck" in the war years.

From the perspective of 2007, many of the refugees have either returned home or have decided that they will remain where they settled. In these cases the reasons for not returning are the lack of economic opportunities, concern for personal safety, or a desire to live in new communities where they are an ethnic majority. Economically 20% of the population remains unemployed in Bosnia if informal employment is considered (UNDP 2002) and across the region unemployment is estimated to be higher in Serbia and Kosovo/Kosova. This contributes to a lack of economic security. In our experience, a lack of security contributes to the need to continue surviving and therefore repressing symptoms of trauma. In other cases the lack of security increases anxiety and contributes to symptoms of trauma. Thus we believe that there is an ongoing and even increasing need for trauma education and therapy resources as the economy improves and recovers.

The consequences of the wars can be seen in an increased level of domestic violence, suicides, alcohol and drug abuse, physical violence, gangs, and organized criminality. Organizations working with traumatized individuals report that the trauma of war veterans is the main cause of domestic violence (MCC 2006).

One characteristic of the post-war societies is the level of denial. Denial can be seen in terms of denying crimes that were committed by one's *own* group. Prosecutions by national courts of war crimes that were committed and which will not be prosecuted by the International Criminal Tribunal for the former Yugoslavia in The Hague (ICTY) have been slow. Individuals that openly discuss crimes committed by "their" group are routinely discounted, challenged, or even threatened. The Youth Initiative for Human Rights (YIHR), an activist group in Belgrade, Serbia recently put up billboards showing pictures taken from exhumations of mass graves and a challenge "to see, to know, to remember" the Srebrenica massacre in 1995. The billboards were quickly covered with graffiti. Likewise a Bosniak former soldier who discussed crimes committed by the army he was a part of was discredited and challenged at a public forum, being asked who had authorized him to speak. In fact he said he was only speaking in his name, but it was the uncomfortable truths that he was saying which were not welcome.

In our work we have been challenged to look for the ways that people make sense of the trauma which happened to them, and their sources of resilience (Good Sider 2003). One of these key sources is the solidarity from strong family and social networks. Although the strength of family networks is clear to any visitor to Southeast Europe, it is hard to document. One way to do this is to note that during the war it was common for family members who had left former Yugoslavia to support those who remained by sending cash or food parcels. This factor is so significant that even today many residents of SEE exhibit resources of cash which can not be explained by the economic statistics. One estimate puts the value of these transfers as high as 20% of GDP (UNDP 2002). Another source of resilience could be resurgence in interest in faith during the last 15 years. This influence is often difficult to see because of the complex role that the religious communities played in the rise and sustaining of nationalism and the strong connections between ethnic and religious identity.

What Types of Trauma Healing are Being Done?

Because of our interest in peacebuilding and trauma healing, we connect with various groups that work at trauma healing. Some of these are projects that MCC has supported financially, but we also see our support in terms of networking, providing resources, and providing professional development for those working in these fields. Although they are working in different ways, we have found a common-enough base of values and a "common purpose" to work together. We look at this from the perspective of mutual capacity building—what do we have to offer and what do we learn/benefit from our association with local organizations. One of the ways that we support them is through regular contacts with their staff and providing consultation and a listening ear to their ongoing challenges. This by no means is a list of all the projects or approaches being used to trauma—only a few with which we are connected.

Bosnia and Herzegovina

The Center for Nonviolent Action (CNA) is an activist organization with groups of trainers in Belgrade and Sarajevo. Their connection with trauma came through focusing on former soldiers. This strategy recognizes that veterans groups have particular legitimacy within their own communities—they are recognized as people who have sacrificed for the group, many of them in terms of injuries. Likewise they have both the potential for support of a nationalist ideology which contributed to the wars, but also the potential to look critically at what they and their societies have lost. As a way of equipping themselves better for this work, CNA asked MCC to provide training in trauma awareness and address the intersection between trauma and reconciliation. CNA has also been using films as a way to increase the impact of their work. The film "Traces" which has been shown on national TV networks, documents the stories of several former soldiers and their reflections on their own participation.

The Franciscan Order of the Catholic Church is also a group that has identified a need to better understand trauma and traumatic healing. As in other areas of MCC's peacebuilding work, this particular cooperation builds on many years and an established trust as a result. One of the reasons for this interest was the Franciscans' sensitivity to those who have suffered in their own societies. Another is the important role of Catholic priests as confessors and pastors. In recent years many have encountered parishioners who are suicidal and have struggled to know how to respond. MCC prepared two seminars that were held in 2005 to provide a background in trauma education and knowledge of how to respond in a pastoral role to people suffering from PTSD. The seminars also addressed how to know the limits beyond which professional assistance is required. This cooperation led to the offering of a course on Trauma and Reconciliation with the Franciscan seminary in March, 2007. This course built on the trauma education approach and was attended by the graduating class of Franciscan priests and laypeople as well as older priests and a seminary professor. The intention is to repeat this class every year.

In 2003-2004, MCC supported a series of seminars for teachers in the Tuzla area. These seminars focused on trauma awareness and fit into the general model of trauma education as mentioned above. One learning from this work is that a high degree of trauma exists among children as identified by teachers and pedagogues (who play a role similar to school counselors in some other countries). In working with this population, many of them discovered their own responses to traumatic stress and came to better understand the connection between current symptoms and the traumatic events of many years ago.

One training project for psychological professionals highlights the needs for trauma therapy in Bosnia and Herzegovina. Gisela Röper and Maria Gavranidou (2003) helped to establish the first clinical psychology program at the Universities of Sarajevo and Banja Luka. Before the war, such programs were only available in Belgrade, Zagreb, and Ljubljana in the former Yugoslavia. This initiative took place in a context of professionals, for example, with social workers and school psychologists, often dealing with their own trauma and not equipped to assist others with their symptoms of PTSD. One of the focus areas was providing supervisions and providing training in clinical supervision as well as defining topics for research.

A common component in all four of these projects is equipping people in "helping professions" who may come in contact with individuals that suffer from PTSD or milder symptoms of traumatic stress.

Another project that MCC supports is with women in the town of Jajce through the organization Viktorija 99. This project of psychosocial help involves groups of women who meet on a regular basis. The project provides a reason for meeting (for example knitting or sewing), a space, and logistical support. Some of these groups also include psychological professionals or trained lay people in listening techniques and identifying symptoms that require a referral to a professional therapist. David Becker (2004) emphasizes the importance of such groups in SEE. For him this is especially important where there may not be adequate resources for therapy, or culturally people may not be open to seek therapy. In the case of Viktorija, contact with an organization that does provide professional therapy helped them to realize that they were not equipped to deal with trauma, and it helped them to describe their project in different terms. This realization is an example of both capacity building and trauma education in action.

The interreligious organization "Face to Face" uses art in trauma healing through the choir Pontanima (Latin for "Soul Bridge"). The 60 member choir sings songs from different religious traditions (Catholic, Orthodox, Jewish, Muslim, and Protestant), and the power of the music is seen in the moments when religious songs from other faith traditions are sung in the cities and town of Bosnia and the region where these songs are understood to be "enemies songs." Singing as a method of trauma healing helps the audience indirectly connect with their traumatic experience and open up for the process of healing. The audience cannot help but feel the effects. People in Southeast Europe are musical and feel the music deeply with their soul; so in listening to the choir, the healing enters in the space that is most sacred, i.e. religious identity. These songs create space for listening to the other that otherwise would not happen. The choir brings an especially strong message of healing when it performs in the towns and cities that have experienced massacres on a large scale. One concert in Banja Luka shortly after the war brought both audience members and the choir itself to tears, a testimony to this powerful healing potential. Similarly, at the beginning, some choir members were not willing to sing Orthodox songs because they associated them with the Serbs who had besieged Sarajevo. However, with time they accepted and embraced these songs.

The organization World Vision supported work with traumatized children in areas with a high degree of traumatization from 1997. The schools that participated in the Creative Activities for Trauma and Stress Diminishment were selected in areas close to former front lines. They are located in areas where refugees and displaced persons are returning after the Dayton peace agreement and where a large percentage of the school population is considered at risk (Children in difficult circumstances) (Badurina, Pašić, Sikima, Zijadic-Husić 2007).

With the support of the school's psychologists and pedagogues, 4 groups of around 20 children in each school were selected that could most benefit from the creative workshops. A component of World Visions's semester-long workshops has been careful pre and post assessments of the children. For the children above the age of 8, this assessment was done through a questionnaire using a battery of indicators, including detailed questions about traumatic events, the Revised Impact of Events Scale and the Birleson Depression Scale. At the same time, a control group was tested in each school (students who were not project beneficiaries). Other 4 person teams also worked in Tuzla, Zenica and the area of Goražde, and until 2004, the teams covered more than 200 primary schools.

Since 2001, the same Sarajevo team has continued working with children but in a focused manner with other World Vision recovery and development programs in schools in the areas of Olovo, in the Federation of Bosnia and Herzegovina and Sokolac and Han Pijesak, in the Republika Srpska. The group from ages 6-8 works with arts, including clay, fingerpaints, and paper. Drawing demonstrates children's complex feelings and is more appropriate for children ages 6-8 than verbal expression. During the 16-week cycle, the following art therapy and diagnostic approaches were used: free drawing, draw the person, draw the person in the rain, draw a house, draw a tree, draw a family, kinetic drawing of the family, kinetic drawing of school etc. Ages 8-10 participate in physical activities focused on different educational games which allow them to know more about their own body, to recognize their own emotions, to deal with unpleasant feelings, to learn new strategies of how to resolve problems in a non-violent way, to build team spirit and belonging to the group, to build a sense of justice and mutual understanding, cooperation, and tolerance.

Ages 10-12 work with drama, music, and dance workshops which have been composed to complement each other and to fulfill the children's needs for free expression of emotions, to enhance their body movement and to encourage exchange of their personal experiences. During the workshops, the following techniques have been applied: relaxation and guided imagery, expression through music, body movement, drama expression, body language, and modes and meanings of verbal and non-verbal communication. The oldest group from ages 12-14 compose a psychological support group which includes the World Vision trainer, teachers, and children. The group encourages children to cope with stress in an active and responsible way. During the workshops, children have been engaged in two consequential components of activities that foster a better understanding of each other and build their self-confidence as well as build capacity of children for non-violent conflict resolution.

The evaluation conducted by the Sarajevo World Vision team demonstrates both a high degree of traumatization in children and a beneficial impact of such creative work. In comparison to a control group, the assessment of PTSD demonstrated a decrease of 40% during the course of the semester-long work. This experience with more than 11,000 children by the Sarajevo team over a period of 10 years also suggests significant findings which could be verified with additional research. For example, they noticed that children who were separated from their parents demonstrated a higher incidence of PTSD than those who had direct experiences of war. Moreover, their assessments show that evidence of PTSD continues to be strong many years after the war and among children who did not experience primary traumatization. Another learning from this project is that symptoms of PTSD can be reduced through careful work, but that it is difficult to interest donors to support a long-term and systematic process of trauma diminishment.

This background of work and interest in trauma led MCC to commission a research project about the approaches and number of organizations and public institutions working in trauma healing in Bosnia (2006). The study was conducted from April—September 2006, and although limited in scope, 170 NGOs and 23 public health institutions were contacted. Of these, 13 NGOs and 4 public health institutions responded that they do work in trauma healing. The majority of these offer individual and/or group therapy but few responded that they do trauma education. One organization responded that they see occupational therapy programs as providing more benefit than ones offering psychological therapy. Most of these organizations are open to any population, but some focus on war veterans, youth and children, or women. All together the organizations reported that they serve around 10,100 beneficiaries a year.

One of the main problems that the responders reported was a lack of donor interest in the problem of trauma. Other problems included a lack of: professional education, supervision and retreat possibilities for professionals and volunteers, human and material capacities, an understanding in the community for those who suffer from PTSD, and the importance of therapy.

Croatia

In Croatia we are in connection with a significant initiative related to trauma healing which is the work of the Coalition for Work with Psychotrauma and Peace (CWWPP) in Vukovar. As mentioned elsewhere, Vukovar is a city that experienced significant devastation and is a potent symbol of Croatia's loss. Vukovar is also one of the most ethnically mixed cities in Croatia as a result of being in eastern Slavonia which was reintegrated into Croatia by agreement rather than by military action. CWWPP provides both individual and group therapy to people who suffer from PTSD and in their reports; this is both a highly needed service and one that is otherwise unavailable in that part of Croatia. CWWPP's approach has been to work with one group over a longer period of time and to include training in communication, identity, and peacebuilding.

Kosovo/Kosova[5]

In Prishtina MCC supports the work of Close to Children. This group of artists began in 2000 in the immediate aftermath of the war and return of Albanian refugees. Focusing within the Albanian community, they created a program in which they work with highly traumatized school children for 3-6 months. During that time children can choose between drama, painting, music, and poetry and are allowed to express themselves using the various artistic media. Although not trained in art therapy, the artists have developed extensive expertise in working with children that have experienced significant trauma. One young boy began by only painting pictures of underwater scenes. When they asked him why, he replied that, "under water the houses can not burn." By the end of their time with him he was drawing normal scenes. The members of the Close to Children team report that more than seven years after the war, new generations of children who did not experience the war directly are still showing signs of traumatization.

Serbia

The Center for Education and Psychotherapy, an organization in Belgrade with a mission to do trauma education and therapy, has a vital connection with the Department of Psychology at the University of Belgrade. This relationship connects formal education in psychology with sensitivity to trauma and trauma healing. Providing individual and group therapy is a significant contribution since therapy is not commonly available and even psychological professionals seem to avoid difficult issues like trauma. Therapy for PTSD sufferers is not widely available in SEE and practicing therapists have told us that many colleagues who complete a therapeutic training either do not see patients (because it is difficult to apply therapeutic theory in practice) or avoid working with trauma victims or perpetrators who suffer from PTSD.

The Center for War Trauma offers therapy with a focus on war veterans. This organization has founded centers for therapy in Novi Sad and in southern Serbia, as well as offering seminars to veterans and psychological professionals. Its work is significant in the way that it brings together Serbian, Albanian, and recently Croatian veterans, provides quality services to a population that has been largely neglected in Serbia, and has created a bridge between offering therapy services and peacebuilding.

The work of the Center supports recent findings that the act of killing another person is a significant cause of PTSD. This form of PTSD has been termed Perpetration-Induced Traumatic Stress (PITS) (MacNair 2002). In a recent conversation, founder Vladan Beara spoke of the difficulty of working with soldiers because of the public ambiguity about what they may have done during wartime. The veterans themselves, according to him, struggle to understand their experience and struggle with the question of why this experience happened to them and how to integrate it into their peacetime lives. Although they have been asked about the ethics of working with a population that includes many perpetrators, their response is that this is exactly a group which needs assistance to avoid hurting further innocent people (for example family members through domestic violence) and to prevent veterans from becoming significant blockers of peacebuilding. Further information about the perspective of war veterans is available in the book *Oh where have you been, my blue-eyed son?* (Beara and Miljanović 2006).

One common framework that peacebuilding organizations use for their work in SEE is that of "dealing with the past." This approach commonly focuses on dialogue between groups from different "sides," with a focus on building self-awareness, and the ability to hear others' perspectives. There is a focus on breaking through denial about crimes committed and the needs for acknowledging them. A recent workshop organized by the Center for Nonviolent Action brought together people working at Dealing with the Past from different perspectives from across the region. Designed for activists that have already passed basic awareness and training on communication, this workshop tried to expose the different perspectives with which individual initiatives work. One of these groups was the Research and Documentation Center (2005), which gathers information about victims of the recent wars, and plays an important part in the ongoing discussion of the losses that happened. This center, whose slogan is "Truth Now, Peace Forever," has meticulously gathered names of the victims in Bosnia and Herzegovina. This has made accurate statistics (much lower than previous estimates) available for the first time and by making a database of victims and statements (without names of perpetrators) publicly available, has contributed to confidence in these statistics. The ICTY in The Hague also presented about their work. This court contributes to the ongoing discussion of the victims and perpetrators during the 1990's as individuals are sought, indicted, and sometimes released to national courts to be tried if their crimes were not the most major.

Within projects working on dealing with the past, education work about trauma narratives and the importance of perceived past traumas as a determinant for acts of violence has been reported to be helpful and a dimension that is not usually covered. Groups like the Center for Nonviolent Action and the Center for War Trauma work directly with former soldiers, many of which were involved in committing acts of violence. Focusing on the connection between trauma, peacebuilding, and reconciliation is helpful to them.

Learnings

We do believe that peacebuilding strategies in areas like SEE need to take into account the traumatic events of the people in the region. Using the term traumatized societies is one way to emphasize that trauma has social consequences as well as individual ones. Particularly if these events are collective traumas, we find that peacebuilding work needs to take into account the importance of group narratives. Such narratives can help to keep the conflict in the present state through the telling of stories and the current impact these stories have on them as individuals and as a group. This activity also contributes to healing of trauma and transformation of the conflict.

One of the benefits of using trauma healing as an entry point for peacebuilding is that it meets people where they are in a conflict situation—where they are wounded. Whereas many conflict transformation strategies focus on the difficult work of encountering the other, trauma healing is something that people can begin while among those of their own group. Although there is a danger of emphasizing victim narratives, it is easy to begin working with a traumatized group by giving them space to tell their stories. In fact this is a key component of trauma healing in our experience and in that of peacebuilders that we interviewed (Puljek-Shank 2003).

For the process of reconciliation to start, it is important to take the first step of retelling the story of what happened, and this story must be shared in an environment that is safe for the whole group. Each group needs to go through this process separately. The process must be led constructively, so that group could be able to name its losses and grieve them. If the group process is not constructive, but it is done for the purpose of strengthening a sense of victimization, then the cycle of violence can continue. When enough time has passed, and a majority of the group has gone through naming and mourning the losses, then the next phase can start—listening to the other group.

There is also an important place for incorporating trauma education into other areas of peacebuilding in traumatized societies, as suggested by Barry Hart's (see Introduction, Figure 1) Peacebuilding Wheel. We believe that Relief and Development projects can be more successful if they include an understanding of the reactions of individuals who have suffered psychological trauma. For example, many large projects in SEE have invested in rebuilding housing as a way of enabling refugee return. However, we find that returnees are often stuck in a pattern of helplessness which to us is connected to their experience of trauma. In addition, the symptoms of PTSD make it difficult to return to the location where traumatic events happened to them. As a result, development projects focused on job creation or rebuilding end up being minimally effective at achieving their goals. Similarly, initiatives in religion and spirituality also benefit from being conscious how they can contribute to healing. An example of this connection is the Pontanima choir in Sarajevo and the examples of healing that have happened at their concerts.

The Peacebuilding Wheel is helpful in that it shows the importance of integrating various components. Trauma healing is a point of entry and a natural connection with the other components. The model emphasizes the importance of explicit values with which peacebuilding work is engaged.

There are various types of organizations that deal with traumatized individuals. Groups that focus on victims are often concentrated on exhumations, return of loved ones, and prosecution of the perpetrators. They do not often see themselves as an important part of the peacebuilding process, or if they do it is only in a limited sense. While there is talk of the importance of reconciliation, it is common to hear people discuss "forgiving but not forgetting." This means that the traumatic event retains its importance in the group narrative. While we are certainly not supportive of forgetting traumatic events, we would like to see victim's groups have a more critical understanding of how they are used and seen by their own group. Victim's groups are often conveniently mentioned around election time to create a negative image of the other group, but are mostly forgotten when their basic human needs should be taken care of or when discussing return to their former homes. Likewise the ICTY is focused on justice in the narrow sense. What is missing is an overarching peacebuilding framework that allows various groups to see their individual efforts as part of one overarching whole and strategy.

Another important lesson is the potential of working with veterans as a peacebuilding strategy. Although this is not our own focus, the two partner organizations (CNA and the Center for War Trauma) that are involved in this work have a clear strategy of peacebuilding in doing so. This is work which requires patience because veterans groups often test the legitimacy of groups who may approach them desiring to help. Moreover, it is work that can best be done by local organizations. The potential here is that these former soldiers can become conscious of the processes by which they were enlisted to fight and can transform their own traumatic experiences and sense of loss (loss of youth, country, and ideals) into positive energy to work for peace. Many soldiers from all sides of the conflict have a clear understanding of what it means to fight in the war, what price they have paid, and how this is not the answer to building peace. After participation in the seminars many of them choose to become involved in peacebuilding work in their communities. The result of their involvement in peacebuilding work marks them as those who ask uncomfortable questions, say how things really happen and reexamine the motives for the wars. Thus, many of them are not able to find a job and are ostracized by their community.

There is the potential for the pain of trauma to be transformed into a motivation for peacebuilding. Some examples that demonstrate this among the partners with whom we work are concentration camp survivors who have come to see their trauma as a source of strength and compassion for others. These people seek dialogue with the other side and keep this dialogue on a continuous level. We are often amazed at the strength of the human spirit that can pull itself above enormous suffering and pain and be able to seek to talk to the other side in the desire for creation of peace that will be long lasting. Many of these individuals are believers and their faith has helped them to work on healing their pain and suffering. They have been able, through their healing to recognize the presence of God in those who were their enemies. This process is a deeply spiritual experience that transforms tragedy into a source of strength. It is also spiritual in the sense of developing a new sense of meaning for their lives, a way to find something good amidst the difficult thing that happened.

One important aspect is that this does not mean that the loss and pain have gone away—they are still present and these people will never again be what they were before. These individuals have become wounded healers, where they carry their wounds with them but do not inflict them on others. They are fully aware of their pain and losses, but there is something strong within them that pushes them to heal, and through this healing process they carry burdens of others (even their former enemies) and enable them to heal (Bartsch 1996).

When we started this work, we drew on the model of the Seminars in Trauma Awareness and Resilience (STAR 2002) which has worked with clergy from various religious groups. In SEE, clergy from all religious groups do not see themselves in a pastoral role as is often expected in North America. This has meant that we expanded our focus to include other helping professions, although clergy remain part of this effort through our partnership with the Bosnian Franciscan Order.

One learning we have is that we believe that the victims of trauma have a responsibility for their own healing. Although this can often be difficult for victims to hear, we see many victims being stuck in the process of waiting for an apology from the "other side." Although we understand the desire for recognition of the injustice that was done and also for justice, often when an apology does come it is not sufficient. Perhaps it is judged to not be sincere, or that there is not a sense of repentance and desire to make things right. Perhaps the apology is tempered by a qualifier, such as "we are sorry for what we did but we also suffered." Healing is a process that the victim needs to engage in for themselves. As one of our partners said, "We do not need to love our enemies, but we cannot let ourselves hate them either because of what that will make us into."

More attention needs to be paid to the aspects of shame. Shame is not often visible on the surface in public debate, in fact there is much more attention paid to claims of victimhood and the justness of each cause. However, shame from past defeats, and the desire to cleanse the group of them, is an important motivator. The strength of such motivators lies partly in being taboos, in not discussing them. Giving voice to feelings of shame helps people to recognize past losses while allowing space to discuss how they have been incorporated into present identities.

Each day brings new possible connections and ways to continue and expand this work in trauma education. Trauma healing and developing new narratives is a generational task, one in which the seeds that are planted my not bear fruit for some time.

Notes

1. Mennonites are one part of the Anabaptist movement which emphasizes pacifism, adult baptism, and congregations as the basic level of organization.

2. For this we are indebted to professors and colleagues at the Center for Justice and Peacebuilding at Eastern Mennonite University, among them Nancy Good Sider, Barry Hart, Carolyn Yoder, and Jayne Seminare Docherty.

3. Bosniak is the term preferred by this ethnic group, which was previously called Muslim according to the 1974 Yugoslav constitution but changed in order to facilitate the distinction between religious and ethnic identity.

4. The Mothers of Srebrenica is a group representing the families of those who were killed in Srebrenica in July, 2005.

5. We separate Kosovo/Kosova to indicate its distinct status at the time of writing as a UN protectorate. Likewise we use both terms to reflect those used by the two largest communities, Serb and Albanian.

References

Badurina, M., Pašić, H., Sikima Ž. and Zijadic-Husić, S. Conversation with authors. Sarajevo. 4 May 2007.

Bartsch, K. and Bartsch K. 1996. *Stress and Trauma Healing: A Manual for Caregivers.* Durban: Mennonite Central Committee, Vuleak Trust, and Diakonia Council of Churches.

Beara, V. and Miljanović, P. 2006. *Oh Where Have You Been, My Blue-Eyed Son?* Novi Sad: Center for War Trauma.

Becker, D. 2004. *Dealing with the Consequences of Organised Violence in Trauma Work.* Berlin: Berghof Research Center for Creative Conflict Management.

Blechman, F., et. al. 2000. *Finding Meaning in a Complex Environment Policy Dialogue.* Fairfax, VA: The Institute for Conflict Analysis and Resolution.

Botcharova, Olga. 2001. "Implementation of track Two Diplomacy: Developing a Model for Forgiveness." In Raymond G. Helmick, S.J., and Rodney L. Peterson, eds., *Forgiveness and Reconciliation: Religion, Public Policy, and Conflict Transformation,* Philadelphia: Temple Foundation Press.

Engle, S. M. 2002. "Mennonite Peacebuilding and Conflict Transformation: A Cultural Analysis." In Cynthia Sampson and John Paul Lederach, eds., *From the Ground Up: Mennonite Contributions to International Peacebuilding.* New York: Oxford University Press.

Figley, C. E., ed. 1995. *Compassion Fatigue.* London: Brunner-Routledge.

Hagan, W. 1999. The Balkans' Lethal Nationalisms. *Foreign Affairs* 78 (4): 52-64.

Herman, J. L. 1997. *Trauma and Recovery.* New York: Basic Books.

Kraybill, R. 1998. From Head to Heart: The Cycle of Reconciliation. *Conciliation Quarterly* 7:4.

Lederach, J. P. 1997. *Building Peace: Sustainable Reconciliation in Divided Societies.* Washington, D.C.: United States Institute for Peace Press.

Lederach, J. P. 2005. *The Moral Imagination: The Art and Soul of Building Peace.* New York: Oxford University Press.

Mack, J. 1990. "The Enemy System." In Vamik D. Volkan, Demetrios A. Julius, and Joseph, V. Montville, eds. *The Psychodynamics of International Relationships: Concepts and Theories. Vol.1.* Lexington: Lexington Books.

MacNair, R. M. 2002. *Perpetration-Induced Traumatic Stress: The Psychological Consequences of Killing.* Westport, CT: Praeger.

Malcolm, N. 1998. *Kosovo: A Short History.* New York: New York University Press.

Mennonite Central Committee. 2006. *Trauma Work in Bosnia and Herzegovina. Sarajevo.*

Moses, R. 1990a. "On Dehumanizing the Enemy." In Vamik D. Volkan, Demetrios A. Julius, and Joseph, V. Montville, eds. *The Psychodynamics of International Relationships: Concepts and Theories. Vol.1.* Lexington: Lexington Books.

———. 1990b. "Shame and Entitlement: Their Relation to Political Process." In Vamik D. Volkan, Demetrios A. Julius, and Joseph, V. Montville, eds. *The Psychodynamics of International Relationships: Concepts and Theories. Vol.1.* Lexington: Lexington Books.

Office of United Nations High Commissioner for Refugees (UNHCR). 1995. Populations of Concern to UNHCR: A Statistical Overview. Available online at http://www.unhcr.org/statistics/STATISTICS/3bfa32e82.pdf.

Puljek-Shank, A. and Puljek-Shank, R. 2003. "Journey of Healing." In Cynthia Sampson et al., eds. *Positive Approaches to Peacebuilding: A Resource for Innovators.* Washington, DC: Pact Publications.

Reich, H. 2006. "Local Ownership" in *Conflict Transformation Projects.* Berlin: Berghof Research Center for Creative Conflict Management.

Republika Srpska Government. 2004. The Events in and around Srebrenica between 10th and 19th of July 1995.

Research and Documentation Center. 2005. Plan of Activities July 2005 – July 2008. Available online at http://www.idc.org.ba/aboutus/RDC%20Plan%20of%20Activities_2005-2008.pdf

Röper, G. and .Gavranidou, M. 2003. Capacity Building in Trauma Therapy and Trauma Research in Bosnia-Herzegovina. *New Directions for Youth Development* 98: 99-110.

Sells, M. 1995. "Some Religious Dimensions of Genocide." In Steven Scholl, ed. *Common Era: Best New Writings on Religion.* Ashland, OR: White Cloud Press.

Seminars on Trauma Awareness and Recovery (STAR) Manual. 2002. Harrisonburg, VA: Eastern Mennonite University.

Sider, N. G. 2003. "Transcendence: Discovering Resources for Posttraumatic Healing and Growth." In Cynthia Sampson et al., eds. *Positive Approaches to Peacebuilding: A Resource for Innovators.* Washington, DC: Pact Publications.

Šuber, D. 2006. Myth, Collective Trauma and War in Serbia: a Cultural-Hermaneutical Apraisal. In *Anthropology Matters Journal* 8. Available online at http://www.anthropologymatters.com/journal/2006-1/suber_2006_myth.htm

Thompson, A. 2000. When the Slaughter Ceases: Understanding and Assisting Traumatized Societies. *Mind and Human Interaction* 11: 162-176.

United Nations Development Program. 2000. Human Development Report Youth. Sarajevo: UNDP.

United Nations Development Program. 2002. Human Development Report Bosnia and Herzegovina. Sarajevo: UNDP.

Vila, P. 2000. *Crossing Borders, Reinforcing Borders: Social Categories, Metaphors, and Narrative Identities on the U.S.-Mexico Frontier.* Austin, TX: University of Texas Press.

Volkan, V. 1990. "An Overview of Psychological Concepts Pertinent to Interethnic and/or International Relationships." In Vamik D. Volkan, Demetrios A. Julius, and Joseph, V. Montville, eds. *The Psychodynamics of International Relationships: Concepts and Theories. Vol.1.* Lexington: Lexington Books.

———. 1996. Bosnia-Herzegovina: Ancient Fuel of a Modern Inferno. *Mind and Human Interaction* 7: 110-127.

———. 2000. *Traumatized Societies and Psychological Care: Expanding the Concept of Preventative Medicine.* Charlottesville, VA: Center for the Study of Mind and Human Interaction.

Yoder, C. 2005. *The Little Book of Trauma Healing: When Violence Strikes and Community is Threatened.* Intercourse, PA.: Good Books.

9

Arts Approaches to Peace: Playing Our Way to Transcendence?

Babu Ayindo

We trust the arts to inform us of our inner urges. They present us with a keen insight as to who we are as well as who we wish to become.

– Bill Cosby

In the last decade, greater recognition has emerged in the "role" of the arts in "mainstream" peacebuilding interventions. Premised on the realization of the limits of the dominant rational approaches to peace education and peace interventions, many artists and peace workers—to use Bill Cosby's phraseology—continue to "acculturate" themselves towards the arts to "validate [their] common humanity."[1] These "arts approaches to peace" have led to in-depth, kinesthetic and experiential learning that is essential when responding to historical pains, problematic multi-cultural encounters or where peace and social justice interventions demand more holistic approaches. In particular, ground-breaking experiments have been undertaken with "arts approaches" in community building, conflict resolution training, facilitation of conflict transformation processes, social justice advocacy, intra-personal and collective healing and, in general, in the quest to break cycles of all forms of violence.

Though accorded considerable attention, current arts approaches are still largely regarded as add-ons and, for the most part, struggling for legitimacy in "mainstream" peacebuilding work. Indeed, numerous are cases where the arts are viewed only as a "tool" to be applied after more serious conflict issues have been logically dissected and concluded. In spite of, or probably because of, its undisputable potential, it is not an exaggeration that the inclusion of courses and initiatives on "arts approaches" in traditional academic programs, training institutes and civil society programs has largely remained minimal and in some occasions, simply tokenistic.

This trend is somewhat ironic for even a cursory historical survey of the evolution of the arts, reveals how our creative expressions were at the core of community building, peacemaking and peace sustenance. Indigenous Knowledge Systems extant in many societies in all continents establish how the arts have always been at the heart of humans' attempt to encounter, and possibly transform, their relationships with other humans, their social structures, nature and the "world beyond." To a large degree, therefore, this discussion represents an attempt to return to the fundamentals of arts and life. In *Decolonizing the Mind*, the Kenyan writer Ngugi wa Thiong'o notes that "drama has its origins in human struggles with nature and with others."[2] Wa Thiong'o reminds us that in pre-colonial Africa (and in other parts of the world), the arts were not sliced away from everyday life. Physically and spiritually, the arts were located at the core of the daily drama of life wherefrom it drew energy, style and definition. For instance, ritualistic theater aimed at correcting the imbalances and disharmony that existed between humans and fellow humans, humans and nature and humans and the "world beyond." Put differently, the arts were a key factor in the making of a culture; in the humanizing of the world. And it is through art that the histories, norms, and values of a community were transmitted imaginatively through narrative, dance, masks and paintings, to mention a few. In other words, if a theoretical validity of arts approaches in peacebuilding may be lacking currently, there is definitely a historical basis for the approach.

Against this background, this chapter is animated by the need to offer a theoretical validity of "arts approaches" in peace education and peace interventions. The working hypothesis is that while the dominant rational approaches to peace work have, in theory and practice, led us to situations of compromise, social order, and occasionally, peace, "arts approaches" bear potential to fully challenge our imagination in the search for creative, viable and sustainable alternatives. Put differently, is it not through the arts that the entire field of conflict transformation can accelerate the movement towards more holistic and transcendental approaches and interventions?

This chapter makes modest contributions in this endeavor drawing on my experience of doing and learning "arts approaches" in various parts of the world. The evidence suggests that if there were greater dialogue between the fields of arts and peace, this discussion would not be necessary. Whether it is in breaking cycles of violence and trauma healing; peace education and training; appreciation and challenging of worldviews, identities and values; social justice research and advocacy; deepening of the spirituality of peace; creation of social and physical spaces for transformation; redefinition and strengthening of human security; and general conflict transformation work, "arts approaches" would find their rhythm and claim their place.[3] But in order for this to intentionally happen, we need to begin by confronting the reality that the field of "arts approaches" is heavily under-theorized and sometimes simply misunderstood.

Critical Theoretical Questions

Writing in 1985, in a fascinating study aptly titled *Social Interaction as Drama: Applications from Conflict Resolution*, A. Paul Hare observed that:

> There is a continuum ranging from everyday life activities that do not have a dramatic quality, through social events that are consciously staged, to theater productions. *In every case, the same psychological variables are at work.* However, the playwrights, directors, actors and critics involved with theater have paid considerable attention to some of the processes involved in the presentation of an idea to an audience. *We must therefore turn to them for source of concepts and hypothesis to be used until more exact terms can be derived.*[4] (italics added).

Hare's assertion that the field of conflict resolution "must" turn to the arts is borne by current trends and patterns in the search for a solid peace praxis. A majority of community based and middle level peace training and direct interventions continue to heavily borrow from the arts. Role playing, simulations and sculpting are perhaps the most popular artistic techniques used in conflict resolution training, peace education and peace interventions. However, by the same token, is it not possible that Hare's assumption, namely, that this borrowing would only be necessary until the conflict resolution field develops its own "exact terms" may have inadvertently stifled in-depth dialogue on the rightful place of the arts in peace education and interventions? In other words, would time come, as Hare seems to suggest, when conflict resolution would no longer need to "turn to" the arts for tools to make it more effective?

This question leads to three cobwebs that need to be confronted and possibly cleared away, before "arts approaches" and peacebuilding can enter into meaningful dialogue. These are: the political history of art, particularly theater; the deficiency in research in regard to the nexus between arts and peacebuilding; and slow development of a solid theory for arts approaches to social change.

Political History of Art

First published in 1979, Augusto Boal's *Theater of the Oppressed* is an epic study on the political evolution of art, especially theater. Not only is the text a solid aesthetic companion of Paulo Freire's landmark *Pedagogy of the Oppressed*, but it also offers a trenchant and compelling historical analysis as well as a theoretical interrogation of contemporary forms and content of art. In the foreword, the Brazilian artist, educator and activist is unequivocal about the primary task of the book: "all theater is necessarily political [...] For this reason the ruling classes strive to take permanent hold of theater and utilize it as a tool for domination. In so doing, they change the very concept of what "theater" is."[5] Boal meticulously proceeds to unmask the ideological and practical manipulation of art and theater that have taken place in history and, above all, how the collective creativity, aesthetics and critical engagement by the majority of peoples have been deliberately whittled away over the years.

In the beginning, Boal celebrates: "theatrical performance was created by and for the people, and could thus be called the dithyrambic song."[6] Indeed there are many indigenous people who do not have an English equivalent for the terms art or theater suggesting an intertwining of life and the collective creative encounter. In "A Brief History of Theater Forms" Alice Lovelace is equally poetic:

> In the aboriginal theater, the community (artists were always part of the community) gathered in the open, under the sky, nature providing the scenery and backdrop. The action was inter-disciplinary, using mask, songs, dance, ritual and unscripted so that the audience/community was free to intervene and shape it. This theater was under the authority of the community. Together they told stories reflecting their values and world view.[7]

Boal notes that it is the aristocracy in the middle ages which subtly invented the superficial division between actors—a select few who could mount the higher level proscenium stage and act—and the majority who would remain seated and watch passively. Even amongst the select group of actors, the aristocracy entrenched their hegemony, values and norms by separating the protagonists—representing the aristocratic class—and the chorus, representing the masses. The process did not end there. With the exit of the aristocracy, the succeeding bourgeoisie class saw the political opportunity in domesticating the arts, particularly theater, which was highly persuasive and had immediate public appeal. With the emergence of the bourgeoisie class, the protagonists created by the aristocrats were embellished even further and as such "became multi-dimensional subjects, exceptional individuals, equally separated from the people, as the new aristocrats—this is the poetics of *virtú* of Machiavelli."[8]

The middle class was equally creative—politically speaking. A new character that typified the values of the middle class was created following Aristotelian poetics. This cult hero, Lovelace tells us, was a member of the aristocracy with a "streak of independence." To date, Hollywood art generally follows this schema where the flaws of this heroic character are severely punished or rewarded when the character upholds the values of his—it usually a he—class. In the creative process, the audience/community, which is a primary party to the unfolding conflict, is not invited to join in generating creative alternatives but rather it is exhorted to remain passive when conflict occurs and wait—yes, wait—for the exceptional middle class hero to liberate them. Unlike the aboriginal theater, the passivity in the creative process is translated into passivity in real life.

And, lest we forget, Boal reminds us in *Games for Actors and Non-Actors*[9] that in Chinese mythology, theater was invented by a woman. Man then took control of theater and domesticated it to primarily advance patriarchal values. Man could not entrust woman with the power and capacity to create and re-create. In the process, critical dialogue–a central element in human interaction and social change–was virtually extinguished as the male-dominated ruling class used theater to construct narratives that entrenched and justified patriarchy, hegemony and domination.

I want to emphasize that to date art, and particularly theater, are still being used to rationalize, sometimes with spiritual overtones, the passivity of the majority oppressed classes. By controlling the ideology, form and content of theater, the distorted creative expressions are virtually sufficient to convince the masses about their "role" in society as passive consumers of art and, above all, entrench an apathy and passivity that is difficult to unlearn or transform. I want to hypothesize that the new bourgeoisie in "modern" nation-states have taken full advantage of technology to propagate an ideology of passivity through art.[10] The bad news, as Boal points out, is that the masses do not just stop acting in the theater (and film), they also stop "acting" in real life!

A more radical change that has taken place, perhaps more germane to our discussion on "arts approaches" to peacebuilding, has to do with dialogue. I think it was the German playwright who said that if cows could dialogue, not all of them would go the slaughter-house. When drama ceased being an inclusive engagement and moved into esoteric spaces, communication was altered in a most fundamental fashion. Let us listen to Lovelace again: "communication was transformed from that which had symbolic meaning and was open to interpretation, to the tightly defined and specific meaning. Language became a barrier, turning the dialogue into a monologue."[11] My experience working in areas of conflict and violence demonstrates how words, indeed words in the predominant English language, simply cannot begin to define or express deep-seated pains and issues. A more symbolic, nonverbal and creative language is required to begin to articulate the pains that people have experience hence the need for "arts approaches."[12]

These historical development in art and theater partly explain why, to date, the word art or theater conjures up images of a building where roles of some "mysterious" artists working in some obscure space and where the un-talented majority literary encroaches. The people no longer can, or have a right to be, creative. While indigenous wisdom teaches us that our Creator and art were at the heart of our very struggles and existence in this life, "civilizations" reduced people's communication with God to one day a week and turned people into passive consumers of arts once every other week – well, if they have the money.

The process of *real politik* diluting the arts is most evident within societies that underwent colonization. In *Wretched of the Earth,* Frantz Fanon elaborates on the phases of transformation that the artist in the colony undergoes in the quest for liberation and in creating relevant culture. In order to redefine her identity and role in society, the artist first imbibes the imposed art and culture of the colonizer. Second, the artist feels a void and tries to remember what she is and an attempt is made to reconnect with traditional art. In the third phase, the artist has to "go native" and shake off the superficial wings of the colonizer.[13] She feels compelled to create art that communicates messages of revolutionary change.[14] Perhaps the artist in "arts approaches" is now on the frontiers of "going native" and redefining the nature, form and content or art in order to create genuine dialogues of peace by peaceful means.

The struggle for redefinition is also evident in the school culture. Being a microcosm of the political super-structure, the school has, by and large, sought to suppress the creative spirit through compartmentalization of knowledge and privileging the rational above the emotional. In the formal school system, education is structured in such a way that as one ascends to the higher levels, the less creative one is expected, or to be more precise regimented, to become. By the time one arrives at university one is expected to be calm, rational and show less affinity to emotions and the dramatic arts. The energy, zest and creative spirit of youth almost dies. In short, the right brain that exudes more aesthetic vibes is heavily under-utilized. It is no wonder that to date, while the majority of university students are drawn from rural Kenya, the university theater companies still think it is revolutionary to "take" theater to the people rather than do theater with the people.

The creative spirit that one finds in kindergarten slowly and systematically disappears as one ascends the academic ladder where logical approaches are canonized. In formal and informal spaces, imagination and creativity are stifled. Instead of emphasizing possibilities as in kindergarten, the academy works particularly hard to separate right and wrong. And, in this endeavor, emotion and creativity are valued even less as one accepts the fallacy that excellence can only be measured through the "only" language of fine words and higher grades.

The unmistakable thread in Boal's *Theater of the Oppressed* is the emphatic call for a new poetics. The definition of art and theater as a resource for self education and social change available to all humans may sound strange to many but it is available. In *Towards a Poor Theater*, the Polish director Jerzy Grotowsky questioned the definitions of theater that skewed the focus from the essentials of theater: namely, body, voice and mind. Grotowsky underlines how current theater practice has swayed away from its very essentials[15] shared by all humans. Though still a minority thought, Boal's idea that all humans possess "essential theater"[16] remains an irresistible call to humans to naturally seek, as Cosby's points out, to "validate [their] common humanity through [their] creative expressions in the arts."

Therefore, in the quest to return the process and products of art to their fundamentals, the reality we must confront is that current theory and practice of art and theater is guided by these dominant and hegemonic ideologies of politics and art. Even within academic institutions and communities, the view that art is for a select few with mysterious gifts is a pervasive thought. In some cases, the political class and those who wield political power in other strata in society continue to control the nature, form and content of art in general and theater in particular.

At one level, artists too must take responsibility for the mystification of art. As privileged captives of this unjust structures (to use the words of Neville Alexander), a majority of artists made the process of art-making an alienated affair where only a few could be allowed to enter the altar of creativity and imagination. While I accept that certain individuals are talented in certain skills more than others, I would like to see this reality being used more as an invitation to others to dialogue in the creative process rather than a superstition for alienating others. In "arts approaches" we aim at overcoming the element where people are spectators in the creative process for they also became spectators of history! I join Boal in echoing that a new poetics is possible.

The good news is, over the past three decades, experiments worldwide are changing this perception about art. For instance, *Theater of the Oppressed, Playback Theater* and *Theater for Development*[17] can be categorized as global movements that attempt to return the nature, form and content of theater to the fundamentals of their historical roots and function. In these forms of art, the people no longer function as passive spectators. Indeed the creative process is no longer esoteric; it is an inclusive rehearsal for social action.

Deficiency in Documentation and Research

The second challenge focuses more on the deficiency in research on the nexus between arts approaches and peacebuilding. Studies that specifically explore the nexus between arts approaches and peace studies and interventions are still very few. Craig Zelizer in USA, Olivier Urbain in Japan and Dessa Quessada-Palm in the Philippines are examples of people who have in the recent past made significant attempts at documenting experiences in arts and peace. This process has been stifled by the tradition of fragmenting knowledge in schools, universities, research institutions and the media. The system of presenting knowledge in "self-contained" compartments has affected both peacebuilders' and artists' ability to discern the web of how entire systems of conflict and possible interventions function.

Whereas arts approaches have been used widely, they have remained substantially under-theorized fundamentally because of lack of documentation. For instance, the rich and extensive experiences of arts approaches in peace work pioneered by artists, Bert Monterona, Tony Apat, Dessa Quesada-Palm and Babu Ayindo for five years at the Mindanao Peacebuilding Institute in southern Philippines are still crying for robust consolidation, cogent documentation and rigorous reflection and theorization. And, this leads us to the third challenge, namely, the articulation of a compelling theory of "arts approaches" in social change.

On a Theory of Social Change

While there is no doubt that practitioners applying "arts approaches" in their work function with a theory in mind, the problem is that this theory is not clearly or well articulated in the field of "arts approaches". I hasten to point out that as a graduate student at Eastern Mennonite University in 1996, it was quite clear that this was a struggle that the field of peace studies, or at any rate as taught at Eastern Mennonite University in 1996, shared with the field of "arts approaches."[18] This is well dramatized by the sheer search of appropriate terms in both peace studies and "arts approaches."

Therefore, in some cases, arts approaches have only provided some "feel good" experience without underlining how arts approaches can actually result in a peaceful and egalitarian world. Or, in some extreme cases even the seemingly liberating arts have been used in the further domestication of the people. Indeed with the proliferation of Non-Governmental Organizations' arts programs in the global south, there has emerged a troubling trend where the arts and theater have been used to beautify unjust systems. In a provocative presentation at a Theater and Education conference held in University of Exeter, UK, in 2002, Syed Jamil Ahmed raised troubling questions about patterns in *Theater for Development* in Bangladesh. Using pseudo-Frerian techniques, urban-based Non-government Organizations mounted supposedly participatory "theater-for-development" programs that basically regimented rural farmers through aesthetically embellished "development messages" to continue producing more raw materials for the development agenda of select few local government agents and multinationals companies. The injustice at the core of such an exchange was hardly questioned and art was used to mobilize farmers to acquiesce to their own oppression!

Again, this is an urgent task for practitioners and theoreticians in the fields of arts approaches and conflict resolution. To lead us to this task, let us underline some lessons, if briefly, from indigenous arts.

The Artist and Conflict: Learning from the Indigenous Traditions

As mentioned earlier, we need to begin by noting that many indigenous societies do not actually have a term for art or theater. We can infer that whereas there are those who were more talented in the arts, it was expected that art was everyone's business. The idea of copyright and intellectual property of artistic and cultural products is therefore a very recent idea. Nowhere is this manifested more than in the songs produced during the antiapartheid struggle in South Africa. To date, no one knows who the original writers of the most popular liberation songs were. More importantly, in the minds of many, it is not even an issue. In her refreshing article, "Mirror, Mediator and Prophet: The Music Indaba of Late Apartheid South Africa" Ingrid Byeley shows how music–or Music *Indaba*[19] as she terms it–transcended the confines of apartheid at various stages of the anti-apartheid struggle, up to when it was dismantled. In her own words, "Music Indaba involved all sectors of the complex South African society, and provided a leading site within the dilemmas of the late Apartheid era which could be explored and resolved, particularly issues concerning identity, communication and social change."[20]

Several other studies reveal the rightful place of the arts, particularly theater, in traditional societies. Chris Wanjala has researched the critical role of the artist among the Batachoni and Babukusu of the Luhya nation in western Kenya.[21] According to Wanjala, the key role of the artist or storyteller is that of a healer and peacemaker. As the custodian of history, the artist sought to nudge the community to transcend conflicts that have resulted from the unavoidable encounters of life. In his insightful study, *Acts of Service*, Jonathan Fox notes:

> Thus the storyteller in an oral culture assumed a special responsibility to tell the story which contained the teaching most important for the community to retain. In this sense he was a priest—a mediator between people and higher ele-

ments—as well as historian and yarn-spinner.[22]

In many indigenous societies, the artist was expected to be at the center particularly during times of crisis. The Ugandan poet Okot p'Bitek is more radical in his assertion. In *Artist the Ruler,* p'Bitek argues that there are two types of rulers in the world: the political chieftain and the artist. Though the artists commands no forces of coercion, she is the more powerful, the poet tells us. And ruling she does not by force but by "proclaim[ing] the laws [...] in the most indirect language; through metaphor and symbol, in image and fable. [She] sings and dances [her] laws. It is taught, not in the schools of law, not in the Inns of Court, but around the evening fire, where elephants and hares act like men"[23]

In an insightful article, "The Mediator as Trickster: The Folkloric Figure as Professional Role Model," Robert Benjamin draws parallels between the current mediation practice and the role of the folkloric figure in resolving conflicts in traditional societies. In every society, Benjamin asserts, a trickster figure exists who thrives on conflict whether by generating or resolving it. He argues that storytelling which is the main "trick" of the Folkloric Figure nourishes human relationships and affirms *communocratic* ideals. Benjamin shows how the mediator challenges the perspectives of the disputants by "editing" their scripts (or narratives) and devising different scenarios to enable all the parties to play in a new drama. Through manipulating the drama the mediator is able to dislodge the parties from their entrenched positions.

Is this not a process of manipulation? Benjamin is insistent that:

> For effective conflict management, pure rational or analytical expertise is not enough. The notion of "come let us reason together," borne from a rational mode of thought and practiced by traditional professionals, is too facile and oversimplified to be effective in complex and protracted conflict. This is not to suggest that mediators should operate by wits and intuition alone, but that the mediator requires both intuitive sensibilities as well as analytical skills. The trickster figure models both.[24]

History provides us with fertile seeds for "arts approaches" to peace and social justice work. Fortunately, there are examples that would help us transcend the narrow and sometimes superficial boundaries erected by the academy and school culture. That is the task to which we shall turn our attention beginning with two recent experiences.

The Art of Reconciliation in Urban Nairobi

Is there, or should there be, a line between art and reality? On which site does art and peacebuilding meet? A lingering experience with a Girls' school in the outskirts of Nairobi in 1997 helps us grapple with these questions. The students at the school had gone on strike and as is characteristic in many Kenyan schools, the students were suspended without much dialogue. However, two weeks after being re-admitted, and in spite of, or perhaps because of, going through some tough disciplinary measures at re-admission, it was evident that the young girls were plotting yet another strike! The school leadership invited Amani People's Theater to "teach" the girls ways of living with all the authority.

Fortunately, at Amani People's Theater[25] a few of us were trained teachers and, of course, all of us as Jennifer Fisher[26] says, were products of the oppressive school culture. The team of facilitators from Amani People's Theater designed a strategy to respond to the situation by undertaking a creative analysis with the students and staff separately then, at some point, assess whether the power issues had been challenged enough to bring the two groups together for dialogue. In the one day intervention, we began by working with the students in three groups while a team of facilitators worked with the teachers. The role plays and sculpting with the students and teachers revealed that tension had considerably built in the school. Interestingly, the students were more than ready to caricature their teachers and show the absurdity of being suspended over "small" issues. These creative processes in small groups took more than four hours in the morning.

In the afternoon, our plan included a process of challenging the perspectives of the students in a Forum Theater process that would encourage broader reflections in their response to conflict. We asked the teachers to stay away from the Forum Theater until we invited them. In the forum we explored what other options the students could consider beyond throwing rocks? The Forum Theater, where an open ended skit developed by one group was performed and discussed, evoked strong emotions. Step by step, the jeering from the students subsided giving way to a more focused discussion and character creation. The facilitation team led a process that creatively analyzed both the problem and possible options given the school and social structures within which the students found themselves.

Following the Forum Theater process, the facilitation team began a process of role playing alternatives to violence as a response from students in a school situation as suggested by the students. The school chef, who had watched with obvious amusement the whole process, volunteered to join the drama where she played the character of a parent. While she was "invisible" all along she suddenly became visible. This had a sobering effect on the process. However, before we even planned for the rest of the school leadership to join us, the headmistress, the head of the school, decided to "gate-crash" into the process at a point when the facilitator was asking the students to volunteer playing the headmistress. In Amani People's Theater we rarely encouraged people to play themselves because of the psychological effect it is likely to have. Again, we knew the involvement of the headmistress could inject negative energies to the whole process.

With the entry of headmistress in the space, the silence was loud as we waited for a volunteer to play the headmistress. It seemed no student was ready to do that, not in the presence of the headmistress. Then like a bombshell, the headmistress volunteered to play the role of the headmistress, or more specifically, to play herself! There was hesitation and silence. The facilitators looked at each other and tacitly decided that the situation merited breaking the rules (whose rules were these, by the way?).

What followed looked surreal. In the safe environment of the People's Theater process, the students and prefects in the drama revealed the key issues they faced–which included lack of communication, frustration by prefects[27], and an administration not ready to listen to them. As the drama built to a climax, the students and headmistress hugged and promised to make the school a community for all of them. In the process, the facilitators—or jokers as Boal calls them–lost their power to dictate the pace.

As the headmistress and students embraced at the end of the process the facilitation team wondered in whispers what our role really was in the process as the boundary from drama to reality was crossed with ease. Or, even whether there was any boundary at all to cross?

Integrating Indigenous African Storytelling, Playback Theater and Forum Theater

In the recent past, when I have worked in contexts of extreme trauma and pain, I have found it useful to create space for the integration of indigenous African storytelling, Playback Theater and Forum Theater.[28] Before I offer some insights gained in using the technique in various parts of the world, let me share an abridged version of an indigenous African narrative that I first heard from my late grandmother, Josfina Ongecha, and which I have adapted given the contextual challenges. I would usually perform the open ended narrative with song, dance and chants:

> When the earth was still young, all the animals in the forest of Hope would gather every evening to sing, dance and just celebrate who they were—and, oh, and who they were not. And, so it was for many years till one evening, during the windy season, the Green Leopard suddenly changed the tradition. In those days, all animals respected each other so much so that the question of fear of each other never arose. But on this occasion, fear entered the vocabulary of the forest as the Green Leopard arrived late, refused to join the cycle of song and dance, and, instead, demanded, in a thunderous roar, that one of the animals prepare him breakfast the following morning.
>
> This had never happened in this history of the forest of Hope. The Green Leopard picked on antelope to prepare him breakfast. But when antelope consulted with the rest of the animals who had now stopped celebrating, they responded in a manner never witnessed in the forest. "Well" they said, "he is the Green Leopard and we do not know why he chose you." Antelope prepared breakfast consisting of his last born child and took it the Green Leopard's cave.
>
> The following day, with an equally loud roar, the Green Leopard, refused, one more time, to join the circle of celebration but, again, demanded that tall giraffe prepare him breakfast the following day. On the third evening, the Green Leopard became even greedier. He chose the small Ma'rabbit and asked her to prepare all her nine children since they were "rather small."
>
> On the following morning, Green Leopard waited at his cave but Ma'rabbit did not turn up. After a while, he stepped out in fury swearing to eat any animal that resembled a rabbit. But as he walked past the great big Mugumo tree he heard some sobs. He peeped and saw Ma'rabbit hiding and sobbing. As soon as Ma'Rabbit saw Green Leopard she explained: "Oh Great one, I prepared all my

> nine children and even added some onions and tomatoes because I love you and respect you. Then on my way to your place, another Green Leopard, grabbed the tray and ran away.
>
> "Another Green Leopard grabbed my breakfast?"
>
> "Oh, yes, the one and only Green Leopard!"
>
> "Where did he go?"
>
> Ma' Rabbit pointed towards the river. With rage, Green Leopard sped towards the river. "I will teach that insolent, recalcitrant Green Leopard a lesson—a lesson for all other animals!" He stumbled with rage at the bank of the river and looked around. There was no Green Leopard. He looked across the bank, but there was no Green Leopard. He roared but no other Green Leopard appeared. Then, just then, he looked into the waters of the meandering river and saw the "other" Green Leopard. He roared in anger looking into the river. He shouted. "You can take away my breakfast and still have the audacity of mimicking every action I do? I will teach you a lesson; I will show you that I am not only in control of the land but also what lies above and below it."
>
> Then with rage, Green Leopard, jumped into the river.
>
> Of course, there was no other Green Leopard in the waters. Worse still, he was drowning. Not quite. He held himself against a branch, some twigs and a rock. When he looked at the bank he saw Ma'rabbit smiling and calling on the other animals to assemble. He pleaded with Ma'rabbit to save him. But they were all singing and dancing their favorite song of who they were—and who they were not—but in a slightly different tune. In tears, he pleaded for Ma'Rabbit to intercede on the behalf of the other animals to save him…

I would usually stop at this point and leave the story open ended. The participants would then work in groups to determine the possible next steps in the narrative. Depending on the character of the group, this would then lead to a Playback, Forum Theater or Visual Arts to explore some of the key issues from the narrative and group presentation that capture the momentum of the time.

I once told this story at Monroe County Jail in Rochester, New York, to two groups of men and women separately. It was interesting how the men's group quickly completed their group work and elected one of them to report with clear logical brevity that since they, as the animals, were not responsible for the Green Leopard falling into their river, they would just let him drawn. In fact, there are inmates who did not participate in the group work since they did not see any "issue" to be belabored. On the other hand, the women's group worked collaboratively and made a presentation where the Green Leopard would be given another chance after new rules and conditions are created and to which Green Leopard would agree to while he is still in the water!

In Freetown, Sierra Leone, one vibrant group led by Alimamy Karbo devised a "solution" where the Green Leopard would disappear into the water but would be held afloat for months by the Crocodile. During all this time, the Green Leopard would witness all the transformation the animals would make as a consequence to his action to ensure no other animal ever imagined turning carnivorous. Eventually the Green Leopard would return to the land, an entirely different world, of which he had little choice but embrace the values of the majority.

In Maridi in South Sudan, one group of leaders-peace makers decided that they would save the Green Leopard but pluck out all his teeth and claws. However, when I returned to Maridi after almost a year for a follow up Trauma Healing workshop[29], some participants recalled the story of the Green Leopard and regretted their "solution." They suddenly realized that after a whole year the Green Leopard had already grown a new set of teeth and claws. It was time to explore another sustainable solution!

In Nadave in Fiji Islands[30], I retold the story one month after the December 5, 2006 coup. One group came up with an interesting solution: Green Leopard was saved only after he promised to become vegetarian. The question that lingered was whether Green Leopard could actually sustain a vegetarian diet.

I must confess that these processes do not always work wonders. I once told this story in Kigali, Rwanda, during a Youth and Conflict Resolution workshop, and in an indefensible lapse of concentration, I talked of the cockroach leading the song and dance of "who we were and who were not." As soon as I uttered those words, the silence was palpable. During the genocide of 1994, the minority Tutsi nation has been referred to as "cockroaches." I cannot tell, to date, why I picked on the cockroaches as characters in the story. Actually cockroaches never featured in my narrative performances. The room fell silent as soon as I mentioned the C-word. And for almost two days of the one week workshop, I was unable to recover. Painfully I learned the lesson of research and checking with indigenous knowledge.

Breaking the Cycle of Violence

The dilemmas that I have explored in different contexts in the creative process of integrating storytelling, Playback Theater and Forum Theater is how to break the cycles of violence at personal and structural level? In the narrative of the animals in the forest of Hope dilemmas are the following:

- Should Ma'rabbit take over the leadership on account of her cunning? And, supposing she did, would she not quickly transform from a vegetarian to a carnivorous? (are we really able to change structures or do structures change us?)
- If the animals were to give the Green Leopard another chance, in what ways would they have to re-organize their lives to ensure that no other animal—not the Green Leopard alone—would turn carnivorous?
- What kind of justice should the Green Leopard and other animals go through to ensure that no other animal would eat their very own?
- What makes humans today behave like the Green Leopard by failing to take the opportunity to reflect when he saw his image in the flowing waters?
- How comes the animals were enthusiastic to celebrate with each other but slow to support each other in times of crisis?
- What does this say about the fundamentals of community life and personal and collective responsibility in breaking the cycles of violence?

My experience shows that pain and violence in most of global south has affected people *en masse*. One on one counseling is simply not possible and in some cases it is not rooted in the tradition and culture. In some cases, defining someone or a people as traumatized is culturally repugnant. Indeed, in many indigenous communities, healing is not viewed through the bio-medical lenses. Ethno-medical approaches conceive a more holistic definition of health and ill-health where, as Alex Kamwaria notes "the body and mind are seen as not only unitary, but also integrated aspects of an individual within the network of social relationships."[31] The state of health, or ill-health, is manifested in the quality of relationship humans amongst themselves as well as their relationship with social structures of governance they have created.

Our experience suggests that current approaches to healing and breaking cycles of violence tend to pay scant attention to the pervasive yet potent nature of structural violence. It is therefore not enough to heal individuals but breaking the cycles of violence work needs to be at the core of work and an agenda to transform social and governance structures so that they become responsive and life enhancing.

Some of the lessons gained, and dilemmas generated, from the integration of Storytelling, Playback and Forum Theater are as follows:

- How can we ensure that the personal stories of pain are woven into the social story leading to social action and transformation?
- How do we respond to localized global conflicts?
- What is our understanding of justice from our cultural perspective? And, what kind of justice would lead us to sustainable peace?
- How do we transform structures so that those who have temporarily healed during the intervention do not simply return to function in structures that traumatize them again?
- How does the field of arts approaches fully benefit from the experiences and wisdom of both genders?

The exploration of this narrative offers the symbolic tools and space to indirectly explore both personal and social narratives of pain and conflict. This would usually be followed by small circles where participants share their own personal stories. Some may volunteer to have their personal stories "played back" or adapted to the larger social narrative that calls for collective social action.

The Nigerian novelist was right when he noted that "when we have an experience or chaos into a story we have transformed it, made sense of it, transmuted experience, domesticated the chaos."[32] Indeed, as Lesley Fordred asserts "stories are not omnipotent, but offer an astonishing resource for reflection and transformation."[33] My grandmother used to tell me that when I hear a story I must re-tell it. Or, if I do not like, I should tell my own story. When I was young I never realized that in retelling, or "playing with structures of given stories" was actually an act of transformation.

Playing Towards Transcendence?

In her refreshing article titled "Rehearsal for Change: Reclaiming the Senses Through Arts Approaches," the Filipino artist-educator, Dessa Quessada-Palm reminds us that

> One of the tragedies brought about by militarism and its accompanying culture of violence is the infringement on personal and collective freedom to experience life with vigor and zest, and the denial of the right to be ensured of safety as people exercise their creative will and critical thinking. As a result of conditioned habits reined in by structures of social control, of trauma and fear, or of inadequate opportunities and spaces that nurture and value dialogue, independence and diversity, more people in militarized contexts are increasingly being denied of a chance to tap fully into their creative potential and to realize their human agency.[34]

Most societies in the world are now either visibly militarized[35] or heavily policed. While the effects of militarism have been analyzed in terms of their "hardware" effects, less attention has been granted to the "software" effects, particularly as they affect three elements of our creative richness as humans. Quessada-Palm rightly notes that

> Our bodies and voices are both receptors and expressive devices that manifest our conditions, values and dispositions. *Work on transforming society will therefore have to integrate the agenda of freeing and rehearsing people's bodies, voices and minds towards an alternative sense of themselves and vision of the world.* (italics added)

Nowhere was this perceptibly manifested than my recent experiences in Fiji Islands. In January 2006 I served as lead facilitator of the inaugural Justpeace Youth peace camp, coordinated by Arieta Koila-Olsson. The sheer zest, energy and urgency of the youth was evident throughout the workshop particularly when the youth engaged the then keynote speaker, acting president Ratu Joni Mandraiwiwi in a viva voce on the social political situation in Fiji Islands.

Only a year later, the 2nd Justpeace Youth camp was held, a year after another coup in Fiji Islands. It was evident that the bodies and voices of young people had been contrived; some youth could hardly be heard when they spoke; walking around the open workshop space was limited and guarded. In my view, part of the "problem" was the fear of the military. No amount of rehearsal of bodies and voices seemed to change the situation particularly for the boys. Fortunately, the Ecumenical Center for Education, Research and Advocacy (ECREA) had invited the military to participate in the workshop. The Republic of Fiji Military Forces (RFMF) assigned an intelligent, warm and perceptive military officer in the person of Major Sam Tupoo who not only actively engaged in the learning process but offered to field critical questions from young people on the historical role of the military in Fijian politics and the dilemmas of the function of the armed forces in a modern nation-state. After his presentation on the third day of the workshop, the change in body, voice and expression in the young people was almost instantaneous. I was humbled by the major's involvement in an envisioning exercise for Fiji Islands. In general , the energy and creativity of youth was regained with vigor. The youth developed beautiful murals with a clear advocacy message for themselves and for political leaders on the Islands.

In contexts of pain and heavy militarization, it is obvious that peace work demands approaches that go beyond the traditional emphasis of mediation and negotiation. The arts provide a language and a process for a deeper analysis of conflict and violence and more cogent non-threatening, almost enjoyable, process where creative alternatives can be explored. Johan Galtung, considered the father of Peace Research, puts it more cogently in his milestone *Searching for Peace: the Road to Transcend*:

> The road to transcending, to developing a praxis for peace, is through transforming the underlying structures and causes of a conflict by promoting a plurality of visions, alternatives and voices, and by building peace work on the search for creative and viable alternatives to violence drawing on the background and experiences of actors at every social level [...] It does not neglect the traditional and cultural approaches to conflict resolution but seeks to build on them, learning from them, strengthening them and generating new approaches and new visions [...] it answers the challenge to creativity and peace based on transcending the structures and causes of violence, which mediation fails to do.[36]

And in order to go beyond compromise, and reach a level of transcendence, we need empathy, creativity and nonviolence, Galtung rightly notes. These are resources found in abundance in "arts approaches." Fortunately, both the history of art and peace theory provide a firm basis for the development of an arts approaches to peacebuilding that will not be locked in the narrow politics of compromise but result in creative alternatives that transcend both our perspectives and theories of social change. If Galtung is right, then the first place to seek empathy, creativity and non-violence is in arts approaches to peace.

Notes

1. Cosby, B. 2004. "Arts of Understanding," in *In His Own Words* by Nelson Mandela. Little, Brown and Company, NY.
2. Ngugi wa Thiong'o, Decolonizing the Mind: The Politics of Language in African Literature (Nairobi: East African Educational Publishers, 1981).
3. See the "Peacebuilding Wheel" as conceptualized by Dr. Barry Hart of the Center for Justice and Peacebuilding, Eastern Mennonite University, Virginia, USA.
4. A. Paul Hare, Social Interaction as Drama: Application from Conflict Resolution (London: Sage, 1985).
5. Augusto Boal, Theater of the Oppressed (London: Pluto, 1979).
6. Boal, Theater of the Oppressed.

7. Alice Lovelace, "A Brief History of Theater Forms: From Aristotle to Brecht, Baraka, O'Neal and Boal" published online at http://www.inmotionmagazine.co./theater/html

8. Boal, Theater of the Oppressed.

9. Augusto Boal, Games for Actors and Non-Actors (London: Routledge, 1992). As the title suggests, Boal shares his experience doing theater in various spaces and people in various parts of the world.

10. Kenya has one of the greatest drama movements in schools. Every year, schools compete from zonal level to national level in the production of plays, dances, narrative performance and poetry. However, the climax of the performances is a "State House concert" with the President, who is head of State and government, as chief guest. In my experience as teacher-director, writer, director and adjudicator, it was evident that teachers and students angled their artistic pieces to fit the "politically correct" message at the time. It was a subtle, yet potent process, where school culture mirrored the national culture.

11. Lovelace, "A Brief History of Theater Forms." For an incisive discussion on "theater without scripts" see Jonathan Fox, Acts of Service: Spontaneity, Commitment, Tradition in the Nonscripted Theater (New York: Tusitala, 1986).

12. Another disturbing trend is to assume that dialogue is taking place because a community project is participatory. In an incisive chapter titled "Participation: The New Tyranny?" Frances Clever shows how many of the participatory projects coordinated by Non-Governmental Organizations (NGOs) were actually disempowering. Regarded as an "act of faith" participation "[h]as been translated into a managerial exercise based on 'tool-boxes' of procedures and techniques. It has been turned away from its radical roots: we now talk of problem solving through participation rather than problematization, critical engagement and class."

13. For an incisive study on the contradictions, paradoxes and ironies of this process of arts (specifically literature), politics and liberation in the postcolony, see Apollo Obonyo Amoko "Against African Literature: Canonicity, Citizenship and the Idea of Africa" (unpublished PhD dissertation, 2004).

14. Cited in Ingrid Bianca Byerley, "Mirror, Mediator and Prophet: The Music Indaba of Late-Apartheid South Africa" (published on line by the University of Illinois, USA).

15. Jerzy Grotowski, Towards a Poor Theater (New York: Simon and Schuster, 1968).

16. Telephone lecture by Augusto Boal to the "Theater and Conflict and Transformation" class at the Summer Peacebuilding Institute class at Eastern Mennonite University, co-facilitated by Jennifer Fisher and Babu Ayindo, June 2000. In his lecture, Boal talked of Essential Theater as the human capacity to imagine and reflect on what is and what it could be. This is what fundamentally distinguishes humans from animals. In Rainbow of Desire, Boal argues that theater is the first of human inventions. As well, it is the invention, which paves the way for all other inventions and discoveries. Theater enables us to observe ourselves and by so doing "discover what it is not and imagine what we could become."

17. See for example, Zakes Mda, When People Play People (London: Zed Books, 1993).

18. I have argued in the article "The Problem with Peace Education: Curriculum, Pedagogy and the Idea of Conflict Resolution" (forthcoming) that part of the reason why peace education trainings and interventions are hardly problematized is that there seems to exist amongst peacebuilding theoreticians and practitioners a tacit but dominant fallacy that to be critical of any peace initiative implies being pro-violence. Therefore, any

'peace education' is necessarily good because to be against it would be morally indefensible.

19. Byerley elaborates that ""Indaba" is a Zulu word meaning both an update on topical matters and a conference, symposium or meeting-place at which members of a group contribute equally towards the solution of a problem. It suggests combined efforts at working towards consensus through discussion of matters concerning the group as a whole. The word, of Nguni origin included Zulu, Xhosa and Swazi nations.

20. Bianca Byerley, "Mirror, Mediator and Prophet."

21. Presentation at the Kenya Drama/Theater and Education Association regional symposium held at the Kenya National Theater, Nairobi, Kenya, December 1997.

22. Jonathan Fox, Acts of Service: Spontaneity, Commitment, Tradition in the Nonscripted Theater (New York: Tusitala, 1986).

23. Okot p'Bitek, Artist the Ruler (Nairobi: East African Educational Publishers, 1986).

24. Robert D. Benjamin, "The Mediator as Trickster: The Folkloric Figure as Professional Role Model" Mediation Quarterly (Winter: 1995) 137. This role of the artiste was often misunderstood as shown by David Kerr, African Popular Theater (London: Heinemann Educational Publishers, 1995). For instance, the colonist "banned indigenous village satirical groups called Halo on the grounds that between conflicting Halo groups were a source of dissension and disorder . . . the District Commissioner did not realize that the Halo groups stabilized village disorders and by driving the groups underground he was fueling the fires of conflict and resistance."

25. Founded in 1994 and based in Nairobi, Kenya, Amani People's Theater applied arts approaches in peace and social justice work. I served as founding artistic director of the ensemble.

26. Jennifer Atieno Fisher "Looking on from Outside; An Evaluation of Amani People's Theater Programs (unpublished), December 2001.

27. Prefects in the colonial British school system are supposed to be leaders amongst the student population who assist the school administration. During my days, prefects were despised as they served as informers and "intelligence gatherers" for the school heads.

28. Another arts group that is undertaking valuable experiments in integrating Storytelling, Playback Theater and Forum Theater is Ubuntu Arts, based in Nairobi, Kenya.

29. Under the auspices of STAR program (Strategies for Trauma Awareness and Resilience) workshops initiated by the Center for Justice and Peacebuilding, Eastern Mennonite University, Harrisonburg, Virginia, USA in collaboration with several organizations.

30. My gratitude to Paulo Paulo Baleinakorodawa and Adi Vasu Chute for their generous advice when I checked with them before the Storytelling-Forum Theater performance whether the narrative would be appropriate in the tense situation in Fiji Islands then. My gratitude also to the late Mimi Turner–Brower and Wilbur Bontrager of Finger Lakes Restorative Justice Center for organizing and guiding the workshops in the correctional facilities and schools in Rochester, New York.

31. Alex Kamwaria "Psychotherapy and Spirituality in the African Context: The Case of Post-conflict Healing Rituals among the Dinka of Southern Sudan" (unpublished, 2006).

32. Cited in Lesley Fordred "Taming Chaos: The Dynamics of Narrative and Conflict" In Track Two, July 1999.

33. Fodred "Taming Chaos"

34. Dessa Quessada-Palm, "Rehearsal for Change: Reclaiming Senses Through Arts Approaches (unpublished, 2006).

35. The World Council of Churches defined militarism as "the result of a process whereby military values, ideology and patterns of behavior achieve a dominating influence over the political, social, economic and foreign affairs of the State." Cited in Yash Tandon, Militarism and Peace Education in Africa (Nairobi: AALAE, 1989).

36. Johan Galtung, , et al. Searching for Peace: The Road to Transcend. (London: Pluto Press, 2000) 78—79. See also his landmark Peace by Peaceful Means: Peace and Conflict, Development and Civilization. (London: Sage, 1996).

10

A Post-Genocidal Justice of Blessing as an Alternative to a Justice of Violence: *The Case of Rwanda*

Vern Neufeld Redekop

Within the context of genocide, human beings imagine and act out ways to maximize the physical, emotional, and hermeneutical suffering of their victims[1] at both the individual and collective levels. Hermeneutics refers to interpretation and meaning-making. For victims, the loss of family, friends and homes calls into question the meaning systems by which they make sense of the world. The deliberate destruction of things of symbolic significance and command rape of women of the opposing identity group are meant to cause suffering at the level of basic values related to the construction of meaning; they intensify hermeneutical suffering. (Anyone who has read or heard accounts of genocide knows the details, which I will not describe here.) The breadth and depth of suffering deliberately caused are overwhelming; the actions, imaginations, and hate-filled

---

Much of the conceptual development is derived from "The Relevance of Teachings of Blessing and Justice of Blessing for Reconciliation in Bosnia i Herzegovina," a paper I presented on October 28, 2006 at a conference on *National Reconciliation, Ethnic and Religious Tolerance and Human Security* in the Balkans organized by the European Centre for Peace and Development. The broader conceptual background is developed in *From Violence to Blessing: How an Understanding of Deep-Rooted Conflict Can Open Paths to Reconciliation* (Redekop 2002)

orientation come together in a form of violence, which in its negative ineffability push the level of injustice to levels approaching infinity. Yet for the perpetrators the violence is justified by memories of their own historic victimization, a mythology of imminent threat at the hands of the victims, and a chauvinistic conviction that they somehow have a right to all that belongs to those they are torturing and killing.

In the wake of extreme violent injustice there is a natural inclination among human beings to do justice violently. This may take the form of reciprocal mimetic violence in which perpetrators are made to suffer, even in ways similar to what they caused their victims to suffer. Another form of violent justice is through punishment that is meted out by a court which proceeds in a context of the rule of law. Forms of punishment have evolved from high suffering death penalties (boiling or burning) to lethal injection to penalties not involving death but some level of suffering. Justice demands that the gross imbalance of individual and collect suffering be redressed—that atrocities not be allowed to happen with impunity, that evil be denounced, that the probability of perpetrators repeating what they have done be reduced to zero. At its most basic level, justice is about the twin concepts of balance and rightness. Cultures are formed in large measure by how they define justice in terms of these concepts.

Given the overwhelming need for justice in the face of genocide, given the human capacity for creative imagination, and given human ingenuity at making what is imagined real, I will develop a new concept of justice, called a justice of blessing, in the hopes that this will make a difference on the ground in Rwanda. This concept of justice is closely related to restorative justice and finds its place in the context of reconciliation. Expressed simply, a justice of blessing is a structured way in which perpetrators commit themselves to take action diachronically for the well-being of the survivors of their genocidal actions. Their orientation, attitude and actions are focused on blessing for the victim/survivor group. Key result areas of blessing are healing, relationships, structural change and transcendence. Healing addresses hermeneutical, emotional, physical and spiritual woundedness. Structural change addresses actual and relative loss and reduces the risk for future victimization. Relationships imply the building of trust. Action is comprised of basic actions, action chains and practices (Macintyre 1981; Ricoeur 1992) the different types of justice making actions address the injustices of genocide directly, indirectly, and informally.

The words, and the concepts they represent, in this dense description are derived through a hermeneutical process that combines a) attention to how they are used within religious/cultural traditions with b) an awareness of the realities and challenges of genocide and c) the on-going development of a conceptual framework for understanding human capacity for violence and for caring. *Justice of blessing* as a concept takes on meaning within the larger framework of mimetic structures of violence and of blessing and within the sub-framework of reconciliation. Its potential needs to be understood in the context of an integral assessment of the losses and woundedness of victim-survivors (individual and collective) as well as the state of perpetrators during and after a genocide. I will develop the concept of justice of blessing in spiral fashion returning to the concept, with a section on justice of blessing, in relation to each the following: 1) mimetic structures; 2) retributive and restorative justice; 3) reconciliation; and 4) an integral assessment of needs; the concept of an integral approach has been developed by Ken Wilber. At its basic level it means to take into account internal and external aspects of a phenomenon at the individual and collective levels. After developing an understanding of justice of blessing in this fourfold conceptual framework, I will present the Arusha Tribunal and Gacaca process as two justice making initiatives in the wake of the Rwandan genocide. I will then show how the concept of justice of blessing can be used heuristically—as a theoretical tool that can be used to discover new insights—to uncover important aspects of these initiatives and how they could be complemented by follow-up actions.

Mimetic Structures of Violence and of Blessing

The story is told of someone who went on to the afterlife and wanted a tour of the premises. She wanted to see hell first. She found grumbling, unhappy people who looked as though they were starving. There were tables of food in front of them but their forks were longer than their arms so they could not get the food in. She went on to heaven where she found happy, well-fed people. The tables of food were the same as in hell as were the long forks. The only difference was—they were feeding each other.

This story illustrates the difference between mimetic structures of blessing and mimetic structures of violence. In this fictional heaven people were contributing to each other's well-being; in hell they were not; in fact, out of their frustration they were probably poking each other with their long forks.

When mimetic structures of violence take over a relational system, people imitate one another in being violent; a pattern is established and the structure takes on a life of its own. The post colonial histories of Rwanda and Burundi can be understood in terms of intertwined mimetic structures of violence involving Hutus and Tutsis. Violence toward one group in one country often inspired violence toward the other group in the other country.

In contrast, when mimetic structures of blessing infuse a relational system, people work toward the mutual well-being of one another. I am told of how, at the village level in Rwanda, this was often the case; Hutus and Tutsis lived together with little regard for distinctions between them.

Mimetic structures are imitative patterns that go on through time. They express and determine the attitudes, orientation and actions of the parties involved. Violence may take many forms: control—restricting the freedom of people; force—inflicting something onto people against their will; extraction—taking something away from people; diminishment—reducing the status or dignity of people; hurt—causing physical of emotional pain; curse—orienting oneself to wish evil on the other; and refusal of help—allowing suffering when one has the means to alleviate it (Redekop 2002).

The concept of blessing comes originally from the Hebrew word ברכה *berekah*—it is associated with on-going well-being and relationships of solidarity and creativity (Fox 2000). Its usage puts in a discursive field that includes sustenance, sustainability, creativity, high ethical standards, flourishing, mutual respectfulness, life, joy, gift, peace, and, over the long term, having descendants who are secure in their place in the world.

By comparing mimetic structures of violence and blessing (See figure 1.), we can see that structures of blessing are characterized by openness, generosity, sharing, creativity and the generation of options. They allow for more complex patterns of interaction.

Mimetic Structure
of

Violence	Blessing
◄———	———►
Deep-rooted conflict	Reconciliation
Closed	Inclusive
Fewer Options	Generative
Acquisitive	Generous
Death oriented	Life oriented
"I had no choice . . . "	Choices

Figure 10.1. Mimetic structures of violence and blessing

There are some concepts that can be drawn from the Hebrew roots that provide added value and meaning to mimetic structure of blessing. From the root metaphor of *barak* as to kneel, we can make a connection between blessing and receptivity, a key concept in Taoism. Receptivity stands in contrast to power, which is an overwhelming value within mimetic structures of violence. But, in so far as mimetic structures of blessing are to provide a context and base for empowerment it suggests both the receptivity to receive from others as well as the action oriented dimension of working to provide to others what they might need. Generosity must be balanced by receptivity for mutuality to work. The Hebrew association of blessing and land speaks to the need to include the environment in the equation. If land/environment is a necessary condition to living well, it becomes a partner in sustaining mimetic structures of blessing. Even though the literal significance of a locutionary act of pronouncing a blessing seems out of place today, that very concept can function heuristically by raising the question of the link between speech and intentionality and hence between speech and the orientation of the locutionary actor. Even the fact that blessings often were intended to extend for generations can play the heuristic role of suggesting that mimetic structures of blessing should be constructed in such a way that they are sustainable through the generations. It links to the Canadian Aboriginal teaching that decisions are to take into account the history of the past seven generations and are to be made in such a way that the benefits will be felt seven generations into the future.

Furthermore, within a relational system marked by mimetic structures of blessing there will be conflict, understood as a clash of identity need satisfiers, interests or desires that can potentially result in mutual hurt. Within such a structure, however, conflict is transformed into an occasion for creativity so that there can be mutual contributions to the well-being of all parties. There is also a discursive field that includes compassion, patience and mercy that can contribute to the on-going restoration of relationships when they get off the rails.

Mimetic structures of violence can be characterized either by indifferentiation, as is the case in mimetic rivalry, or differentiation, as is the case in scapegoating. Mimetic structures of blessing can be marked by a movement toward a blessing of indifferentiation in cases of dehumanization—that is, points of commonality and shared humanity are found—or blessing of differentiation, which is needed when rivals are too close and may need more distance—psychological or physical—between them.

Blessing is used to connote a life-oriented, creative impulse oriented toward the mutual well-being of Self and Other.[2] Within a mimetic structure of blessing Self and Other feed one another at many different levels of reality. If blessing becomes mimetic, both parties are at the same time receptive and generous. Symptoms of blessing are joy, confidence, self-esteem, peace, dignity and respect.

Justice of Blessing (1)

At its core, a justice of blessing works within a meta-ethical framework of blessing. That is, it is oriented toward establishing structures of blessing within which people contribute to the well-being of one another. This raises many questions about whether or not this is feasible or even desirable in the wake of severe human atrocities.

Within the framework of mimetic structures, reconciliation can be perceived as the process by which those in a mimetic structure of violence reduce the hold that violence has on them and begin to construct mimetic structures of blessing. However, the actions associated with the mimetic structure of violence may end up being asymmetrical; that is, one of the parties stands out as being more significantly victimized as is the case in genocide. In this context a justice of blessing can be seen as a process by which the legacy of past violence is dealt with in a systematic way. Former perpetrators become agents of blessing as they do what is necessary to work toward the well-being of victim/survivors. What they do, how they do it, and from what distance (psychological or physical) must be determined through dialogue with, and giving priority to, victim/survivors. Every effort needs to be made to enhance the security of those victimized.

How this might happen will become more clear when it is seen within a better developed framework of reconciliation. However, we will first put justice of blessing into the context of other conceptions of justice.

Retributive and Restorative Justice

For victims, attending to the need for justice is a necessary, if not sufficient, condition for healing. The idea that violent, oppressive actions can be taken with impunity adds to the sense of injury. "With impunity" means without punishment, accountability or negative consequences. It points to a fundamental, almost visceral understanding of injustice. The primal call for justice is a call for perpetrators of violence to suffer not only any negative consequences that might naturally come their way as a result of violence but negative consequences imposed upon them by the victims, those in solidarity with victims, or by the state acting as a third party.

This primal sense of justice manifests itself first as vengeance and, at second order, as retributive justice—a justice based on punishment. French thinker René Girard, develops the concept of mimetic violence, that is, that violence, once introduced, is imitated, and reciprocated (Girard 1987; Girard 1988). Victims define for themselves a need for violence to be balanced, what was done to them or their loved ones should be done to the perpetrator. However, as Girard points out, violence is always returned with interest; hence there is a spiral of ever increasing violence.

An initial act of violence not only inflicts harm, but it also creates a relative imbalance in a capacity to act. The one traumatized by the loss of a loved one, injury or loss of possessions is put at a grave disadvantage in terms of the horizon of the future. It is this relative imbalance that needs to be addressed.

Roots of Retributive Justice

"Justice" is a word with many meanings. Its roots go back through Latin to Greek (Kolbert 1979) with a significant Hebrew interface (Schrenk 1964). Originally it had connotations of what is right, or what is done to make right, or the process of indicating what is right. *Right* in turn had to do with balance (Sharpe 2004), particularly in the wake of structural imbalance (Hahnel 2005). It meant to do what was customary—i.e. the way we are used to doing things defines rightness—and eventually was linked with the very concept of law.

Justice can also be conceived as finding a right balance of goods, that is, that which enhances well-being—economic, physical, rights, power, or recognition. The challenge is to define what "right balance" means in a particular case. This is a matter of both process and comparison with a standard (Rawls 1999). The standard may be defined through a statement of rights, or laws, a moral code, or cultural tradition. Laws may either help to define the degree of harm (tort law) or the degree of offence to the community (criminal law).

Retributive Justice

In the case of one party causing suffering to another party, one way of attempting to balance the situation is for the party responsible for the suffering to be caused to suffer in a commensurate way through revenge or retributive justice (Walgrave 2004). Strict justice means that the suffering of the perpetrator must come as close as possible to that caused by the initial act of violence. However, much is a matter of interpretation. If victims are not only hurt or traumatized by fear, but also interpret the harmful action as having disgraced their honour, they feel that much more that something has been taken from them and hence the debt owed by the perpetrator is that much greater. Likewise, when it comes to "repaying the debt," this too is a matter of interpretation. Those who look to time spent in prison as a way of paying a debt to society, have a currency of prison time such that the more grave the offence the longer the sentence. The sentence then becomes a measure of the degree of injustice inherent in the wrongdoing. Those who interpret their victimization as having been severe and who witness a perpetrator getting a small sentence will perceive the system as having committed a further injustice by not according to their crime the severity they have felt. Yet all this is a matter of interpretation—first a system of interpretation of severity in terms of sentence and second a particular sentence as reflective of the degree of victimization. At a meta-level this assumes a debt to society on the part of the perpetrator which in turn presupposes that wrongdoing needs to be punished.

There are analogical comparisons to be made in the case of large intergroup conflicts. In these situations, the groups themselves become the agents of retributive justice-making and inevitably there are mimetic rounds of revenge-based violence.

The fatal flaw in a violence-based paradigm of justice is that the victim, who initially is indignant at the violence done to them, gets drawn into a mimetic structure of violence (Redekop 2002). The victim desires more than anything that violence be done to the other, to the perpetrator. The perpetrator, who is hated, becomes the model for the victim. The victim then appears to be left with a profound negative aporia—for the perpetrator to be violent with impunity is untenable; to become violent in response means that the perpetrator becomes the model whose actions and attitudes are mimetically appropriated and the victim becomes like the hated one. In addition, to become obsessed with a passion for violence is not a helpful, life-giving option for the thoughtful victim. Furthermore, there is the risk that violence overall will be increased over the long term, particularly if the perpetrators being punished become scapegoats for communal problems beyond the violence for which they are responsible (Girard 1989; Redekop 1993).

This retributive approach assumes that the violent action can be imputed to a well defined perpetrator (Ricoeur 2000). A well defined perpetrator must be one who is capable of deciding spontaneously to engage in violence. The perpetrator must be able to be held accountable for the violence. Perpetrators have their own histories and identity needs. They are located within communities and cultures. In some cases clear decisions are made to harm innocent victims. In many cases, perpetrators consider themselves to be victims and are acting out of their own desire for vengeance for perceived violence and injustice done to them in the past.

These difficulties with retributive justice call for rethinking of the very concept of justice. There are some options that have been developed: something short of strict justice—mercy, forgiveness, restorative justice, relational justice. Before examining these options, it is important to enunciate some principles that should be present within any justice-making processes. First, the needs of the victim should be addressed. Second, the victim should be an actor throughout, that is, the victim should have options and should be empowered to decide upon different courses of action. Third, no further harm should be done to the victim and the victim should be better off at the end of the process. Fourth, any accrued benefits—absolute or relative—coming from the violent action should be transferred from the perpetrator to the victim/survivor. Fifth, as much as possible, the perpetrator should be given an opportunity to play an active role in the justice making process. Sixth, there should be an equitable balance established as a result of the process. Seventh, the process should play an exemplary and pedagogical role within society such that it has the effect of reducing the likelihood of similar types of violence in the future.

Croatian theologian Miroslav Volf, points out that a response short of strict justice is called for (Volf 1996). This means that at least there will not be an increase in violence within the response. Perpetrators are held accountable and may be punished but care is taken to limit the degree of punishment in order to decrease the possibility of violence being on the increase.

Restorative Justice

If the essential sct of justice values is positive and constructive, the emphasis is put on making things right, and the paradigm is known as restorative justice (Zehr 1990). That is, first and foremost, rather than cause additional suffering on the part of the perpetrator, balance is sought by attending to the well-being of the victim (Johnstone 2004). In this case, if the violence involves theft or injury to property, the property is restored to the victim.

Restorative justice puts the emphasis on a mediated negotiation by which the perpetrator agrees to do everything possible to make things right. This may include such things as apology, payment of reparations, and constructive symbolic actions. The emphasis is on restoring the relationship that existed before the initial violence, assuming that the relationship was positive.

Extending mercy means that the victim and/or the community recognize that full restitution is not possible and that strict retribution would not result in positive consequences and thereby what is expected from the perpetrator by way of restitution or suffering is reduced. Mercy functions then as a gift. To use the mercenary metaphor of accountability that is often used associated justice, it means that the debt accrued on the part of the perpetrator for having been violent is metaphorically stroked from the record books, or at least significantly reduced. The concept of grace which is etymologically linked with gift would suggest that metaphorically there is a justice fund set up whereby in a situation of mercy, the debt is paid from this fund with no strings attached. Mercy can be extended by any individual or body charged with bringing justice to a situation.

Forgiveness is much like mercy but with different connotations. In forgiveness the victim that does the forgiving becomes an actor who voluntarily gives up the right to seek redress or to seek a balancing violence in the form of punishment to be perpetrated against the perpetrator. Forgiveness can occur without any interaction with the perpetrator. There is a reflexive dimension in that the forgiveness is a gift the victim gives herself; that is, it releases the victim from the hold of negative memories. Many victims also need to forgive themselves for they blame themselves for decisions made before the violence in the language of "If only I had . . ." Forgiveness is a letting go of the need and right to make the perpetrator suffer on the part of the victim. Forgiveness may take place without mercy; that is, the victim/survivor may go through a psychological process of forgiveness but the bodies responsible for justice may not necessarily grant mercy.

Justice of Blessing (2)

Restorative justice has tended to focus on a discursive process whereby a decision is made concerning the obligations of the perpetrator to the victim and the community in the wake of a crime committed. The discursive process may take the form of a victim-offender mediation session, a sentencing circle, a recommendation by a third party to a judge that an alternative sentence be given in line with the principles of restorative justice.

A justice of blessing resembles restorative justice in that the opportunity is made for a perpetrator to undertake actions that make things right. However, it builds on the concept by shifting the emphasis from a synchronic one-time decision to a diachronic a change of orientation whereby the perpetrator binds himself to a commitment to work towards re-empowering the victim over the long haul without knowing what this might entail. Being a perpetrator of genocide has both legal and human implications. The commitment to work toward blessing of the victim could be made public within a legal setting and the follow-up could involve institutions with a quasi-legal orientation. Besides the formal aspects, a justice of blessing includes indirect approaches to blessing such as blessing through shared economic development and informal approaches such as hospitality and acts of generosity and kindness.

Reconciliation

Reconciliation can be understood as both a goal and a process. The first part of the goal is to get out of mimetic structures of violence. At this stage, people can co-exist without hurting one another and without fear of attack. The second part of the goal is to establish a mimetic structure of blessing.

Reconciliation as a *process* may be understood as a complex set of exchanges that include a number of elements (Figure 2). At times, the process is directed through a conscious well-defined effort to achieve reconciliation, in other instances, the process may take place at the tacit level with different actors intuitively taking a variety of initiatives. Invariably, the process will include some or all of the following elements (Redekop 2002) organized under the rubrics of *Pre-requisites*; *Meta-requisites*; *Discursive and Symbolic Processes*; *Key-Result areas of Healing, Structural Change and Renewed Relationships*; and *Justice of Blessing*:

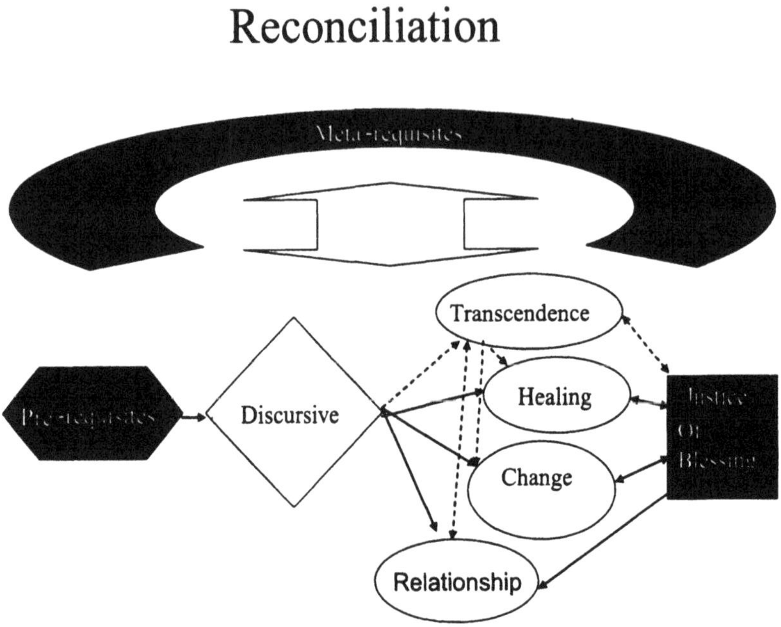

Figure 10.2. Process of reconciliation

Pre-Requisites

1. Vision and mandate: either one of the parties or a third party has a vision and desire for reconciliation and obtains a mandate to work to that end.
2. Safety: the safety of the parties needs to be assured. This means that overt violence must be halted. Sometimes a legal framework needs to be in place to assure the safety of potential victims. Safety also means that the parties do not intimidate each other.
3. Immediate survival needs: reconciliation processes can be demanding both cognitively and emotionally. Hence it is important that parties are assured of having their immediate physical and emotional needs sufficiently met to function through the process.

Meta-Requisites

1. Teachings: the process of reconciliation is directed by a framework, values, root metaphors and mental models that provide motivation and insight to keep the process going. Teachings may take the form of stories of previous reconciliation processes, traditional proverbs and customs, or analytical insights. Education for reconciliation includes the development of skills (Huyse 2003) and generation of new beliefs and attitudes about both the conflict and the other party (Bar-Siman-Tov 2004).

2. Gradual Reciprocated Initiatives in Tension-Reduction (GRIT) (Osgood 1966): one party may decide to make a low-risk gesture of goodwill; if the other party reciprocates with a similar gesture the first party may take another positive initiative (Osgood 1966). Gradually the tension dissipates and the parties are prepared to enter into another level of discourse to address the deep-rooted conflict.
3. Institution Building: in the face of large scale violent events, the various sub-processes need to take place within institutions that could include Truth and Reconciliation commissions. If there is to be a justice of blessing, this could demand an institution within which there is ongoing follow-up.

Discursive and Symbolic Processes

1. Dialogue: at some point parties will enter into a dialogue in which they are motivated to truly understand one another. Dialogue means that meaning flows freely between the parties (Bohm 1997). There is also open disclosure of the emotional dimensions of the conflict.
2. Truth-telling: in addition to the dialogue there may be a need to formally establish the truth of what occurred. Ideally this will lead to a shared acceptance of the same presentation of the history of the conflict. Analysts, historians[3] and lawyers may play a role in this and it may involve a formal process (Lederach 1997).
3. Expressions of acknowledgement of harm done, remorse, and apology: eventually those who have committed acts of violence will understand the impact of these acts on the other party. As they acknowledge a) what they have done, b) the hurt it has caused, c) feelings of remorse over having caused the harm, and d) a desire to not commit the same acts in the future, they will be able to offer an effective apology.
4. Expressions of victimization, openness to forgiveness: those victimized will express to the perpetrator and third parties what they have experienced. As they hear an acknowledgement of their hurt from the perpetrator along with apologies and expressions of remorse they may become open to forgive. Forgiveness means to give up an impulse or right to make the perpetrator suffer in response to the suffering caused by the perpetrator, implying moral judgment, the humanity of the perpetrator, and a desire for a renewed relationship (Bole, Drew Christiansen, & Hennemeyer 2004; Shriver 2001; Volf 2005).
5. Justice and mercy: justice involves making some judgment about what would restore a sense of balance to the relationship. Where violence has involved theft or destruction of possessions, these can be restored. When there is emotional pain, torture, or loss of life, it is impossible to return parties to their previous state. Some things may be done by way of compensation or compensatory actions to alleviate the loss. Some form of mercy or generosity of spirit may be combined with positive balancing measures to craft a profound forgiveness (Lederach 1999).

Key Result Areas

1. Re-orientation of relationship: this may demand inner changes of identity, attitude and orientation in relation to the other (Bar-Siman-Tov 2004). Both parties and the relationship itself will be transformed such that both parties will contribute to mutual empowerment.
2. Healing of traumas and memories: in order for the reconciliation process to be sustained and for both parties to flourish, it is important that as much as possible emotional traumas and memories be healed. Reconciliation rituals may play a role in this process (Schirch 2005) as can various forms of therapy (Herman 1997), cognitive reframing and spiritual disciplines and practices (Hermann 2004).
3. Transformation of structures: reconciliation is not complete if the structures left in place continue to victimize. For example, hegemonic structures, in which one party systematically dominates another party, involve economic, political, physical, and/or discursive dimensions (Redekop 2002). Action has to be taken in each of these areas to address systemic imbalances. New laws, customs, economic regulations and institutions may be needed to sustain the reconciliation process (Kriesberg 2004).
4. Transcendence: Transcendence implies that those disempowered by either trauma, shame or depression are brought to a new level of reality whereby they achieve a measure of wholeness that gives them a new sense of agency. Transcendence can be understood in terms of transformation, achieving a higher level of consciousness or the result of spiritual events, experiences and disciplines. As one victim/survivor put it, it is getting from the ditch onto the road again.

Reconciliation is not a linear process; rather it is cyclical and iterative. Not all of the elements above may be present each time and some may have to be addressed repeatedly.

Justice of Blessing (3)

The root concepts out of which "justice" emerged, also produced the concepts of righteous, virtue, and goodness. These suggest a paradigm of justice called relational justice in which the goal is first and foremost to produce good, mutually empowering relationships. Within this paradigm, justice as seeking a balance, becomes a part of a bigger process of reconciliation. As such there are specific justice-making aspects of the process in line with restorative justice and there are broader dimensions of justice-making as reversing hegemonic structures, laws and customs that may have contributed to victimization are adjusted for long-term achievement of justice within larger relational systems (Napoleon 2004; Redekop 2002).

The link between healing, justice and reconciliation is complex just as identity-based conflict is complex. For some victims, the need for meaning is achieved through justice-seeking processes. This in turn, may help to reduce the trauma. For some victims, the result of justice and reconciliation processes may address their need for security and hence reduce the fear component of their trauma. If the very process empowers the victim to take action and to make choices, their sense of agency and self-esteem are enhanced. If the hurts of the victim are recognized by the community and acknowledged by the perpetrator, the feeling of being fundamentally violated may diminish. In like manner, the process may address the needs of the perpetrator who also is in need of healing (Staub & Pearlman 2001). If the victim is allowed to see the humanity of the perpetrator and if both parties can acknowledge a shared humanity, this too will help in spiritual and emotional healing. Given the complexity of the situation, it is impossible to predict in which of these areas healing is most needed and in which, given the imperfect realities, positive redress will be achieved.

A justice of blessing is meant to adjust the balance between victim and perpetrator, to make thing right, over the long term. In its first phase, it establishes the loss and woundedness on the part of the victim and the motivation and role of the perpetrators. The key is to get the perpetrators to admit to their violent actions, acknowledge the loss and woundedness that resulted. Where people were killed, nothing can restore the situation but perpetrators can commit themselves to working for the long-term well being of victims and groups of victims without knowing in advance what that might mean. There would be two temporal dimensions to the justice process. In the short term, stolen lands and property would be returned, to the degree possible. In the long term, there would be a commitment to periodic accountability sessions in which the healing and personal growth of the victims would be acknowledged and new needs derivative of the victimization would be identified. A plan of action would be undertaken to address these needs and at each subsequent accountability session, a report would be given on action taken. On-going remorse would be communicated along with thanks for every act of graciousness on the part of victims. This would be the formal part of the process. Informally perpetrators would find ways to go beyond what was required in terms of contributing to the well-being of victims and victims groups. Over time, a new constructive relationship would be formed.

Assumptions of a Justice of Blessing (see figure 3).

- What is destroyed can not be restored.
- The perpetrator is oriented toward enhancing the well-being of victims.
- Victims are oriented toward rebuilding their lives.
- It starts with returning property that has been stolen.
- There is a shared imagination and vision of long term best case scenario.
- Early on there are short term objectives defining actions, attitudes, and orientation that address healing, structural change and relationship renewal.
- There are accountability nodes through time.
- Each accountability node takes stock of what has been accomplished in terms of key result areas and establishes short term goals to set the trajectory until the next accountability node

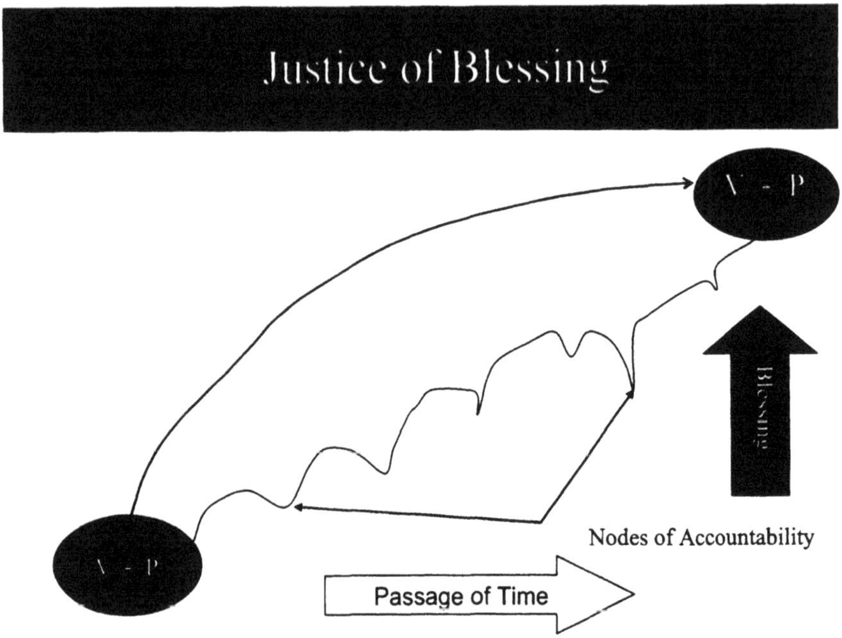

Figure 10.3. Justice of Blessing (1)

At each of the nodes of accountability there is an integral assessment of loss and woundedness.

An Integral Assessment of Victims' and Perpetrators' Needs

In the case of genocide, mass killing or other severe human atrocity, the damage done stretches human capacity for comprehension, understanding, and empathy. The needs of victims are enormous. Perpetrators are caught in a web of denial, shame, self-justification and psychological guilt. The concept of a justice of blessing is meant to address the following challenges:

1. The woundedness resulting from atrocities is both profound and complex with an inner and outer side at the individual and collective levels.
2. The negative effects of atrocities continue for a long time affecting several generations.
3. The failure of perpetrators to take responsibility is a function of a self-justifying meaning system rooted in a particular historical consciousness and a fear of the violent consequences should they own up to what they have done.
4. Victim/survivors feel further victimized by every act of denial on the part of perpetrators.

The theoretical and conceptual development will be along the following lines: first, the introduction of key concepts and pre-understandings, each with its own theoretical base; second the development of a framework that can help to analyse the experience of loss and woundedness on the part of victims; third, the presentation of a framework that can be used to examine the experience of perpetrators; fourth, in the light of the overwhelming challenges that become evident, to describe what is required theoretically (or strategically) of a justice of blessing and finally to make some observations of how a justice of blessing might be operationalized.

Key-Concepts

A *relational system* involves a Self and an Other who are brought into contact with one another in an on-going significant way. This may be because they live in the same place, they work together, or events have brought them together. A relational system may be characterized by mimetic structures that orient Self and Other either toward violence or blessing.

Mimetic structures, as was mentioned above, are patterns of thought and action that are oriented toward a particular way of being in the world in relation to others. The violence within a particular relational system may be anywhere along an axis from symmetrical to asymmetrical. At the symmetrical end of the axis, both parties have been violent to each other. Each party has been victimized and each has done its share of violence. At the asymmetrical end, one party has been severely victimized and has done relatively little to harm the other side.

An *integral approach* to any phenomenon, as developed by Ken Wilber, acknowledges that interior and exterior aspects need to be considered as do individual and collective as the figure 4 shows. An integral framework includes stages, waves and lines of development in each of the four quadrants. It is beyond the bounds of this chapter to develop all aspects of an integral approach; suffice it to say that the dotted lines in each quadrant show that there is development from simple to more complex in each of these areas.

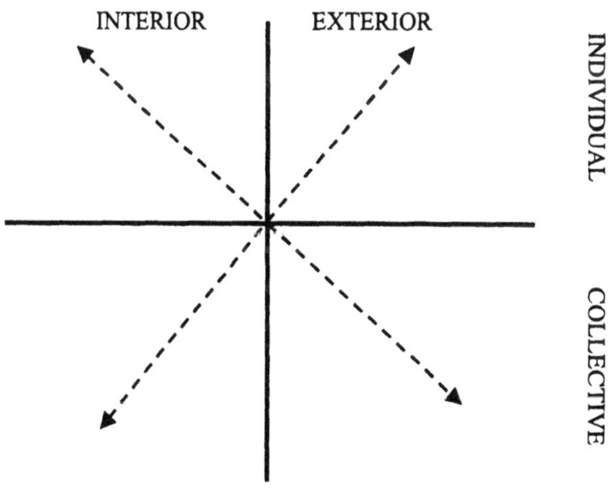

Figure 10.4. Integral approach

Human Identity Needs are theoretical constructs that help to understand what motivates people. Needs for meaning, connectedness, action, security and recognition are closely associated with emotions (see Figure 5). When they are threatened, they invoke anger, sadness, depression, fear and shame respectively. The need categories are universal but the satisfiers are a function of experience and culture. These need categories are evident in all quadrants. On the interior-individual side, people experience directly the emotions associated with a threat to identity need satisfiers. On the exterior-individual side, it can be observed that certain actions would constitute a threat to identity need satisfiers; the observable emotional reactions confirm that this is happening.

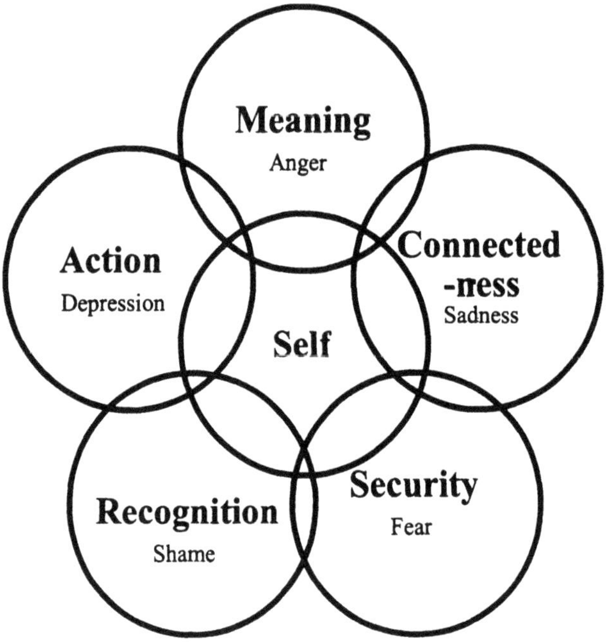

Figure 10.5. Human identity needs and emotions

Victims' Integral Framework of Loss and Woundedness

Taking an integral approach to victimization highlights the fact that there is an objective or exterior side of victimization and a subjective or interior side. The exterior can be described in terms of loss while the interior is constituted by various types of woundedness. Loss and woundedness can be experienced in any of the identity need areas. For example, the destruction of a central place of worship for a community can call into question a meaning system, diminish a sense of connectedness, reduce the potential for community action, induce fear and insecurity and take away a symbol of recognition. This type of analysis will not be followed for each of the kinds of loss and woundedness presented below.

	Interior	Exterior
Individual	Trauma —Woundedness •Hermeneutical •Emotional •Spiritual •Relational •Self	Loss of •Loved ones •Property •Security •Capacity •Status •Place Bodily Damage
Collective	Threats to •Continuity •Coherence •Imagination Vitality •Capacity Victim Mentality Loss of Complexity Rigid Boundaries	Loss of •Members •Property •Capacity •Status •Place •Culture •Language

Figure 10.6. Integral approach to victims

The elements of each of the quadrants in figure 6 will be described.

Exterior—Individual

Human Loss—primary victims lose their lives; secondary victims lose people who are close to them. This has a profound impact on their need for connectedness.

Material Loss—victims often lose property which is either stolen or destroyed. This may include land, houses, artwork, religious artefacts, money, or other material or intellectual goods.

Loss of Status—one form of violence is to pass discriminatory laws; for example, the Nuremburg Laws passed in Germany by the National Socialists prohibited Jews from holding many positions.

Loss of Security—victims may feel very vulnerable to additional violence.

Loss of Capacity—violent acts may clearly incapacitate people so that they can no longer do what they did before. This is most clear when people have lost arms or legs but there are less visible forms of this phenomenon. Someone may have fears that stand in the way of doing certain things.

Loss of Place—many victims are uprooted and have to leave their homes or the territories where they used to live. Place implies space with symbolic, historic and emotional meaning attached to it (Brueggemann 2002).

Bodily Damage—victims may have damaged organs or lose arms or legs.

Interior—Individual

Hermeneutical Woundedness—hermeneutics is concerned with interpretation and meaning-making. Victims of atrocities may find that their World of Meaning is shattered. They cannot make sense of anything. For some it means that basic values are dismissed. Another form of hermeneutical woundedness is that everything is interpreted in terms of their victimization. Also, the memory of violence is always present and colors everything. Victims may also lose capacity to generate meaning; the logotherapy of Holocaust survivor Victor Frankl addressed this phenomenon in particular. Victims are also left with the big question, "Why?" Victims have recounted that they talk about the genocide every day.

Emotional Woundedness—there may be emotional memories that overwhelm an individual such that the horror of the atrocity is re-enacted internally again and again and again.

Spiritual Woundedness—for some, it may mean that they no longer have faith in God. For others, it may mean that they cannot connect to transcendence in other ways. They cannot see the beauty in nature or people; they cannot take delight in things working out; they cannot discern any higher purpose in life.

Relational Woundedness—victims may lament the broken relationships; friends with whom one partied the night before, killed one's family the next day. There may be disassociation, a withdrawal from people. Some lose a capacity to build trusting relations. For some, the projection of a bitter attitude repulses people.

Woundedness of the Self—the accumulation of this inner woundedness can result in the identity of the self being wounded. This is a profound sense of not being well. The extreme form would be the "Muselmänner" of the Nazi concentration camps—walking "dead" persons with no meaning or direction.

Exterior—Collective

Loss of Loved Ones—within the group there is a sense that friends, relatives and members of the group are forever lost.

Bodily and Psychological Harm—there may be a high number of handicapped people that need special attention within the group.

Property Loss—Community centers, churches, synagogues, mosques, temples, memorials, statues or any other properties with special meaning to groups may have been damaged or destroyed.

Loss of Capacity—with the killing, deportation or relocation of large numbers of a group, the capacity for collective action is diminished. Often leaders are the first to be killed or sent into exile. Significant skill sets may no longer be present within a community.

Loss of Status—groups may lose political, economic or social status; this brings about a threat to a need for recognition resulting in a feeling of shame.

Loss of Place—groups that have eradicated from an area through forced dislocation or mass murder lose connection with places that have historical, symbolic or spiritual significance to them. Armenians for instance feel a powerful sense of loss of connection to parts of Turkey where they were the first inhabitants and feel a connection to the land that goes back hundreds, if not thousands of years.

Culture—genocide may succeed in wiping out enough people, places and things that an entire culture may be lost. Krakow before the Shoah was one of the most significant centers of Jewish culture; at the end of the war it was wiped out as a Jewish centre. Whatever was distinctive about its expression of Judaism was lost.
Language—many languages have been forever lost as a result of atrocities and deliberate policies of cultural genocide.

Interior—Collective
Threat to Continuity—within communities that have been subject to atrocities their may be a fear that as a distinct community they will not survive. Not only have group members been killed but out of fear, members of the community may deny their group identity, choosing to assimilate within a population or identify with another group. Many European Jews, for instance, have converted to Christianity.
Threat to Coherence—events may have been so traumatic that positive elements that provided a shared identity and meaning system may be undermined. There may be internal conflicts over interpretations of events and responses to them that disrupt the life of the community.
Threat to Imagination—a vision for the future maybe limited as a group focuses on reliving and recounting its chosen traumas which take the role of defining mythologies.
Threat to Vitality—there may be a lack of energy to do things.
Threat to Capacity—a collective may have lost so much in terms of skills, property and resources that they may be limited in what they can do. Before the wars of the 1990s, for example, the former Yugoslavia had an indigenous oil industry; now all of the processing and retailing of oil products is by multinational corporations based outside the region.
Victim of Injustice—a group may take on a victim mentality that becomes defining of identity.
Loss of Complexity—Victim groups may resort to simple identity markers, losing tolerance for a rich and diverse fabric of identities (Sen 2006).
Rigid Boundaries—with a loss of complexity comes rigid boundary markers with clear ways of indicating who is excluded. For example, Rwandan Hutus and Tutsis in Canada who have intermarried feel excluded from both groups.

Perpetrators' Integral Framework of Justification, Denial, Gain, Shame and Guilt

Ken Wilber's integral framework can also be used to map out the experience of perpetrators. In this case, it is important to look at three different aspects of perpetrators' experience: during conflict (see figure 7), after conflict (see figure 8), and the circumstance in which perpetrators accept the responsibility for their actions (see figure 9).

	Interior	Exterior
Individual	Hermeneutics of Justification Emotional gratification Internal validation Historic vindication Fear of not joining in Dehumanization	Violent Actions Recognition of violence Celebration of victories
Collective	Hermeneutic of Justification Vindication for chosen traumas Mimesis of chosen glories Dehumanization	Violence unleashed by many Uncontrolled acquisitions Pressure on all to join in Defiance

Figure 10.7. Integral approach to perpetrators during atrocity

Exterior—Individual

Violent Actions—during a genocide or mass murder individuals participate in violence. Some work at the level of organizing and inciting violence, some are at the front end of actually carrying out the murder, rape and torture and some expedite the violence by providing information about the location of victims, turning victims in, cheering on the violence, or simply refusing to do anything to stop the violence.

Recognition for Violence—violence against the victim is an obvious collective value so individuals who excel at this get praise from those around them. They might even be promoted or otherwise rewarded for their efforts.

Celebration of Victories—as a village is destroyed or a group of victims killed there may be a celebration at an individual as well as collective level.

Interior—Individual

Hermeneutics of Justification—within the perpetrator, actions against victims are interpreted as being justified. This could be on the basis of the victim having perpetrated evil in the past, a current perceived threat, or an understanding that the victim is less than human (metaphors are used in this regard: vermin, pestilence, cockroaches, lice, etc.)

Emotional Gratification—participation in violence can provide an emotional high: there is success at meeting goals for number of people killed; the excitement at the challenge of the hunt and eventual success; the release of energy through violent action.

Internal Validation—the combination of justification and gratification along with recognition from peers provides a sense of validation for one's efforts.

Historical Vindication—where there is a mythology of past perceived injustice on the part of victims there is a sense that finally there is justice.

Fear of not joining in—not every perpetrator is enthusiastic about joining in; there may be moral inhibitions but the fear of reprisal if one does not join in starts the process. Once violence is initiated it is hard to stop since stopping indicates that previous actions were wrong so there is deep self-judgment if this happens.

Dehumanization—as violence continues, dehumanization of the victim becomes ever more complete.

Exterior—Collective

Violence Unleashed by Many—there can be massive involvement in atrocities at all levels.

Uncontrolled Acquisitions—the perpetrator group takes goods from their victims. At an extreme, during the Shoah there was a warehouse at Auschwitz-Birchenau called Kanada that held material taken from incoming inmates; wares were distributed among Nazi officials and officers.

Pressure on All to Join in—both to support and validate the effort there is collective pressure for all members of a perpetrator identity group to join in; those that resist often become victims themselves. This was the case with moderate Hutus in Rwanda during the genocide and with Serbs who did not join in ethnic cleansing in Bosnia and Herzegovina in the 1990s.

Defiance—perpetrators often express defiance toward any community that tries to stop them.

Interior—Collective

Hermeneutics of Justification—within the perpetrator community there is a discourse that justifies the atrocities.

Vindication for Chosen Traumas—along with the justification is a framing of the action such that it is interpreted as justice or vindication for past actions in which perpetrators were victims.

Mimesis of Chosen Glories—in the "victory" over victims there can be a reliving of past glorious memories when the perpetrator group vanquished its enemies.

Dehumanization—is on-going with the use of metaphors described above.

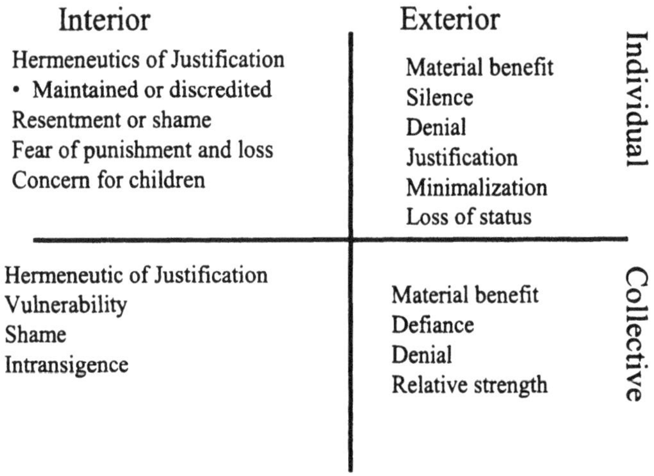

Figure 10.8. Integral approach to perpetrators after conflict

Exterior—Individual

Material Benefit—after the period of genocide and mass murder, perpetrators may be left with land, money and other goods taken from victims.

Silence—many perpetrators remain silent about their actions.

Denial—some deny that atrocities took place.

Justification—statements are made by some that justify violent actions.

Minimalization—the involvement of individual perpetrators is often minimalized.

Loss of Status—individual perpetrators lose status if there is any body to hold them to account for genocide or crimes against humanity.

Interior—Individual

Hermeneutics of Justification—within the individual perpetrator is a hermeneutical framework carried over from the violent action that is used to interpret events in such a way as to justify the action. Either the genocidal action is maintained to have been necessary under the circumstances or the individual involvement is framed as "I had no choice . . . " or "I was simply following orders . . ." This framework of justification is either maintained persistently for a long period, perhaps till death, or it is discredited with the amassing of evidence. If it is discredited it may result in hermeneutical woundedness as perpetrators realized the wrongness of what they have done. This woundedness may simply become chronic, resulting in despondency, negativity and negative coping mechanisms or it may lead to taking responsibility.

Resentment or Shame—as violence gets exposed as genocidal there may be resentment at being judged or a profound feeling of shame.

Fear of Punishment and Loss—if there are accountability institutions (tribunals, indictments, sentences) there may be a fear of being charged, apprehended and punished.
Concern for Children—if the truth were to come out, there would be a fear of losing face in front of one's children.

Exterior—Collective
Material Benefit—perpetrator groups can continue to benefit from what they have acquired and if they are not subject to punishing measures, they have the benefit of relative strength in relation to the victim group
Defiance—collectives and their leaders may be defiant toward any community trying to judge them for their actions.
Denial—frequently atrocities are denied or minimized.

Interior—Collective
Hermeneutic of Justification—groups may continue to justify their actions and deny atrocities.
Vulnerability—along with the justification may be a vulnerability if the global community is holding them accountable.
Shame—as they become associated with a crime against humanity and get negative recognition there are feelings of shame.
Intransigence—the combination of all of the above may lead to a resolve to resist taking any responsibility for deadly actions.

Interior	Exterior	
Trauma – Needs healing Hermeneutical woundedness Shame Relief Fear of punishment and loss Concern for children	Expression of willingness to make reparation Dialogue Reveal truth	Individual
Hermeneutic of self-criticism Vulnerability Shame Fragility	Expression of willingness to make reparation Apology Symbolic conciliatory acts Relative strength	Collective

Figure 10.9. Integral approach to perpetrators who accept responsibility for their actions

Exterior—Individual
Expression of Willingness to Make Reparation
Dialogue—the individual enters into interactive processes where there is a mutual exchange of personal meaning.
Reveal Truth—the individual reveals what happened and provides vital information to families

Interior—Individual
Trauma—there are deep emotional wounds and perhaps PTSD.
Hermeneutical Woundedness—the meaning-making capacity has been turned upside down; what was once viewed as justified has now been re-framed as an atrocity or crime against humanity.
Shame—there is interior negative recognition with a resultant sense of loss of worth.
Relief—it is no longer necessary to cover up the truth or to fear that it might be revealed.
Fear of Punishment and Loss
Concern for Children—what will happen to the family name? Will the children disown the parent? Who will provide if a parent goes to prison? How will the parent be remembered?

Exterior—Collective
Expression of Willingness to Make Reparation
Apology
Symbolic Conciliatory Acts
Relative Strength—if many of the "Other" group have been killed; they cannot be brought back and there will still be relatively greater numbers of the perpetrator group.

Interior—Collective
Hermeneutic of Self-Criticism—the perpetrator group may come down hard on itself.
Vulnerability—if the truth is out and power dynamics have shifted, there may be reprisals.
Shame
Fragility

Justice of Blessing (4)

What may have to happen is that a mechanism like a truth commission may be the starting point. People could be given the option of moving into a justice of blessing process at any time. This would demand that both victims and perpetrators would be open to a joint, long term process. There may be a need for a sequential or concurrent series of justice processes that would include criminal tribunals and short-term restorative justice programs. Educational programs about the atrocity and its impact could be a significant part of the justice of blessing overall program.

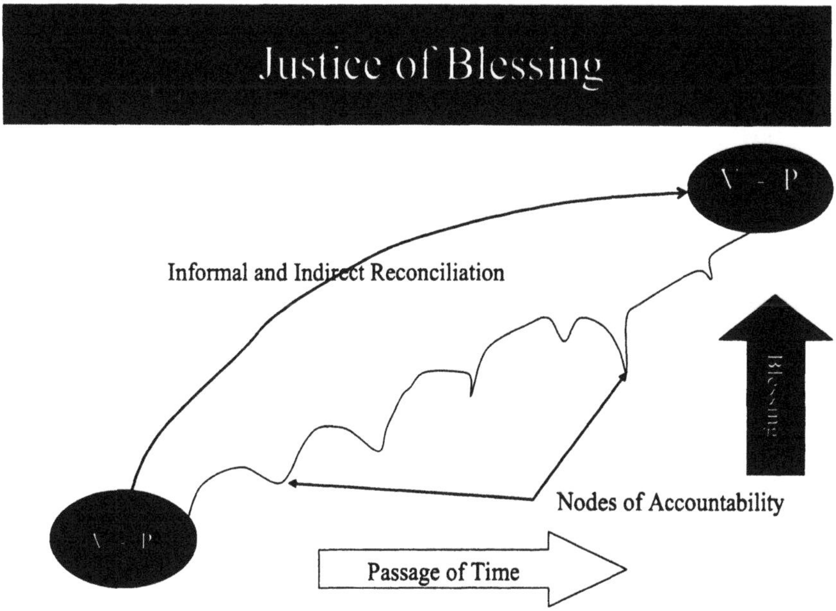

Figure 10.10. Justice of Blessing (2)

In this diagram (figure 10) it is indicated that through time there is a transformation from a mimetic structure of violence to mimetic structures of violence. The nodes of accountability are times to take stock of the situation in terms of the key result areas along with the changes in the integral frameworks of the perpetrators and victims. This means that on the exterior side, there are actions that can be verified such as restitution of property. It is important that participants in the accountability sessions also reflect on their own interiority. That is, they take stock of their sense of woundedness, emotional states, and how they interpret the situation. Stories may need to be repeated and reframed; expressions of remorse would likewise have to be repeated. Transformational processes would continue to occur.

The distance in time between accountability sessions could vary from 3 months to one year. Over time it might make sense to have such sessions every three to five years.

It should be noted that there is room for parallel reconciliation processes—indirect and informal. Indirect processes are comprised by joint actions toward supra ordinate goals or constructive development projects. Examples would be reconciliation through economic development and reconciliation through joint celebration of the restoration of cultural buildings and monuments. Informal reconciliation happens through positive interactions between people from different groups in the course of their everyday lives.

Justice-Making Processes in Rwanda

The justice-making challenges facing Rwanda in the wake of the 1994 genocide were overwhelming. The genocide had been organized by the Government; thousands of machetes had been procured in advance and were distributed; the *interahamwe* militia was organized to systematically track down and kill all Tutsis; *Radio et Télévision Libres des Mille Collines* (RTLM) was used to motivate people throughout the country to participate in the genocide; about 750.000 people played a direct role in the killings and many others a supporting role; the genocide was ended by the Tutsi-dominated *Rwandese Patriotic Front* (RPF) which defeated the Government and formed a new Government. Many of the *genocidiares* went to camps in the Democratic Republic of Congo; and 120,000 people were put into prison.

Identity cards specifying Hutu, Tutsi or Twa were done away with and discursive distinctions are officially not allowed; however, everybody still thinks in these categories and the question in everyone's mind is always "Where were you during the genocide and what did you do?" The judicial system was decimated by the genocide since not only Tutsis but moderate Hutus had been killed as well. To deal with this situation, the United Nations established an international tribunal based in Arusha, Tanzania to try those responsible for orchestrating the genocide. The judicial system started to try some of the perpetrators but the rate was so slow that it would have taken a century to try all those in prison. To speed up the process and involve the community, the traditional *Gacaca* process was modified for the purpose of trying and sentencing large numbers of alleged perpetrators. I will describe both the Arusha Tribunal and *Gacaca* process in greater detail, before showing how a justice of blessing might be applied to the situation.

The International Criminal Tribunal for Rwanda

The International Criminal Tribunal for Rwanda (ICTR) was established by the Security Council of the United Nations in 1994 and will complete its work by 2010 (Jallow 2006; *The Tribunal at a Glance*). From 1995 to 1999 there were six judgements including Prime Minister Jean Kambanda, who pleaded guilty. It was the "first time that a head of government was convicted for the crime of genocide (*The Tribunal at a Glance*). From 1999 to 2003 there were nine judgements with 14 accused; three of the accused were from the media, the first time since the Nuremberg trials. The court "noted that it was 'critical to distinguish between the discussion of ethnic consciousness and the promotion of ethnic hatred'." (*The Tribunal at a Glance*). In its third mandate there were judgements. Currently 28 people are being tried in 11 trials. Ministers, military leaders, Bourgmestres and other leaders have all been brought before the tribunal.

Witnesses are brought to Arusha for the trial. They are offered protection and separate housing along with childcare and specialized medical care. Witness Support Assistants are available on a 24 hour basis.

Judges and prosecutors come from many countries. Up to nine judges may be active at any one time. A Judicial Records and Archives Unit keeps track of records, which are digitized.

The ICTR works against a culture of impunity for leaders in genocide. Their sentences are long prison terms which are served in different African countries. Most victims feel however that the ICTR has not been efficient enough, some say it even corrupt, given the limited number of leaders who have been sentenced over a twelve year period, in comparison with the millions of dollars spent over the same period. They also denounce what they consider as injustice in terms of treatment, those leaders detained in Arusha being well treated in comparison with the miserable life the survivors are subjected to. Many women who were contaminated with HIV-AIDS (often deliberately) during the genocide have no access to treatment while the perpetrators in Arusha are provided with anti-AIDS drugs.

The Gacaca Process

The *Gacaca* process in the post-genocide era is derived from a traditional process meaning literally justice on the grass. Legislation in 2001 provided a framework within which the country was divided into regions, sectors and cells. Within each cell a *Gacaca* court is established with 9 judges, known by their traditional name of *Inyangamugayo,* who are people with integrity who make decisions together on different cases. In each cell there are also 7 deputy judges. Decisions can be appealed from a cell to a sector level to the regular court system.

Within the post-genocide justice framework, there are 3 levels of genocidal crime (originally there were four). The first level involves those responsible for planning and inciting genocidal murder and committing rape. These need to be tried in the regular system. Levels 2 and 3 are brought before the *Gacaca* courts. These include perpetrators of murder or assaults causing death and other crimes like assault and property crimes (Majtenyi 2005). The *Gacaca* process starts with the classification of the crimes of the individual. In a significant number of cases there is a guilty plea. The *Gacaca* court is convened outside with the nine *Inyangamugayo* judges sitting at a table or on a bench facing the community. The accused might sit on either side—visible to the judges and the community. The whole community is summoned; it is anticipated that the assembly will be comprised of 200 people from the cell. “Each inhabitant is a lawyer, a prosecutor and a witness at the same time.” (*Gacaca Jurisdictions: Achievements, Problems and Future prospects*). If there are not sufficient people available cells are combined.

The charges are brought against the offender and anyone from the community can speak to the issue of guilt or innocence. At the end the panel of judges determines guilt and recommends a penalty. The prison terms range from one to thirty years.

Many perpetrators being tried in *Gacaca* hearings spent time in prison. Significant numbers were released when they pleaded guilty to crimes. To get a feel for the situation, I examined the list of 3,714 names of accused in the Southern city of Butare. Most of them were released because of a guilty plea; the others were either minors or senior citizens.

Of the perpetrator group, some have been living freely in the community. Those who are released from prison are sent to an *Ingando*, meaning a camp of solidarity, for several months of training and preparation for integration into the community. However, while these releases are crucial in a reconciliation perspective, they undoubtedly brought back a sense of despair for the survivors whose loved ones perished at the hands of those very people who came to share their daily lives as neighbors.

From the perspective of the Government of Rwanda, *Gacaca* is a cornerstone for reconciliation because

- It removes suspicion, the guilty party is denounced.
- It helps to eradicate the culture of impunity.
- It enables people to live in peace and harmony once again.
- It enhances collaboration between the inhabitants in disclosing the truth on the genocide events.(*Gacaca Jurisdictions: Achievements, Problems and Future prospects*)

It is meant to remove suspicion, dispel rumours, and provide penalties "intended to integrate the guilty person into society and to enable him to collaborate with others in the reconstruction of the country (TIG) . . . [It] helps the victims of genocide to know where the bodies of their relatives were thrown so they can burry them in dignity." (*Gacaca Jurisdictions: Achievements, Problems and Future prospects*)

There are 12,103 *Gacaca* courts, over 9,000 at the cell level. With deputies, there are 169,442 judges. 26 per cent of these are women. (*Gacaca Jurisdictions: Achievements, Problems and Future prospects*)

Since it was initiated, there have been a number of problems with the Gacaca process. Witnesses have been intimidated and killed (Karasira; Majtenyi 2005). Recent reports from Rwanda indicate that this is a current troubling trend. As of July 2006, only 6,267 out of 63,000 cases have been tried (Twahirwa July 31, 2006). There have been complaints that even though guilty parties who have plead guilty have been released from prison, those some who are innocent are being held (they are tempted to plead guilty to minor crimes they did not commit just to get out) (*Report IV: "The guilty plea procedure, cornerstone of Rwanda's justice system"*, 2003). Culturally, for a perpetrator to declare his crimes in front of victim is an act of defiance rather than an expression of remorse as would seem appropriate. Many of the guilty are denying their involvement and some who do plead guilty and confess are harassed by fellow prisoners. When the numbers of victims identified by perpetrators are added up, they do not come anywhere near the actual number of those killed. In some areas, there are no survivors to provide evidence against the perpetrators. In a number of instances, judges were disguised perpetrators, and were later removed. Support for survivors falls far short of what is needed (*Survivors Fund*, 2006). Also, how records of *Gacaca* courts are kept is another important issue. It is essential that these be properly kept for future documentation and research purposes. While the Government vision for *Gacaca* is grand, the results fall far short of expectations. In spite of these problems, the fact remains that it is a very innovative approach to dealing with an overwhelming problem. It takes a traditional process deeply rooted in Rwandan culture and adapts it to deal with a new reality. It has taken time to establish the infrastructure and work out the difficulties. Lists of accused are now posted on the internet. There is an attempt to coordinate sessions so they do not conflict with other events that demand the presence of community members.

The Potential for a Justice of Blessing in Rwanda

That there is a need for a justice of blessing in Rwanda is quite evident. Up to 750,000 people may have played a fairly direct role in the genocide (*Gacaca 2004: More Suspects, More Challenges?*), (Twahirwa July 31, 2006) and over 100,000 are playing role as judges. The current Tutsi population is probably around a million people[4]. It is divided into the following groups (figure 11).

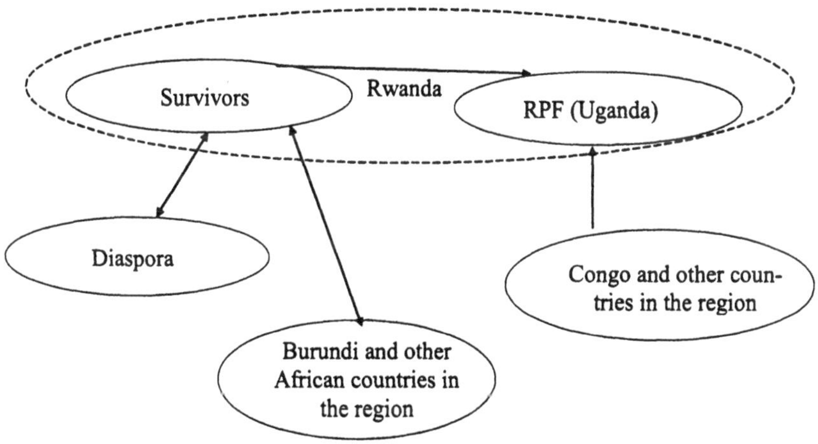

Figure 10.11. Batutsi inside and outside Rwanda

It is important that all Batutsi (this is the plural form of Tutsi in Kinyrawanda) have occasion to participate in justice of blessing processes. Many are in tremendous need, especially the thousands of households headed by children (*Gacaca 2004: More Suspects, More Challenges?* 2004).

The Arusha Tribunal has played the following important roles: key leaders have been held accountable in that their role in the genocide has been clearly established; the fact of the genocide is clearly documented, and witnesses have been protected. In a country where impunity was the norm for decades, these trials by an international penal court goes a long way in signalling a real change in the mindset. The more of the truth of the genocide that is made publicly available, the easier will be the healing process. Research is needed on the archival material and books written and documentaries made with the results. Beyond that, it is important that those leaders who are now serving long prison terms in various countries be invited to be part of a justice of blessing process. They could, initially through their writings, express remorse and offer words of comfort and support to the survivor communities. A justice of blessing means that perpetrators will use their skills and energy to empower the victims and the victim communities. It cannot be said *a priori* what specifically this might entail, but those that planned the genocide are bright and well organized people. If they put their minds to working towards healing, relationships, structural change and transcendence, they could undoubtedly come up with helpful actions. In addition to what they might do for victim groups in Rwanda, they would have a contribution to make to the global community. If they were to reflect on the patterns of thought that motivated them to participate in genocide and what might have changed the situation, they could develop ideas useful for genocide prevention in other places.

Within the *Gacaca* processes could be commitments to reassemble regularly over the coming years to assess their progress as communities working toward reconciliation. This would mean empowering survivors and reintegrating perpetrators. In doing so, and in acknowledging and documenting their progress, they could demonstrate to one another and to the world that they are capable of rebuilding humanity in the wake of overwhelming and unspeakable human tragedy. As constructive values of truth, generosity, honesty, critical thinking, interconnectedness and hard work coalesce, a vibrant sense of peoplehood and economic life could emerge. Rwanda could become a mimetic model for countries around the world that have experienced atrocities.

A sub-process could involve perpetrator accountability sessions in which a group of perpetrators who accept responsibility for their actions would hold individuals accountable who might be reluctant to own up to what they had done. Within these sessions it would not be a matter of accusations coming in the form of "you" statements but rather "we" statements—"We have done this and you are one of us . . ." This idea is an adaptation of a Canadian Aboriginal approach to child sexual abuse in which an alleged abuser is teamed up with someone who will accompany him along the path of taking responsibility. This person is a former abuser. There is also a meeting with other abusers so that the person does not feel alone in the process of taking responsibility.

Within a justice of blessing framework, each perpetrator could be encouraged to "adopt" one survivor and work towards that person's well-being.

There are now a number of cases of victims showing forgiveness to those who killed their families and of establishing a relationship with these people. Recently one such case was featured in a documentary aired on the ABC network in the United States. Other victims have truly transcended the rut of negativity and trauma that is a frequent consequence of this order of violence. The phenomena of forgiveness and transcendence suggest that first, it might be a good idea for those who have had these experiences to come together to share experiences, and second, these experiences should be used sensitively as potential mimetic model for others. I say "sensitively" since victims should not be pressured into forgiveness or reconciliation; they should not be made to feel guilty if they cannot forgive.

In order that justice of blessing be comprehensive, the truth of the Hutu massacres of Tutsis must be accompanied by the truth of reprisals—these did not involve the same numbers at the time of the genocide but for the Hutu victims, the pain too was profound. Post-genocidal revenge killing needs to be taken into account as well. Rwanda needs to move quickly to develop political parties that cross the dividing lines of Hutu and Tutsi that unite peoples around shared constellations of values.

At another level of relational systems, a justice of blessing could address the roles of colonial and post-colonial powers in historical events leading up to the genocide and failure to intervene to stop it when it started. At this level there has been reluctance on the part of leaders to take responsibility for what happened and to passionately embrace a responsibility to play a long-term role in re-empowering all the peoples of Rwanda.

Likewise, considering the role of churches in the genocide (Ndahiro 2004; Redekop & Gasana 2007, a justice of blessing would suggest that they play a role in modelling and supporting the taking of responsibility for past actions. To that end, they could start by re-examining the Christian biblical text with a hermeneutics of blessing so as to re-create teachings of blessing that could inform reconciliation processes throughout the country (Redekop 2007).

Notes

1. In a strict sense, victims of genocide and other atrocities have been killed. However, their friends and relatives who survive are also victimized. Likewise those who are raped, tortured, hunted down, captured and confined are also victimized as are their children who often suffer secondary effects. When the term "victim" is used it refers to all who are members of a group that has been singled out for violence; in most cases reference is made to people who are still alive for whom issues of justice are a pressing need.

2. Ibid., 255-283.

3. For an example see *The Scholars' Initiative: Confronting the Yugoslav Controversies* organized by Purdue historian Charles Ingrao. It is a project within which over 200 historians from different sides of the conflict as well as neutral institutions work together to prepare consensus documents. One of these is "Ethnic Cleansing and War Crimes, 1991-1995" (Calic 2006) to which 24 scholars contributed.

4. Currently people are not officially identified as Hutu or Tutsi. At the end of the genocide there were roughly 250,000 Tutsis left and since then an estimated 800,000 have returned.

References

Appleby, R. S. 2000. *The Ambivalence of the Sacred: Religion, Violence and Reconciliation.* Lanham: Rowan & Littlefield.

Bar-Siman-Tov, Y. 2004. "Dialectics between Stable Peace and Reconciliation." In Y. Bar-Siman-Tov ed., *From Conflict Resolution to Reconciliation.* Oxford: Oxford University Press.

Bohm, D. 1997. *On Dialogue.* New York: Routledge.

Bole, W., Drew Christiansen, S., & Hennemeyer, R. T. 2004. *Forgiveness in International Politics. An Alternative Road to Peace.* Washington, D.C.: United States Conference of Catholic Bishops.

Brueggemann, W. 2002. *The Land: Place as Gift, Promise, and Challenge in Biblical Faith.* 2d ed. Minneapolis: Fortress Press.

Calic, M.-J. 2006. Ethnic Cleansing and War Crimes, 1991-1995. Retrieved December 1, 2006, from http://www.cla.purdue.edu/academic/history/facstaff/Ingrao/si/scholars.htm

Capra, F., & Steindl-Rast, D. 1992. *Belonging to the Universe: Explorations on the Frontiers of Science and Spirituality.* San Francisco: HarperSanFrancisco.

Chanteur, J. 1992. *From War to Peace* (S. A. Weisz, Trans.). Boulder: Westview Press.

Fox, M. 2000. *Original Blessing: A Primer in Creation Spirituality.* New York: Jeremy P. Tarcher/Putnam.

Gacaca 2004: More Suspects, More Challenges? 2004. Retrieved November 14, 2006, from http://www.internews.org.rs/articles3.htm

Gacaca Jurisdictions: Achievements, Problems and Future prospects. (15/07/2006). Retrieved November 13, 2006, from inkiko-gacaca.gov.rw

Girard, R. 1987. *Things Hidden Since the Foundation of the World.* Stanford: Stanford University Press.

———. 1988. *Violence and the Sacred.* Baltimore: Johns Hopkins University Press.

———. 1989. *The Scapegoat.* Baltimore: Johns Hopkins University Press.

Hahnel, R. 2005. *Economic Justice and Democracy.* New York and London: Routledge.

Herman, J. 1997. *Trauma and Recovery.* Basic Books.

Hermann, T. 2004. "Reconciliation: Reflections on the Theoretical and Practical Utility of the Term." In Y. Bar-Siman-Tov ed., *From Conflict Resolution to Reconciliation.* Oxford: Oxford University Press.

Huyse, L. 2003. "The Process of Reconciliation." In D. Bloomfield, T. Barnes & L. Huyse eds., *Reconciliation After Violent Conflict: A Handbook.* Stockholm: International Institute for Democracy and Electoral Assistance.

Jallow, H. B. 2006. Address by Hassan Bubacar Jallow, Prosecutor of the ICTR, ICTR Newsletter, October 2006. Retrieved November 14, 2006, from http://69.94.11.53/ENGLISH/newsletter/oct06/oct06.pdf

Johnston, D., & Sampson, C. eds. 1994. *Religion: The Missing Dimension of Statecraft.* New York: Oxford University Press.

Johnstone, G. 2004. "How, And In What Terms, Should Restorative Justice Be Conceived?" In H. Zehr & B. Toews eds., *Critical Issues in Restorative Justice.* Monsey, NY: Willan Publishing.

Juergensmeyer, M. 2001. *Terror in the Mind of God: The Global Rise of Religious Violence.* Berkeley: University of California Press.

Karasira, P. Gacaca: Justice for All or Injustice for Some? Retrieved December 8, 2006, from http://www.inkiko-gacaca.gov.rw/En/EnGacaca.htm

Kolbert, C. F. 1979. "The Legal Background." In Justinian: *The Digest of Roman Law—Theft, Rapine, Damage and Insult.* New York: Penguin.

Kriesberg, L. 2004. "Comparing Reconciliation Actions within and between Countries." In Y. Bar-Siman-Tov ed., *From Conflict Resolution to Reconciliation.* Oxford: Oxford University Press.

Lederach, J. P. 1997. *Building Peace: Sustainable Reconciliation in Divided Societies.* Washington, D.C.: United States Institute of Peace Press.

———. 1999. *The Journey Toward Reconciliation.* Scottsdale, Penn.: Herald Press.

Majtenyi, C. 2005, January 21, 2005. Gacaca Genocide Trials Set to Open in Rwanda. Retrieved November 14, 2006, from www.voanews.com/english/archive/2005-01/2005-01-21-voa33.cfm?renderforprint

Macintyre, A. 1981. *After Virtue: A Study in Moral Theory.* Notre Dame: University of Notre Dame Press.

Mooren, T. 2002. September 11, 2001 and the Future of Monotheistic Religions. *Mission,* 9(1), 39-64.

Napoleon, V. 2004. "By Whom, And By What Processes, Is Restorative Justice Defined, And What Bias Might This Introduce?" In H. Zehr & B. Toews eds., *Critical Issues in Restorative Justice.* Monsey, NY: Willan Publishing.

Ndahiro, T. 2004. "The Church's Blind Eye to Genocide in Rwanda." In C. Rittner, J. K. Roth & W. Whitworth eds., *Genocide in Rwanda: Complicity of the Churches?* St. Paul, MN: Aegis

Osgood, C. 1966. *Perspective in Foreign Policy.* Pal Alto: Pacific Books. Paragon House.

Pert, C. 1997. *Molecules of Emotion: The Science Behind Mind-Body Medicine.* New York: Touchstone.

Rawls, J. 1999. *A Theory of Justice.* Cambridge, MA: Harvard University Press.

Redekop, V. N. 1993. *Scapegoats, the Bible and Criminal Justice: Interacting with René Girard.* Akron, PA: Mennonite Central Committee.

———. 2002. *From Violence to Blessing: How an Understanding of Deep-Rooted Conflict Can Open Paths to Reconciliation.* Ottawa: Novalis.

———. 2007. "Teachings of Blessing as an Element of Reconciliation: Intra and Inter-Religious Hermeneutical Challenges and Opportunities." In M. Courville ed. *The Next Step in Studying Religion: A Graduate's Guide.* London: The Continuum International Publishing Group.

——— and Gasana, O. 2007. "Implication of Religious Leaders in Mimetic Structures of Violence: The Case of Rwanda." In R. Simkins ed. *The Contexts of Religion and Violence. Journal of Religion & Society Supplement* Series 2. (pp. 117-37) The Kripke Center; http://moses.creighton.edu/jrs/toc/2007SS.html

Report IV: "The guilty plea procedure, cornerstone of Rwanda's justice system". 2003. Retrieved December 3, 2006, from http://www.penalreform.org/publications/Gacaca/R4-The-Guilty-Plea-Procedure-Jan2003.pdf

Ricoeur, P. 2000. *The Just* (D. Pellauer, Trans.). Chicago and London: The University of Chicago Press.

Schirch, L. 2005. *Ritual and Symbol in Peacebuilding.* Bloomfield, CT: Kumarian Press.

Schrenk, G. 1964. "The Concept of Law in the OT" (G. W. Bromiley, Trans.). In G. Kittel ed., *Theological Dictionary of the New Testament* (Vol. 2). Grand Rapids: Eerdmans.

Sen, A. 2006. *Identity and Violence: The Illusion of Destiny.* New York: W. W. Norton and Company.

Sharpe, S. 2004. "How Large Should The Restorative Justice "Tent" Be?" In H. Zehr & B. Toews eds. *Critical Issues in Restorative Justice.* Monsey, NY: Willan Publishing.

Shriver, D. W. 2001. "What is Forgiveness in a Secular Form?" In S. Raymond G. Helmick & R. L. Petersen eds., *Forgiveness and Reconciliation: Religion, Public Policy, and Conflict Transformation.* Philadelphia and London: Templeton Foundation Press.

Staub, E., & Pearlman, L. A. 2001. "Healing, Reconciliation, and Forgiving after Genocide and Other Collective Violence." In S. Raymond G. Helmick & R. L. Petersen eds., *Forgiveness and Reconciliation: Religion, Public Policy, and Conflict Transformation.* Philadelphia: Templeton Foundation Press.

Steele, D. 1990. *Theological Assessment of Principled Negotiation as a Role Model for Church Involvement in the Mediation of International Conflict.* (Unpublished)

Survivors Fund. (November 7, 2006) Retrieved November 14, 2006 from http://en.wikipedia.org/wiki/Survivors_Fund

The Tribunal at a Glance. Retrieved November 14, 2006, from 69.94.11.53/English/factsheets/1.htm

Twahirwa, A. July 31, 2006. Justice Eludes Many 1994 Genocide Survivors. Retrieved November 14, 2006 from http://www.ipsterraviva.net/Africa/viewstory.asp?idnews=752

Volf, M. 1996. *Exclusion or Embrace: A Theological Exploration of Identity, Otherness, and Reconciliation.* Nashville: Abingdon Press.

———. 2005. *Free of Charge: Giving and Forgiving in a Culture Stripped of Grace.* Grand Rapids: Zondervan.

Walgrave, L. (2004). "Has Restorative Justice Appropriately Responded to Retribution Theory And Impulses?" In H. Zehr & B. Toews (Eds.), *Critical Issues in Restorative Justice.* Monsey, NY: Willan Publishing.

Zehr, H. (1990). *Changing Lenses.* Scottsdale, PA: Herald Press.

11

The Role of Religious Peacebuilding in Traumatized Societies: From Withdrawal to Forgiveness

Mohammed Abu-Nimer

> *Past the seeker as he prayed came the crippled and the beggar and the beaten. And seeing them . . . he cried, "Great God, how is it that a loving creator can see such things and yet do nothing about them?" . . . God said, "I did do something. I made you."*
>
> — Sufi Teaching

Religious beliefs, rituals, and institutions have been widely associated with causing and triggering violence, perpetuating reality of ethnic and cultural divisions among states, ethnic groups, and even family members. It is not new to assert that religious leaders have used their followers' faith to instigate political conflict and justify new economic, social, and cultural policies. Religious ideologies have been used to sustain oppressive systems such as Apartheid in South Africa, racial separation in United States, removal of natives form their lands in places like Latin America, Australia, most of African countries, and Palestine. Religious identities have been utilized to effective mobilizing support for both state and nonstate terrorist activities. Al Qaeda is a classic example in Muslim societies, but Christian evangelicals, Jewish ultra orthodox militant groups, as well as Buddhist monks in Sri Lanka have done the same by supporting or legitimizing violence against civilians.

Although many justifications have been made by scholars and practitioners for a greater role of religion in formal and informal negotiation processes, the two primary ones are: First, for individuals and societies who view the world primarily through their religious identity, there is a strong commitment, ability, and conviction that their conflict is religious and therefore its resolution can only be processed through religious tracks. Second, religious identity has provided for thousands of years sources of energy and guidance for most humans on ways to handle their lives.

Thus, it is not a new invention to incorporate religious values, rituals, or actors in peacebuilding processes. Chinese, Islamic, Greek and Christian European civilizations have heavily relied on their religious institutions to settle interpersonal, community, tribal, as well as violent state conflicts. It is important for us to recognize that currently we are primarily engaging in the task of systematizing and conceptualizing the constructive role of religion in the field of peacebuilding.

In general, the core objective of peacebuilding activities in traumatized or intractable conflict societies is the transformation of conflict relationships. The desired change is from confrontation to cooperation, mistrust into trust, deadlock into option generation, misconception into understanding the root causes of the conflict, dominant into more symmetrical relationship, superiority into respect of individuals and group rights and avoidance into confrontation of the conflict symptoms and causes. Religious peacebuilding has an important role to play in contributing to these conflict transformation processes.

Possible Roles in Religious Peacebuilding

Like in other conflict situations, in the context of traumatized societies, religious peacebuilding roles and activities can vary form an actual mediation intervention to individual pastoral care. In each of these roles, religious leaders and clergy can directly and consciously contribute to the overall peacebuilding efforts carried out by many forces in the society. Some of these roles include:[1]

Spiritual Care: Religious leaders and clergy can attend to the human, moral, spiritual needs of people in conflict, people who are bereaved as well as political activists. In Sri Lanka, many of the Buddhist Monks and Hindu priests have provided comfort to bereaved families and individuals who attend their temples seeking healing powers and community solidarity. A Tamil Catholic priest from Muthur in North East Sri Lanka, described his worked with local Christian communities, who were facing a threat from the Liberation Tamil Tigers Ealem (LTTE) and Government bombing, as *life saving*[2]. "In the last four months, I have spent most of my time with my parish attending to their fears and trauma—with each bombing and attack on the villages there are hundreds of Internally Displaced Peoples (IDPs) that need our help.[3]" Not all religious institutions pay attention to such roles, however, in many Christian seminaries, pastoral counseling and guidance is an integral part of the training of many pastors and priests. For Muslim clergy, such a role is often assumed as part of the traditional cultural leadership associated with imams. Following 9/11 attacks, Christian clergy stepped in to offer care for the survivors or victims families. The STAR Program at Eastern Mennonite University offers a "space" for religious and other care givers to process and deal with their own stress and trauma. It also provides participants an educational opportunity to study trauma recovery in relationship to peacebuilding and restorative justice.

Presence and observation: Religious clergy and activists can provide an active, watchful, supportive, moral presence during times of major confrontation or great moral challenge. In an intensive and intractable conflict, human rights groups are often active and report various types of violations. However, their presence is not always systematic, thus an outside or external group may fulfill an important function of moral presence, which may prevent further human rights violations by militant groups. The Christian Peacemaker Team (CPT), has been active in Hebron, Palestine, since 1993. Their systematic presence and observation have allowed them to gain the confidence of many Palestinians and Israeli Jewish peace groups. Their reports from Hebron throughout the last 13 years have been informative and their work has provided valuable space for the voices of local residents of Hebron to express their experiences with the occupation. The CPT members stay with members of the Palestinian community and report on Israeli army as well as settlers' harassment of local Palestinians. Their observations have provided a base for many advocacy and human rights groups who featured their reports outside of Palestine.

Accompaniment: There is a long religious tradition of this action or role. Prophets (Mohammed, Jesus, Moses) and nonviolent activists like Gandhi and King have acted in this capacity when they joined crowds of people who were protesting or fleeing for their safety. To stand by and walk with those who are endangered or morally challenged is especially powerful and active role by religious leaders or organizations. Informed by their faith, a Catholic priest, Father Roberto C. Layson and a Muslim partner, Mike P. Alon work together in Pikit, Mindanao area (Southern Philippines)[4] work together for peace, reconciliation and mutual respect among communities. They have both overcome personal loss and now work to help others through offering facilitating dialogue. Both have accompanied many Internally Displaced Persons or IDPs and have provided housing for thousands of refugees throughout the last decade. In Sri Lanka, the Non-violent Peace Force (NPF) has operated in the North East (especially Jaffna area) and several of its members, motivated by their faith, have been accompanying Tamil refugees and residents to the LTTE offices to inquire about the fate of their relatives[5].

Obviously the risk of taking or acting in this capacity in a high tension conflict zone is much greater than other activities. The NPF team in Sri Lanka has recently reported some of the risk involved:

> In the context of this tension (i.e. bombing and military operation in North East), after witnessing the aftermath of the bombing of the market and assisting several of the injured people to a hospital, our Trinco Team was attacked by an angry crowd of Sinhala youth while returning to the office. The crowd surrounded the NP vehicle which was marked with the NPSL sign and flag. Members of the crowd slapped and punched the driver, FTM Charles Oloo Otieno, who was trying to turn the vehicle and move away from the hostile scene. Parts of the truck were ripped from the side. The team was also threatened with a

hand grenade. Before they could leave from there heavy stones were thrown at the vehicle, smashing the side and back windows. Luckily the team was not seriously physically injured. However, the whole event took place 30 feet (10 meters) from a police/army checkpoint and the forces present made no attempt to intervene. The team recovered quickly from the attack and continued work the next day, hence it provided protection for the delivery of relief to those displaced by the violence.[6]

Fact-finding, assessment: Accessing factual information in conflict zones is a tremendously challenging task. Conflict parties expand their fights to manipulate information dissemination channels. Thus objective venues for information gathering and dissemination become scarce and often the existing channels serve a propaganda function for the political parties. Religious clergy can operate more freely because of their moral status, especially if they are outsiders who seek out a balanced understanding of the conflict, assess the conflict dynamics, and recommend a way forward.

The International Fellowship of Reconciliation (IFOR) has mobilized a special program for its fact finding mission in Israel Palestine. The interfaith delegation program has organized many delegations to visit the occupied territories in Palestine and issues a daily journal and final report upon their arrival back in USA. Their efforts of brining hundreds of delegates from different faith groups including various Christian denominations, Jews, Muslims, Buddhists, has been covered by local and international media as well[7].

From 2001 until the present (2007) IFOR has organized 20 interfaith peacebuilding delegations with an average of 15 members in each delegation. These religious groups have also conducted important follow-up activities. Often peacebuilding programs face real challenge in sustaining their efforts beyond the specific event or action that they organize, however the interfaith peacebuilding program has created a mechanism for follow up and reentry activities too. As they describe their mission: "Delegations are only the first step . . . Our deeper goal is to build, support, and sustain a network of informed citizens who can influence opinion in their local communities throughout North America. We're making a difference—because our delegates come home energized and committed to convey what they have seen on their delegations."[8]

Good offices: In intractable conflict areas communication lines between official and average citizens from different groups have been severed by the conflict. In most conflict cases, due to the high level of distrust and emotional and psychological injuries, many people and leaders on all sides have reduced their contacts with the "other." Often a discourse of national or ethnic "loyalty test" is developed based on the measure of having any contacts with the "other" or enemy. Those who take the risk of communicating directly with the enemy are subject to public shaming and campaigns aimed at disqualifying their national loyalty or sense of patriotism. Religious leaders or activists have managed to open these channels of communication by insuring a simple space for good office function. For example, Bishops and Ulamas in Mindanao, Philippines, due to their public recognition and important social and cultural role in the two societies (Christian and Muslim) have taken the role of providing auspices or gathering certain militant elements under their religious office. They open lines of communication, carry messages between the Philippine government, army generals, and Moro National Liberation Front (MNLF) or more recently Moro Islamic Liberation Front (MILF) leaders.

Provide auspices: The lack of secure space in a conflict situation has allowed religious leaders to host or act as a host for talks and providing "protective cover" for parties to meet. For many decades, leaders of the MRA (Moral Rearmament) have utilized special and often spiritual gatherings to bring together many political and community leaders from conflicting societies.[9] Their houses in the UK, USA, Switzerland and India have been sites for these gatherings of community leaders from divided societies such as Lebanon, Palestine, Rwanda, India, etc.

Conciliation: The deadlock and stalemate in intractable conflicts produce lack of trust, misunderstanding, and inherent suspicion of the other intentions. Religious leaders have contributed a great deal in helping to move the parties toward nonviolent interaction and a negotiated settlement by reducing fears, suspicions, misunderstandings and misperceptions. The dialogue and training space offered by the various interfaith groups has been effective in changing the views and perceptions of many participants on the need to support negotiation. For example, Mindanao Peace Institute (MPI) has launched an annual gathering for interfaith grassroots leaders to learn negotiation, mediation, and problem solving skills which can be utilized in their community development role[10]. (See: http://cpn.nd.edu/MPIbrochure2005word1.pdf)

Another example of such work by religious leaders had been applied by the Center for Strategic and International Studies (CSIS) in the Balkan. Hundreds of Orthodox Serbs, Muslims Bosnians, and Catholic Croatians were trained by the CSIS staff and trainers in peacebuilding skills. In one of these training for Muslim Imams, a participant stood in front of 70 other imams and community members and said: "if we had such space in our society two decades ago, we would have saved many lives." [11] David Smock from United States Institute for Peace (USIP) captured the nature of the efforts by religious leaders:

> The inter-faith dialogue work in Bosnia organized by Reverend David Steele of the Center for Strategic and International Studies (CSIS) is worthy of mention. While not a faith-based organization itself, CSIS effectively facilitated many inter-faith dialogues and helped to found the local Center for Religious Dialogue to continue this work. Steele developed an approach to organizing dialogues that has proved effective over several years in Bosnia, Serbia, Kosovo, and Macedonia. His methods are based heavily upon personal storytelling, which uses the participants' experiences to help them relate to members of other faith communities. In addition to employing personal testimony, his approach emphasizes the importance of acknowledging responsibility for wrongs committed against the other group, forgiving injuries inflicted by the other group, and developing strategies to address the issues of justice that have generated and sustained intergroup conflict. The CSIS cases in Bosnia demonstrate that enlightened action by faith-based NGOs can contribute to inter-religious reconciliation in places where religion is a source of conflict. These NGOs can

bridge religious divisions, diminish the level of animosity, and focus attention on the shared responsibility to rebuild society.[12]

Facilitation and Mediation: Religious leaders can play a more active role in intractable conflicts situation when there is a lack of initiatives to settle conflicts. For example, traditional religious leaders have been engaged in conducting actual negotiations to help disputants agree upon the terms of an agreement or by conducting face-to-face discussion between the conflicting parties. Intractable and deep rooted conflict dynamics bring social and cultural imbalance into the communities and power relations are out of their functional order. Thus, as we see in many indigenous groups they have developed an important role for religious figures to restore social and spiritual balance into the community. An imam in a traditional Muslim community will see his role in society to restore order and bring parties a compromise, especially if he is formally asked by the parties to settle the conflict. Laura Nader (1978); Cathy Witty (1982); Abu-Nimer 2003; 1996; 1997 have examined these mediation and arbitration processes and compared them across cultures. In their stories of peacemakers from Asia, they featured "Ms. Hadja Manondog, an impressive and strong Muslim woman who bases her work for peace and reconciliation on her belief in the Koran. She travelled all the way from the remote area where she lives to be interviewed because she feels that there is a need for a book of inspiring stories, to share with others—especially children. Hadja is happy to share her story. Concerning the idea of sharing stories about beliefs and practices she says: 'If you have faith, you do no wrong.'[13]

On a higher level of religious representation, the Bishop-Ulama Forum (BUF) in Mindanao, Philippines is a forum for religious leaders who have acted in various situations to settle crisis in Muslim-Christian relations on the local, regional, and national levels.[14]

Finally, in the classic case of Rhodesia's (Zimbabwe) religious institutions or groups have been highly effective in settling a conflict and brining the parties to the table with some tangible results. Ron Rayville 1994, has examined the contribution of the Sant'Egidio community, MRA, the Catholic Church, along with Quaker and Mennonite groups. These religious actors have collectively and separately facilitated political processes in their own unique ways, which resulted in agreement between the rebel and the white led government.[15]

David Smock (2004) presents another case of successful intervention:

> The most dramatic example of religious peacemaking over the past two decades is the mediation orchestrated between 1989 and 1992 by the Community of Sant'Egidio, which brought an end to the civil war that had ravaged Mozambique for more than a decade. Sant'Egidio is an international movement composed of Catholic laity whose principal focus prior to the Mozambique mediation was to serve the needs of the urban poor. Don Jaime Goncalves, Catholic Archbishop of Beira, was familiar with Sant'Egidio from the time he had spent in Rome. Although all other parties had failed, he thought Sant'Egidio might succeed in bringing the governing Front for the Liberation of Mozambique (FRELIMO) together with the Mozambican National Resistance (RENAMO) insurgents. After many months of patient probing, Sant'Egidio succeeded in

making contact with the RENAMO leadership and encouraging Mozambican government officials to meet with them. The mediation work of Sant'Egidio in Mozambique illustrates how savvy religious organizations, building on their neutrality and compassion and utilizing the skills of other institutions, can bring feuding parties together and perhaps help end civil wars.

Advocacy and lobbying: In a reality filled with fear, suspicion, and trauma, to work for peace and justice is a dangerous task. The consequences can be dire to the activists, however being a religious leader often gives the person a higher moral ground to argue for certain values and changes. Thus abuse and violation of basic human rights have been the main focus of many religious peace activists. The religious activists have confronted their own government and defied its political rules or laws by witnessing or meeting the enemy.

Nevertheless, when they bring the message home (parliament, president, or other formal offices) they confront their own constituencies and are often received with shocking responses. When a Catholic priest in the mid-1990s asked his community or parish to pray for all victims of the conflict and not only the Catholic ones, over half of the parish members responded by leaving the church.[16] Another example is a story of the Buddhist monks who insisted on meeting the LTTE (define and labeled as a terrorist group by the Sri Lankan Government and Sinhalese majority opinion) prior to the historic ceasefire agreement in 2002. They were advocating for peace and strongly lobbied for stopping the war among their political leaders. Condemned by many other Buddhists in Sri Lanka, those monks were taking a stand that cost them alienation, threats to their lives, and possible imprisonment. Advocacy to stop the violence is also a classic role of religious peacebuilding in such context. Rabbis, imams, pastors, and priests meet regularly with US official urging them to constructively intervene in the Middle East to stop the violence and war. Such calls have even been extended to the war on Iraq in recent years[17].

Intervention through Inter-Religious Peacebuilding

Having identified some possible roles and risks for religious peacebuilding in intractable conflicts involving high stress and trauma, the following section looks at the basic strategies and preparation for many of these interventions.

Obviously there is a need for some preparatory stages for the initiation of the intervention, first preparing the inter-religious or intra-religious team through a process of values and attitudes clarification. This is a necessary step for clarifying the purpose and views of the inter-religious team on the various aspects of the conflict. It is often assumed by intervention teams that they share the same values or common views regarding the dynamics and causes of the conflict. However, they are surprised with the first set of activities on the ground that they differ in their perceptions regarding the conflict and its solutions. Such differences affect their decision making capacity throughout the intervention process. In a nonviolent march in Bethlehem, Palestine in December 2005, the Christian priest and Muslim Imam, who were surrounded by Israeli army officers trying to prevent them from entering Jerusalem, began a debate about the best strategy to diffuse the situation or confrontation with the Israeli army officers. Also in interfaith dialogue groups, participants assume that because they share the same views about what needs to be done, then they must share the same feelings, attitudes, or perceptions of the causes and motivations for action. As a result the organizers either postpone or skip such processes of clarifications, but they are surprised to find out that participants have different agenda or purpose for supporting the same actions.

Another part of the preparation efforts is to realize or become more aware of limits and strengths of the religious actors capacity to operate or even to change the situation. Religious leaders are not the only force or actor who determines the dynamics and settlement of the conflicts. Naturally their role is limited and they can not be expected to respond to all aspects of the conflict. Developing such realization among the inter-religious intervention team is crucial to reduce their typical post intervention frustration and burn out. Holding realistic as well as an optimistic view of reality and recognizing the limits of inter-religious peacebuilding can certainly assist religious actors and activists in identifying their successes and evaluating their limitations and failures in a proportional perspective.

An initiative known as the Alexandria Declaration in which Jewish, Muslim, and Christian leaders met for the first time in Alexandria, Egypt in 2002 and issued a declaration of peace was certainly a breakthrough into the Middle Eastern religious leadership role into the conflict.[18] The initiative started as a three-day summit in Alexandria, Egypt in January 2002 between senior Christian, Jewish and Muslim leaders and resulted in the First Alexandria Declaration of the Religious Leaders of the Holy Land, which condemned violence and pledged to work for peace. A Permanent Committee for the Implementation of the Alexandria Declaration (PCIAD) was established from the signatories and other spiritual leaders who have since met regularly.[19]

Such an initiative, regardless of its visibility, is unable to shift reality on the ground within a short period of time (even within a 2 year period!). In interviews with Muslim and Christian Palestinian clergy in 2003, they cited the failure of the Alexandria Declaration in achieving peace between the Israelis and Palestinians. Developing a realistic set of expectations and agreeing for the short term and long term intervention objectives, without relying solely on "divine miracles" is certainly a necessary preparatory step for inter-religious peacebuilding.

A third necessary preparatory step for inter-religious peacebuilding in such habituated conflict systems,[20] is the development of inter-religious peacebuilding skills. Having strong faith is not enough to insure effective peacebuilding intervention in conflict situation, definitely not within societies where there is high levels of traumas. Developing a systematic set of skills for the inter-religious team is a necessary condition for their success and capacity to intervene in the conflict situation. The major skills which are needed for such training are not necessary different form the typical training a secular team would receive. Thus, it can include communication skills, facilitation and mediation strategies, basic and advanced conflict analysis tools and trauma awareness education. There are also some basic skills that relate to inter-faith peacebuilding which might also enhance the team's capacity to intervene, such skills should include: sensitivity to utilizing cultural and religious rituals, the use of primary and secondary languages, and mechanisms for joint and separate prayers as well as basic knowledge of other faith groups' belief systems.

Obviously more preparatory activities can be generated beyond these three basic steps. The principle for this stage of intervention is to be as comprehensive and inclusive in constructing the inter-religious team.

Level and Extent of Inter-Religious Intervention

The nonviolent technique does not depend for its success on the goodwill of the oppressor, but rather on the unfailing assistance of God.

— Cesar Chavez

As mentioned earlier, intractable and deep rooted conflicts are complex systems and it is essential for an inter-religious team to realistically and strategically identify their objectives and goals prior to their intervention. Similarly, identifying the level of intervention is crucial for the potential impact of inter-religious teams. Conflict intervention can be, as mapped out by John Paul Lederach (1997), on three levels: community leaders and civil society, political and religious elites, or bottom up grass-roots communities.

Developing a strategy to maximize the possible impact of the religious factors and actors in any given conflict is a crucial segment of the intervention process. The inter-religious teams or group can devise a plan to address the manifestations of conflicts in their communities based on their capacities, entry points, and level of resources available. For example, inter-religious peacebuilding in Palestine and Israel has focused mainly on civil society or professional community members; they have not been able to systematically inject their efforts on the political elite levels. Similarly in Egypt and Lebanon inter-religious activists, like in many other inter-faith meetings and programs, have focused on educating each other about the basic elements of each faith, and mostly aimed at exploring similarities in beliefs and rituals. Few activities and program have designed their process to explore genuine differences (political or theological) (Abu-Nimer, Khoury, and Welty, 2007—USIP).

In many traumatized and intractable conflict realities, the conflict dynamics have contributed to and being sustained by the public impression and discourse that any attempt to change the nature of the conflict is doomed to failure and those who carry it are either naïve or have hidden agenda. Devising the inter-religious intervention plan is a necessary condition to impact such a society and it is essential, as well, to avoid the typical image of a naïve and idealistic person of faith who does not understand the conflict.

In the case of religious peacemakers, the challenge to break away form this impression is doubled due to their spiritual and universalistic message. Most of inter-religious peacebuilding adopt the narrative of justice, peace, harmony, or human brotherhood and so forth. This discourse is in direct contrast with the nature of traumatized or conflict habituated systems. A clear and strategic intervention plan will certainly help inter-religious actors in battling this public discourse.

Identifying the entry point, in most conflicts, religious factors and forces constitute only a part of the overall conflict dynamics and processes. Even in the Israeli-Palestinian conflict, in which many analysts have mischaracterized it as a religious conflict, most Israelis and Palestinians will described their conflict as political, nationalistic, or territorial. Obviously there are groups on the two sides who have framed the conflict mainly through religious ideologies and belief systems (Hamas and rightwing Israeli Jewish religious groups). Thus, it is crucial for inter-religious teams to expand their work and search for an entry points in the conflict which will not necessary confine them to their limited religious constituencies.

Palestinian and Israeli inter-religious groups can be effective in reaching out to nonreligious factors in their societies. In fact, secluding themselves and their activities within their small religious communities (preaching to the same "political converts") is one of the short comings of this type of intervention. Being able to identify, link, and network with other peacebuilding groups in society is a necessary strategy for inter-religious peacebuilding in such complex conflict reality.

The same lesson was shared by a Buddhist monk and Christian priest from the inter-religious peace foundation in Sri Lanka, in 2007 when they reflected on their peace efforts since the ceasefire agreement in Sri Lanka in 2002.[21] For three years, the group has worked mainly within their clergy constituencies; however in 2006 they shifted their strategy to reach out to wider segments of the Sri Lankan communities.

Clarifying criteria for measuring success or impact of the inter-religious intervention is another step in designing an effective strategy. Achieving clarity on the impact the inter-religious peacebuilding team is aiming for is a central factor in sustaining their efforts and vision. Many inter-religious groups develop too high and unrealistic macro objectives for their teams or intervention strategies. An example would be a Muslim and Christian group of clergy in Egypt who decided to conduct a monthly study circles to explore the commonalities and differences of beliefs in their respective faiths. Such a group has to determine the type of impact and success of their work. Changes in macro political relations or policy decision that affect the Muslim-Christian relations on the ground is not necessarily a criterion of success for such activity. However, some changes in the individual knowledge of another's faith is certainly a measure of success and even some changes in individual attitudes towards the other is a possible outcome of the intervention. The process of internalizing such realizations and determining the extent of the success can influence the motivation and commitment of the group members.

Interfaith Dialogue

A spiritual person tries less to be godly than to be deeply human.
— Rev. William Sloan Coffin, Jr

One of the central methods utilized by religious peacebuilders is the development of an interfaith dialogue space for people from various wounded communities to share their views, pain, injuries, and beliefs. Inter-faith dialogue is powerful and can be constructed as a sacred space for people to heal and establish new relationships across ethnic and religious divides. Stories and examples of inter-faith dialogue participants who were transformed by their experience have been widely documented by researchers and practitioners (see Abu-Nimer 2007, Gopen 2002, Smock 2002, Appleby, 1999). The existing literature clearly points out to the transformative power of the inter-faith dialogue forums or space.

Through dialogue, participants who held negative images and dehumanized their enemies learned to appreciate the diversity and complexity of other opinions and beliefs. In other cases, inter-faith journeys have produced collective action and advocacy for protection of human rights as in the case of Christian and Muslim leaders in Mindanao or the FOR interfaith delegations to Palestine.

The inter-faith space can provide a healthy environment for many of the participants who have been paralyzed by their conflict dynamics and processes. The relationship they build in the inter-faith group offer them a platform to express their pain and injuries, especially when these are publicly shared with the "enemy;" and a burden is lifted off the shoulders of both victim and victimizers. A Palestinian woman in an interfaith group in Jerusalem declared in an interview in 2004, "I come here to let them know what we go through everyday as a result of the occupation. They do not know. But when I share with them what happened to me in the check point, they can not deny my pain any more."

Evaluation reports of inter-faith dialogue groups in conflicts such as Mindanao, Sri Lanka and Israel—Palestine have recorded an impressive set of achievements in the short term, allowing for an individual-level shift in attitudes about the other group. Participants reported a sense of relief and satisfaction from their safe interaction with members of the other faith groups (see reports on such groups in Abu-Nimer, Khoury, 2007).

Nevertheless, inter-faith dialogue space is not enough to transform the conflict or to bring change into its political processes. The lack of input of these interfaith groups into the formal political system or lack of input into the wider political movements for change was identified as a problem of inter-religious peacebuilding in these conflict areas. Suggestions made by certain participants who reached such painful realization included:

1. Being more strategic in selecting the participants for the inter-faith group.
2. Prior to the inter-faith dialogue, devise a plan on how to bring the success and outputs into the political macro elite level.

3. Avoid inter-faith dialogue for short terms, but insist on long term commitment as a condition for participation.
4. Establish systematic formal or informal linkages with existing peace groups who work for change and improve relations among communities.
5. Shift the power relations among members in the inter-faith group to be symmetric as opposed to mirroring dominant power relations in the actual conflict.
6. Provide more professional training and skills for the inter-religious actors.

Conclusion

Inter-religious peacebuilding is a one significant segment of the Peacebuilding Wheel (see Barry Hart's Wheel in the book preface). This part of the wheel will be less effective if religious actors are not fully linked to the other conflict transformation processes in action. However, it is neither accurate nor realistic to expect religious actors to magically or divinely transform the society, which has been trained and habituated for many decades to live in a conflict mentality and has conditioned its members' behaviors and beliefs to sustain the destructive dynamics of the conflict.

There is a wide range of activities and roles that can be developed and applied by religious actors for peace in any given society. Obviously the selection and determination of the type of activities carried out should be solely shaped by the individuals involved, their level of risk taking, the resources available and type and nature of their awareness.

In addition to the potential roles discussed in this article, Annex 1 offers a more detailed list of possible religious peacebuilding roles and activities. Although the list was developed for people in the Northern Hemisphere, nevertheless, many of these proposed activities can be carried out anywhere in the world. The list was developed by *"Living as Peace Maker in A broken world: http://www.cctpp.org/documents/sp_study_resource.pdf."*

Finally, a word on the ethics of intervention and exportation of inter-religious peacebuilding strategies and methods. It is not for international organization or any other external entity to dictate the pace and nature of these inter-religious intervention for peace. What works in Harvard Square does not necessarily work in Jerusalem!

Despite the above challenges, the contribution of the inter-religious peacebuilding field is being conceptualized and gradually recognized by scholars in international and religious studies. Even politicians have begun realizing the positive and powerful role that religious leaders can play in the processes of negotiation and political settlements conflict resolution. However for the future development of the inter-religious peacebuilding field, more research is needed to explore questions such as:

1. What are the specific forces and factors that allow the inter-religious peacebuilding to be effective?

2. What are the ideal conditions for inter-faith dialogue setting?
3. What are the unique features of inter-faith dialogue setting as opposed to secular dialogue processes? Are they really unique?
4. What specific role can inter-religious peacemakers play in a formal negotiation processes when they are shaped by power politik dynamics?

Annex 1.
Living as Peace Maker in A broken world
http://www.cctpp.org/documents/sp_study_resource.pdf

CATEGORIES OF SUPPORT BY REGIONAL AND LOCAL RELIGIOUS BODIES FOR PEACEBUILDING IN OTHER COUNTRIES

A. Sending people, financial resources, and providing training and support for peacebuilding efforts in other countries

1. Sending people to a particular country to work with people from that nation in peacebuilding efforts;
2. Equipping international students through courses and events in the U.S. to provide leadership to peacebuilding in their own or another country;
3. Providing training, curriculum, and other assistance to indigenous peacebuilding efforts abroad;
4. Participating in established ecumenical accompaniment processes;
5. Monitoring elections at the request of indigenous groups;
6. Raising money for particular indigenous peacebuilding projects;

B. Relationship building among people who are in conflict with each other

1. Bringing people together in the U.S. whose ethnic group or related communities are in conflict in a particular country (e.g. Catholics and Protestants who are from or whose families were from Northern Ireland);
2. Engaging in interfaith dialogue with people whose religions are in conflict in a particular country (e.g. Christian, Muslims and/or Jews in Israel/Palestine, the Balkans, etc);

C. Educating in the U.S. about the need for peacebuilding in particular countries and developing relationships building between those engaged in peacebuilding in another country and people of faith in the U.S.

1. Establishing partnerships between judicatories and religious bodies in the U.S. and peacebuilding efforts in particular countries;
2. Sending people to a specific country to learn about the conflict in that nation so that they can make presentations in the U.S. and enlarge support for peacebuilding in that country;
3. Sponsoring events, including worship experiences, on the conflict in a particular country;
4. Assuring press coverage for events on conflicts in particular countries;
5. Preparing opinion pieces and letters to the editor lifting up peacebuilding efforts in particular countries;
6. Crafting denominational, ecumenical and interfaith theological statements about the importance of peacebuilding in a particular nation and/or the importance of peacebuilding around the world;
7. Developing mass media presentations such as "Faces of Forgiveness" on the Hallmark Channel, especially working with local PBS and other media outlets;
8. Creating an e-mail network to provide information to regional and local

faith-based groups on peacebuilding activities in other countries;

9. Developing curriculum and other educational tools to educate adults in the U.S. about the conflict in a particular nation;
10. Educating children on the conflicts in a particular country by sponsoring events on these topics, preparing curriculum, and offering hands-on projects like preparing school kits;
11. Educating U.S. college and seminary students on the need for peacebuilding in particular countries, including educational experiences in that country;

D. Public education in the U.S. about conflicts and peacemaking opportunities that arise from faith-based peacebuilding work in particular countries

1. Developing and implementing strategies for public education (outside of the religious community) and action on the conflicts in particular countries, including public policy advocacy;
2. Providing information and opportunities to those in the faith community concerned about conflicts in a particular country to share their concerns with their congresspersons and other policy-makers.
3. Arranging for people engaged in peacebuilding in other countries to visit congresspersons, editorial boards and other leadership.

Notes

1. The list is based on a training session on religion and peacebuilding and a handout developed by Cynthia Sampson, Eastern Mennonite University, SPI 2000. There are other lists of possible peacebuilding role and activities. See the annex (1) for this chapter.
2. LTTE is a rebellious group that seeks to represent the Tamil minority (20-22%) in Sri Lanka and since early 1980s has been fighting for their equal rights and self determination from the Majority Sinhalese (Buddhist) government.
3. Catholic Priest Muthur , Interview Tricomalee January 20-07.
4. The stories of Father Roberto C. Layson and Mr Mike P. Alon are set in Pikit Municipality. Both Mike and Fr Bert have suffered and overcome personal loss and are now working for peace, reconciliation and mutual respect among communities through facilitating dialogue. Mike and Fr Bert work together closely on peace-building in Pikit. See full story of their work in the forthcoming book: You Can Inspire: Personal Stories form Asia, CISE, 2007.
5. In December 2002, 130 delegates from 47 nations chose Sri Lanka as the site of the first Nonviolent Peaceforce pilot project. The Nonviolent Peaceforce is recruiting, training, and sending 50 international civilians to help establish a foundation for sustainable peace in Sri Lanka.
6. Sri Lanka Interim Report—April 2006 April 25, 2006. See Website: http://nvpf.org/np/english/srilanka/slqreport3_6.asp.html
7. http://www.ifpbdel.org/reports.html
8. http://www.interfaithpeacebuilders.org/us/default.html
9. MRA is also known as Initiatives for Change (I of C). Following World War II, Moral Re-Armament (MRA), as it had become known, launched a program of moral and spiritual reconstruction to foster change in private and public life based on a change in motivation and character. It worked for reconciliation between France and Germany, and between Japan and many other Asian neighbors. It was involved in the process of decolonization, and in forging industrial teamwork and harmonious race relations. It was also active in inter-religious relations and in the struggle for the rights of indigenous peoples. In an event in Washington DC, I of C sponsored a panel of Christian, Muslim, and Druz Lebanese who promoted reconciliation and healing among Lebanese (for further information, see: http://www.iofc.org/en/abt).
10. Since 2000, Catholic Relief Services (CRS), the Mennonite Central Committee (MCC) and the Catholic Agency for Overseas Development (CAFOD) have joined efforts and resources to bring together peacebuilders and practitioners from thirty-one (31) countries for the Mindanao Peacebuilding Institute. The MPI, as envisioned, provides a unique experience in that it brings together a wide range of people with vast experience, knowledge and skills in peace-related work. The intensive training in areas such as religious peacebuilding, conflict transformation, community-based peacebuilding and other themes increases people's skills, drawing on the shared knowledge of both the participants and the facilitators. The Institute has become a venue where participants strengthen their commitment to peacebuilding work. The diversity of conflict types around the world is highlighted by the more than 700 peacebuilders who have participated in the past Institutes (2000 to 2004), coming from areas such as Bangladesh, Belgium, Bulgaria, Cambodia, Croatia, East Timor, Germany, India, Indonesia, Korea, Kosovo, Madagascar, Myanmar, Pakistan, Papua New Guinea, Senegal, Sri Lanka, Vietnam, the former Yugoslavia, and the Philippines. Former participants and facilitators represent local and international humanitarian organizations, local NGOs, youth groups, church-based organiza-

tions, people's organizations, local and international networks, corporate foundations, academic institutions, women's groups, and socio-civic groups.

11. April 2001, Sarajevo Training for Muslim Bosnian Imams, Sponsored by CSIS program.

12. Divine Intervention Regional Reconciliation Through Faith, by David Smock From *Religion, Vol. 25 (4)—Winter 2004).*

13. See full story of their work in the forthcoming book: You Can Inspire: Personal Stories form Asia, CISE, 2007 (forthcoming).

14. BUF has been operating for almost a decade and its members have met systematically to explore possible ways to reduce interelgious violence and bring more security and stability to the Moro-Christian relations in Mindanao and Philippines. The group is widely known and has been consulted by the Philippine president and other national leaders on various occasions.

15. Ron Kraybill, 1994: Doug Johnson and Cynthia Sampson, Edited Book.

16. Based on the story of the Catholic priest in EMU in Sumer 1997.

17. For example, on July 31, Dr. Maher Hathout, Rev. George Regas and Rabbi Leonard Beerman met with Senator Dianne Feinstein (D-CA) and Senator Barbara Boxer (D-CA) in their Senate office building in Washington DC to discuss the recent crisis in the Middle East. The three religious leaders expressed a commitment to peace and human rights and articulated the need for an immediate cease-fire to the escalating violence in the Middle East. (see: http://www.mpac.org/article.php?id=393)

18. *First Declaration of Alexandria of the Religious Leaders of the Holy Land*

In the name of God who is Almighty, Merciful and Compassionate, we, who have gathered as religious leaders from the Muslim, Christian and Jewish communities, pray for true peace in Jerusalem and the Holy Land, and declare our commitment to ending the violence and bloodshed that denies the right to life and dignity.

According to our faith traditions, killing innocents in the name of God is a desecration of his Holy Name, and defames religion in the world. The violence in the Holy Land is an evil which must be opposed by all people of good faith. We seek to live together as neighbors, respecting the integrity of each other's historical and religious inheritance. We call upon all to oppose incitement, hatred, and the misrepresentation of the other.

1. The Holy Land is holy to all three of our faiths. Therefore, followers of the divine religions must respect its sanctity, and bloodshed must not be allowed to pollute it. The sanctity and integrity of the Holy Places must be preserved, and the freedom of religious worship must be ensured for all.
2. Palestinians and Israelis must respect the divinely ordained purposes of the Creator by whose grace they live in the same land that is called Holy.
3. We call on the political leaders of both parties to work for a just, secure, and durable solution in the spirit of the words of the Almighty and the Prophets.
4. As a first step now, we call for a religiously sanctioned cease-fire, respected and observed from all sides, and for the implementation of the Mitchell and Tenet recommendations, including the lifting of restrictions and return to negotiations.
5. We seek to help create an atmosphere where present and future generations will co-exist with mutual respect and trust in the other. We call on all to refrain from incitement and demonization, and to educate our future generations accordingly.
6. As religious leaders, we pledge ourselves to continue a joint quest for a just peace that leads to reconciliation in Jerusalem and the Holy Land, for the common good of all our peoples.

7. We announce the establishment of a permanent joint committee to carry out the recommendations of this declaration, and to engage with our respective political leadership accordingly.

Signatories:
His Grace the Archbishop of Canterbury, Dr. George Carey
The Sephardi Chief Rabbi Bakshi-Doron
The Deputy Foreign Minister, Rabbi Michael Melchior
Rabbi David Rosen, President of the WCRP
The Rabbi of Savyon, Rabbi David Brodman
Minister of State for the Palestinian Authority, Sheikh Tal El Sider
Representative of the Greek Patriarch, Archbishop Aristichos
The Melkite Archbishop, Archbishop Boutrous Mu'alem
Representative of the Armenian Patriarch, Archbishop Chinchinian
The Bishop of Jerusalem, the Rt. Revd. Riah Abu El Assal

19. Network for Interfaith Concern, for further details see: http://www.anglicannifcon.org/InterfaithInit.htm.

20. Conflict Habituated system is a term coined by the Institute for Multi Track Diplomacy (IMTD) in reference to certain individual and group beliefs about their conflict processes and dynamics. Most of these characteristics involve feelings of helplessness, distrust, lack of community, disempowerment, polarized views of reality, simplified solutions to the conflict, lack of creativity or well to engage constructively with the other, unwillingness to learn new information about the other, developing negative mythologies about the enemy.

21. Colombo Sri Lanka, interview January 16, 2007 leaders of Inter-religious Peace Foundation.

References

Appleby, Scott. 1998. *The Ambivalence of the Sacred: Religion, Violence, and Reconciliation.* New York: Rowman and Littlefield.

Abu-Nimer Mohammed, Amal Khoury, and Emily Welty. 2007. *Unity in Diversity: Interfaith Dialogue in the Middle East.* Washington, D.C.: United States Institute of Peace Press.

Abu-Nimer, Mohammed. 2003. *Nonviolence and Peacebuilding in Islamic: Theory and Practice.* Gainesville, FL.: University Press of Florida.

———— Religion, Dialogue, and Nonviolence Actions in Israeli-Palestinian Conflict. *International Journal of Politics, Culture and Society* Vol. 17, No. 3 (Spring 2004)

———— "The Miracles of Transformation through Interfaith Dialogue: Are you a Believer?" in David Smock, ed., *Interfaith Dialogue.* Washington, D.C.: United States Institute of Peace Press.

———— Conflict Resolution and Islam: Some Conceptual Questions. *Peace and Change*, Vol. 21, January, 1996 (22-40).

Diamond, Louise, and John McDonald, eds. 1996. *Multi-Track Diplomacy: A Systems Approach to Peace.* West Hartford, Conn.: Kumarian Press.

Gopin, Marc. 2000. *Between Eden and Armageddon: The Future of World Religions, Violence, and Peacemaking.* New York: Oxford University Press.

Kraybill, Ron. 1994. "Transition from Rhodesia to Zimbabwe: The Role of religious actors." In Douglas Johnston and Cynthia Sampson eds. *Religion: The Missing Dimension of Statecraft*. New York: Oxford University Press.

Nader Laura and H. Todd. (Eds). 1978. *The Process-Law in Ten Societies*. New York: Columbia University Press.

Lederach, J. Paul. 1997. *Peace Building in Divided Societies*. New York: Syracuse University Press.

Salem, P. *Bitter*. 1994. *Legacy: Ideology and Politics in the Arab World*. New York: Syracuse University Press.

Smock David, Divine Intervention Regional Reconciliation Through Faith, From *Religion*, Vol. 25 (4), Winter 2004).

Smock David, ed. 2002. *Interfaith Dialogue and Peacebuilding*. Washington, D.C.: United States Institute of Peace Press.

Witty, Cathy. 1980. *Mediation and Society: Conflict Management in Lebanon*. New York: Academic Press.

Part III

Trauma Healing in Croatia, Columbia and Australia

12

Daring to Dream: Learning about Community Trauma, Accountability and Building the Future in Post-War Forums in Croatia

Arlene Audergon

Trauma and injustice from violent conflict impact all of us, up close and at a distance. Dynamics around past trauma and injustice lead to new rounds of conflict. Outrage, pain and silence around injustice and trauma from violent conflict are combustible fuel. The fuel doesn't just blow up on its own. Throughout history, and in our current world scene, government and military state terror tactics readily exploit these dynamics, as do terrorist tactics, to stir new rounds of violence.[1] Grappling with community trauma and issues of accountability throughout society—so that we are less susceptible to such tactics—is of critical importance to peace-making and violence prevention.

Take a moment to think about how easily you can unconsciously fall into repeating rounds of conflict, at your own kitchen sink, especially where you've been hurt. Conflicts repeat with partners, family, colleagues or inside your own heart. If life teaches us something as individuals, it may be that just when you think you've worked out how to not fall back into an old pattern, it comes back once more. At the same time, life challenges us to become conscious and grow into a sense of responsibility and choice in how we deal with even the most painful difficulties life brings.

Considering all the violence in our world, it is natural to feel a sense of despair or hopelessness. But, can we dare to imagine taking responsibility for our history and future? Can we seek justice and accountability without being taken into revenge? Can we find ways to include the tragedy and traumas of our personal and collective history into our hearts without repeating them? Can we imagine a world where we actively work with the history and conflicts from which we suffer, rather than fall into repeating them?

In this chapter, I suggest steps in this direction, with learning from large forums in Croatia from 1996-2001, and in 2006, where participants worked with issues of how to reconcile and move forward, given community-wide trauma and unanswered questions of justice and accountability.

I introduce the nature of the projects and how it all started. I discuss some of the ideas and methods of Process Oriented Psychology, developed by Arnold Mindell, in their application to conflict resolution and community building. I particularly focus on dynamics of community trauma and accountability, illustrating with stories from the forums in Croatia. I consider how community based work on trauma and accountability links with the work of tribunals, truth commissions, and other means that society has for grappling with its past and future, such as media or arts. I look to participants in our forums in Croatia, who modelled the possibility of grappling with the war, discovering how they played a part, and assuming leadership in building their communities and creating the future.

Worldwork: Daring to Dream for Croatia

It was 1994; the former Yugoslavia was at war. Two women from Croatia heard about an important method for working with conflict, developed by Arnold Mindell and colleagues, called 'world work'.[2] They travelled to Slovakia, joining 300 participants from 30 countries in an intensive conference over ten days, inside a gigantic gymnasium in the small town of Stupava, near Bratislava.

There were extraordinary and heated interactions, conflict and transformations as the large group and small groups worked together on a wide range of themes, including racism; gender; attitudes around sexual orientation; mental health; attitudes between east and west; and issues for central and eastern Europe after the fall of the former Soviet Union.

'World work' is based on Mindell's far-reaching concept of 'deep democracy'.[3] Deep democracy refers to potential creativity within groups and communities when there is an opportunity to interact with facilitation among all points of view. Deep democracy also means including all dimensions[4] of group life: the content and issues; the underlying polarization of roles; and the deepest creative and sentient level that underlies conflict.

One morning, the group turned its focus to the violence in the Balkans. Tanja Radocaj spoke about her distress and began to formulate a vision. Could it be possible to bring these methods of facilitation to Croatia, to work with conflicts among Serbs, Croats and Muslims? Mirela Miharaja, also from Croatia, joined her in the dream. Tanja and Mirela then spoke to my colleague Lane Arye and me, asking if we would come to Croatia. We supported them to follow their dream and promised that if they got a group together, we'd be there.

Building Sustainable Community in the Aftermath of War

Osijek 1996

We went to Osijek, Croatia for the first time in Spring 1996. The four day forum was organized through the International Rescue Committee (IRC). It was made up of participants from all around Croatia, and also Bosnia. People later said that this gathering in Osijek was the first time Croats, Serbs and Muslims came together to talk about the war and how they could begin to go forward as a community. Years later, people still talk about the deeply moving and transforming experiences in that first forum in Osijek

Forums: 1997-2001

The work continued with a new project led by Tanja Radocaj and later Nives Ivelija, of Udruga Mi, which means Organization 'us' or 'we', a non-governmental organization in Croatia, with cooperation and financial support from the United Nations High Commission for Refugees (UNHCR), and other sources, including Open Society Institute (OSI), Office of Transition Initiatives (OTI), USAID, Threshold Foundation, Office for Security and Cooperation in Europe (OSCE), as well as several embassies. Udruga Mi, had a special role to bring together key players from all war-affected regions in Croatia. Lane Arye and I facilitated the forums. Participants were from 35 local and international NGOs (Non-governmental organizations), 27 government organizations, 12 Red Cross branches and 6 local governments. Four day forums occurred twice a year in Split, Stubicke Toplice, Trogir, Topusko, Brac, Dubrovnik, Supetar, Nasice, as well as an afternoon forum in Vukovar. Additionally there were regional meetings, a newsletter, and a training group.

Several hundreds of participants attended the forums. Each four-day forum had 70-90 participants. Participants included a wide range of people, from those directing organizations to those in grassroots services, from social workers to youth, and lawyers to mayors. They were a very mixed group of Croats, Serbs, Muslims, and other and mixed ethnicities

The idea was to bring together people working in the field with issues pertaining to reconciliation and community building. In a group of Serbs, Croats and Muslims, each with their own war experiences, the conflicts and issues they met in their communities were present among themselves. By not only talking about the problems in their communities, but working on their direct interactions, we entered sensitive and sometimes volatile territory, and the groups found pathways forward as key players and leaders in rebuilding their communities. Their experiences in these forums were directly applied to their home communities, affecting communication and relationship between organizations, as well as the contributions of individuals and organizations in human services, reconciliation efforts, economic development, and community leadership.

Forum 2006

We returned to Croatia in November 2006. Udruga Mi coordinated a project to support regions in Croatia that had been hit the hardest during the war, and were struggling to survive, economically and to rebuild community. These communities had been devastated and many young people left these communities after the war. The project included support for economic community projects as well as this forum. It was supported by the UNHCR, and the Dutch embassy. This time Jean-Claude Audergon (an international facilitator of Process Oriented Psychology, as well as my partner), Lane Arye and I facilitated together as a team.

Welcoming and Deep Democracy

When we welcome people in forums, we usually say something about how the wisdom and direction forward is within the group. We say a few words about Mindell's concept of 'Deep Democracy',[5] and the wisdom of communities, when all views, feelings and dimensions of our experience are included. We soon invite people to speak about issues in their community, what is on their hearts, and we go through a sorting process to find out how the group would like to focus, knowing that there are so many important issues, and we will not be able to do it all. We explain that the forum will involve large group discussion, small groups, as well as opportunities to work with specific issues or projects. We briefly share a few facilitation methods, so the group knows where we are coming from.

Roles and Ghost Roles

When facilitating, we sometimes represent 'roles'. 'Roles' help to represent a polarization of positions, and people can step into each spot to further differentiate these positions. Roles, however, are more than viewpoints. Roles also represent a deeper structure to the interaction or conflict. For example in most conflicts, we see the role of who is suffering, and the one who caused this suffering. In a conflict usually everyone identifies with the role who is suffering, and the one who caused the suffering is a 'ghost role'[6]. That means it is implied but not directly represented. It can be very useful, when someone is able to represent a ghost role, within the interaction

We also remind people that the use of roles is for the purpose of deepening the dialogue. While at one point, a role is further differentiated by people guessing into it, in a kind of role 'play', at another moment these roles become extremely personal. By stepping very personally into these underlying roles that structure our conflicts and interactions, it is possible to relate more consciously with one another in community, rather than feeling swallowed up and at the mercy of repeating conflict.

Another reason to use roles is that a role is not identified with one individual. It is bigger than any single viewpoint and needs many voices to fill it out thoroughly. At the same time, each individual is bigger than any one role. This makes people freer to speak without being locked into one role. They can speak their mind and step out again, or even change to the other role. This helps individuals to become aware of their own wholeness, as well as supporting fluidity in the group dialogue.

Hot Spots

We also mention that while facilitating we will notice 'hot spots'.[7] These are points where something is said that is sensitive or controversial. The 'hot spot' sizzles. It may be subtle or strong. Everyone intuitively recognizes such moments, where everyone goes silent, changes the subject, or tempers may flare. When ignored, hot spots return, and may become volatile if ignored over time. They are points where conflicts escalate, cycle, or where people retreat and go hopeless. What is exciting is that hot spots are also points of potential transformation. They are doorways. A hot spot can also be understood as a point of instability that appears to lead to chaos, and with awareness is a turning point from past (the repeating conflict) to the possibility of a different future.[8]

Community Trauma and Accountability

Imagine a group gathered after the war, to talk about how the country will reconcile and move forward. How do you begin to talk among people you don't know or trust? But how will you ever trust and work closely with colleagues to rebuild community if you are not able to talk about the central issues shaping your lives and work? How do you talk together in a group filled with people who were fighting on the opposite side of a war, and "when we know that all men of a certain age were involved in the fighting"?

Especially in the early forums, people did not want to say their names, because it would indicate if they were Serb, Croat or Muslim. People formulated what they wanted to say in carefully chosen words and such complex sentences that it was hard to understand, in order to avoid touching hot spots or sensitive or volatile issues.

Questions needed to be asked: Is it good idea to open such potentially volatile issues? If so, how do we do it in a way that won't just set things off again? Is it safe? Can it make it worse? Is it better to just try to forget? And if we do not find forums to process the violence of the past, what then?

Distance, Museum Pieces, and Weeping

People were hesitant and terrified to touch anything to do with their war experience or ethnic/national background, because it might stir up conflict and touch their own or other' pain. They did not want to touch upon the pain, for fear they would cry. And they were afraid to cry for fear their tears would never stop.

There's a story from our first forum about distance to our emotions and one another, and bridging that distance. It is also a story that reflects the well of pain around community wide trauma. During our first gathering, there was several participants form Sarajevo, Bosnia and Herzegovina. At one point a woman from Sarajevo said to the other participants 'You hold us apart. You treat us like museum pieces. You look, but don't touch'. She and her colleagues had recently suffered from the terrible violence as Sarajevo was under siege. There was a silence in the room, and then one woman stood up and crossed the room, and sat on the floor facing her. She said 'It's true. I keep you at a distance. I saw images of Sarajevo on television. At that point the war in Croatia had stopped, and though I lived less than a couple hundred kilometres away, I watched, but I couldn't feel it. And I remember I was glad it was there and not here.' Both women now had tears in their eyes and then everyone in the room began to cry, too. I remember looking around the room and seeing tears streaming on everyone's faces. Lane and I were crying too. The group continued to share their experiences of distance, and pain. The interpreter cried, too, and was very upset with herself, because she felt this was not professional. When we told her it was okay, she broke down and wept, as others pitched in to interpret.

By acknowledging the distance in that moment, the distance was bridged and an extraordinary sense of connection grew. Everyone recognized how they had kept distance to their own pain and to one another. And everyone recalled their feeling of isolation, as the world, at a distance, had sat by and watched it all on television.

Hot Spots, Touching Community Trauma and Accountability

Hot spots are not only charged and potentially volatile points of conflict. If you touch a hot spot in a region that has been at war, you touch a vein of community-wide trauma. [9] When facilitating groups and communities who have experienced violent conflict its important to understand how hot spots touch dynamics of community trauma and how to work carefully with them. Hot spots are also a direct link to history, unresolved and open questions about what happened, the missing people, and who is accountable.

When you hear about community trauma after violence, people sometimes refer to psychological illness. While it may certainly be useful to recognize and treat psychological symptoms in various ways at an individual level, thinking only in terms of individual pathology can exasperate the sense of distance, misunderstanding and isolation. It misses the fact that we are not talking about a community of ill people, but rather a community of people who have been at war, or a community of people who have suffered atrocities, and are trying to come to terms with their community story, as well as individual stories.

One reason people usually try to avoid touching the hotspots of their interactions is the fear of triggering trauma. Ignoring hot spots, however, leaves you at their mercy, creates stress, and increases danger of escalation. Choice and awareness is needed. Rather than waiting to fall into the dynamics surrounding hot spots, it can be protective to go directly and carefully to these spots with choice and with special tools of facilitation. In the forums we would often speak about the group's wish to protect itself, and encourage this, by going slowly at these hot spots, by including the group in a sense of responsibility and choice about how to go forward, and inviting everyone to join us in the facilitation.

Accountability and Conscience

During one forum, there was an atmosphere of high tension surrounding unanswered questions and suspicions. Where were you? Why did you stay? Why did you leave? One man became very agitated, broke into a sweat and in great distress jumped up to leave the room. His trauma was triggered. He said he was frightened that touching on these volatile issues would be too much. We were able to ask whether he wanted to stay or go, and if he wanted to stay, what would he need to be able to? And also what would others need so that we did not exclude anyone? He said he very much wanted to stay and for this discussion to happen, but did not believe it was possible. He wished there was a way that could take care of everyone there, and the trauma so many have suffered.

We thanked him for his protective message. At this point a woman spoke about the terrible tension in their home communities, from the constant questioning and accusations. On top of the traumatic experiences suffered, you had to also endure suspicions. She then said something that led to a transformation in the group. She said "The roles of the questioner and the questioned are both inside of me". She then told about a terrifying and traumatic story, in which under threat of her life she made certain choices that put her friend's life in danger along with her own. They lived through it, but the painful self-questioning about the risk she'd taken with her friend's life had never stopped. As she spoke, a stillness came over the room, as everyone realized how they suffered not only from the suspicions among them and within their communities, but from their constant inner questioning. One by one people shared very personally about their own inner accusations and doubts, how they grappled with their own conduct under the pressure of the times. Several people said the most difficult thing was the constant doubts about whether they made the right choices that affected their loved ones, families, and communities. Several people said if it was only their own life in danger, that would be okay—but it was the sense of responsibility for others. One man spoke very personally about being in a public position and having to make decisions that could affect the lives of his whole community.

The explosive atmosphere, the panic, jumpiness, and fear of setting off trauma, was transformed, as the group actively entered a shared process of reflection, conscience and accountability The person who had been so anxious was profoundly relieved, saying he had not dreamed that this kind of dialogue could possibly happen in a group of Serbs, Croats and Muslims. At one point he told me he needed to make sure he was not in a dream. [10]

One Part Goes Forward and One Part Replays

A dynamic of trauma is that people may feel distant or cut off from their emotions, unable to touch the subject for fear of triggering painful and traumatic memories. In individuals, this 'splitting' is a well known characteristic of trauma. A person may feel simultaneously cut off from the experience, and at the same time at the mercy of the experience that takes over in outbursts of emotion, or repeats in flashbacks, nightmares and visceral symptoms.[11] At the point of the traumatic experience, one part of the person went forward, to function, survive. There was no time or capacity to feel, react, or deal with the magnitude of the experience. Life appears to go on, but the traumatic experience is there just below the surface, and replays, without choice.

A way to understand why trauma repeats in visceral experiences, flashbacks and nightmares is that the story is seeking a witness, some part of ourselves who can perceive it. At the point of the traumatic event, it was not possible to include it into the narrative of the person's individual experience. There was no part of the personality able to take it in, react and in some way to integrate it into life. It replays as if waiting to be heard, seen, responded to and included. This is simultaneously a psychological, social and political process. The traumatic experience belongs not only to the individual's personal story, but to the community's story, and our world's story. [12]

A way to understand the dynamics of community wide trauma or collective trauma is that similarly to how one part of the individual goes forward to survive, while the traumatic story remains locked in time and replays, the whole community also has to move forward to try to rebuild, and the community wide trauma remains and replays. One form of replay is in the traumatic experiences of large numbers of people in community. Another replay is in outbursts or new rounds of violence or retribution. Community trauma needs to be included into the community narrative or collective history. The untold stories need to be told. The holes in information need to be filled. There needs to be a process of accountability and there needs to be a community grappling with its conscience.

Accountability throughout Society

The ability for people during the forum to reflect internally upon their personal conscience and accountability does not replace looking to community relationships and accountability issues between Serbs, Croats and Muslims.

Rather, it was a part of grappling with justice and accountability and community trauma at all levels. The learning from these forum experiences helped us to begin to formulate a vision that justice and accountability and community trauma need to be grappled with at all levels of society: there is a need for an international process of criminal accountability, such as the International Tribunal; there is a need for forums and methods of dialogue throughout community to work with conflict and accountability between groups; there is a need for discussions and questions about responsibility for one's own group; and an internal grappling with conscience and sharing of these stories. All levels are needed and each impacts the other. Most of all, there is an uncanny source of wisdom and direction in community, when interactions can be followed carefully and accurately.

In the forums, we often heard pleas for accountability, for the atrocities committed. People wanted someone on the other side, to stand opposite them, and say that they/or their community did this terrible thing. With this was a plea to assume responsibility for one's community, in order to talk to people, find the still missing graves, and missing information. As in conflicts everywhere it was difficult for people to take accountability. Everyone identified more easily as the one who suffered, who was part of a group who had been hurt by the other side. The one creating the suffering or who can assume any responsibility became a 'ghost role'.

Croats spoke of the 'ethnic cleansing' and atrocities in 1991. When Croatia announced its independence from the former Yugoslavia, Serb paramilitaries living in Croatia, backed by the Yugoslav Army (JNA), took over the Krajina region of Croatia, accompanied by forcing out Croats, atrocities and killing. Serbs spoke of the killing and ethnic cleansing when the Croatian army came in 1995 and seized the area back. Now Serbs were forced out and killed. And in discussing this cycle of violence, discussions also quickly returned to open wounds and lack of accountability for what happened in World War II, World War I, and to the 14th century.

I remember in one forum discussion, a conflict cycled between Serbs and Croats living in Croatia. Some were despaired, others cynical, that we would ever emerge from this mess. Then two women spoke, one Croat and one Serb, one after the other. They were both elders in their community, who had personally suffered great loss and tragedy. Each spoke so personally and eloquently that the group was riveted and very moved in their hearts. The Croat woman spoke about the atrocities committed in her villages by Croats. A Serb woman spoke about the atrocities in her village carried out by Serbs. That they spoke about the crimes of their own group, with such a deep sense of sorrow and remorse, made a profound impact.

Tribunals

As the question of sending war criminals to the Tribunals came to the news, we noticed discussions about accountability were more possible in the community forums. There was a need to differentiate criminal accountability from what it means for a society to grapple with its conscience and issues of responsibility at a community, relationship and personal level.

One purpose of a criminal Tribunal is to create the possibility for society to have this dialogue. By bringing those most responsible to the International Tribunals, the rest of society might begin to discuss what happened and their part.

When the question arose of sending Croat war criminals to The Hague, we could see that some people in our forums (and some people throughout society) believed that no Croat should be held accountable for what happened in the military operation and ethnic cleansing of 1995. They felt that these were defenders and heroes, in relation to what had happened in 1991, and that even atrocities were excused within this context.

But many believed that warlords on all sides must take criminal responsibility. For some the Tribunals brought a sense of hope that there would be accountability and closure, and a chance to put the war behind us. Some felt that once criminals were held accountable, there would be no more need to talk about accountability—that accountability was only a criminal matter. Others felt that it was insufficient to leave all matters of responsibility on the war criminals, and that criminal accountability was only one level of a much broader discussion that was needed throughout society. In relation to broader community discussions, some felt that we should only be responsible for our personal actions. Others felt that it is essential that we assume responsibility in some way for our own group's actions.

An important learning is that while many people think that this sort of debate and these differences in views might prevent a process of accountability from going forward, it is in fact, this kind of debate throughout society that is an essential part of the process of grappling with accountability.

Truth Commissions

Tribunals make an essential contribution to society's recognition that accountability is needed, that there needs to be a bottom line. This bottom line is that having power is not an excuse for impunity. Everyone must be accountable.

Truth commissions, particularly the famous model from South Africa, provide a model that accountability is not only about criminal justice, but also about telling the full story. It is not only about acknowledging what happened, and providing the necessary missing information for people to learn what actually happened to their loved ones, but also about showing remorse for one's actions. In South Africa, many also were given the possibility of amnesty, if they came forward in this way to bring out the truth. Behind the Truth and Reconciliation Commission was the idea that the whole society needs to find a way to tell and grapple with its story, for everyone to be able to move forward.

One of the essential characteristics of the South Africa Truth commissions was the input and support in their design came from many levels of society. It was not something that was imposed on community. It engaged many people and the hearts of the country. It also reflected the vision and determination of Mandela to free both the oppressor and the oppressed, in order to go beyond the oppressive system in trying to build a new country and different future.

Vision of Facilitated Community Interaction in Tandem with Tribunals and Truth Commissions

A vision emerges of facilitated community forums, using the principle of 'deep democracy'. Such forums, in tandem with Tribunals and Truth Commissions, would support societies to get to know their histories and conflicts, with opportunities to process community-wide trauma and issues of accountability and to connect in community to our creative resources and leadership. Such forums would be one part of a wider trend of communities reflecting on the past and future, through media, arts, education and more.

Facilitation and Eldership

For this to happen, facilitation is needed. This includes not only designated facilitators able to deal with hot spots, and support all sides of conflict. Facilitation also needs to be fostered as that part in all of us that is interested and cares for the potential creativity and direction that emerges out of a real conflict among all parts, rather than one side dominating another. Mindell sometimes refers to 'eldership'[13], as that quality that cares for the past and future, takes all sides, and is able to make a stand. It is that part of us that can transcend the polarizations, but welcome and facilitate conflict.

Trauma and the Missing Witness

We need to ask ourselves in society if and how we will deal with past atrocity and trauma, and if not, what then. First there is no time to tell and respond to the story, as one must move forward to survive. Later it may feel too late. There is also a wish to move forward, and leave the tragic past behind. Those who would rather not consider their accountability may say, it's in the past, so let's forget it. This augments the original split from the story, which in turn augments its intrusive symptoms. People say there are so many people who have problems worse than me. People say I can't hear another story, there are too many. Some say they don't want to burden their neighbours, who have more than enough of their own troubles. Sometimes the stories are too horrendous—it feels unspeakable.

Or, someone wants to tell the story, but there is a lack of response. Some will say they have heard too many stories, or are exhausted or cynical. Or, the reaction in the listener is frozen, mirroring the lack of response in the teller, who is also cut off from her feelings. Silence may be from shock, from caring but not knowing what to say, and sometimes from indifference. Silence in turn reinforces the trauma. The story in search of a witness continues. The distance and silence make for a missing feedback loop. So the story replays and replays, without closure.

Collective Trauma and the Privilege to Forget

When thinking about dynamics of collective trauma, the part that goes forward may be the part of society that can go forward and forget. The part that remains and replays is represented by those who suffered the injustice and atrocities, who must go on telling the story. Those who would like to forget the story say isn't that a long time ago? Isn't it time to stop talking about it? This has nothing to do with me. For example, you see this dynamic in the USA, where although each of us has our own opinions and input about such broad and important collective issues, it is usually white people who say its time to forget about our treatment of Native Americans and African Americans, though there has been no real process of accountability or bearing witness to the atrocity and corresponding trauma, nor recognition of how privilege has been built on the backs of those who suffered. In this way 'forgetting' or splitting off our atrocious history is a part of the dynamics of collective trauma.

To Talk about Trauma or to Not?

In our recent forum in Croatia, our hosts thought that people may not even bring up the war, focusing on other matters of community building, now that it has been many years since the end of the war. But, at the first opportunity to choose the topic, the group spoke about war and the problems of reconciliation and moving forward.

Someone suggested that society needed to make space to talk about widespread trauma. Others disagreed and said it was important to not tread upon old wounds.

We made two roles, to bring out these two positions further. One role was 'It's essential to talk about community trauma'. The other role was 'It's essential to forget the past, so that we can move forward.'

The side that said we should not talk about traumatic experiences thought that bringing up old wounds would keep us stuck in the past. They said we needed to pull up our boots and get on with it. Several people, speaking from the first role responded saying 'the reason to talk about trauma is not because we want to stay in the past, but so that we can heal and move forward'.

A surprising thing happened at this point. Those who adamantly said we must not talk about traumatic events began to talk about the traumatic events they had suffered—as if in passing. One told of having seen all his relatives killed in front of him. Another told of having to take a live grenade from a small child's hand. A young woman spoke about losing her father, which she never knew what happened, and his body was never found.

The stories came out so fast that in the telling and hearing of these stories, there was no emotional reaction. They were told as if it's just a normal, everyday thing, and it is—so many people have had such experiences. This lack of emotional reaction to the terrible experiences is a feature of community trauma, however, and can support the splitting off of traumatic experiences, which leaves them to replay. We therefore slowed things and asked people to express feeling reactions to these personal stories.

Those who had told the stories stayed with their position, saying that we all just needed to toughen up and not become emotional over these things. When someone expressed sorrow about the young woman losing her father and that his body was still missing, she said 'what difference does it make—the only thing that matters is going forward with an active life.'

While the group had taken two sides on the question of whether they felt it was a good idea or not to talk about trauma, the traumatic stories had come forward. The two sides spontaneously formed a circle and everyone listened to each other now with respect, realizing that although they did not agree, what they shared was that each had a personal way of grappling with the trauma, and each shared the same goal of being able to move forward in their individual lives and as a community.

Being Personal—Responsibility and Love

The group went on to look at participants' specific projects in these regions that had been hit hardest during the war, and had important group interactions around the relationship between NGOs and Government organizations, and issues in community relationships between Croats, Serbs and Muslims. At the last session, people gathered closer together in the large circle, and several people said how important it was for them to have been able to talk about issues in the forum that were normally not discussed. One man said 'when we arrived in this room, it felt like sitting on nails, and now it's like sitting on a sofa together'. People began to say thank you to one another in very personal, felt ways. Then a man said that he would like to especially say a word of appreciation to the young woman who had spoken about her missing father, for her active contribution to the forum. He then spoke about an organization he had established, to help families look for the bodies of those who were missing in the war. After appreciating her contribution and spirit, he said to her without hesitation or doubt, "I will find your father." She burst out crying, and at first ran from the room. Someone checked on her. We could see that she had been deeply touched by what he said, and how he said it. She came back a moment later, saying how moved she was by the whole experience. She thanked the man who said he would find her father and they hugged. Everyone present felt the impact of this clear and simple step of what it meant to stand for one another, to step into the role of the 'missing' elder and care and take accountability for our past and our future.

Trauma and Beyond: Our Future

In one of our forums in Croatia, people spoke about how they all felt blocked from any attempt to build bridges between communities, Serb, Croat and Muslim. They described an attitude, a 'ghost role' that says "How can you associate with them. You are betraying loyalty to your own group." As people experimented with how they might deal with this situation, 'this ghost role' refused to allow it, and people became exhausted and despaired. It reminded them of the situation just before the war, when their loyalties had been manipulated into violent war. Yet they realized how they still perpetuated this notion of loyalty and betrayal. At this moment, two people sat on the floor, and said "We are your children". They were making a 'role play' to represent the children who suffered from their block to reconcile and move forward. Speaking very intimately and personally, others stepped into this 'role' and began to talk about their children. They spoke about the details of the traumatic scenes their children had endured. Some spoke about how their children had known only war. They spoke about their worries and attempts to keep them safe. As they reached out to each other as parents, the group grew very close. And they vowed to each other that when they went home, they would be loyal to each other, their children and future.

I have been touched again and again by the ability some people have to meet and transform the most difficult situations. There is nothing more personal than a traumatic experience that has shaken you to the core, and nothing more private than the journey towards finding contact to our deepest sentient and creative resources to find our way forward. At the same time these stories are not only personal and it is a collective task to find our way.

Our societies need to also make that journey to find our deepest collective resources and direction, in dealing with collective trauma and accountability. It is essential that we ask ourselves in societies everywhere what we will do with our histories of oppression, injustice and atrocity, and the community-wide trauma and unanswered questions of accountability in the wake of violence. Discussions have started and many more are needed in the fields of human rights, international development, conflict resolution, peacebuilding, journalism and media. Peacebuilding and conflict prevention, and their relation to dynamics of accountability and trauma involve the whole society and the whole of us, from psychology and personal development to spirituality, from education to law, from tribunals and truth commissions to community forums and town meetings; from journalism, film and the arts to personal relationship.

Collective Conscience

I had assumed at one time that the worst trauma accompanied gruesome unspeakable tragedies, and this is sometimes true. But, I learned that often the most serious trauma comes from haunting self-questioning, and feeling of guilt, conscience and responsibility. I remember one man who was very traumatized and unwell. His story was that a close friend (a Croat) had come to him (a Serb) in a state of great distress, saying he had heard that there were people being killed—should he flee? The man had assured his friend that he would be okay, and believed due to his position he could personally see to it. He could not, and it cost his friend his life.

One way for society to help those who wrestle with their conscience, and to reckon with collective trauma, is for the wider society to join in the soul-searching process. Collective trauma needs a collective conscience, interested in our future—interest in accountability for our own actions, and assuming responsibility for one's own group and others.

Closing

Whether we have experienced personal trauma, or have had the fortune not to have had such experiences, as a world we have all taken part in the collective dynamics of trauma. Whether we talk about violence from the past, or from today, it is still fresh. We have taken part both in pain and silence that is passed through generations. We have taken part in shock, and in the privileges gained through others' suffering, and we have been a part of groups that inflicted suffering on others, and/or have suffered as a particular ethnic/religious/national group and as a human being. We also take part through our compassion, through our wish to make a difference.

The forum participants found room in their hearts for the most painful experiences, and heated issues of accountability, and for a renewed sense of life and possibility, that people often said they did not expect to feel again. The level of friendships that grew from these forums was profound and continues. And we still hear of how forum participants took their learning into further work, taking on a sense of leadership and eldership in their own communities.

Depending on which side of the bed I get out of, I can envision a world that brings awareness along into our social and political interactions. I see a great need and trend for us to recognize the relationship between dynamics of collective trauma, accountability, peacebuilding and conflict prevention, in relation to the atrocities and conflicts in our world. I also see a trend and great need for us to explore the interplay between personal, relationship, community and collective processes, and to find room in our hearts both for our brutal history and for the possibility we can shape a different future.

Notes

1. Audergon, A. (2005) The War Hotel: Psychological Dynamics in Violent Conflict, London: Whurr/ Wiley.

2. See www.worldwork.org

See Mindell A. (1995) Sitting in the Fire: Large Group Transformation Using Conflict and Diversity, Portland, OR, Lao Tse Press; Mindell A. (1993) The Leader as Martial

Artist, San Francisco, CA: Harper Collins; and Mindell A. (2002) Deep Democracy of Open Forums. Charlottesville VA: Hampton Roads See also Audergon, A (2005) The War Hotel: Psychological Dynamics in Violent Conflict, London: Whurr/ Wiley and Totton N. (2000) Psychotherapy and Politics, London: Sage Publications.

3. Mindell A. (1993).

4. Mindell, A. http://www.aamindell.net/deep-democracy.htm (April 2007).

5. Mindell A. (1993) The Leader as Martial Artist, San Francisco, CA: Harper Collins.

6. Mindell A. (1993) The Leader as Martial Artist, San Francisco, CA: Harper Collins, p. 25; Mindell A. (2000)Quantum Mind, Portland OR: Lao Tse Press p.550.

7. Mindell A. (1995) Sitting in the Fire: Large Group Transformation Using Conflict and Diversity. Portland, OR: Lao Tse Press.

8. Audergon A. (2005); Audergon, Arlene *'Hot Spots: Post-conflict trauma and transformation'* Critical Half Vol. 4, No 1 (July 2006), Women for Women International.

9. Audergon, Arlene: ' Collective Trauma: The Nightmare of History', in Psychotherapy and Politics International, Volume 2, Number 1, 2004, Whurr/Wiley Publishers Ltd London.

10. Audergon A The War Hotel: Psychological Dynamics in Violent Conflict, London: Whurr/ Wiley 2005.

11. Hermann J (1997) Trauma and Recovery: The Aftermath of Violence-From Domestic Abuse to Political Terror, New York: Basic Books; Audergon A. (2005) p. 173-207.

12. Audergon A. (2005).

13. Mindell A. (1995) Sitting in the Fire: Large Group Transformation Using Conflict and Diversity, Portland OR: Lao Tse Press; Mindell A. (2002) Deep Democracy of Open Forums, Charlottesville VA: Hampton Roads.

13

Opening Space for Healing in Colombia

Bonnie Klassen

Since the beginning of the 2003 demobilization process led by the Colombian government with the United Self-Defense Forces of Colombia (Autodefensas Unidas de Colombia—AUC), discussions about how to deal with the country's worst human rights violators have peppered the newspapers, radio shows and television news. The halls of Congress have heard numerous debates about how to balance truth, justice and peace. Non-governmental organizations have organized countless forums to analyze the issues.

Yet, many aspects remain unclear and many questions unasked. The government continually alters its approach and its policies in response to the AUC[1]; so one can not help but conclude that the government is improvising its strategy. The Minister of Internal Affairs and Justice did not assure many souls when he publicly affirmed, "We are working with a method of trial and error." (Revista Semana 10 April 2006). Can new laws alone bring peace? How do the procedures put in place for the AUC demobilization relate to broader peace-building processes with all of the Colombian armed groups?[2] Instead of promoting isolated, partial processes, can Colombia find a framework for healing and lasting peace that addresses the overall dynamics of violence? How must the current process change to fit coherently into this framework?

This chapter addresses these broader questions while focusing on alternatives for the AUC process in particular. The author would argue against separating this process from the larger task of peace-building with all of the armed groups in Colombia. Yet at the same time, the existing dynamics between the government and the AUC require specific observations, rather than just theoretical contributions towards general issues. The proposed alternatives for the process in progress should open, rather than close, doors for healing Colombia as a whole.

A Brief Walk through History

In the 200 years since Colombia became a Republic, the population has only enjoyed five years of relative peace (Posada 15 November 2003). It is a society of victims and perpetrators, where the distinction between one and the other often disappears. The diverse forms of violence affect Colombian people as individuals, but also as a whole society; millions of people are affected simultaneously by the same realities. In a society that suffers collective traumatization, where everyone seems to carry too much fear and pain to live truly healthy lives, healing also needs to unfold collectively.

Although the root causes of the Colombian conflict lie in the structures of exploitation and exclusion generated by the Spanish invasion in the early 1500`s (Gonzalez 2000), the current internal armed conflict started with the unsatisfactory resolution of the civil war, called "La Violencia", between Conservatives and Liberals that tore the country apart between 1948 and the late 1950´s. Insurgent or guerrilla groups formed during the mid 1960´s in response to the economic exclusion and political intolerance perpetrated by the peace agreements signed by the Conservative and Liberal elites in 1957. Private security armies and paramilitary groups later formed as a reaction to the insecurity caused by the insurgents. Many of these groups joined together in 1997 under the leadership of Carlos Castaño to form a loose federation known as the Autodefensas Unidas de Colombia (AUC).

However, the current conflict dynamics are infinitely more complicated than what this four sentence explanation can portray. Many factors have shaped the foundations and the development of Colombia's internal armed conflict. Moreover, as happens in many protracted armed conflicts, the principle issues that sparked the war are now intertwined with myriad other significant issues that feed the on-going confrontation (Cousens 2001). All of the armed groups function out of a complex mix of motives: economic, political, social, cultural and military. A closer examination of the factors that have fed the AUC over time can illustrate this reality.

Socio-economic inequalities: The *Comisión de Estudios sobre la Violencia* (Commission of Studies on Violence) concluded in 1987 that the violence in Colombia has more to do with the high percentage of people living in absolute poverty and the deep socio-economic inequalities than with the armed groups themselves (as cited in González 2000). Violence does not just come out of the barrel of a gun; it is also fuelled by the suffering of those who live in miserable conditions. Desperate people use violence as a means to seek change and the poor can view membership in an armed group, such as the AUC, as a source of employment or power[3].

At the same time, violence also aggravates the inequalities. Particular economic groups, drug cartels and large land-owners created private armies in Colombia to protect their interests and to expand their monopoly over economic resources (Así Va el Diálogo 2004; Human Rights Watch 2005). Several studies have shown the connection between AUC presence and the concentration of property, drug trafficking and the consolidation of economic mega-projects that violate the interests of the local population (Mondragón Jan. 2001; Programa Andino de Derechos Humanos Oct. 2003; Kirk 2003)[4]. The Consulting Office for Human Rights and Forced Displacement (CODHES) estimates that the AUC and the drug cartels forcibly took over approximately 5 million hectares of land from 1997-2003 (El Tiempo 21 Dec. 2004)[5].

Political Control: Alongside the economic interests that motivate the creation of private armies, the dominant political leaders' desire to maintain power and repress minority opposition groups strengthens these armed actors. Selective assassinations and disappearances committed by the paramilitaries weaken alternative political groups and maintain the power imbalance weighted towards the traditional political-economic elite, thus breaking down public democratic processes. The AUC itself has gained considerable political influence in many regions and on a national level, radically changing the electoral tendencies in at least 180 municipalities of Colombia and obtaining control over a significant sector of Congress (Human Rights Watch 2005; El Tiempo 1 Oct 2006; El Tiempo 26 Sept. 2004)[6]. During the second semester of 2006, the Supreme Court of Justice began to process dozens of cases of congressional members, government functionaries and regional politicians accused of maintaining alliances with the AUC, thus highlighting a historic reality that the media suddenly scandalized as "para-politics".

The Role of the State: These dynamics do not limit themselves to the AUC. It is more accurate to talk about the historic widespread phenomenon of paramilitarism and private armies (Garcia-Peña 2004). Overall, the State has not maintained a permanent presence in much of Colombia's territory and therefore illegal armed groups (guerrilla and paramilitary groups) have filled these gaps (Callejón con Salida 2003). In addition, with regards to the private armies propagated by powerful elite, the State has often turned a blind eye rather than seeking to regain monopoly over the use of force (Gonzalez 2000). The State has not functioned as an impartial entity protecting the common good, but rather has allowed certain groups to use private armed actors to impose their interests. Moreover, human rights organizations have extensively documented the collaboration between State Armed Forces and private defence groups.[7]

Psychological Factors—individual and collective trauma: Personal psychological elements have also played a significant role in the growth of private armies. The principle AUC leaders, as well as many of their combatants, all suffered insurgent attacks on their family members. As they absorbed this "chosen trauma" into their identity, they felt entitled, as victims, to always act with reference to the initial violation against them (Volkan and Itzkowitz 2000; see Revista Cambio 2 Aug. 2004). The desire for revenge and fear of future attacks generate a mobilizing psychological framework that supports systematic violence against a profoundly "bad" enemy, in this case the guerrilla groups (Suárez-Orozco and Robben 2000). In a context of 98% impunity (Garay 2002), the private self-defence groups easily convince themselves that they are acting in favor of justice by eliminating the insurgent groups. This deep sense of "righteousness" has given AUC members the psychological strength to commit horrific attacks against civilians accused (often falsely) as guerrilla supporters[8].

Additionally, centuries of violence in Colombia have produced a widespread acceptance of aggression as a means to deal with conflict. Deep traumas stretch from one generation to the next because no adequate process has helped people digest their pain (Gampel 2000). Repressed pain then expresses itself in a variety of ways, including cycles of violence within the family and the community. Many youth join one of the armed groups to escape violence at home and then paradoxically perpetuate the violence they detest (Neme 2005). These dynamics fuel all of the armed groups.

Ideological factors and International influence: The ideologies behind the National Security Doctrine of Colombian President Turbay (1978-1982) and the Democratic Security policies promoted by current President Uribe provide an intellectual framework for the violence committed by the AUC in connection with the State Armed Forces. Politicians have injected fear in the population and then justified exaggerated militarism and diverse mechanisms that infringe on human rights as necessary strategies to ensure people's safety. Certain violations become "heroic acts of service" (see Lagos 2000). Based on this ideological foundation, politicians created legal private armies, such as the CONVIVIR[9], which provided unofficial approval and logistical support for the AUC. In addition, international players, particularly the United States' government, have fed the militarization of Colombian society by promoting military solutions and providing massive amounts of weapons[10].

Effects of Paramilitarism

What has resulted from the tacit promotion of paramilitary groups? During the last 15 years alone, the violence perpetrated by the AUC has forced two million Colombians to flee their homes[11], assassinated, massacred and disappeared thousands of community leaders, campesinos, human rights defenders, peace-builders and workers' union promoters[12] and diverted millions of dollars away from social programs[13]. The horrific violence sows profound fear in people's hearts. Displacement robs people of everything familiar, including their identity, and weakens their capacity to cope. Although many victims of violence demonstrate an astounding level of resilience, the large scale violence in certain regions has broken down the social fabric and fragmented many communities.

The urban population in Colombia that receives the victims of violence as they flee the countryside has generally responded with indifference, suspicion and rejection. Paradoxically, encounters with victims produce such anxiety that city dwellers seem to block off their sense of empathy and compassion[14] (Suárez-Orozco and Robben 2000). Victims have had no social space to share their stories. Instead, they are stigmatized as weak and politically dangerous. When they seek health services, housing, education or employment, doors shut quickly. This exclusion becomes toxic, breeding anger and distrust that later become a seed-bed for new violence (Suárez-Orozco 2000).

The So-Called Peace Process with the AUC

Clearly, in light of the intense and ongoing violence, any step to reduce the AUC's activities is positive. Yet, should we simply content ourselves with a small step in the right direction? What are the future implications of the current demobilization process?

President Uribe began to pave the way for dialogues with the AUC soon after taking office in August 2002. On December 1, 2002, the AUC declared a unilateral ceasefire and talks between this group and the government began. On July 15, 2003, the two sides signed the Agreement of Santa Fe de Ralito in which the AUC committed itself to "demobilizing the totality of its members in a gradual process . . . that would culminate by December 31, 2005." On May 13, 2004, the government and the AUC signed an agreement to establish a 368 square kilometer zone in Santa Fe de Ralito, municipality of Tierralta, where official dialogues continued. The demobilization process itself extended longer than originally planned, but the Colombian High Commissioner of Peace, Luis Carlos Restrepo, announced on April 17, 2006, that the AUC no longer existed, after 30,944 members had demobilized (Revista Cambio 11 June 2006).

The total number of officially demobilized paramilitaries is more than double the number of AUC combatants said to exist when the dialogue process began (Revista Semana, 10 April 2006; El Tiempo 10 July 2006). The government's High Commissioner for Peace recognized that in the first round of demobilizations a large number of common delinquents and drug-traffickers "demobilized" in the name of the AUC (Human Rights Watch 2005). With many of the groups that demobilized later, over half of the people were not combatants but rather members of the community that had provided "social support" to the AUC and were now hoping to receive the monthly subsidy offered by the government to ex-combatants (El Tiempo 10 July 2006).

Unfortunately, contrary to this general tendency of "over-demobilization", one particular group of ex-combatants has not formally demobilized: child soldiers. Of the estimated number of 5000 under-aged members of the AUC, only 212 appear in the lists of ex-combatants. The AUC commanders sent most of the children to their homes without any kind of accompaniment, in order to avoid charges for recruitment of minors (El Tiempo, 15 June 2006).

The demobilization process itself unfolded in the following sequence. The AUC commanders decided which combatants to demobilize at a given time and gathered them together "concentration zones". Ex-combatants identified as potentially guilty of committing atrocious crimes remained in the "concentration zone" to wait for an ambiguous judicial process[15] while the majority of ex-combatants returned to their homes as "reinserted people", free of any legal process against them (Human Rights Watch 2005). Unfortunately, since the Colombian justice system has not identified the author of the vast majority of crimes, many AUC members responsible for assassinations, disappearances and massacres left undetected (Sánchez 2000).

The reinserted ex-combatants receive free housing, a basic salary, and some education, but do not receive effective job training or adequate psychological accompaniment for their re-entry into civilian life. Only 10% currently have regular, legal employment (El Tiempo, 10 July 2006).[16] A significant number of demobilized people maintain links to illegal activities (Desmobilizar a los Paras).

In evaluating the process, it is important to keep in mind that the AUC is a loose federation of armies, without strict control over all of its members. To further complicate matters, two AUC commanders with a great deal of information and authority, Carlos Castaño and Miguel Arroyave, were assassinated between March-September of 2004[17]. Overall, the process has generated more anxiety than relief. The violence continues. The legal framework in response to the serious crimes committed by AUC members is unclear and inadequate. The victims remain invisible and unheard.

Ongoing human rights violations and violence: The government signed an agreement with the Organization of American States (OAS) to monitor the AUC ceasefire and demobilization process on January 23, 2004. However, the OAS representative, Sergio Caramagna, operates without a well-defined mandate and with a very limited budget (Mercado and Gómez, 2005, El Tiempo, 1 February 2005). Neither the ceasefire nor the demobilization process has been fulfilled in reality. The State Human Rights Ombudsman's Office *(Defensoría del Pueblo)* and non-governmental organizations documented permanent violations of the ceasefire[18].

Later, the OAS documented several regions where demobilized AUC groups continue to operate as if they had not demobilized, often in collaboration with State security forces. In five departments of the country, demobilized AUC members have committed massacres, offered security services to drug-traffickers, called people to mandatory community meetings and sold arms. The OAS also reported cases of new recruitment by paramilitary groups in at least six departments (MAPP/OEA 2006). Moreover, by October 2006, news reports revealed State intelligence documents referring to the existence of up to 44 new illegal paramilitary-type armed groups (www.indepaz.org.co). Even the AUC commanders have recognized that many demobilized combatants never fully demobilized[19].

Ernesto Baez, a political spokesperson of the AUC, predicted that "this new paramilitary generation will be more violent and bloody than the previous ones" (Revista Cambio 11 June 2006); they will not be reigned in by a hierarchical structure since the AUC federation no longer exists. Moreover, "third generation paramilitaries" have focused more on maintaining control over specific economic interests than on continuing the anti-insurgent military campaign (Revista Cambio 11 June 2006)[20]. The OAS reports that demobilized AUC members continue to control illegal economic activities in many regions of the country (MAPP/OEA 2006).

The Justice and Peace Law: In response to international pressure for a legal framework around this process, the government presented versions of an Alternative Penalties Law in 2003 and 2004 without obtaining Congressional approval. By the beginning of 2005, seven different laws had been proposed by diverse Congress members. Essentially, the diverse proposals implied different levels of condemnation and dismantlement of the paramilitary phenomenon and fulfilment of the victims' rights to truth and reparations (Human Rights Watch 2005). Throughout this time, the AUC leaders insisted that they would not spend any time in prison, nor would they give back the land or wealth acquired through illegal means (Revista Cambio 2 Aug. 2004).

After months of political manoeuvring, Congress finally approved the Justice and Peace Law—Law 975 on July 25, 2005. Although Law 975 includes elements of justice and truth not contemplated in the Central American peace processes, thus advancing positively towards building sustainable peace, international experts expressed concern that it does not comply with international norms of justice and that it will actually facilitate the consolidation of organized crime structures. The United Nations High Commissioner for Human Rights in particular communicated these concerns and affirmed that, if not carefully implemented, the law could obscure "the State's responsibilities in crimes committed by paramilitaries . . . due to action or omission" (UN Commission on Human Rights, 2006).

In concrete terms, the law asks demobilized combatants to confess their crimes, but does not impose any sanctions on those who give false information or omit facts. Neither does it require individuals to turn over all illegally obtained assets such as property or financial holdings nor to disclose information about structures or sources of funding. In reality, the law permits high levels of impunity because it provides an unfeasibly short amount of time for the Attorney General's Office to investigate each case before pressing charges. The victims have no space to tell their experience of history. Many AUC members guilty of terrible crimes against humanity have already been released because the judicial system could not gather clear evidence against them in the amount of time available (El Tiempo 18 Oct. 2006). Moreover, the consequences that the AUC commanders eventually condemned of crimes against humanity will actually face remain unclear.

And the victims? With regards to the reparation of their victims, the AUC commanders promised to hand over 100,000 hectares of land, only a small fraction of the 4-6 million hectares that State entities identify as land held by narco-traffickers and AUC members (El Tiempo 17 Sept. 2006). Law 975 created a Commission for Reparation and Reconciliation, however it does not have any real power to implement a reparation process; it merely has an advisory role. The Reparation Fund only has 25,601 hectares of land, clearly insufficient to respond to three million displaced people (El Tiempo, 13 June 2006). So, the Commission of Reparation and Reconciliation has focused on symbolic reparation without offering much hope of material reparation to the victims.

Building a Framework for Healing and Sustainable Peace

Now, instead of just criticizing the current situation, it is time to ask what opportunities we should try to create out of this reality. What would it mean to promote a process that contributes to healing? How can the process go beyond demobilizing combatants to truly terminating the common use of private armies to protect particular interests? Can the process also open doors for a lasting peace process with the insurgent groups who have been fighting for more than 40 years, who have committed terrible atrocities too and who also maintain their struggle for a complicated mix of motives? How can we generate hope?

Many academics who have written about peace processes agree that these require a broad infrastructure that addresses the underlying causes and the current manifestations of violence while also generating a new vision for the future that will respond to the basic human needs for security, identity, participation, equity, dignity and meaning (Lederach 1998; Cousens 2001; Orr 2001; Fisher 2001; Abu-Nimer 2001). In Colombia, this means confronting and reaching some consensus about the economic, political, judicial, social, psychological, cultural and moral causes of the conflict. It means also countering the consequences of the protracted armed conflict, such as the destruction or lack of economic infrastructure, the lack of employment for thousands of ex-combatants, the mass number of internally displaced people, political polarization, the lack of governance, corrupt State security forces, millions of traumatized people and a culture of distrust and violence. No formulas or magic frameworks exist to solve this myriad of issues. Moreover, each local community has unique priorities for peacebuilding, as their experience of the armed conflict has also been unique (Callejón con Salida 2003).

A process for building lasting peace unfolds over a long period of time. It always has fragile points that could crack and unleash new waves of violence. Sustaining such a process with the AUC, as with all of Colombia's armed groups, requires a variety of supports, such as: a) concrete positive experiences that allow people to taste the transformation that the process seeks (Chupp 2003), b) socio-political and cultural structures that absorb the tensions inherent to these processes and that strengthen life-giving forces (Doe 2003; Schwoebel and McCandless 2003) (c) spaces of trust for dialogue about complex issues on local, regional and national levels (Chupp 2003), d) a deep sense of joint responsibility among all sectors and strata of society, highlighting common interests for building solutions in a participative way (Porter and Mancau 2003; Kumar; Lederach 1998; Orr 2001), e) long-term funding and logistical support from other countries and agencies, who do not impose their external agendas or generate dependency (Chupp 2003; Lambourne 2001), f) modest short/medium term goals (Cousens 2001) and g) effective systems for monitoring agreements (Orr 2001). It is always better to slowly reach concrete, coherent, viable agreements than to quickly write ambiguous, unrealistic treaties that no one will implement (Rasmussen 2001).

Does Colombia have some of these basic conditions to sustain a true peace process? Throughout the centuries, Colombians have demonstrated profound resilience to the violent forces around them. Certain sectors, such as women's groups, the indigenous people and some religious communities, have maintained firm positions for non-violence and a deep vision for a just and sustainable peace, despite persecution by the armed groups[21]. They absorb cycles of violence and give birth to new forces for life.

Other dynamics that currently contribute to the violence, if amended, could contribute to conflict transformation. Although the *media* should not gloss over the terrible realities of the armed conflict, it does need to increase its efforts to publicize positive steps towards peace made by *all* of the armed groups. Positive information, if provided by credible sources[22], would help build trust in the possibilities for change and shift people's attitudes about specific groups. Many more *spaces for dialogue*, without fear of repression for expressing specific positions, need to open up on local, regional and national levels (Callejón con Salida 2003). The peace processes in general need to become more *participative*, with the inclusion of diverse sectors of society[23] and respect for *local peacebuilding processes*, rather than criminalizing local dialogues[24]. The peace process also clearly needs additional technical support, from national and international organizations, to *verify* the fulfilment of agreements reached. Finally, national interests must shape the support from the *international community* rather than the interests of donor countries[25].

Returning now to the AUC process, how can the country work through economic, political, legal-justice, social, psychological, cultural and moral issues at this juncture, with a vision for facilitating broader healing processes, inclusive of the insurgent groups? The following ideas apply specifically to the AUC process, but most aspects also connect to the underlying causes and dynamics of the insurgent groups. While it helps to look at each aspect separately, the different elements connect very closely with each other.

Socio-economic policies: Economic monopolizing forces, and specifically certain national and international companies, helped create the AUC and benefited from their existence. Force allows the economic elite to hold onto its wealth and land. Absurdly, large landowners spend large sums of money maintaining private armies to protect their land, but would not share these same resources with their marginalized neighbours. When a minority controls basic resources to the detriment of the majority, the potential for violence remains high, even when the tensions are not overtly evident (McCandless 2001). How can natural resources and wealth become sources of stability instead of instability? Is there any way to generate a more rational, shared use of resources in Colombia? If so, private armies would lose part of their reason for existing.

First, those who have benefited from the violence must return their gain to the many victims who lost everything (Abu-Nimer 2001). This is a monumental task; no one can "put everything back where it was." However, the victims will find it very difficult, if not impossible, to feel compassion for their attackers and heal relationships if these same attackers end up living very comfortably while the victims suffer in poverty (Green and Pearson d'Estrée 2003). Displaced people need viable opportunities, with appropriate security, infrastructure and technical conditions, to return to the land if they wish[26], even if they can not always return to their own land. This does not mean leaving the victimizers with nothing. It means that everyone has "enough".

Secondly, the State needs to take a much more effective role in generating distributive justice, whereby everyone perceives the distribution of wealth and services as equitable (Lambourne 2001). Distributive justice also implies a sustainable use of natural resources, protection from contracts with multinational companies that do not benefit the Colombian people as a whole[27], and fair labour conditions for all workers. When the State has sent a clear message that a few can not benefit disproportionately from the country's wealth, when the population does not fear scarcity, then no one needs to use force to maintain or obtain a monopoly over wealth. Theoretically, these transformations would also weaken the insurgent groups' justification of their armed struggle, diminish their sources of support or spheres of influence and could perhaps open doors for dialogue.

Unfortunately, some problems, when left unattended, become much more complex over time. Centuries of economic exclusion in Colombia sparked the creation of many parallel underground economies, such as the notorious illicit drug trade. These very lucrative illegal economies fund the vast majority of the AUC's activities (Sierra and Sierra, El Tiempo, 15 May 2004)[28] and Colombia finds itself entirely entangled in the global drug trade knot. Economic justice will loosen the knot—many people would gladly make a living legally if they could find viable alternatives—but it will not untie it entirely. As long as millions of people do practically anything to consume drugs like cocaine, certain groups, particularly armed groups in need of a stable income will continue to provide the supply. In other words, wealth redistribution and viable development projects can address the supply side of the drug problem in an environmentally sustainable way[29], but the demand issue requires a much more global approach. Cocaine-consuming countries need to dramatically increase education and rehabilitation strategies to dry up the demand and break this factor of violence in Colombia.

In general terms though, distributive justice is a fundamental tool for dismantling the private defence system in Colombia. By natural course of events, these transformations seem quite unlikely. The necessary shifts lie within the realms of both attitudes and structures. Can economic policies in Colombia focus on the common good rather than private interests? Can those who have more than enough share the wells of resources instead of building walls? The State can not impose these changes and expect to create lasting peace. Can cycles of moderate reforms, dialogue and then more changes help create the deeper transformations necessary? Can the economic elite learn by experience that sharing will give them real security? Can this learning process occur quickly enough to prevent desperation among those who live in misery?

Political structures: The implementation of distributive justice presupposes the existence of a legitimate State. Yet a principle cause of violence in Colombia is the fragility of democratic political structures and the lack of nonviolent mechanisms for resolving conflicts of interest between diverse sectors of society. How can Colombia transform its internal, and even external, power relationships so as to create a legitimate state, making the use of repression via paramilitary groups unthinkable? Healing the nation means moving beyond the traditional dynamic of the powerful vs. the powerless to a relationship of co-creators among all Colombians (White 2003). New policies must result from basic consensus-building methods, not decisions imposed by a few via force. These political processes must connect to real systems of accountability, not just generate procedures that appear democratic. Broad political participation helps sustain "social patience" when socio-economic transformations occur slowly (Kumar 2001).

These political shifts will require a much more organized and better educated civil society with the capacity to dialogue, mobilize people and amplify moderating voices. Grassroots groups need to understand the diverse societal conflicts, analyze alternatives, and articulate preferences (Assefa 2001). Weak sectors of society need to work internally first, to strengthen their identity and vision, before dialoguing with the rest of society[30]. A strong civil society will make broad political participation fruitful.

Strengthening democratic political structures also means providing adequate security and guarantees so that diverse political candidates can run for public positions under equal conditions and so that community leaders can express themselves freely (Kumar 2001). After the AUC's bloody history of assassinating alternative social or political leaders and human rights defenders, the ex-combatants need to sustain a true ceasefire for a significant period of time until the Colombian people begin to trust their right to participate. Members of the State Armed Forces who have directly or indirectly collaborated in the persecution alternative leaders must also face the consequences of their actions so as to build trust in the Armed Force's respect for human rights[31].

The peace process itself must put into practice these new political assumptions and structures. A process strong enough to endure must ensure the participation of all different sectors and strata of society (Lederach 1998). The elite negotiators can not make decisions about how to dismantle the AUC alone. Such significant decisions require the empowered participation of the Colombian people as a whole, not just a handful of "representatives" (Schwoebel and McCandless 2003). Peacebuilding practitioners have suggested different methods to allow for broad participation in a manageable, but meaningful way, such as Appreciative Inquiry Workshops (Rios and Fisher 2003) or Dialogue Groups with adequate mechanisms to balance power (Hubbard 2001). Reconciliation can happen when people feel an adequate level of control over the process, when they escape the powerlessness imposed by violence.

What will make transformation towards just political mechanisms possible? Again, the powerful must realize that they will be much more secure if they share power and trust participative processes than if they abuse power to eliminate those who think differently. Colombia needs a shift in paradigms whereby politics is no longer an exercise of seeking personal power but a process of building just relationships (Rasmussen 2001).

Alternative Justice: This quest for just relationships leads us to ask what justice requires in response to so many past violations. How can a broken country find healing and reconciliation? Can justice create a positive future and not just react to the past?

In many circles, the word "justice" is associated with punitive actions that focus on making the perpetrators suffer. Yet, if justice would make right the wrong done, it must focus on and empower the *victims* of the wrong done, those who must choose between rebounding their pain with aggression, carrying it on to the next generation, or seeking an alternative path of freedom from violence[32]. As Colombian social investigator Hector Mondragón concluded, "in the victims' salvation, we will all find salvation" (Interview 2005). By regaining control over their lives, by rediscovering their own capacity and value, by reaffirming their identity as people beyond their victimhood, the people who have suffered violence find a compelling life force that leads towards healing. Healing can not occur if victims define their self-image based on past painful events and do not take steps towards becoming survivors capable of contributing life to others. They need to regain control instead of letting the past control them (Bartsch 1996; Schwoebel and McCandless 2003; Good Sider 2003; Puljek-Shank 2003; Pratt Ewing 2000). Their needs must guide the process towards justice. Otherwise, Colombia will remain a nation full of victims—for all sides of the conflict view themselves as victims—who compete with each other over who has suffered more.

Many Colombians have suffered *multiple traumas* and have had no space to digest and transform these experiences. They simply adapt to a continually hostile environment and perpetuate the hostility so that their adaptations make sense (see Good Sider 2003). These victims need accompaniment, on an individual and collective level, to heal and rediscover meaning in their lives. They need a social context that embraces them and provides them with practical assistance, instead of one that rejects them[33] (Suárez-Orozco and Robben 2000; Bartsch 1996).

Prioritizing the individuals that most need psychological-spiritual accompaniment does not mean simply picking out the victims of the "worst" crimes (de Levita 2000). Many factors besides the event itself, such as the victim's interpretation of the event, previous state of health, level of self-awareness, and age influence how deeply the victim's life will tear apart. A broad network of professionals needs to accompany communities to identify and work with those who demonstrate lasting symptoms of trauma.

If the justice process focuses on the victims first, then perhaps appropriate ways to work with the *perpetrators* will become clearer. While the justice process should not operate contrary to Colombia's international commitments to uphold human rights, Colombians will not find healing and reconciliation by simply following the standard recipes of national or international law. A traditional punitive approach will not help perpetrators repair the damage they have done, particularly if the State takes possession of the perpetrators' wealth.[34] Punishment will not guarantee any fundamental change in the perpetrators' lives.

Alternative judicial procedures would allow both victims and offenders, from all sectors and strata of society, to participate in identifying violations and defining the consequences. This process would give victims greater control over the consequences than in traditional procedures. At the same time, it could help perpetrators analyze more consciously the nature of their actions and their capacity to repair the wrong done based on the victims' real, expressed needs. The perpetrators' analysis will not necessarily lead to repentance, but it does push them to take responsibility for the wrong they have done.

Undoubtedly, the diverse participants in such a process will view justice differently, and the results will not satisfy everyone. However, active participation will help each affected person view the process of defining justice as more fair, thus coming closer to procedural justice. Satisfaction with the process can have as much importance as satisfaction with the consequences. "Solutions" imposed by the State on both victims and perpetrators will likely generate new cycles of frustration and revenge, leading the country farther away from reconciliation (Estrada-Hollenbeck 2001; Assefa 2000).

Since considerable evidence points to historic collaboration between the State and the AUC[35], the AUC's victims distrust the State's capacity to represent them in the negotiation of consequences.[36] The State has no interest in dealing harshly with the AUC for fear that the AUC will bring to light all the evidence of State collaboration, as AUC commanders have threatened to do.[37] For this reason, the State should play a primary role in applying justice, but all of society must participate in building justice.[38]

Direct participation by both offenders and victims can help regulate the *reparation process* so crucial for restorative justice. Large-scale State-run reparation programs tend to provide uniform answers to all victims' needs and break any connection with the offenders. A participatory process would make visible the perpetrators' efforts to compensate for their destructive actions. These actions symbolically provide a degree of guilt release for the offenders and a degree of assurance for the victims that the violations will not occur again. A participatory process could also come closer to providing what specific victims really need to rebuild their lives. It is worth noting that the State will need to participate in the reparation process not so much as a facilitator but rather as an actor in the Colombian conflict, responsible for some of the wrong done. External facilitators must accompany the reparation process to ensure greater objectivity. If people observe that the process truly seeks to rectify the wrong done and rebuild the lives of those who have suffered, they will have more trust in the possibility of creating lasting peace (McCandless 2001).

All ex-combatants, regardless of what they have done and what consequences they must face, need significant support during their transition back into society, otherwise they will continue to revert to criminal behaviour as a way of survival (Doyle 2001). They need release from the psychological mechanisms that led them to obey certain authorities at all cost and generated "learned disinhibition" (Suárez-Orozco and Robben 2000). They need extensive training in new productive and relational skills. Child soldiers need special attention in their process of recuperation and re-entry into society. They may have committed acts of violence, but they are also victims of recruitment of minors. The line between offender and victim disappears in these cases. Overall, former combatants need to develop an identity beyond their past experience carrying large guns around the jungle.[39] If justice, in its most constructive and reparative sense, means righting what has been wrong, then it also requires healing the offenders.

Rebuilding Relationships—Reweaving the Social Fabric

How can supportive relationships, so necessary to reweave the strands of the country's social fabric, form between Colombians after such a protracted, polarizing conflict? Processes of structural transformation and participatory justice will become practically impossible if not sustained by concrete interpersonal relationships between people of diverse backgrounds, with at least minimal levels of trust. Relationship building will unfold slowly because the layers of distrust and hate run deep. Trying to force the process will only abort it (Assefa 2000). However, certain tools can help hold up the reconciliation process.

Truth-telling by both victims and perpetrators of violence, recognizing that the line between the two often blurs, can convey the deeper meaning behind the brutal acts and the expressions of pain. Human relations evolve out of stories and memories (Volkan, as cited in Green and Pearson d'Estrée 2003). Yet stories also make people vulnerable, as many courageous Colombians who have told the truth and died as a result could testify. Therefore, the testimonies must be told in a safe environment with careful facilitators that validate each person's experience, even if other perspectives exist.[40]

The testimonies of wrong done and pain suffered by people of all sectors and strata of society would contribute to raising truth from the dead and affirming the victims' pain, giving the stories both a judicial and a political dimension. Some voices in Colombia argue that uncovering the horrible past will only incite revenge. Yet, denying the past is like expecting a wound to heal without cleaning it. Truth alone can be merely descriptive, hollow of any spiritual meaning, but without truth, transformation becomes very difficult. Truth gives life and freedom, even if no one's hearts and minds are big enough to hold the full meaning of the inexplicable pain (Green and Pearson d'Estree 2003; Suárez-Orozco and Robben 2000; Pratt Ewing 2000). In some cases, the truth can also have very practical implications, such as helping family members find the corpses of the "disappeared", or simply know "what happened" for their own mental health and healing (Robben 2000; Lagos 2000; Santamaría 2000).

Beyond providing information, stories also humanize people[41] and help build empathetic connections with each other, particularly if the truth-tellers own their actions and express their emotions (Henderson 2003; White 2003; Green and d'Estreé 2003). When we discover a spark of humanity in our "enemies" and seek to find the best in them, when we acknowledge the other's pain (as victims or perpetrators), we open the door for transformation. When we view others with their complex multiple identities rather than just with the identity of "belonging to the enemy group", we give them space to change; we begin to find common threads that tie us together (Schirch 2001).

Discovering this "spark of humanity" in the enemy does not mean denying the wrong done; it means working on the assumption that no person is entirely bad, that the line between good and evil runs through people and not between them. It allows victims to view the perpetrators with "compassionate anger" (Doe, as cited in Good Sider 2003). Society must still hold perpetrators accountable, but facing consequences and repairing the wrong done should make perpetrators more human not less.

Stories open the door for alternative, life-giving narratives of what has happened so as to draw limits around the trauma, without justifying the wrong done and without providing arguments for victims' revenge. If the stories shared from all sides of the conflict explore the causes and perceptions behind the violence, they can help build a common version of history and a meaning for the past that, when internalized on a personal and collective level, generate attitude changes and a vision for an alternative shared future (White 2003; Green and Pearson D'Estrée 2003; Pratt Ewing 2000).

A variety of methods, such as interviews between people from different perspectives of the conflict (Whitney, Liebler and Cooperrider 2003), conversations over shared meals (Henderson 2003), regular, facilitated dialogue around specific topics (Assefa 2001), public rituals, story-telling among people with similar experiences (Green and d'Estrée 2003) and truth commissions could assist in eliciting a massive number of stories. The truth told by some will help others break their silence. Most importantly, the methods used must focus on building a safe, sacred environment where truth can dwell and acknowledged pain can heal. For that reason, these processes unfold best in small groups, focusing on a manageable number of issues, and gradually expanding to affect wider circles (Assefa 2001). A multitude of smaller groups allow much broader participation, and a much deeper, more complex exploration of each case (van der Merwe 2001). Projecting the results from the small-group into broader society would then help identify of general tendencies.

The truth-telling processes would best take place simultaneously and connected to the strategies for establishing socio-economic, political and judicial justice. The psychological process makes alternative justice processes possible[42]. Alternative justice processes could respond adaptively to the discovery of new information and to the shifts in perceptions by all sides of the conflict. Reconciliation does not imply building relationships at the expense of justice, but rather the construction of just relationships.

Some people who have committed crimes within the armed conflict will still flee from any procedures that push them to face the truth and renounce their ill-gotten wealth. The perpetrators who resist involvement in the alternative procedures self-select their submission to the arbitrariness and impersonal nature of the regular punitive system. Investigations would open against them, and include the verifiable information shared by others who stand up to tell the truth. Without doubt, in this scenario the perpetrators face a better future by telling the truth themselves and facing the consequences agreed upon with their own participation.

A further step in the process of building relationships would involve people from different sides in the conflict *working together* on common, life-giving tasks. For example, a Mennonite congregation in Colombia accompanied reinserted combatants from both insurgent and paramilitary groups. After adequate psychological and pastoral support, these ex-combatants from opposite sides have worked together on income-generating projects. They realized that they share many of the same experiences, and saw each other as humans again. Bringing ex-combatants together to re-build the infrastructure that the conflict has destroyed could create a profound symbol of hope.

This discussion of reparation, truth-telling and story-sharing opens the door to mention forgiveness, with the caveat that *forgiveness* does not negate the need for these other elements. Perhaps for some, forgiveness can occur as a discipline or "because the Bible says we should forgive"[43]. However, generally this kind of "head" forgiveness needs the validation of "heart" forgiveness for true healing to occur (Bartsch, Interview 2004). Suggesting forgiveness too quickly sparks anger. People need time to mourn (Puljek-Shank 2003). They must walk their own path, at their own pace, towards realizing that forgiveness frees them from letting the past event control and manipulate them. However, only the victims themselves can forgive, just as only the offenders can repent, make amends and change their behaviour. Certain societal processes can facilitate forgiveness and conversion, but ultimately it will depend on personal-private processes, not on collective-public events (Gopin 2001).

Just relationships will not arise naturally out of judicial procedures; therefore Colombians need to rebuild *relational covenants* with new values. These include non-violence, respect, a sacred awe for life, open communication, shared power, transparency, accountability, security based on mutuality, among other values, in order to restore people's basic trust in each other, and in society's institutions. Trust slowly allows people who stood on different sides of the conflict to take moral responsibility for each other's well-being. Trust does leave people vulnerable, but not any more so than violence does. Alongside the political, economic and judicial processes, these cultural transformations can prevent violence from blazing up again in the future.

One fundamental relational value is a true *respect* for cultural, religious and ideological diversity. In examining the armed conflict in El Salvador, Mark Chupp concluded that "civil war is the ultimate breakdown of a society's ability to peacefully manage its differences" (2003). Often the lines of diversity become excuses for excluding certain groups, with the assumption that the available resources will not stretch to reach everyone. If people assume that "the country has enough" to allow everyone a dignified life, the reasons for drawing exclusive lines diminish. If at the same time, the nation has established adequate procedures for making decisions and reaching consensus on critical issues, diversity does not remain a threat. The final step then requires letting go of stereotypes and mindsets that devalue diversity.

A second important cultural shift means eliminating the widespread militaristic mentality and embracing the power of *nonviolence*. Hundreds of thousands of Colombians make a living as security workers (official, private, legal or illegal) because their fellow Colombians assume that men with guns guarantee security. The weapons left by the ex-combatants loop back into the hands of private security forces. It is time to destroy both the excess weapons and people's blind trust in armed protection.

Thirdly, Colombians, collectively and as individuals, need to balance their exploration of past pain with a *positive vision* for the future in order to hold onto hope. They need to celebrate each small step towards healing. Rituals, art, drama, humour and music may help to express emotions, memories, hopes and ideals when words do not suffice (Schirch 2001). These practices help to release the past without denying it, and root a vision for a positive future in reality before it entirely materializes. Perhaps the fact that few living Colombians can remember a time of peace in their country is an obstacle for building peace; people struggle to build what they can not imagine. Rituals and art can open people's minds to new possibilities and make transformation viable.

Colombians need to recover many positive, valuable aspects of their cultures. Throughout history, what has given Colombians life and held the threads of society together? Many of the indigenous groups traditionally resolved community conflicts nonviolently. How can Colombians reclaim their heritage of nonviolent relationships, rather than holding onto the oppressive and violent models of the Spanish invaders? During recent years, many local communities have resisted pressures from all of the armed groups. Hundreds of hidden heroes have held onto love and compassion even when these values seemed absurdly naïve. How can Colombians recognize that this courage and resilience potentially belongs to all of them? Reaffirming and publicly projecting inspiring elements of Colombians traditions and experience can help to heal their identity and self-image (Schirch 2001). Positive identity then reinforces the reconstruction of the country's moral fibre.

The hardest thread to weave into this whole process of healing Colombian society is the one that runs through *each individual*. Justice and peace depend on broad societal structures, but they start within each person's heart (Henderson 2003). Only the moral and spiritual strength of each person can make all of these transformations possible. Repentance, forgiveness, healing and reconciliation come to those who have cultivated humility, self-awareness and the ability to confront the evil within on a deeply personal level (Gopin 2001; Abu-Nimer 2001). Are Colombians willing to stare deep into the mirror at their own souls for the sake of healing themselves and their nation? Each healed heart becomes a seed of life for healing the nation.

Healing for Colombia's people and land will not arise automatically out of a few signed agreements and minor tweaks to the judicial system. The nation's trauma will recede to a manageable level when Colombians collectively participate in transforming structures and attitudes to meet everyone's needs and alleviate everyone's fears. Fear will disappear when Colombians can listen to each other's stories and see their brothers and sisters before them. Healing will come when Justice and Mercy have met together, when Justice and Peace have kissed (Psalm 85).

Notes

1. The government has shifted from proposing practically no penalties for the AUC to placing the top leaders of the AUC in a maximum security prison, with many diverse positions in between, over time.

2. The current legal framework theoretically applies to all of the illegal armed groups; however, it was clearly created in response to the AUC demobilization process in particular. Since it will only apply to crimes committed before the law's approval, it appears less pertinent for the other armed groups that continue to function at present.

3. This is particularly true for people joining the AUC, due to the higher "salaries" paid by this group.

4. More than half of Colombian territory lies in the hands of a few families who do not even work the land (Mondragón 2001). Meanwhile, small-scale farmers (campesinos) do not have access to enough land to make agricultural production viable.

5. "Rodrigo", AUC commander of the "Bloque Metro" affirmed himself that the union between the AUC and narco-traffickers led to a major agrarian counter-reform (El Tiempo 17 Sept.2006).

6. AUC supported candidates in Magdalena, Córdoba, César, Sucre and Antioquia won up to 96% of the votes in their municipalities, sometimes without even campaigning at all (El Tiempo 1 Oct.2006).

7. See reports such as "La Sexta Divisi6n: Relaciones Militares-Paramilitares y la Política Estadounidense en Colombia (New Cork: Human Rights Watch, 2001), as an example of many documents demonstrating this link.

8. The AUC has been known to cut people up into pieces with chain-saws or machetes (e.g. the Mapiripán massacre in July 1997, killing 60 villagers), bash people against rocks until they die (e.g. the Chengue massacre in January 2001, killing 26 people), play soccer with people's heads and other gruesome acts (Kirk 2003, 176; Vivas, 1999).

9. The CONVIVIR were promoted during the 1990's, particularly by leaders such as the current President who was governor of Antioquia at the time. The CONVIVIR were later declared illegal in 1998, but the private security structures had already consolidated by that time.

10. Since 2000, the United States has given Colombia USD 4.7 billion. Colombia is the third largest recipient of US assistance, and by far the largest outside of the Middle East. Of that aid, 80%—at a rate of $1.5 million per day—has gone to Colombia's police and military (www.usiponline.org).

11. There have been approximately 3.5 million people displaced since 1985 (www.codhes.org); the AUC is responsible for at least 56% of these cases (Callejón con Salida 2003).

12. The AUC is responsible for most of the 10.174 people massacred between 1994-1999. According to the Association of Family Members of Disappeared and Detained People—ASFADDES, 6.370 people were disappeared between 1994-2004 (El Tiempo, 16 Sept.2004); the AUC were responsible for 84% of these cases (Callejón con Salida 2003).

13. For example, hundreds of millions of dollars were taken from the subsidized health system in La Guajira and used by the AUC (El Tiempo 24 Julio 2004).

14. Pastor Jorge Moreno reflected after his region suffered massive displacements due to combats between the AUC and the FARC: "I heard about people's cold treatment of displaced people, but I didn't think my town would be capable of such heartlessness. Now I see that it is true. Everyone here rejects the displaced people, treating them as worst element of society."

15. The government has made a list of 2695 ex-combatants that should be processed judicially (El Tiempo 18 Oct 2006).

16. Many spent their time loitering outside the reinsertion houses in Bogotá with nothing to do, until one of these houses was bombed and the city government pressured the national government to locate the ex-combatants elsewhere. Dozens of reinserted combatants (not named for security reasons) that the Mennonite Church has accompanied described their total frustration with the lack of real government support. Some said they wanted to return to "the mountains" i.e. to fight, because "at least we knew how to survive there."

17. In both of these cases, evidence suggests that they were assassinated by other AUC leaders who did not share the same positions or who did not want certain information to become public.

18. The Colombian Commission of Jurists reported that the AUC assassinated or "disappeared" 1899 people between December 2002, when the ceasefire was declared, and August 2004 (as cited in Human Rights Watch 2005). By the end of 2006, Senator Gustavo Petro, an opposition party leader, announced that a total of 3005 people assassinated by the AUC since the ceasefire had been declared.

19. To give an example of this phenomenon, the Commander of the Bloque Resistencia Tayrona, Hernán Giraldo, instructed his men during the demobilization

process to store away a significant portion of their weapons "in case we have to re-organize ourselves again" (Revista Cambio 11 June 2006).

20. This shift in motives may explain why the new paramilitary-type groups have even been waging war against each other in the main cities of the country. When the author visited Altos de Cazucá, the epicentre of the new generation paramilitaries in Bogotá on September 29, 2006, two people had just been killed or disappeared as a result of this territorial battle between paramilitary groups an hour before.

21. Examples would include the Grassroots Women's Organization that resisted collaborating with the AUC when this armed group took control of Barrancabermeja in 1999, the massive non-violent indigenous mobilizations in Cauca to protest the presence of armed actors on their land and to retrieve their kidnapped leaders (Sept-October 2004), the Sanctuary for Peace Churches promoted by Justapaz and the Communities for Peace in Urabá and other regions of the country.

22. Here lies part of the challenge: mass media in Colombia is controlled by two of the main economically elite families and is considered biased towards the State Armed Forces.

23. The current President has practically ignored the existence of the National Peace Council, the legally constituted State and Civil Society body with representatives from diverse sectors that has the function of advising the President in peace-building processes.

24. The current government has closed all doors for community leaders or municipal governments to dialogue and negotiate with armed actors, even for humanitarian reasons. Those leaders who have participated in such dialogues have often been imprisoned.

25. The U.S., a main donor country, designed its major military aid plan, known as Plan Colombia, contrary to the Colombian government's initial petitions and against the wishes of significant sectors of Colombian society.

26. The current government's policy of pressuring displaced people to return to their land without any security guarantees, or with heavy but unsustainable military presence, and without the necessary tools and materials to start over does not respect displaced people's basic rights to safety and to a voluntary return. Returns require strong economic, physical, political and judicial structures (Hart 2001).

27. There are many examples of arrangements unfavourable for Colombia. For example, for about 20 years, the Colombian government practically paid Exxon to take coal out of Colombia due to an agreement that Colombia would pay Exxon if international prices did not exceed certain levels (Posada). There is considerable concern that the Free Trade Agreement with the U.S. will lead to a greater economic monopoly over Colombian natural resources and food sovereignty by foreign companies, as Colombian producers will have to compete with highly technified and subsidized producers from the U.S. The Free Trade agreements could add pressure rather than relieve it (see Cousens 2001).

28. The FARC also finances much of its activities through taxes charged on coca-growers.

29. The current punitive method of eradication of coca-growing through indiscriminate aerial fumigations has destroyed thousands of hectares of food crops, contaminated water sources and causes illness and death among animals and people (Bowman and Klassen 2003).

30. Some projects, such as Planeta Paz and the Permanent Assembly of Civil Society for Peace have attempted to strengthen and organize specific sectors of civil society since 1998. It is too early to evaluate the lasting impact of these initiatives, but they have helped to open dialogue.

31. For example, the assassination of three labour union leaders in Arauca, August 3, 2004, the massacre of seven people in the Peace Community of San José de Apartadó, February 21, 2005, car bombs prior to the 2006 Presidential elections, were all committed by members of the State Armed Forces.

32. Because this paper has focused on the AUC demobilization process, it has not highlighted the deep pain suffered by victims of insurgent violence. However, it is clear that processes of justice in Colombia must place victims of all of the armed actors, from across the political spectrum, on equal ground.

33. Currently, the Colombian government provides subsidies, housing and education for ex-combatants, but has generally not lived up to its obligations to provide at least the same level of support to displaced people and other victims. This difference can clearly give the message to victims that they are "worse" than their victimizers, thus seriously blocks the healing process.

34. This is the current practice.

35. The AUC commanders themselves declare that the State has provided them with their weapons and point to the State as their creator (Sierra and Sierra, El Tiempo 15 May 2004).

36. The government's focus on "forgiveness" and minimal consequences seem to validate this fear. If the victims of AUC violence were currently in power, or if the current government were judging the insurgent groups right now, it would likely focus more on strict, punitive justice (Assefa 2000).

37. For example, one of the AUC commanders, Ernesto Baez, assured that if they have to go to prison, they would ensure that all of Colombia's Presidents since the 1980's would have to go too (Sierra and Sierra El Tiempor, 15 May 2004). This author perceives serious difficulties in the current process precisely because it does not include the insurgent groups. The State will not admit its collaboration with the AUC because this would give the insurgent groups a significant political advantage at a time when the guerrillas face no pressure to confess anything. The AUC will not take responsibility for the wrong it has done if the State does not assume responsibility for its role in these violations. This one-sided dynamic will make it much more difficult to find the truth (Assefa 2000, 97). It is worth noting that there are practically no other cases in the world where paramilitary groups demobilize before the insurgent groups. (Callejón con Salida 2003).

38. The idea that citizens should or have to apply and enforce justice is very common in Colombia; this concept is precisely what has led to the creation of so many private armies. For that reason, the distinction between defining justice and applying/enforcing justice is important (Sánchez 2000).

39. The fact that the former insurgent members that demobilized in the late 1980's are still referred to as "reinserted people" or "ex-combatants" contributes to their difficulty in successfully integrating into society. The label immediately gives them an identity that leads many other people to reject them.

40. For this to happen, Randy and Amela Puljek-Shank highlight the need for what they call "prophetic listening" (2003).

41. Humanization of an enemy is not an easy process by any means, considering the strong psychological mechanisms that people activate to continually affirm the "badness" of their "enemies", e.g. the fundamental attribution error: blaming one's own faults on environmental factors while blaming the other's faults on their character (Berkowitz, as cited in Fischer 2001), the strong tendencies to avoid cognitive dissonance by ignoring or reframing information contradictory to one's assumptions. However, through dialogue and regular contact, people can begin to view their enemies with greater complexity.

42. Humberto Lagos argues that alternative methods are necessary because tribunals can not function if they have no capacity to discover the truth, and tribunals alone have not always been very successful in doing just that (2000).

43. This has been a common response heard by the author when facilitating trauma workshops among church leaders, even though they themselves admit that they don't feel entirely satisfied with this answer.

References

Abu-Nimer, M. 2001. "Education for Coexistence in Israel: Potential and Challenges." In Mohammed Abu-Nimer, ed. *Reconciliation, Justice and Coexistence.* New York: Lexington Books.

Así Va el Diálogo con los "Paras". 2004. Bogotá: Indepaz.

Assefa, H. "Coexistence and Reconciliation in the Northern Region of Ghana." In Mohammed Abu-Nimer, ed. *Reconciliation, Justice and Coexistence.* New York: Lexington Books, 2001. 165-186.

Assefa, H. 2000. "Experiencias de Lucha contra la Impunidad en Africa." In Leonel Suárez Gil, ed. *Reparación, Reconstrucción y Reconciliación.* Bogotá: Editorial Códice Ltda.

Bartsch, K. and Bartsch, E. 1996. *Stress and Trauma Healing.* Durban: Vuleka Trust and Diakonia Council of Churches.

Bartsch, K. Personal interview. October 25, 2004.

Bowman, J. and Klassen, B. 2003 (July) Unpublished Trip Report: Field Trip to Fumigated Municipalities in el Sur de Bolivar.

Chupp, M. 2003. "Creating a Culture of Peace in Post-War El Salvador." In C. Sampson, M. Abu-Nimer, C. Liebler, and D. Whintey, eds. *Positive Approaches to Peacebuilding.* Washington D.C.: Pact Publications.

Cousens, E. M. 2001. "Introduction." In E. M. Cousens and C. Jumar, eds. *Peacebuilding as Politics.* London: Lynne Rienner Publishers.

Cultivos Proscritos y Política Antidroga. 2003. Bogotá: Indepaz.

de Levita, D. 2000. "Child Psychotherapy as an Instrument in Cultural Research: Treating War-Traumatized Children in the Former Yugoslavia." In Antonius C.G.M. Robben and Marcelo M. Suárez-Orozco, eds., *Cultures under Siege: Collective Violence and Trauma.* Cambridge: Cambridge University Press.

Después de un año de haber sido aprobada, la Ley de Justicia y Paz sigue sin ser aplicada. *El Tiempo.* 13 June 2006.

Doe, S. G. 2003. "Proventive Peacebuilding in the Republic of Guinea." In C. Sampson, M. Abu-Nimer, C. Liebler, and D. Whintey, eds. *Positive Approaches to Peacebuilding.* Washington D.C.: Pact Publications.

Doyle, M. W. 2001. "Peacebuilding in Cambodia: Legitimacy and Power." In E. M. Cousens and C. Jumar, eds. *Peacebuilding as Politics.* London: Lynne Rienner Publishers.

En Demobilización, paras ocultaron a niños que hacían parte de sus filas, advierte Procuraduría. *El Tiempo.* 15 June 2006.

Estrada-Hollenbeck, M. 2001. "The Attainment of Justice through Restoration, Not Litigation: The Subjective Road to Reconciliation." In Mohammed Abu-Nimer, ed. *Reconciliation, Justice and Coexistence.* New York: Lexington Books.

Fisher, R. J. 2001. "Social-Psychological Processes in Interactive Conflict Analysis and Reconciliation." In Mohammed Abu-Nimer, ed. *Reconciliation, Justice and Coexistence.* New York: Lexington Books.

Florez, L. B. 2005. "Desplazamiento Forzado: Un impacto territorial."

Galán, C. F. and Edulfo P. 2005. "Extras: el as bajo la manga de los uribistas." *El Tiempo.* 13 Feb. 2005.

Gampel, Y. 2000. "Reflections on the Prevalence of the Uncanny in Social Violence." In Antonius C.G.M. Robben and Marcelo M. Suárez-Orozco, eds. *Cultures under Siege: Collective Violence and Trauma.* Cambridge: Cambridge University Press.

Garay, L. J. 2002 *Colombia: Entre la Exclusión y el Desarrollo: Informe Controlaría General de la República.* Bogotá: Alpha-Omega.

García-Peña J. D. 2004. La Relación del Estado Colombiano con el Fenómeno Paramilitar: por el Esclarecimiento Histórico. *Tierralta: A la Hora de la Verificación.* Bogotá: Indepaz.

Gobierno y Fiscal, en roces por paras sin juzgar. *El Tiempo.* 18 October 2006.

González, F. 2000. "Una Nación Fragmentada: Una Aproximación a la Violencia Colombiana." In Leonel Suárez Gil, ed. *Reparación, Reconstrucción y Reconciliación.* Bogotá: Editorial Códice Ltda.

Good Sider, N. 2003. "Transcendent: Discovering Resources for Posttraumatic Healing and Growth." In C. Sampson, M. Abu-Nimer, C. Liebler, and D. Whintey, eds. *Positive Approaches to Peacebuilding.* Washington D.C.: Pact Publications.

Gopin, Marc. 2001. "Forgiveness as an Element of Conflict Resolution in Religious Cultures: Walking the Tightrope of Reconciliation and Justice." In Mohammed Abu-Nimer, ed. *Reconciliation, Justice and Coexistence.* New York: Lexington Books.

Green, P. and Pearson d'Estrée, T. 2003. "The Positive Power of Voice in Peacebuilding." In C. Sampson, M. Abu-Nimer, C. Liebler, and D. Whintey, eds. *Positive Approaches to Peacebuilding.* Washington D.C.: Pact Publications.

Hart, B. 2001. "Refugee Return in Bosnia and Herzegovina." In Mohammed Abu-Nimer, ed. *Reconciliation, Justice and Coexistence.* New York: Lexington Books.

Henderson, M. 2003. "Initiatives of Change." In C. Sampson, M. Abu-Nimer, C. Liebler, and D. Whintey, eds. *Positive Approaches to Peacebuilding.* Washington D.C.: Pact Publications.

Hubbard, A. S. 2001. "Understanding Majority and Minority Participation in Interracial and Interethnic Dialogue." In Mohammed Abu-Nimer, ed. *Reconciliation, Justice and Coexistence.* New York: Lexington Books.

Human Rights Watch. "Colombia: Librando a los paramilitares de sus responsabilidades." URL: http.//www.hwr.org (31 January.2005).

Jorge 40 es la cabeza de la operación en que dineros de la ARS han pasado a los paras. *El Tiempo* 24 July, 2004.

Kumar, C. 2001. "Peacebuilding in Haiti." In Elizabeth. M. Cousens and C. Jumar, eds. *Peacebuilding as Politics*. London: Lynne Rienner Publishers.

Kirk, R.. 2003. *More Terrible Than Death*. New York: Public Affairs.

Lagos, H. 2000. "Derechos Humanos y Mesa de Diálogo en Chile." In Leonel Suárez Gil, ed. *Reparación, Reconstrucción y Reconciliación*. Bogotá: Editorial Códice Ltda.

La Manzana de la Discordia. *Revista Semana*. 10 April 2006.

Lambourne, W. 2001. "Justice and Reconciliation: Postconflict Peacebuilding in Cambodia and Rwanda." In Mohammed Abu-Nimer, ed. *Reconciliation, Justice and Coexistence*. New York: Lexington Books.

La Paramilitarización de Colombia. *El Tiempo*. 26 Sept. 2004.

Lederach, J. P. 1998. *Construyendo la Paz: Reconciliación sostenible en sociedades divididas*. Bilbao: Bakeaz.

MAPP/OEA. "Sixth Quarterly Report of the Secretary General to the Permanent Council on the Misión to support the Peace Process in Colombia." (6 February 2006).

McCandless, E. 2001. "The Case of Land in Zimbabwe: Cause of Conflict, Foundation for Sustained Peace." In Mohammed Abu-Nimer, ed. *Reconciliation, Justice and Coexistence*. New York: Lexington Books.

Mercado, B. and Gómez S. "Luego de un año de funcionamiento de la misión de la OEA, no se logra afinar desmobilizaciones." *El Tiempo*. 1 Feb 2005.

Mondragón, H. Personal interview. 27 March 2005.

Mondragón, H. "Plan Colombia: Gasolina al Fuego." URL:http://www.nadir.org/initiatv/agp/free/colombia/mondrag2.html (January 2001).

Moreno, Jo. E. Personal interview. 21 September 2004.

Neme, J. Member of the Colombian Coalition against the Use of Children and Youth in the War. Personal Interview. 15 February 2005.

ONG revela que paramilitares se han quedado con 5 milliones de hectáreas de tierra entre 1997 y 2003. *El Tiempo*. 21 Dec. 2004.

Orr, R. C. 2001. "Building Peace in El Salvador." In. Elizabeth M. Cousens and Chutan Kumar, eds. *Peacebuilding as Politics*. London: Lynne Rienner Publishers.

Porter, T. W. and Mark C. M. 2003. "Engage Conflict Well." In C. Sampson, M. Abu-Nimer, C. Liebler, and D. Whintey, eds. *Positive Approaches to Peacebuilding*. Washington D.C.: Pact Publications.

Posada, F. Personal Interview. November 15, 2003.

Pratt Ewing, K. 2000. "The Violence of Non-Recognition: Becoming a 'Conscious' Muslim Woman in Turkey." In Antonius C.G.M. Robben and Marcelo M. Suárez-Orozco, eds., *Cultures under Siege: Collective Violence and Trauma*. Cambridge: Cambridge University Press.

Proceso de Paz: Cronología de Negociación. *Revista Semana*. 13 Feb. 2005.

Programa Andino de Derechos Humanos—Universidad Andina Simón Bolívar. "El Desplazamiento Forzada en Colombia: Acumulación de Capital y Exclusión Social." Revista Aportes Andinos No.7. Globalización, migración y derechos humanos. URL: http://www.uasb.edu.ec/padh (October 2003).

Puljek-Shank, A. and Puljek-Shank R. 2003. "Journey of Healing." In C. Sampson, M. Abu-Nimer, C. Liebler, and D. Whintey, eds. *Positive Approaches to Peacebuilding.* Washington D.C.: Pact Publications.

Rasmussen, J. L. "Negotiating a Revolution: Toward Integrating Relationship Building and Reconciliation into Official Peace Negotiations." In Mohammed Abu-Nimer, ed. *Reconciliation, Justice and Coexistence.* New York: Lexington Books.

Reacción a la Multiplicación de los Paramilitares. *El Tiempo.* 10 July 2006.

Rios, M. O. and Fisher, D. S. 2003. "Appreciative Inquiry as a Tool for Conflict Resolution." In C. Sampson, M. Abu-Nimer, C. Liebler, and D. Whintey, eds. *Positive Approaches to Peacebuilding.* Washington D.C.: Pact Publications.

Robben, A. C.G.M. 2000. "The Assault on Basic Trust: Disappearance, Protest and Reburial in Argentina." In Antonius C.G.M. Robben and Marcelo M. Suárez-Orozco, eds., *Cultures under Siege: Collective Violence and Trauma.* Cambridge: Cambridge University Press.

Salvatore Mancuso Amenaza con Tomar de Nuevo las Armas si no hay Solución Radical a su Extradición. *El Tiempo.* 5 Dec. 2004.

Sánchez, A. 2000. "Justicia, Verdad y Reparación hacia la Reconciliación." In Leonel Suárez Gil, ed., *Reparación, Reconstrucción y Reconciliación.* Bogotá: Editorial Códice Ltda.

Santamaría, C. 2000. "Guatemala: Recuperación de la Memoria Historica In Leonel Suárez Gil, ed., *Reparación, Reconstrucción y Reconciliación.* Bogotá: Editorial Códice Ltda.

Schirch, L. 2001. "Ritual Reconciliation: Transforming Identity/Reframing Conflict." In Mohammed Abu-Nimer, ed. *Reconciliation, Justice and Coexistence.* New York: Lexington Books.

Schreiter, R. 1992. *Reconciliation: Mission and Ministry in a Changing Social Order.* Maryknoll, NY: Orbis Books.

Schwoebel, M. H., and McCandless, E. 2003. "Toward the Theory and Practice of Appreciative Inquiry in Complex Peacebuilding and Development Contexts." In C. Sampson, M. Abu-Nimer, C. Liebler, and D. Whintey, eds. *Positive Approaches to Peacebuilding.* Washington D.C.: Pact Publications.

Secretos de las tierras arrebatadas por "paras". *El Tiempo.* 17 September 2006.

Se les atribuye la mayoría de las 1969 masacres entre 1994 y 2003 a los Paramilitares. *El Tiempo*, 16 Sept 2004.

Sierra, Luz María and Alvaro Sierra. "Un Día en el Corazón de las Autodefensas Unidas de Colombia." *El Tiempo.* 15 May 2004.

Suárez-Orozco, C. 2000. "Identities under Siege: Immigration Stress and Social Mirroring among the Children of Immigrants." In Antonius C.G.M. Robben and Marcelo M. Suárez-Orozco, eds., *Cultures under Siege: Collective Violence and Trauma.* Cambridge: Cambridge University Press.

Suárez-Orozco, M. M. and Antonius C.G.M.Robben. 2000. "Interdisciplinary Perspectives on Violence and Trauma." In Antonius C.G.M. Robben and Marcelo M. Suárez-Orozco, eds., *Cultures under Siege: Collective Violence and Trauma.* Cambridge: Cambridge University Press.

Tres senadores en la lista de "Jorge 40". *El Tiempo.* 1 October 2006.

United Nations Commission on Human Rights. 2006 (January).Report of the High Commissioner for Human Rights on the Situation in Colombia.

United Nations Development Program. 2003. El Conflicto, Callejón con Salida. *Informe Nacional de Desarrollo Humano: Colombia*_Bogotá.

Un Paso Adelante, dos atrás. *Revista Semana*. 10 January 2006.

Van der Merwe, H. 2001. "Reconciliation and Justice in South Africa: Lessons from the TRC's Community Interventions." In Mohammed Abu-Nimer, ed. *Reconciliation, Justice and Coexistence*. New York: Lexington Books.

Vivas, B. Public Testimony. 5 October 1999.

Volkan, V. D. and Itzkowitz, N. 2000. "Modern Greek and Turkish Identities and the Psychodynamics of Greek-Turkish Relations." In Antonius C.G.M. Robben and Marcelo M. Suárez-Orozco, eds., *Cultures under Siege: Collective Violence and Trauma*. Cambridge: Cambridge University Press.

White, A. 2003. "Rewriting Narratives in the New South Africa." In C. Sampson, M. Abu-Nimer, C. Liebler, and D. Whintey, eds. *Positive Approaches to Peacebuilding*. Washington D.C.: Pact Publications.

Whitney, D., Liebler, C., and Cooperrider, D. 2003. "Appreciative Inquiry in Peacebuilding." In C. Sampson, M. Abu-Nimer, C. Liebler, and D. Whintey, eds. *Positive Approaches to Peacebuilding*. Washington D.C.: Pact Publications.

14

Healing Trauma among Australia's 'Stolen Generations'

John Bond

Professor Judy Atkinson probably knows more about healing the trauma confronting Aboriginal Australians than anyone else in the country. As an Aboriginal, she experiences this trauma from the inside. And as Professor of Indigenous Australian Studies at Southern Cross University, she works to build bridges between Indigenous healing practices and Western trauma recovery processes. Her book, *Trauma Trails—Recreating Song Lines*[1], is a study of the transgenerational effects of trauma among Aboriginal Australians, and her findings in the search for healing.

The causes of this trauma are not hard to find. Since Britain's colonization of Australia began in 1788, the story of the Aboriginal people has been one of dispossession, massacre and disease. The oldest living culture on the planet came close to extermination—and is still under serious threat today, with Aboriginal languages dying steadily. Aboriginal people are a despised minority in the land to which their ancestors came at least 60,000 years ago. They die 20 years younger than the rest of the population. They are imprisoned at 14 times the rate of the rest of the population. And most Australians, living with a suppressed guilt at having taken their land and left them in wretched conditions, do not want to know about the past. There is little enthusiasm for history courses in Australian schools.

The 'Stolen Generations'

One of the most pernicious of the cruelties practiced on Aboriginal people by the colonizers was the removal of tens of thousands of their children from their families with the aim of assimilating them into Western culture.

Assimilation was Australia's policy through most of the 20th century. Everyone, no matter their origin, was expected to adopt the culture of white Australia. Until the 1960s, non-white people were forbidden permanent residency. But where did the Aboriginal population fit into this policy?

At the time it was widely assumed that full-blood Aborigines were a dying race. But the number of people of mixed Aboriginal and white parentage was growing steadily; and since they were usually born of white fathers and Aboriginal mothers, most of them grew up in Aboriginal communities.

This alarmed the authorities, who looked on Aboriginal culture as worthless. In their view, if they denied these children access to Aboriginal culture, the children would turn naturally to the culture of white Australia. Western Australia's so-called Protector of Aborigines, A. O. Neville, put this view bluntly. Either Australia would "have a population of one million blacks," he told a national conference, or "we could merge them into our white community and eventually forget that there were any Aborigines in Australia."[2]

So, from the late 1800s, the authorities adopted a practice of removing the children from their Aboriginal families and placing them in white institutions, often run by churches, or with white foster parents. Some white Australians spoke out against the practice—but their views were over-ridden by the authorities, whose approach to social planning was shaped more by eugenics than by simple humanity.

The Effects of Removal

The removal policies were traumatic for all concerned. Widely throughout the country, Aboriginal families lived, year after year, with the fear that their children would be snatched from them. When a Government patrol officer appeared, the children would scatter into the bush. Some families fled to isolated places or kept moving ahead of the authorities. This caused constant disruption in many Aboriginal communities, destroying any chance of the stability on which advances in health, education and economic development depend.

The most severe trauma has been among the removed children. The long-term impact on them has varied widely, depending on the situation to which the child was taken, and the amount of the love and attention he or she received. Some have coped with the trauma of losing their families, and flourished. They still have to cope with the emptiness resulting from the silence about their birth families, and the denial of their Indigenous heritage. But their state of wellbeing is far better than those who were placed with unsatisfactory foster parents or in institutions. Many of these children have never overcome their loss, and their lives have become an anguished story of social malformation. At least one academic study has found that, after removal from their families, the children's scholastic achievement deteriorated markedly.[3]

The least trauma sensitive places were the institutions. The staff included many caring people. But they were unable to give the children the attention they needed, and many children grew up starved of affection. There was also staff that was wholly unsuitable, as the evidence of physical and sexual abuse makes clear. Most institutions were seriously under-resourced, and the living conditions of some were deplorable, even by the standards of the time.

Above all, however, the institutions were given an impossible task—to prepare part-Aboriginal children to take their place in a society which treated non-white people as second-class. In many institutions the children were taught to stay away from Aboriginal people. They learned to be ashamed that they were black. Most girls were trained with the expectation that they would become domestic servants, and boys were expected to become stockmen, or learn a simple trade.

Many who adopted or fostered these children tried to ignore the social attitudes to non-white people, reasoning that if they treated the child as an equal, the rest of society would too. Normally this did not happen. As the children reached twelve or thirteen they found their white friends dropping away. It became harder to get a friend of the opposite sex. Unwanted and alienated, the children couldn't withdraw into Aboriginal company like their cousins back home.[4]

Though their experiences were different, both the children from the institutions and those in foster homes have faced the same problems. Not accepted by the whites, too ashamed to join the blacks, all too often the stolen generations were left in the middle. One of the best-known of them, Bob Randall, explained his feelings:

> Growing up 'colored' in a world of black and white has been a constant struggle for all Aborigines of mixed descent. Those of us who were taken away from our mothers as young children were taught that we were better than our Aboriginal families, but not good enough to be equal in white society. We were not allowed to speak our language or learn about the culture of our mothers. We were given a mediocre education because the Government believed that we were less intelligent than whites and could only be trained for menial work. The traumas we members of the stolen generations carry in our memories, and the identity questions we still live with, have been passed on to our children, creating a deep wound in the spirits of Aboriginal families right across Australia.[5]

The Effect on the Next Generation

In 2004 the Telethon Institute for Child Health Research conducted the largest survey ever on the health of Aboriginal children in Western Australia.[6] The Institute Director, Professor Fiona Stanley, outlined the results in a speech in the Great Hall of Parliament House, Canberra, in 2005.

As researchers we have known that the pathways to health and wellbeing depend on parents providing a loving, nurturing, safe and educational environment for their children. We also know that one of the most powerful factors in wellbeing is how well your parents cared for you in the early years of your life. Parents who as children did not receive the love and care they needed are much less likely to be caring parents themselves. Hence we knew that the forced removal of children over 70-80 years of the 20th century would have had a profound effect on the parenting of subsequent generations. But we did not have the data to prove it.

The survey studied both the children and the adults who brought them up—normally the parents, though sometimes aunts, uncles or other foster parents—whom the survey describes as 'carers':

Our survey was so large (over 5000 children) and representative that estimates of health and wellbeing can be reliably compared between those who were and were not removed. We found that of today's children and young people (0-17 years), 12.3% of their carers had been forcibly removed from their families.... It is clear that the practice continued well into the 1970s and beyond in Western Australia.

The carers had higher rates of alcohol consumption and gambling (than the average for Aboriginal people), were twice as likely to have been arrested or charged, half as likely to have someone with whom they could share their problems, and much more likely to have contact with psychological/mental health services. The effects on the children—the next generation—were profound. They are twice as likely to have emotional and behavioral problems, to be at high risk for hyperactivity, emotional and conduct disorders, and to abuse alcohol and drugs.

The Effect on the Non-Indigenous Population

Studies about Perpetration Induced Traumatic Stress (PITS) in numerous countries demonstrate that cruelty results in trauma not just in the victim but in the perpetrator too. Much of the history of white settlement in Australia can be seen as influenced by guilt and self-justification arising from the expulsion of Aborigines from the most productive land, ruthless destruction when they resisted, and a determination to control those who were left. Among the people who implemented the removal policies is much evidence of this kind of stress. Some examples are clear. The son of a policeman wrote:

My father was a good and conscientious policeman, serving from 1922 to 1946. When I was seven or eight, he would sometimes come off duty and sit crying and sobbing like a child. All he would say to me was, 'Son, don't ever be a policeman. It's a dirty job.' When I was 16, we went on a fishing trip. Sitting around the camp fire, I asked him why he had cried. He told me that when he went on duty those mornings, his sergeant would order him to accompany two welfare officers to Cummeragunga, a mission station, to give them protection

> when they entered nice, clean, simple homes of [Aboriginal] people and bodily removed children from loving mothers and fathers.[7]

More subtle was the effect on those who looked after the children, who often felt that they were left carrying the consequences of a tragically misguided policy. One person who adopted an Aboriginal child wrote:

> We were told that the child had been detained in the Home for ten months after his birth because of a 'chest infection'. And that his mother was dead. We didn't understand the identity issues that would arise for an Aboriginal boy growing up in a white family. When eventually we did, we sought out his birth family, and he was able to meet up with three sisters. One sister had been trying to find him for a very long time. Thirty-five years after we adopted him, we discovered that his mother had not only been alive, but unwilling to give him up. That was the real reason he had been kept in the Home. We were devastated to discover that we had unknowingly contributed to their separation.[8]

In Canada this aspect of trauma has been recognized, and there has been an extensive program of dialogue, particularly between the Aboriginal former inmates of the Residential Schools to which they were removed, and the staff of those institutions. This has contributed to healing on both sides. Nothing comparable has taken place in Australia—a symptom of the denial which is still widespread among white Australians.

Self-Help Healing

This denial has meant that, for decades, no professional help has been offered to Aboriginal people to recover from the trauma induced by their removal. They have had to develop their own processes towards healing. Especially important has been the close bond maintained between those who grew up together at a particular institution. When, in recent years, stolen generations people in Western Australia were offered counseling, they replied, "You should have come twenty years ago. We have had to work out how to counsel each other, and help each other through the bad times."One participant in Professor Atkinson's healing programs said:

> Saddest thing is we [Aboriginal people] don't even realize that we've got all the coping mechanisms and we've been healing ourselves all these years. If this was pointed out, things would really start to happen. We would build on it, because we know things are wrong, but we don't know what to do about it.

National Inquiry into the Separation Policies

Some of the stolen generations became active in Aboriginal organizations, and agitated for an inquiry into the policies and practice of removing children from their families. They endured a long and often heart-breaking struggle. But eventually, in 1995, the Federal Government agreed. To chair the inquiry they chose a former High Court judge, Sir Ronald Wilson. During the next two years, the inquiry heard from, or received submissions from, 777 people and organizations, of which 535 were Indigenous people who gave evidence about their experiences of forcible removal.

By the time the inquiry reported in 1997, an election had brought in the new Federal Government of John Howard. Their view was that Aboriginal interests had won too many concessions thanks to an undue sense of guilt among white Australians, and they took steps to "swing the pendulum back", as the new Prime Minister expressed it. Then Wilson's report, *Bringing Them Home*, landed on their desk. Its 680 pages told in heart-rending detail of the agony endured by Aboriginals as a result of the forced removal policies.[9]

Australians had grown up believing that these children were altruistically taken out of wretched conditions to be offered all the benefits of white society. Now a national inquiry described the immense harm caused by the policies. For eight months the government made no response except to say that there would be no apology, and no compensation would be paid. Several government ministers attempted to discredit the report.

The public reaction was totally different. *Bringing Them Home* sold in far greater numbers than any comparable report, and the tone of letters to the newspapers showed that many people were horrified by their Government's cold-hearted response. Most may not have understood much about Aboriginal culture, but everyone could understand the pain of a mother whose child has been forcibly removed. This polarization made the stolen generations a frequent media topic. When the Government made a statement such as "There never was a stolen generation" (since, they argued, the removal of 10% of children did not constitute a generation), the media responded with agonizing stories of people who had been removed.

Speaking a few weeks after the release of the Report, Aboriginal Social Justice Commissioner Mick Dodson told an Aboriginal conference:

> We have seen a most extraordinary turn of events in this country. Day after day and week after week the newspapers and airwaves have been jammed with talk about our families and children. Day after day the letter pages in the papers are filled with the reactions of ordinary Australians who are horrified at the truth that they never knew. Never before have so many Australians turned their attention to our families. Never before has Australia really known or cared about our children, children taken from the arms of their mothers, taken from their culture.[10]

At that stage the Government had showed every sign of ignoring the report, yet as community concern welled up, the tone of official pronouncements softened. Eventually the Government announced its response—they would put $63 million into adopting a few of the report's recommendations. Link-Up services—which bring together Aboriginal families separated by the removal policies—received Government funding, as did counseling services for the stolen generations.[11]

However, the sums invested were totally inadequate to meet the need. Where Canada, faced with a similar situation, has invested hundreds of millions of dollars in its Aboriginal Healing Fund, Australia has invested only tens of millions. This has meant that few stolen generations people are able to receive help from health professionals.

Some of the stolen generations sought redress through the courts. The Government paid expensive lawyers to oppose them. The best-known case, in which two members of the stolen generations sued the Government for wrongful treatment, lasted 107 days, costing over $10 million. In his judgement, in August 2000, Justice O'Loughlin accepted that both had been abused in the institutions to which they had been taken, but he could not find that the Government bore any responsibility for this abuse, even though Government officers had removed the children to the institution. Crucial documents could not be found, and witnesses had died, he pointed out. So the case was dismissed.[12]

Response of the Australian community

Perhaps it was this intransigence that galvanized so many Australians. Stolen generations people live in every town, and in most suburbs of our cities. Many non-Indigenous Australians would have encountered them at some stage—at school, in clinics or welfare offices. Though few questioned the official view that these people had been removed from wretched conditions to be offered all the benefits of Western society, many must have been uneasy at this explanation. Still, Aboriginal Australians did not *fit in* Australian society. Alienated as they are by traumatic experiences in childhood, they are often unable to make friends with their neighbors and their neighbors, having no concept of what they have endured, are unable to bridge the gulf of misunderstanding. Often the stolen generations' only friends are those they grew up with in their institution.

Since the report appeared, however, in local communities throughout the country, many of these neighbors have reached out to the stolen generations, building bridges across the gulf. The person principally responsible for this was Sir Ronald Wilson. He had been profoundly affected by the inquiry.

> It was like no other I have undertaken. Other inquiries were intellectual exercises, a matter of collating information and making recommendations. But for these people to reveal what had happened to them took immense courage and every emotional stimulus they could muster.
>
> At each session, the tape would be turned on and we would wait... I would look into the face of the person who was to speak to us. I would see the muscles straining to hold back the tears. But tears would stream down, still no words being spoken. And then, hesitantly, words would come.

> We sat there as long as it took. We heard the story, told with that person's whole being, reliving experiences which had been buried deep, sometimes for decades. They weren't speaking with their minds; they were speaking with their hearts. And my heart had to open if I was to understand them.[13]

This affected Sir Ronald profoundly. "I came to this inquiry as a man over the hill at 73, with fifty years behind me as a hardboiled lawyer, mixing it with all sorts of antagonists," he told an overflow audience in Canberra, the national capital, "and yet this inquiry changed me. And if it can change me, it can change our nation."

That was no rhetorical statement. He retired from public office at the end of the inquiry, and so was free to make his views known. From then on he spoke publicly in forum after forum, drawing crowds in their hundreds.

> Children were removed because the Aboriginal race was seen as an embarrassment to white Australia. The aim was to strip the children of their Aboriginality and accustom them to live in a white Australia. The tragedy was compounded when the children, as they grew up, encountered the racism which shaped the policy, and found themselves rejected by the very society for which they were being prepared.[14]

Sir Ronald asked for apologies from Australian governments, churches, the police and all who had been involved in implementing the removal policies—and led the way himself. "I was a leader of the Presbyterian Church in Western Australia at the time we ran Sister Kate's Home, where removed children grew up," he said. "I was proud of the home, with its system of cottage families. Imagine my pain when I discovered, during this inquiry, that children were sexually abused in those cottages." He and the Presbyterian Church apologized wholeheartedly to the Aboriginal people.

His actions struck a chord. In the following months, most of Australia's State parliaments and churches held formal ceremonies to hear from representatives of the stolen generations, and to apologize for their role in this tragedy. They were profoundly moving events, which sent a burst of hope through the Aboriginal community that perhaps a new day was dawning. These ceremonies have contributed to the healing process. As Professor Atkinson writes: 'Ceremony is the observance or practice of a ritual which gives meaning to aspects of the life story. Telling and listening to stories can be ceremonial and therefore healing. In ceremonies we celebrate the awareness that our lives are sacred.'[15]

Sorry Day

A bigger ceremony was yet to come. One recommendation of the *Bringing Them Home* report was that a Sorry Day be held annually to commemorate the tragedy. This had been proposed by several of those who gave evidence to the inquiry, when asked what could help the healing process.

Sorry is a potent word. As Sir Ronald said, "It indicates understanding, a willingness to enter into the suffering, and implies a commitment to do more."[16]

In Aboriginal English it has a further meaning: when Aboriginal people come together to grieve—usually when a death occurs—they describe this as "sorry business". So a Sorry Day would be meaningful to both Aboriginal and non-Aboriginal Australians.

The Federal Government was not interested. But could a Sorry Day be held on a community basis? Sir Ronald consulted spokespeople for the stolen generations, and they jointly invited thirty people, Aboriginal and non-Aboriginal, to meet and consider this question. At that meeting, in January 1998, the participants unanimously decided to try. They chose 26 May as the day, since the report had been tabled in the Federal Parliament on May 26, 1997, and elected Carol Kendall, a widely-respected member of the stolen generations, as co-chair of the informal committee. The other co-chair was a non-Aboriginal Australian, Greg Thompson, since the committee wished to include all Australians in developing the Day. In a statement the committee described Sorry Day as

> A day when all Australians can express their sorrow for the whole tragic episode, and celebrate the beginning of a new understanding. . . . Indigenous people will participate in a Day dedicated to the memory of loved ones who never came home, or who are still finding their way home. . . . Sorry Day can help restore the dignity stripped from those affected by removal; and it offers those who carried out the policy—and their successors—a chance to move beyond denial and guilt. It could shape a far more creative partnership between Indigenous and non-Indigenous Australians, with immense benefit to both.

A former Governor-General of Australia, Sir Zelman Cowen, accepted their invitation to be a patron. Then in March the idea was launched to the nation through the media. The response exceeded all expectations. The Sorry Day Committee was merely a group of people with almost no money, and no ability to organize events across the nation. But that did not matter, because people organized their own events. Aboriginal and non-Aboriginal Australians met to plan. Artists painted, musicians composed, writers and playwrights wrote. A well-known actor created *Sorry Books*—manuscript books in which people could express their apology. More and more books were produced as demand grew from schools, public libraries, and town councils. Soon several thousand books were in circulation, and nearly a million people wrote messages, many of them telling of personal experiences which prompted them to contribute to a Sorry Book.

When the day arrived, it was commemorated by thousands of events. There were theatrical presentations, cultural displays, and town barbecues. Universities, government departments, local councils, churches held gatherings to hear from stolen generations people. In many of them, the Sorry Books were ceremoniously handed to local Aboriginal elders. Over half of the 30-minute national TV news that evening was devoted to Sorry Day events, and to the heartfelt response of Australia's best-known Aboriginal leaders.

Why did Sorry Day touch such a chord? One of the deepest human pains is that of a mother who loses her child or a child its mother. Yet the gulf between Aboriginal and non-Aboriginal Australians was simply too immense for even this pain to flow across it. Bringing Them Home exposed this gulf, and many Australians were shocked. Sorry Day was a chance to accept blame, and to do something about it. As one person expressed it:

> I thought back to my primary school classroom in Tumut (New South Wales). I can name every person in that class except the four Aboriginal boys who sat at the back of the class, never asked a question, stuck with each other in the playground, never played with the rest of us. When I read *Bringing Them Home*, I began to understand what they had probably endured, and why they felt so alienated from the rest of us. And I felt ashamed.

The Federal Government was taken aback by the strength of the Day. They had no idea how to respond to a campaign which included many people active on their side of politics. So they stayed silent and aloof. But the stolen generations were deeply moved. For the first time, they felt that the Australian community understood what they had gone through. The effect of this could be seen in innumerable ways. One example was given by the Aboriginal Commissioner who carried responsibility in the Aboriginal and Torres Strait Islander Commission for health issues.

> In the past, when I visited non-Indigenous health officials, I found a resistance to my argument that Indigenous people faced particular health issues, and health professionals needed to be trained to recognize these. Since Sorry Day I have discovered far more openness to these ideas.[17]

Now, many of the stolen generations felt, the way was open towards healing. From across the country many of them met together. Out of their discussions came a decision to launch a "Journey of Healing". A prominent stolen generations woman, Lowitja O'Donoghue, became its patron.

Journey of Healing

The Journey of Healing's underlying concept is that, if the wounds are to be healed, both government and the community, Aboriginal and non-Aboriginal, have a vital role. It offers every Australian the chance to be part of healing this deep national wound. And many have responded. It has included many of the features advocated by Professor Atkinson. She draws upon the work of Raphael, Swan and Martinek.[18] 'In trauma the self feels fragmented, with a resultant sense of loss of identity,' they write. 'The fragmented self is unable to establish and maintain stable relationships. . . . For many Aboriginal people the fragmentation of self has been compounded by the enforced physical separation of people from their families and communities.'

How to overcome this fragmentation? In her experience, she writes, "The single most important restorative need for people who have been victimized is a supportive and caring family and community." She uses healing circles to create a supportive environment. As one participant explained:

> My changes started in sharing stories, feeling strong because of the support of others, bonding into a family, coming to know that I was lovable, learning we are all unique and important. . . . People can only heal when they know themselves to be of value, and have a sense of their own worth. . . . Healing occurs with people sitting together, maturing through their stories.[19]

She has reached these conclusions through hundreds of hours of interaction with victims of trauma. But this interaction only confirmed what she knew from her own experience. As she would be the first to agree, it does not take an academic to know that a supportive environment is vital to healing. Or that enabling a traumatized person to tell their story—should they wish to tell it—can be a step towards healing. These are home truths, innately understood by people of every background.

In Australia in the late 1990s, these home truths were applied on a massive scale in response to the revealing of the extent of the harm caused by the removal policies. It happened in the absence of Government leadership, through the spontaneous conviction of hundreds of thousands of Australians, expressed in a myriad of events and initiatives in local communities across the country.

Hundreds of events are arranged each year, principally on the anniversary of Sorry Day, bringing together Aboriginal and non-Aboriginal Australians. In many places, radio stations invite stolen generations people in the neighborhood to tell their stories. All over the country, ordinary Australians are learning what many of their Aboriginal compatriots endured, not in the abstract but through people they bump into in the supermarket.

When their local community understands the problems that stolen generations people face, some of these problems can be overcome. As a result, people who have felt alienated for years are experiencing the welcome of their local communities. In a supportive environment, they can begin to heal.

In some cases community groups have developed methods of implementing recommendations of the *Bringing Them Home* report which the Government had ignored. In Western Australia, for instance, a Bringing Them Home Committee was formed. It raised tens of thousands of dollars, and used this to implement the recommendation that stolen generations people should be enabled to "return to country"—to visit the area from which they were removed. Especially for those incapacitated by illness or old age, who needed an assistant to travel with them, this had often been prohibitively expensive. But now many were able to go.

In 2001 Brian Butler was the Commissioner responsible for stolen generations issues with the Aboriginal and Torres Strait Islander Commission. 'Wherever I go, I see spin-offs of the Journey of Healing,' he told a meeting of the National Sorry Day Committee that year. 'The work you are doing as Committees is important, but your effect has gone far wider than that. It is developing into a widespread social movement.'[20]

A Million People Walk for Reconciliation

In the year 2000 the Council for Aboriginal Reconciliation arranged a walk across the Sydney Harbour Bridge, for all who wanted to show their support for reconciliation between Aboriginal and non-Aboriginal Australians. Many of the stolen generations walked behind a banner proclaiming the Journey of Healing. But not all wanted to take part. One stolen generations woman, Val Linow, was very angry. She phoned the organizers to say that after all she had been through, there was no possibility of healing for her, and she would only walk if they got rid of the banner. She had been removed from her family at the age of two, and had been cruelly treated and abused.

One organizer listened to her story, and suggested that, even if she could not walk behind the Journey of Healing banner, she could still take part in the walk. This she decided to do, carrying a sign stating, "Stolen Generations—I am not a myth."

A quarter of a million people walked. It was the largest demonstration in Australian history. As at Sorry Day, people made their views known in their own way. Some paid for a skywriting plane, which wrote "Sorry" in the sky above the Bridge.

For Val, it was a life-changing experience. As she wrote later: "As for the march across the Bridge, seeing that sign "Sorry", I know at last I'm not alone, and seeing the white Australians joining in with the Aboriginals, I felt peace, as if everything in life has its meaning. Part of me was trying to heal, but most of my healing was the walk over the Bridge."[21] She is now active in the Journey of Healing in Sydney.

Her story is a powerful illustration of the role of commemoration in the healing process. As Danieli writes: 'Commemorations can fill the vacuum with creative responses and may help heal the rupture . . . between the survivors [of victimization] and their society. It is a shared context, shared mourning, shared memory. The memory is preserved. . . . The nation shares the horrible pain.'

These events have given many of the stolen generations the determination to launch out on their personal journey of healing. In many cases, this takes immense courage. As Judy Atkinson points out:

> Change is hard work and painful. All healing is self-healing. The person walking with a participant acts as an educator to an emerging new knowledge, helping to strengthen the deepening understanding of the self, and helping to build bridges of communication between the person and others. The task of healing is to facilitate people's discovery of themselves, their own nature, and their place in the world and value to the world. As people come to know themselves better, they become increasingly able to be with another person in the same process, without judgement or prejudice.[22]

> Healing is facing up the fact that you've got choices. There is no need to live all your life in your pain. Knowing you have choice is itself healing, and it shifts you from that place you never thought you could get out of. Healing is knowing you can change things in your life. In taking this power to yourself,

> you become more able to work towards change within the systems that have previously functions abusively on you. Healing therefore must not be considered an outcome, but a process of engagement and understanding, of change and growth.[23]

Memorial to the Stolen Generations

After the Sydney Harbour Bridge walk, every other Australian city organized a similar walk. A million people took part in walks for reconciliation that year. The Federal Government could not ignore such a demonstration. Prime Minister John Howard announced that a central area in Canberra would be set aside "to perpetuate in the minds of the Australian public the importance of reconciliation, and will include a memorial and depiction of the removal of children from their families."

Memorials make a vital contribution to healing. They are usually politically sensitive, because they are a permanent commemoration. This was true of the memorial in Canberra to the stolen generations. The Federal Government, refusing to accept any responsibility for the harm caused by the removal policies, at first developed the memorial themselves, without any consultation with the stolen generations.

Exclusion of the very people who were being remembered provoked demonstrations and criticism, even from party colleagues such as former Prime Minister Malcolm Fraser. The project ground to a halt.

Some of the Sorry Day Committee went to see the Government minister in charge of the project. "This memorial could be immensely healing," they said, "if it comes out of genuine consultation. We are prepared to consult the stolen generations, former staff of the institutions to which they were taken, and those who fostered or adopted children, with the aim of reaching consensus on the design of the memorial."

Eventually the minister accepted this proposal. Consultation teams were organized who travelled throughout the country, meeting with several hundred people, bursting with ideas. These ideas were brought together in three days of passionate meetings in Sydney. Through the heartache, people listened to each other, and shifted from hard-held points of view. By the end, there was consensus on a provisional text. Further consultation refined the text, and it was presented to the Government. The Government, which had attempted to minimize the harm caused by the policies, was reluctant to accept the agreed text. But it had little strength to its argument since those who had carried out the policies, and those who had been victims of them, had reached consensus. Finally they approved the text.

Today the memorial stands between the High Court and the National Library, where hundreds of people pass it daily. The text begins: "This place honors the people who have suffered under the removal policies and practices. It also honors those Indigenous and non-Indigenous people whose genuine care softened the tragic impact of what are now recognized as cruel and misguided policies." At the dedication ceremony in May 2004, the National Sorry Day Committee released a statement.

> As South Africa's Truth and Reconciliation Commission has shown, a public acknowledgement of shameful past practices is a crucial first step in healing the wounds caused by those practices. This memorial will inform Australians from all over the country and, we hope, will inspire a new determination to overcome the continuing harmful effects of the removal policies.[24]

This is desperately needed. Today thousands of Aboriginal people struggle because their removal left them vulnerable to despair within themselves and abuse by others. Perhaps this is why Sorry Day has become a fixture on the national calendar, despite the Federal Government's lack of support.

Gradually the Government's attitude is shifting also. At a major event in the Great Hall of Parliament in May 2007—the tenth anniversary of the *Bringing Them Home* report—the Federal Minister for Health, Tony Abbott, was one of the speakers.

> The forcible removal of Indigenous children from their families is an episode in our history of which we are rightly ashamed. . . . The fundamental premise on which it was based—that children were better off away from their black families—was wrong, indeed repugnant. It was a policy based on race not reason. We should have known it then. We certainly know it now, and we do have to atone for it.

Now the Sorry Day Committee is working more closely with Canada, and recently hosted a visit by Phil Fontaine, National Chief of Canada's Assembly of First Nations. Mr. Fontaine was the first Canadian Indigenous leader to publicly expose the abuses with the Residential Schools to which tens of thousands of Indigenous Canadians were removed in policies similar to Australia's. He has been at the heart of negotiations with the Canadian Government which have resulted in the Government agreeing to put C$4.8 billion into measures aimed at healing the harm done by the policies of "aggressive assimilation"—as they are known in Canada. C$2.2 billion of that sum will go in compensation to those who were removed to these schools. And a Truth and Reconciliation Commission will be established to discover the full story of these removals and their impact on the Indigenous community.

Conclusion

The Executive Director of Canada's Royal Commission on Aboriginal Peoples, after a visit to Australia, said that whereas Canada has done much more at Government level to resolve the grievances of those who removed, Australia has done much more at a community level. "Both are needed for healing to take place," he concluded.[25]

There are steps which only Governments can take. One is to apologize for the policies implemented by their predecessor Governments. The other is to sit down with representatives of the stolen generations, and reach agreement on what Governments can do, and what programs they can fund, to repair the damage. The removal policies grew out of the white authorities' determination to control almost every aspect of the lives of Aboriginal people. The harm this caused is now recognized. Healing depends on abandoning this control by involving the victims of those policies fully in measures towards healing.

But the community can also play a role in trauma healing. Professional counselors sometimes underestimate the role that untrained people can play. And there is no doubt that professional training is a tremendous asset. But where the trauma is widespread, as among Aboriginal Australians, many who suffer may not receive any help unless the wider community is enlisted.

The Australian experience shows that in many people there is an innate understanding of the steps needed to heal trauma. When encouraged to get involved, they have known how to help—caring for the person in practical ways, giving them the opportunity to tell their story should they wish to do so, making them feel welcome in their locality. And through this involvement, they have been given the opportunity to see their society through Aboriginal eyes.

This opens a way to genuine reconciliation between Indigenous Australians and the wider community. When denial of the ugly side of our history is overcome, and the guilt which accompanies this denial, it will be a freeing experience for all Australians. If we can learn to accept the truth about our history, that will engender a new respect for Aboriginal people. This is vital. This fragile continent faces grave ecological challenges in the next few years, and scientists have stated that these challenges will only be met through the application of both Aboriginal experience and Western expertise. That teamwork depends on the growth in respect and appreciation between the communities.

Notes

1. Trauma Trails—Recreating Song Lines by Judy Atkinson, Spinifex 2002.
2. Speech at Commonwealth-State Native Welfare Conference, Canberra, 1937.
3. *A rape of the soul so profound; the return of the Stolen Generations* by Peter Read, St. Leonards, N.S.W.: Allen and Unwin, 1999. 'As part of a court case, I was asked to examine the case histories of ten Aboriginal people all removed from the same area within a ten year period. Every one of them declined catastrophically in both personality and intelligence as they were then measured.' Professor Read details this survey on p. 172-175.
4. These descriptions of the conditions of institutions to which Aboriginal children were removed, and the attitude of the wider Australian community towards these children, are taken from 'The Stolen Generations', a booklet published by Senator Trish Crossin, Australian Senate, 2000, and compiled by Peter Read, Wayne Connop and John Bond. Professor Read, Deputy Director, National Institute for Indigenous Studies, Australian National University, is widely regarded as Australia's leading historian on the policies which separated Aboriginal children from their families. Wayne Connop is an Aboriginal lawyer whose family has been directly affected by the removal policies.
5. Bob Randall, Songman, ABC Books, 2003.

6. Western Australian Aboriginal Child Health Survey, conducted by the Telethon Institute for Child Health Research, April 2005.

7. Lang Dean, letter to *The Age* newspaper, October 1997.

8. Keith McEwan, interview, September 2006.

9. See www.austlii.edu.au/au/special/rsjproject/rsjlibrary/hreoc/stolen/ for the full report.

10. M Dodson, Proceedings of Second Aboriginal and Torres Strait Islander Child Survival Conference, Townsville, June 1997. p. 24-5.

11. See www.health.gov.au/internet/wcms/publishing.nsf/Content/health-oatsih-pubs-bth.htm for the Government response to the report.

12. The transcript and conclusions of this court case can be read at www.austlii.edu.au/au/journals/AILR/2001/36.html

13. Interview for *For a Change* magazine, London, January 1998.

14. Speech at Old Parliament House, Canberra, 28 October 1997.

15. Atkinson, p. 202.

16. Interview for *For a Change* magazine, London, January 1998.

17. ATSIC Commissioner for Health, speaking at meeting of ATSIC Board with representatives of the National Sorry Day Committee, 1999.

18. 'Intergenerations aspects of trauma for Australian Aboriginal people'. This essay was a chapter in the International Handbook of Multigenerational Legacies of Trauma, Pg 327-39. Plenum Press, New York, 1998.

19. Atkinson, p. 211.

20. Minutes, NSDC national conference, 2003.

21. Letter to John Bond, June 1998.

22. Trauma Trails, Atkinson, p. 252.

23. Trauma Trails, Atkinson, p. 201.

24. For fuller account, see *For a Change* magazine, London, August 2004.

25. Tony Reynolds, Interview with John Bond, 2001.

The Way Forward: Policy Development and Implementation

Barry Hart

The authors of this book speak to the variety of threats and destructive actions facing individuals, communities and entire societies due to violent conflicts and structures. These conflicts impact people's security, identities, human rights, economic well-being and emotional health. Add to this the threat of global warming and other factors of rapid change related to global politics and economics, and it becomes clear that new thinking, polices and actions are needed that will influence the short- and long-term safety, health and livelihood of people and the planet. A global effort is required to break cycles of violence and contribute to the restoration of people's relationships, social structures and natural environment.

Building peace in traumatized societies affected by local and global issues requires analyses of causes of violence and what sustains this violence structurally *and* emotionally. The examination and transformation of a range of social, political, economic, cultural and psychological factors involved in this process requires the development of innovative polices and leadership at every level of society. As these leaders develop a more complete awareness of how *interdependent* the people they serve are and how their own dependence on and interaction with them is essential for communal and social stability, they will choose to create more just and equitable policies and practices. As emerging progressive leaders, they will take into consideration how their communities and societies are influenced by external factors—whether economic, political or environmental—and adjust accordingly to meet constituent needs.

Policy development and implementation[1] to aid building and sustaining peace in societies deeply impacted by large-scale acts of violence and structural injustice also requires a greater engagement of the people directly affected by this violence. Along with civil society organizations in partnership with local and national governing bodies, the people who have suffered from violence become important participants in the creation of more comprehensive policies and practices regarding social reconstruction and capacity building. Engagement in this way helps establish and add to the development of socio-political and economic mechanisms that reflect and meet the safety, identity and healing needs of individuals and groups at multiple levels of society.

As people impacted by violence demand and are given the opportunity by leaders to contribute to the social reconstruction of their communities and societies, they are no longer seen (or experience themselves) as passive victims or bystanders. They are acknowledged as people who are able to face past humiliation and pain, integrate and transform it. Through this process they become an important factor in the prevention of future violence and destruction. Leadership that creates the political, dialogical and emotional space for this transformative process to take place helps people (re)discover their natural resilience and develop it through educational, cultural and spiritual practices. With its focus on *strength within*, resilience contributes to healing traumatized individuals or communities through helping people deal with, learn from and overcome their trauma experience.

As just noted, it is important for victims of violence to be included in the development of policies and their implementation related to social reconstruction and overall public health. Perpetrators of the violence should also be part of this process.[2] Perpetrators' acknowledgement of and accountability for their actions through a justice system that includes a significant *restorative justice* component become an important factor in social reconstruction.[3] Restorative justice values and practices are concerned with peoples' needs and rights as well as their relationships and the structures that provide and maintain them. It works toward the reestablishment of the human bond broken by acts of violence and examines *why* perpetrators used violence in the first place.

The reasons behind perpetrators' acts of aggression and use of force often reflect their own victimization, where historical trauma, or more current issues of human rights abuse and economic disparity, was never addressed. Once given the opportunity to tell their stories about these recent or historical grievances, the information becomes part of the analysis of violent events and can be incorporated into policies, strategies and practices for the prevention of future conflicts. Furthermore, when perpetrators' narratives are told directly to victims or to the society through transitional justice or other truth-telling processes, they become potential aids to the healing of victims, perpetrator and society in general. Significant antidotal evidence points to this constructive change, but more research is needed to determine if transitional justice, that includes retributive and restorative justice and truth commission processes make a difference in psychological recovery, reconciliation and overall societal reconstruction after large-scale violence.[4]

What *is* clear, though, is that breaking cycles of violence in these complex conflicts requires the involvement of victims and offenders, civil society members and leaders from every sector of society. It also requires a true partnership between the people, their leaders and civil society, with this partnership extended to include international NGOs and in most cases the various agencies and member states of the United Nations. Through this collaborative effort, comprehensive policies and practices for societal reconstruction, with their important political, economic, cultural and psychological components, can be developed and implemented in societies emerging from violent conflict.[5]

The Role of the United Nations in Building Peace and Healing Trauma

The newly established United Nations Peacebuilding Commission[6] is tasked to "promote an integrated approach to post-conflict peace building and play a central role in addressing the problem of armed violence." This statement from the 2007 Geneva Declaration on Armed Violence and Development[7] reflects a concerted effort by the United Nations and its member states to comprehensively address the results of violent conflicts and prevent future ones. Forty-two countries have resolved through the Geneva Declaration to "promote sustainable security and a culture of peace by taking action to reduce armed violence and its negative impact on socio-economic and human development." These countries intend to work individually and collectively to promote peaceful settlement of conflict, uphold human rights and build sustainable peace in communities and societies deeply impacted by violent conflict.

This group of member states recognizes that the security of people and development of their political and economic infrastructures is critical to the promotion of peace, human rights and dignity for all peoples. The declaration also speaks clearly to the human costs and public health needs of those affected by these conflicts. It does not directly address the psychosocial or trauma healing issues of people deeply impacted by violence and war. To incorporate these issues more fully into the discourse, the following points are suggested:

- Human security involves the physical security of people and their psychological health as well as identity safety. The overall health of people is directly tied to their ability to make individual and collective choices about their emotional well-being and related involvement in rebuilding their communities, regions and states.
- Choices are made within contextually and culturally appropriate frameworks, with methodologies that help both victims and perpetrators to positively and creatively integrate the pain, fear, anger and hatred that help cause conflict and result from it.
- An integrated peacebuilding approach that includes trauma healing and other psychosocial practices is critical for the prevention of inter- and trans-generational transference of trauma, which in tern helps break the cycle of violence for future generations.

The social and political stability of post-complex conflicts that the Geneva Declaration speaks to will be further enhanced as member states and others involved in the stabilization and peacebuilding process include identity and worldview *reconstruction* as part of its policymaking and related practice. Along with psychological and spiritual issues, identity and worldviews fall into the category of intangible factors that need attention as part of conflict and post-conflict reconstruction.

Identity concerns people's existential needs and values, with met needs reflecting a sense of well being and safety; and where values include social and/or religious principles that speak to a sense of community and mutual accountability. Worldview is a set of lenses that people construct based on culture and language and provides a common framework for people and a way of *seeing* and creatively *acting* in the world. As part of complex and violent conflicts, identities and worldviews are threatened, manipulated and often stripped away and in the process people lose their sense of safety, interdependence, meaning and autonomy.

Identity and worldview abuse are part and parcel of what leads to violent conflict and these interrelated factors are major causalities of this abuse. If identity and worldview needs are not recognized and addressed in the policies that influence the practices of individuals, international NGOs and the United Nations and other groups wanting to help rebuild deeply wounded societies, there is the danger of future violence and more unjust structures. Therefore, in conjunction with the tangible needs of communities and societies devastated by conflict, such as infrastructure renewal, economic and judicial restructuring, the intangible issues that address how people think, feel and see the world are needed to complete the peacebuilding equation. Inclusive policies and practices for peace and social reconstruction after conflict offer the means to meet *both* the immediate and long-term material and psychological needs of the people most affected by the conflict.

Policy Development and Implementation: Government, Civil Society and NGO Interaction

Strategic peacebuilding policymaking includes the involvement of key individuals and organizations that have *access* to the physical setting and people in conflict. Those that intervene in the development of policy need the *power* of expertise, resources and relationships to see the process through. For these interventions to be effective, they need to be "woven into the formal infrastructure of the states, either existing or under construction."[8] Civil society and national and international NGOs, through their knowledge of context, access to financial resources and ability to influence the public through educational and economic programs, and who enter the context with a set of values that reflect the needs of the people they serve, are able to enhance the policymaking and implementation process by working directly with governing structures.[9]

Developing policy within a larger peacebuilding framework also requires an understanding that not all conflicts and their contexts are the same and that there may be historical, cultural and/or current political factors that prove difficult to overcome. Ongoing conflict and governance issues in Afghanistan, Iraq and the Sudan are the most notable examples of conflicts where internal instability and external geopolitical and economic interest further complicate an already complex set of circumstances. However, the work initiated by the NGO Search for Common Ground in Burundi in 1995 related to increased involvement of civil society in the local policymaking process,[10] and the current activities of 3D Security Initiative and InterAction[11] as they attempt to influence United States Government domestic and foreign policy, are examples of the outsider/insider interface that is part of the changing scenario of policy development and implementation.

Advancing these partnership approaches to policymaking, for the creation of policies that fully include trauma healing education, practices and values—such as caring for the wounded and using methodologies that reflect contextual needs and sensitivities—will lead to more effective polices and transformative practices. As part of this *partnering for change*, instituting an information and/or educational component for policy makers would enhance their knowledge of the peacebuilding process and the role of psychosocial values and practices necessary for effective peacebuilding.[12] The statement that is consistently raised when providing educational programs about peacebuilding and trauma healing to grass-roots and mid-level actors is, "We need this, but so too do our leaders." Thus, *partnering for understanding* regarding violent conflicts with their complex mix of material and psychological issues needs to be encouraged and directly linked to policy development and implementation.

An increased understanding of this *web-like* set of variables and practices would benefit from its own guidelines and procedures for policy development and implementation. The recommendations in the following section are an attempt to add to this discussion and further partnership thinking and action.

Recommendations for a Way Forward

Policies that represent the most comprehensive and effective ways of building peace and just structures to sustain this peace are those that reflect a policymaking process that is analytical and committed to change. This process, at a minimum, should also include the following:[13]

- A multi-level identification of the key insider/outsider actors—both natural allies and those who may be antagonistic to the suggested policies.
- A focus on relationship and trust-building with these actors and eliciting and learning from their input and expertise.
- An understanding that human security, rights and development are central to policymaking and need to be the focus of policy development and implementation.
- An awareness of time factors, since hurried decision, though sometimes necessary, will not result in the best policies and implementation methods.
- The creation of educational, dialogical and planning *spaces* that allow for the greatest understanding of the issues and the most constructive policymaking procedures.

- The appropriate use of media power to inform the public about the policymaking process and encourage policymakers to develop comprehensive and positive polices of change.
- Monitoring and evaluation procedures for implemented polices and a final external evaluation tool to assess outcomes and future needs.

The way forward for governments, civil society, and international bodies building peace after large-scale violent conflict or long-term structural violence is to focus on relationships. Changing the political, economic and sociocultural systems that support these relationships is essential and requires visionary thinking and leadership. It further requires a pragmatism that insists on doable and just practices and outcomes. The development and implementation of policies that reflect this process and address peoples' material, relational and psychosocial needs will aid peacebuilding practices and advance social reconstruction and growth.

Notes

1. Ross drawing on Edelman defines policy as "the distribution of tangible and symbolic benefits in society." He further states that policy "has substantive and symbolic dimensions and both are important in determining who participates, how they participate, and what groups seek from policy and from its implementation." Moreover policies according to Ross "grow out of grievances that are articulated as political claims for which state and/or nonstate action might provide a remedy." See "Adding Complexity to Chaos: Policymaking in Conflict Situations" in *NGOs at the Table: Strategies for Influencing Polices in Areas of Conflict*. Fitzduff, M. and Church, C. (eds.), Rowman and Littlefield, Lanham, MD. 2004.

2. During the 1991-1995 wars in the former Yugoslavia, for example, members on all sides believed they were the true victims of these conflicts. See Chapter 16 for details about how victimization is perceived in this region of the Balkans.

3. Restorative Justice has its historical roots in customary law of traditional societies. In the United States, Europe and New Zealand, it is a victim-offender based process used mainly within the criminal justice system. It central tenants are: Putting right wrongs and harms, "by focusing on harms and needs, addressing obligations, involving stakeholders and using inclusive collaborative process." See Zehr, H. *The Little Book of Restorative Justice*. Intercourse, PA: Good Books (2002).

4. See Chapter 10 for research regarding the interface between transitional justice and trauma healing.

5. There is still the issue of governments not wanting NGOs, civil society or the international community getting involved in state matters. External political or economic pressure can encourage governments to change their attitudes on this matter. More positively stated, political and economic *incentives* can be offered to encourage reluctant governments to change direction and engage *outsiders* in the policymaking process.

6. The United Nations Peacebuilding Commission was established in December 2005 as ". . . an intergovernmental advisory body that will be a new forum to bring peacebuilding stakeholders in a selected country together to coordinate their overall strategies, and particularly to identify gaps in the international community's effort to support sustainable peace in transitioning countries." (see Global Partnership for the Prevention of Armed Conflict Report, 5 September 2006).

7. To view the entire document see: http://www.iansa.org/issues/documents/armed-violence-and-development-geneva-declaration.pdf.

8. See "Stepping Up to the Table: NGO Strategies for Influencing Policy on Conflict Issues" in *NGOs at the Table: Strategies for Influencing Polices in Areas of Conflict,* Fitzduff, M. and Church, C. (2004).

9. These same groups work outside governing structures as advocates for policy change, using their resources to apply pressure on policymakers. Or, they may work in parallel with governing structures to garner public support for particular policies.

10. See note 8 above.

11. See Chapter 12 for an explanation of the 3D Security Initiative and http://www.interaction.org/about/index.html for InterAction's role in engaging policy-makers.

12. It is also important for members of NGOs, civil society and the peacebuilding community writ large to learn the *language* and understand the practices of government actors and policymakers.

13. Adapted from *Peacebuilding Policy Consultations and Dialogues: A Study of the Canadian Experience* (July 2001); and *NGOs at the Table: Strategies for Influencing Policies in areas of Conflict* (2004).

Index

Contributors

Mohammed Abu-Nimer is a professor at International Peace and Conflict Resolution (IPCR) and director of the Peacebuilding and Development Institute, American University. He is also a founder and director of Salam: Peace and Justice Institute. He has worked for over two decades on interfaith dialogue and peacebuilding in United States and many parts of the Muslim world. His recent publications include: *Unity in Diversity: Interfaith Dialogue in the Middle East* (USIP, 2007); *Interfaith Dialogue as Guide for Muslims* (IIIT, 2007); *Nonviolence and Peacebuilding in Islam: Theory and Practice.* (Gainesville, University Press of Florida 2003); *Reconciliation, Justice, and Coexistence: Theory and Practice* (New York, Lexington 2001).

Arlene Audergon, Ph.D., is a conflict resolution facilitator and psychotherapist. With her partner, Jean-Claude, she is co-founder of the UK training in Process Oriented Psychology, RSPOPUK and C FOR, an organization devoted to violence prevention, multi-cultural dialogue and creative capacity in community to resolve conflict and shape the future. Dr. Audergon co-lead a UN sponsored project in Croatia, 1996-2001 and 2006, facilitating large forums for post-war reconciliation in all war-affected regions and is currently working on a further project among post Yugoslavia countries. Arlene is author of *The War Hotel: Psychological Dynamics in Violent Conflict* (Wiley, 2005). She has published several articles and chapter contributions on collective trauma, accountability, conflict transformation and politics and psychology. Working also in theatre, Arlene co-directed SPIRIT with Improbable Theatre, a piece about war which played at the Royal Court Theatre in London, and in numerous festivals internationally. Arlene lives in London where she also enjoys her private practice. See www.cfor.info.

Babu Ayindo is an independent consultant in the design and facilitation of conflict resolution and peacebuilding processes; researcher and trainer in arts, peace education and development communication. He has extensive experience in applying "arts approaches" in peacebuilding in various parts of the world. Babu served as Senior Lecturer and Coordinator of the Dag Hammarskjöld Peace Centre at Mindolo Ecumenical Foundation, Zambia. He has also served as adjunct faculty at the Institute of Justice and Peacebuilding at Eastern Mennonite University (USA); Mindanao Peacebuilding Institute (Philippines); the National Youth JustPeace Camp (Fiji Islands) and the Peacebuilding and Development Institute of The American University (Washington, DC). He is co-author of the acclaimed *When You Are the Peacebuilder* as well as several articles on the arts, peace and politics. He holds a B.Ed. from Kenyatta University in Nairobi, Kenya and M.A. in Conflict Transformation from Eastern Mennonite University, USA. Babu does organic farm work with his wife Miriam, and children, Biko, Sankara and Che for he firmly believes that genuine and sustainable just-peace begins when people have access to quality food.

Judy Barsalou has over two decades of experience researching and working on issues related to the Middle East and international peace and conflict. In 2008 she joined the Ford Foundation, where she serves as Representative for the Middle East and North Africa in its regional office based in Cairo. Previous posts she has held include the Vice President of the Grant and Fellowship Program of the United States Institute of Peace; Executive Director of the Middle East Research and Information Project, which publishes Middle East Report; Director of Academic Programs at the Institute of Government Affairs, University of California at Davis; and Program Officer at the Ford Foundation, first in its New York headquarters and then in its Cairo office. She has written extensively on the Middle East but her most recent publications have focused on the challenges of teaching history in divided societies and the role memorialization in social reconstruction.

Rezarta Bilali is a Ph.D. candidate in social psychology with a concentration on Psychology of Peace and Prevention of Violence at University of Massachusetts, Amherst. She holds a M.A. in Conflict Analysis and Resolution from Sabanci University in Turkey. Ms. Bilali's research interests include investigation of group identities and collective memories, international images, and social trust. Since 2006, Ms. Bilali has been part of the academic team working with Radio La Benevolencija's reconciliation project in Great Lakes Region in Eastern Africa.

John Bond was Secretary of the Sorry Day and Journey of Healing movement from 1998 to 2006. He was awarded the Medal of the Order of Australia in 2007 "for services to the community through the activities of the National Sorry Day Committee." John has enlisted hundreds of thousands of Australians in initiatives to heal the harm caused by tragically misguided past policies towards Aboriginal Australians. He is now a member of Australia's Stolen Generations Alliance: Australians for Healing, Truth and Justice, an organization set up in 2007 to expand the work of the Journey of Healing. He lives in Canberra, Australia's capital city, where he has frequent interaction with political leaders on the issues of Aboriginal rights, and has organized many events in the national Parliament. By profession he is a writer and editor, and writes frequently for the media. John has worked with Initiatives of Change (formerly Moral Re-Armament) for the past 35 years, including 10 years in Africa, mainly in Ethiopia and Zimbabwe.

Barry Hart is associate professor of conflict and trauma studies in the Center for Justice and Peacebuilding at Eastern Mennonite University. He has extensive experience in trauma healing and conflict transformation research and training through his work in Northern Ireland, Liberia and the Balkans. In 2005 Barry coordinated the working group on trauma healing at the United Nations conference on civil society and the prevention of armed conflict. In 2007 he co-chaired the first international academic conference on the relationship between peacebuilding and trauma recovery. His publications include *Transforming Conflict through Trauma Recovery Training* and *Transforming Conflict: Creating Spaces for Change*. Barry is the Academic Director of the Caux Scholars Program in Caux, Switzerland. He received his M.Div. degree from Eastern Mennonite Seminary and a Ph.D. from the Institute for Conflict Analysis and Resolution at George Mason University.

Riva Kantowitz is assistant professor at Sabanci University in Istanbul, Turkey where she teaches in the Programs in Conflict Analysis and Resolution and Social and Political Sciences. Her research and practice interests include understanding the social-psychological effects of war at the communal and societal level, and how they relate to effective peacebuilding, development, and trauma healing processes across cultural settings. Riva has worked in Latin America, Southeast Asia and Southeastern Europe with various organizations including the United Nations Development Program and the Center for International Conflict Resolution at Columbia University. As the recipient of Fulbright-Hays and David L. Boren Fellowships, she has also conducted extensive field research in Guatemala examining the effects of war on indigenous communities. Riva is currently engaged in comparative research on social trauma with Kurdish communities in Southeastern Turkey. She earned a Ph.D. in Social-Organizational Psychology with a concentration in Conflict Resolution at Columbia University and received her undergraduate degree in history from Bryn Mawr College.

Bonnie Klassen has been the Mennonite Central Committee Representative in Colombia since MCC opened an office in this country in 2002. Previously she worked for five years in the Colombian Mennonite Church Center for Justice, Peace and Nonviolence—JUSTAPAZ, as the assistant to former Director Ricardo Esquivia. Through both of these positions she has worked very closely with Anabaptist and other Protestant church projects in response to victims of Colombia's armed conflict and a variety of peace-building initiatives. She also participated actively in the Permanent Assembly of Civil Society for Peace, where she served on the National Executive Committee for one year. Bonnie Klassen completed her undergraduate degree in social psychology and peace and conflict studies at the University of Waterloo and Conrad Grebel College, respectively.

Evelin Lindner is a social scientist with an interdisciplinary orientation. She holds two PhDs, one in medicine and another in psychology. Her book *Making Enemies: Humiliation and International Conflict* was published by Praeger/Greenwood in 2006. She is currently establishing Human Dignity and Humiliation Studies (www.humiliationstudies.org, HumanDHS) as an international platform for further work on dignity and humiliation. She designs her life as a global citizen in order to be able to build HumanDHS globally. She teaches as an associate professor and guest professor at universities in Norway (University of Oslo, and Norwegian University of Science and Technology (NTNU) in Trondheim), and is affiliated with the Maison des Sciences de l'Homme in Paris, and Columbia University, New York, while teaching as visiting guest professor wherever her path leads her. For example, among others, Japan (International Christian University, and Rikkyo University, Tokyo), Israel (Hebrew University, Jerusalem), Australia (Queensland University), or Costa Rica (United Nations-mandated University for Peace).

Laurie Anne Pearlman, Ph.D., is a consultant on psychological trauma. She has published numerous articles and co-authored several books on both direct and vicarious trauma, including *Risking Connection* (2000). She speaks nationally and internationally on direct and vicarious psychological trauma. Dr. Pearlman serves as president of TREATI, directs the clinical associates program for the Headington Institute, and serves on the practice committee of the American Psychological Association's trauma division and the complex trauma task force of the International Society for Traumatic Stress Studies. She has collaborated with professor Ervin Staub on peace-building and trauma recovery in Rwanda since 1999. Dr. Pearlman has received awards for her clinical, scientific, and media contributions from the Connecticut Psychological Association and the International Society for Traumatic Stress Studies.

Amela Puljek-Shank received an M.A. degree from Eastern Mennonite University's Center for Justice and Peacebuilding. She co-wrote the chapter "Journey of Healing" in *Positive Approaches to Peacebuilding: A Resource for Innovators* (2003) and "Trauma and Reconciliation" in *20 Pieces of Encouragement for Awakening and Change* (2007). Amela has worked in the field of facilitation with Seeds of Peace Program in Greece, the United States and the Balkans. She has taught trauma healing and recovery in the Summer Peacebuilding Institute at Eastern Mennonite University. Currently Amela is working with Mennonite Central Committee as a co-representative for Southeast Europe and holds trauma healing seminars and workshops.

Randall Puljek-Shank is co-representative for Southeast Europe with Mennonite Central Committee and lives in Sarajevo. He also previously worked with relief and peacebuilding projects in Bosnia and Herzegovina from 1995-1996, has taught classes in social movements and been a trainer and consultant to peacebuilding projects in Croatia, Serbia, and Bosnia-Herzegovina. He holds a M.A. in Conflict Transformation from Eastern Mennonite University. He co-wrote the chapter "Journey of Healing" in *Positive Approaches to Peacebuilding: A Resource for Innovators* (2003) and also wrote "Mennonite Experience with Interfaith and Ecumenical Work in Southeast Europe" *in Borders and Bridges: Mennonite Witness in a Religiously Diverse World* (2007).

Vern Neufeld Redekop teaches in the graduate program in Conflict Studies at Saint Paul University. In his former role as President of the Canadian Institute for Conflict Resolution, he developed and lead a series of two-day interactive, generative seminars and worked with a Rwandan and Bosnian on Community-Based Conflict Resolution programs in their respective countries. His theoretical and practical insights found expression in his book *From Violence to Blessing: How an Understanding of Deep-Rooted Conflict Can Open Paths to Reconciliation.* Subsequent research has focused on protest crowds and police, the role of the church in the Rwandan genocide, reconciliation between Nuers and Dinkas in South Sudan, the concept of "teachings of blessing," the nature of structural violence within economic systems, and the potential for reconciliation through economic development.

Abikök Riak is director of grants acquisition and management for World Vision U.S., supporting World Vision offices in Asia, Middle East and Eastern Europe. She previously worked with World Vision International as peacebuilding coordinator for the Asia Pacific region and as program officer for the Sudan program. She was also a researcher and technical writer for the Institute for Food and Development Policy. Her publications include chapters titled "Mainstreaming Local Capacities for Peace in a Federal Organization" and "What Are We Trying to Develop? Lessons Learned from the Philippines in Community Leadership" in the recently published book *A Shared Future: Local Capacities for*

Peace in Community Development. She is a contributing author to *Options for Aid in Conflict: Lessons from Field Experiences*, edited by Mary B. Anderson. She has a B.A. in economics and history from Bluffton University and an M.A. in city and regional planning from the University of North Carolina at Chapel Hill.

Lisa Schirch is professor of peacebuilding at Eastern Mennonite University (EMU) and program director of the 3D Security Initiative which promotes conflict prevention and peacebuilding in U.S. security policymaking. With colleagues in the Center for Justice and Peacebuilding at EMU, Schirch consults with a network of strategic partner organizations involved in peacebuilding activities throughout the U.S., Latin America, Africa, Asia, and Europe. Schirch has worked in over 20 countries. A former Fulbright Fellow in East and West Africa, Schirch has written four books and numerous articles on conflict prevention and peacebuilding. Her current research interests include civil-military dialogue and the intersection of climate change, sustainable development, social marketing, the media arts, and conflict prevention. She is a frequent public speaker and has TV and radio experience discussing U.S. foreign policy. She holds a B.A. in International Relations from the University of Waterloo, Canada, and a M.S. and Ph.D. in Conflict Analysis and Resolution from George Mason University.

Margaret Smith is Scholar in Residence at the School of International Service at American University. She is the author of *Reckoning with the Past: Teaching History in Northern Ireland*, published by Lexington Books in 2005. She was for five years an associate of the Program on International Conflict Analysis and Resolution at Harvard University. Before completing her Ph.D. she worked for the conflict resolution organization Initiatives of Change in the U.S. and Europe, as well as in Papua New Guinea and Australia. She has taught history, political science and conflict resolution at the college level. Her academic interests include theories of nationalism and ethnicity, historical memory and ethnonationalism, the Northern Ireland conflict, comparative ethnic conflict, human rights, and international organizations.

Ervin Staub is Professor and Founding Director of the Ph.D. program in the Psychology of Peace and the Prevention of Violence, Emeritus, at the University of Massachusetts at Amherst. He has studied the roots of altruism, the origins of violence including genocide and mass killing, as well as prevention, psychological recovery and reconciliation, with many publications, including books such as *The Roots of Evil: The Origins of Genocide and Other Group Violence* (1989); and *The Psychology of Good and Evil: Why Children, Adults and Groups Help and Harm Others?* (2003). He is past President of the Society for the Study of Peace, Conflict and Violence and of the International Society for Political Psychology. He has worked in many applied settings, including schools to promote altruism, active bystandership and reduce aggression, with police to reduce the use of unnecessary force, and since 1998 in Rwanda and the Great Lakes Region of East Africa. He is the recipient of varied awards. See www.ervinstaub.com.

www.ingramcontent.com/pod-product-compliance
Ingram Content Group UK Ltd.
Pitfield, Milton Keynes, MK11 3LW, UK
UKHW021035150926
475561UK00003B/114

9 780761 840350